GREAT LIVES
FROM
HISTORY

GREAT LIVES FROM HISTORY

American Women Series

Volume 1
A-Chi

Edited by
FRANK N. MAGILL

SALEM PRESS

Pasadena, California   Englewood Cliffs, New Jersey

∞ The paper used in these volumes conforms to the
American National Standard for Permanence of Paper for
Printed Library Materials, Z39.48-1984.

Library of Congress Cataloging-in-Publication Data
Great lives from history. American women series /
edited by Frank N. Magill.
    p.   cm.
Includes bibliographical references and index.
    1. Women—United States—Biography. 2. Women—
Canada—Biography. 3. Women—United States—His-
tory. 4. Women—Canada—History. I. Magill, Frank
Northen, 1907-   . II. Title: American women series.
HQ1412.G74   1995
305.4'0973—dc20
ISBN 0-89356-892-9 (set)   94-38308
ISBN 0-89356-893-7 (volume 1)   CIP

PUBLISHER'S NOTE

Great Lives from History, American Women Series, is the sixth set in an ongoing series providing coverage of the lives, careers, and achievements of historically significant individuals from antiquity to the present. Previously published sets have covered figures from American history, from British and Commonwealth history, and from world history spanning the period from early human history up to the late twentieth century. This latest series is the first to focus specifically on the achievements and accomplishments of women. Given the abundance of scholarship that has been published during the 1980's and early 1990's in the field of women's history, it has become clear that there is an important need among students, researchers, and general readers for more up-to-date coverage of the lives of distinguished North American women. The editors have sought to provide a well-rounded assemblage of such women, one that includes individuals who have achieved fame and international recognition for their accomplishments as well as lesser-known figures whose achievements are equally deserving of attention.

The *American Women Series* includes 408 articles on 409 women whose lives have had a distinct impact on North American society and culture. Areas of achievement for these individuals range from government to the arts and from medicine to women's rights, including architecture, business, diplomacy, education, literature, music, politics, religion, social reform, and theater and entertainment. The range of figures covered is wide in time as well, from early figures such as Colonial poet Anne Bradstreet and explorer Sacagawea of the Lewis and Clark Expedition to contemporary figures such as Nobel Prize-winning author Toni Morrison and Cherokee leader Wilma Mankiller. In broad fields, such as the sciences, in which the contributions of women have often been overlooked, there is coverage of figures in a variety of individual disciplines, including astronomer Maria Mitchell, computer scientist Grace Hopper, biologist and environmental writer Rachel Carson, and astronaut-physicist Sally Ride. Early women's rights activists such as Elizabeth Cady Stanton, Lucy Stone, and Susan B. Anthony are included alongside such later figures from the women's movement as Bella Abzug, Gloria Steinem, and Betty Friedan. The *American Women Series* also profiles forty-five African Americans, eleven Asian Americans, eight Hispanic Americans, eight Native Americans, and seven Canadians.

While this set has many distinctive qualities that differentiate it from the five previous entries in the *Great Lives from History* series, it shares several features that distinguish this series as a whole from other biographical reference works. The articles combine breadth of coverage (in contrast to the brief entries typical of many biographical dictionaries) with a format that offers the user quick access to particular information needed (in contrast to the longer, unformatted entries found in many encyclopedias).

The format for these articles, which average two thousand words in length, follows the easy-access standard adhered to throughout the series: Each article begins with ready-reference listings, including dates and places of birth and death, areas of achievement, and a short statement on the individual's overall contribution to her discipline and to the world. The remainder of the article is divided into four parts. The *Early Life* section provides facts about the individual's upbringing and family life and covers her life up to the point at which her major work began. The *Life's Work* section provides a straightforward chronological account of that period during which the individual's most significant achievements were made. The *Summary* section constitutes an evaluation of the individual's contributions to or impact on history, providing an analysis of the individual's life and achievements in the larger context of North American culture and women's history. The final section is an annotated bibliography, which is intended to serve as a starting point for further research. The works included in this section are chosen for their accessibility through most libraries.

An index by "Areas of Achievement" allows the user to gain access to historical personages by their fields of endeavor and appears at the end of each volume. Volume 5 contains two additional reference features designed to aid users of the set: a "Biographical Index" and a "Time Line." The "Biographical Index" lists all of the figures covered in the set and includes cross-references from other names by which the individual may be known. The "Time Line" places these individuals in chronological order based on their date of birth.

Special thanks are extended to our contributors, scholars from disciplines as ·various as the broad array of personages covered: general historians, intellectual historians, and historians in the fields of art, literature, science, and women's studies, to name only a few. We wish to acknowledge the efforts of these specialists and thank them for making historical scholarship available to the general reader. Their names appear at the ends of the articles and in a roster listing contributors and their academic affiliations, to be found in the front matter to Volume 1.

CONTRIBUTING REVIEWERS

Elizabeth C. Adams
Frostburg State University

Amy Adelstein
Independent Scholar

Richard Adler
University of Michigan—Dearborn

Eleanor B. Amico
University of Wisconsin—Oshkosh

Deborah Elwell Arfken
University of Tennessee, Chattanooga

Mary Welek Atwell
Radford University

Sue Bailey
Tennessee Technological University

Ann Stewart Balakier
University of South Dakota

Rosanne M. Barker
Sam Houston State University

Alice Ogden Bellis
Howard University School of Divinity

Cynthia Breslin Beres
Independent Scholar

Charles Merrell Berg
University of Kansas

S. Carol Berg
College of St. Benedict

Milton Berman
University of Rochester

Terry D. Bilhartz
Sam Houston State University

Cynthia A. Bily
Adrian College

Margaret Boe Birns
New York University

Nicholas Birns
Western Connecticut State University

John Braeman
University of Nebraska, Lincoln

Catherine Coleman Brawer
Curator, The Maidenform Museum

John A. Britton
Frances Marion University

Mary Hanford Bruce
Monmouth College

Joyce I. Buchea
Independent Scholar

Jeffrey L. Buller
Georgia Southern University

Jennifer Burton
Harvard University

Ursula Burton
Independent Scholar

Karen A. Callaghan
Barry University

Charles Cameron
Independent Scholar

Allison Carter
Rowan College of New Jersey

Elisabeth A. Cawthon
University of Texas at Arlington

Susan Chainey
Sacramento City College

Richard G. Cormack
Independent Scholar

David O'Donald Cullen
Collin County Community College

Su A. Cutler
Kalamazoo Valley Community College

Carol Damian
Florida International University

Kwame Dawes
University of South Carolina at Sumter

Laurie Dawson
University of Texas, San Antonio

Mary Jo Deegan
University of Nebraska, Lincoln

Bill Delaney
Independent Scholar

James E. Devlin
State University of New York College at Oneonta

Betsy Downey
Gonzaga University

Sarah Smith Ducksworth
Kean College of New Jersey

Joyce Duncan
East Tennessee State University

Anna Dunlap
University of Tennessee, Knoxville

Robert P. Ellis
Worcester State College

Penelope J. Engelbrecht
DePaul University

Nancy Erickson
Erskine College

Thomas L. Erskine
Salisbury State University

Kimberly K. Estep
Wesleyan College

John W. Fiero
University of Southwestern Louisiana

Bonnie L. Ford
Sacramento City College

Catherine Francis
Towson State University

Carol Franks
Portland State University

Timothy C. Frazer
Western Illinois University

Julie Foegen Frederick
Duluth News-Tribune

Richard G. Frederick
University of Pittsburgh, Bradford

Mary Pierce Frost
Sonoma State University

Jean C. Fulton
Maharishi International University

Robert L. Gale
University of Pittsburgh

Lynne M. Getz
Appalachian State University

Douglas Gomery
University of Maryland

Karen Gould
Independent Scholar

Lewis L. Gould
University of Texas at Austin

Larry Gragg
University of Missouri, Rolla

Lloyd J. Graybar
Eastern Kentucky University

J. Greco
Suffolk Community College

Jennifer Padgett Griffith
University of Georgia

Marlene San Miguel Groner
State University of New York at Farmingdale

Laurie Schwartz Guttenberg
Nassau Community College

Gillian Greenhill Hannum
Manhattanville College

Sandra D. Harmon
Illinois State University

Fred R. van Hartesveldt
Fort Valley State College

Carol P. Harvey
Assumption College

Margaret Hawthorne
South Hadley High School

John R. Holmes
Franciscan University of Steubenville

Roberta M. Hooks
Potsdam College

William L. Howard
Chicago State University

Marsha M. Huber
Otterbein College

E. D. Huntley
Appalachian State University

Duncan R. Jamieson
Ashland University

Willoughby G. Jarrell
Kennesaw State College

Jan Jenkins
University of Arkansas at Monticello

Maude M. Jennings
Ball State University

Jeffry Jensen
Independent Scholar

Sheila Golburgh Johnson
Independent Scholar

Yvonne Johnson
Collin County Community College

Michelle L. Jones
Muskingum College

Marcella Joy
Independent Scholar

CONTRIBUTING REVIEWERS

Margaret Foegen Karsten
University of Wisconsin—Platteville

Anne Kearney
Jefferson Community College

Susan E. Keegan
Mendocino College

Nannette Fabré Kelly
Imperial Valley College

W. P. Kenney
Manhattan College

Pamela Kett-O'Connor
Independent Scholar

Joseph C. Kiger
University of Mississippi

Anne Klejment
University of St. Thomas

Grove Koger
Boise Public Library

Marilyn Kongslie
Independent Scholar

Christian Koontz
University of Detroit Mercy

Beth Kraig
Pacific Lutheran University

Jane Kristof
Portland State University

Mildred C. Kuner
*Hunter College of the City University
of New York*

David Z. Kushner
University of Florida

Eugene Larson
Pierce College, Los Angeles

Vera Laska
Regis College

Ray Leadbetter
Andrews University

Douglas A. Lee
Vanderbilt University

Virginia W. Leonard
Western Illinois University

David Lester
Richard Stockton College

Gregory A. Levitt
University of New Orleans

Kriste Lindenmeyer
Tennessee Technological University

Thomas Lisk
North Carolina State University

James Livingston
Northern Michigan University

Janet Alice Long
Independent Scholar

Janet Lorenz
Independent Scholar

N. Jane McCandless
West Georgia College

Sandra C. McClain
Georgia Southern University

Robert McColley
University of Illinois at Urbana-Champaign

Jean McConnell
Eastern New Mexico State University

Irene E. McDermott
Independent Scholar

Melissa A. McEuen
Georgetown College

Margaret McFadden
Appalachian State University

Susan MacFarland
Wesleyan College

James Edward McGoldrick
Cedarville College

Jennifer McLeod
California State University, Chico

Timothy J. McMillan
Humboldt State University

Patricia McNeal
Indiana University—South Bend

Sally Ward Maggard
West Virginia University

Edward A. Malone
University of Missouri, Rolla

Bill Manikas
Gaston College

Suzanne M. Marilley
University of Notre Dame

Annette Marks-Ellis
Antelope Valley College

Elizabeth L. Marshall
Independent Scholar

Toni Marzotto
Towson State University

Patricia Masserman
Independent Scholar

Deborah T. Meem
University of Cincinnati

Linda J. Meyers
Pasadena City College

Edmund Miller
Long Island University, C. W. Post Campus

Jane Ann Miller
Dartmouth College

Christian H. Moe
Southern Illinois University at Carbondale

Joycelyn K. Moody
University of Washington

Jay Mullin
*Queensborough Community College of the
City University of New York*

Donna Mungen
Los Angeles Times

Susan Nagel
Independent Scholar

Nkeonye Nwankwo
California State University, Long Beach

Elvy Setterqvist O'Brien
Independent Scholar

Patricia Okker
University of Missouri, Columbia

Judith A. Oliver
Robert Morris College

Lawrence J. Oliver
Texas A&M University

William T. Osborne
*Florida International University and
Florida Memorial College*

Linda Rohrer Paige
Georgia Southern University

Judith A. Parsons
Sul Ross State University

Robert L. Patterson
Armstrong State College

Betsey Pender
University of North Florida

Donna Perry
William Paterson College

Sheryl Perry-Yannaccone
San Diego State University

Rebecca Phillips
West Virginia University at Parkersburg

Marjorie J. Podolsky
*Pennsylvania State University, Erie
Behrend College*

Janet M. Powers
Gettysburg College

Norma Fain Pratt
*Center for the Study of Women
University of California, Los Angeles*

Verbie Lovorn Prevost
University of Tennessee, Chattanooga

Edna B. Quinn
Salisbury State University

Colin Ramsey
University of Arkansas at Little Rock

Michaela Crawford Reaves
California Lutheran University

Kim Dickson Rogers
Independent Scholar

Carl Rollyson
*Baruch College of the City University
of New York*

Mitchel P. Roth
Sam Houston State University

Joseph R. Rudolph, Jr.
Towson State University

Constance B. Rynder
University of Tampa

Wendy Sacket
Independent Scholar

Dorothy C. Salem
Cuyahoga Community College

Jean Owens Schaefer
University of Wyoming

J. Christopher Schnell
Southeast Missouri State University

Elizabeth A. Segal
Ohio State University

R. Baird Shuman
University of Illinois at Urbana-Champaign

B. R. Siegfried
Brigham Young University

Charles L. P. Silet
Iowa State University

Andrew C. Skinner
Brigham Young University

CONTRIBUTING REVIEWERS

Jane A. Slezak
Fulton Montgomery Community College

Genevieve Slomski
Independent Scholar

A. J. Sobczak
Independent Scholar

Raymond J. Sobczak
Independent Scholar

Katherine Socha
Independent Scholar

Katherine R. Sopka
Four Corners Analytic Sciences

George Soule
Carleton College

Elisa Kay Sparks
Clemson University

David L. Sterling
University of Cincinnati

Louise M. Stone
Bloomsburg University

Carla Stoner
San Diego State University

Jean Strandness
North Dakota State University

Darlene Mary Suarez
San Diego State University

James Sullivan
California State University, Los Angeles

Glenn L. Swygart
Tennessee Temple University

Marcia G. Synnott
University of South Carolina

Emily Jane Teipe
Fullerton College

Terry Theodore
University of North Carolina at Wilmington

Sarah Thomas
Independent Scholar

Kenneth William Townsend
Coastal Carolina University

Catherine Udall Turley
Arizona State University

Diane C. Vecchio
University of Wisconsin—Whitewater

Mary E. Virginia
Independent Scholar

Carol M. Ward
Clemson University

Harry M. Ward
University of Richmond

Dover C. Watkins
University of Texas at Arlington

Linda S. Watts
Drake University

James M. Welsh
Salisbury State University

Derrick Harper West
Independent Scholar

Dexter Westrum
Ottawa University

Thomas Willard
University of Arizona

Cynthia J. Williams
Hobart and William Smith Colleges

Donna Glee Williams
North Carolina Advance Center of Teaching

Judith Barton Williamson
Sauk Valley Community College

Susan Wladaver-Morgan
Western Association of Women Historians

Ken Wolf
Murray State University

Shawn Woodyard
Independent Scholar

Clifton K. Yearley
State University of New York at Buffalo

Laura M. Zaidman
University of South Carolina

Philip Zampini
Westfield State College

Laura Weiss Zlogar
University of Wisconsin—River Falls

LIST OF BIOGRAPHIES IN VOLUME ONE

LIST OF BIOGRAPHIES IN VOLUME ONE

GREAT LIVES
FROM
HISTORY

BERENICE ABBOTT

Born: July 17, 1898; Springfield, Ohio
Died: December 9, 1991; Monson, Maine
Area of Achievement: Photography
Contribution: Abbott devoted her life to photographing the products of human ingenuity and creativity. She also became one of the earliest "experts" in the field of photography, a lecturer on its philosophy and technique, an inventor of photographic equipment, and a promoter of photography as a form of both art and communication.

Early Life

Bernice (she added another "e" while in Paris in the 1920's) Abbott was born in rural Ohio on July 17, 1898. Her parents were divorced while she was still an infant, and as a result, Bernice rarely saw her older brothers, her sister, or her father. An unhappy and often lonely childhood led Bernice to become self-reliant at an early age. After attending public schools in Cleveland and Columbus, Bernice entered Ohio State University to study journalism, but she soon became bored with what she considered a dull, freshman routine.

In the winter of 1918, Bernice borrowed twenty dollars to buy a train ticket to New York. One of her former classmates, Sue Jenkins, had encouraged Bernice to seek a new life in the city, and so she offered Bernice a place to sleep in her Greenwich Village apartment. Once established, Bernice enrolled at Columbia University, but she found her neighborhood's artists, actors, and playwrights much more interesting than her journalism studies, so she dropped out of Columbia in order to pursue her growing interest in the arts. Bernice was most interested in sculpture, but she also landed a few small roles in local plays. In 1921, when the New York art world seemed at odds with her personal artistic goals, Bernice bought a one-way ticket to Paris.

Paris offered Bernice a satisfying artistic environment, although she made more money posing for sculptors and painters than she did producing her own sculpture. In 1925, she abandoned sculpture and went to work full-time as an assistant to Man Ray, a well-respected portrait photographer. After printing many of his negatives and operating a camera on her own time, Bernice was encouraged by two of Man Ray's patrons, Peggy Guggenheim and Robert McAlmon, to open her own Paris portrait studio. They lent her the money to set up, and within a year, Bernice became one of the city's most sought-after portrait photographers.

Life's Work

Berenice Abbott's prosperous business was supported by clients who admired her photography. Among her sitters were playwright Jean Cocteau, *The New Yorker* correspondent Janet Flanner, novelist James Joyce, fashion designer Gabrielle "Coco" Chanel, and Sylvia Beach, owner of the Left Bank book shop known as "Shakespeare and Company." Abbott's reputation as a portrait photographer was spread by word of mouth, since she never advertised or pursued prospective clients.

In addition to perfecting her portrait work while in Paris, Abbott admired and studied the photographs of a little-known French photographer named Eugène Atget. The bulk of his life's work had not been created in a portrait studio, but out on the streets of Paris in the early years of the twentieth century. After Atget's death in 1927, Abbott bought fifteen hundred of the photographer's glass-plate negatives and eight thousand of his prints. She spent decades trying to find a publisher to show Atget's work to the rest of the world. Her recognition of the value of Atget's City of Paris project revealed Abbott's critical eye. From her early years as a photographer, she began to develop a philosophy about photography and its purposes in a modern society. Abbott's words about visual images came to be nearly as important as her photographs themselves.

In 1929, Abbott returned to New York City for a brief visit, but she was so overwhelmed with the vitality of the city that she decided to move back to the United States. She wanted to photograph New York—its architecture, its historical places, and its streets. Soon after her move that same year, the stock market crashed and the resulting economic depression made business difficult. Nevertheless, Abbott stayed afloat financially by taking on commercial work. Her pictures appeared in a number of popular magazines including *Fortune, Vanity Fair*, and *The Saturday Evening Post*. In her spare time, Abbott explored the city's streets with her camera in hand. Enjoying the diversity of New York's neighborhoods, Abbott carefully observed the various architectural styles, from the old brownstones to the modern skyscrapers. Upon noticing that some older structures had been demolished to make way for new buildings, she realized that she needed to record the process of change in the city. Abbott recognized that photography could play a role in historical preservation as well as tell the story of a city's present condition. After collaborating with architectural historian Henry Russell Hitchcock on a documentation of pre-Civil War architecture in several eastern seaboard cities, Abbott returned to New York more convinced than ever of her responsibility to document what was, in her opinion, the most vital American city.

Abbott's goal to capture New York City in photographs sustained her throughout the 1930's. Institutional support for her documentary project came first from the Museum of the City of New York, which exhibited forty-one of Abbott's photographs in 1934. As a result of this exhibit, she was offered a teaching position at the New School for Social Research, and her success encouraged her to seek outside funding for her photography. Officials at the Federal Art Project of the Works Progress Administration, one of the public works programs set up by President Franklin Roosevelt's administration, decided to provide financial support for Abbott's ongoing project, known thereafter as "Changing New York." The federal government's backing resulted in wide exposure for Abbott's photographs, which were sent to federal galleries throughout the United States. In addition, the Museum of the City of New York, a cosponsor for "Changing New York," opened a show of Abbott's pictures in October of 1937. An overwhelming public response to the exhibit and Abbott's soaring reputation led E. P. Dutton to offer to publish her pictures in book format as *Changing New York*. In 1939, the finished product appeared, containing ninety-seven of Abbott's photographs, along with commentary by art critic Elizabeth McCausland. That same year, the Federal Art Project cancelled the ongoing "Changing New York" project, a decision that led Abbott to focus more intently upon her teaching and her philosophy of photography.

Throughout the 1940's and 1950's, Abbott spoke and wrote about photography as a medium and the role of the photographer in modern society. In addition to several important published articles, her books and catalogs included *A Guide to Better Photography* (1941), *The View Camera Made Simple* (1948), and *A New Guide to Better Photography* (1953). Ever conscious of the atomic age that World War II had ushered in, Abbott encouraged photographers to study, to understand, and to document scientific subjects. She herself experimented with magnetic fields, energy transformation, electric currents, and various types and directions of waves and wavelengths. Emphasizing the photographer's responsibility to communicate reality, Abbott wrote in 1951, "The photograph may be presented as finely and artistically as you will; but to merit serious consideration, must be directly connected with the world we live in." For Abbott, the world had become one dominated by science and technology. Her pictures of scientific subjects were widely exhibited, particularly after she won the respect of her associates on the Physical Science Study Committee, where she served as principal photographer from 1958 to 1961.

After completing a documentary project that took her the length of U.S. Highway 1 from Maine to Florida, Abbott moved to Maine in the mid-1960's. Before her move she managed to find an interested publisher for Atget's work, and *The World of Atget* finally appeared in 1964. In the next twenty-five years, her reputation continued to expand further as exhibitions of her work were shown at such places as the Smithsonian Institution's Museum of History and Technology, the Museum of Modern Art, the Witkin Gallery in New York City, and the International Center of Photography. In 1989, the New York Public Library sponsored a major retrospective of her work in an exhibition which traveled to cities throughout the United States and abroad. In her later years, Abbott chose people and places in the state of Maine as the primary subjects for her camera's eye. She died in Monson, Maine, in 1991.

Summary

Berenice Abbott lived through an age that witnessed great technological changes in many realms, particularly in her own field of photography. When she began in the early years of the twentieth century, she carried a heavy 8 x 10 view camera and a tripod around with her, but as lighter cameras, faster-speed films, and new processes replaced the old, Abbott was there to take advantage of these changes and help advance the medium of photography. As a result she aided in generating recognition for photography as a recognized medium of communication as well as a respected form of art. Her early exhibitions of photographs on museum walls broke new ground, since some art critics and artists believed that photographs should not hang on the same walls as paintings. Yet Abbott's arguments for photography as a viable way of informing while simultaneously uplifting humanity won widespread acclaim. She constantly emphasized the power of human creativity and noted that every person had both the need and the ability to be creative.

Every aspect of Abbott's life and career was marked by her independence. She never felt limited because she was a woman. While managing her own business affairs, Abbott pursued photographic projects that she thought needed attention, even though other projects could have generated more income. For her, the process of recording life was a necessity to understanding life itself.

Bibliography
Abbott, Berenice. *Berenice Abbott*. New York: Aperture Foundation, 1988. In addition to a perceptive essay by Julia Van Haaften, the book contains a list of collections that include Abbott's work, a list of her exhibitions shown over a sixty-year period, and a bibliography of works by and about Abbott.
_____. *Photographs*. Washington, D.C.: Smithsonian Institution Press, 1990. The book contains a brief introduction by David Vestal and a foreword by Muriel Rukeyser, but its strength lies in the photographs and in the accompanying explanations Abbott provided for her scientific work.
Daniel, Pete, et al. *Official Images: New Deal Photography*. Washington, D.C.: Smithsonian Institution Press, 1987. A comparative examination of the different types and uses of photographs produced by federal government employees in the 1930's. It is particularly useful for understanding the impact of photography during the Great Depression.
Mann, Margery, and Anne Noggle, eds. *Women of Photography: An Historical Survey*. San Francisco: San Francisco Museum of Art, 1975. A collection of fifty brief but insightful biographies of female photographers. In their introductions, the editors note the important contributions of women photographers to the medium since its inception. Among the book's strengths are listings of the depositories and other locations where each woman's photographs may be found.
Mitchell, Margaretta K. *Recollections: Ten Women of Photography*. New York: Viking Press, 1979. Based on an exhibition of the same name sponsored by the International Center of Photography, the book includes biographical sketches written by the photographers themselves with additional commentary by the editor. Abbott discusses the source of her independence and tendency toward risk-taking.
O'Neal, Hank. *Berenice Abbott: American Photographer*. New York: McGraw-Hill, 1982. The most thorough biography available on Abbott. In addition to O'Neal's observations and research, there are lengthy observations by Abbott about the numerous photographs included in the book. Reproductions of her works are excellent.
Sundell, Michael G. "Berenice Abbott's Work in the 1930s." In *Prospects: An Annual of American Cultural Studies*. Vol. 5, edited by Jack Salzman. New York: Burt Franklin, 1980. A scholarly treatment of Abbott's "Changing New York" project.

Sundell contrasts Abbott's documentary work with that of Eugène Atget, arguing that Abbott belonged to a quite different age. There are thorough examinations of Abbott's keen interest in specific building projects as they grew to dwarf the old New York City.

Melissa A. McEuen

GRACE ABBOTT

Born: November 17, 1878; Grand Island, Nebraska
Died: June 19, 1939; Chicago, Illinois
Area of Achievement: Social reform
Contribution: A leading Progressive reformer, Abbott worked for social justice both within and outside of government, especially for the health, safety, and fair treatment of immigrants, women, and children.

Early Life

Grace Abbott was born on November 17, 1878, in Grand Island, Nebraska, which, though it was the county seat, still had a frontier feeling. Her Quaker mother, Elizabeth Griffin Abbott, came from a strongly abolitionist family, graduated from Rockford (Illinois) Female Seminary, and became an educator; at the time of her marriage in 1873, she was working as a high-school principal in Iowa. Othman Ali Abbott, Grace's abolitionist Canadian father, served as an officer in the Union Army in the Civil War, read law in Illinois, and, in 1867, moved to Nebraska where he practiced law.

The interests and work of both parents had a powerful influence on the four Abbott children, especially Grace and her elder sister Edith, who became lifelong partners in the pursuit of social justice. Their mother worked for the cause of woman suffrage, hosting and making arrangements for suffragists who traveled through Nebraska; she showed keen concern for the injustices suffered by American Indians. She encouraged all of her children to prize education and sought to provide them with better opportunities than were available in rural Nebraska; for example, in spite of economic hard times, she managed to send Grace and Edith to the World's Fair in Chicago in 1893. Their father also encouraged them, often taking them to the courthouse to observe the judicial process and discussing court cases and politics with them; he treated women's political opinions with respect. No less than their brothers, the sisters were expected to study, work, think about political and social issues, be articulate, and make a contribution to improve the world.

Initially, those contributions remained close to home. The depression of the 1890's hit midwestern farmers hard and soon caused financial problems for professional families such as the Abbotts. Although their mother had hoped to send her daughters to Rockford Seminary, they went to work teaching school to help their family pay its debts. Despite these obligations, both used their free time to continue their educations. During summer vacations, they took courses at the University of Nebraska and later the University of Chicago, from which Edith earned a doctorate in economics in 1905 and Grace a master's degree in political science in 1909.

Life's Work

Even as children, Grace and Edith Abbott had exhibited different but remarkably complementary personalities and skills. While Edith was more private, reserved, and scholarly, an analytical thinker, Grace confidently approached life as a series of challenging problems to solve by organizing and getting people to work together. Grace was always the one who came up with practical ways to achieve their shared goals and had no qualms about confronting new people and situations. Virtually from Grace's arrival at the University of Chicago on, the Abbott sisters frequently worked as a team, with Edith providing Grace with statistics and analysis on which to base policies and Grace offering her sister new information uncovered during the implementation of policies.

While still working on her master's degree, Grace Abbott took a temporary position with the Juvenile Protection Association in 1908; the job consisted of keeping children from poor neighborhoods away from dangerous activities. Soon after, she moved into Hull House, the famous settlement house headed by Jane Addams, which she and Edith used as their home base for nearly the next ten years. A strong recommendation from social worker Sophonisba Breckinridge, Edith's university mentor and friend, launched Grace in her first major professional post as director of Chicago's Immigrants' Protective League in 1908.

Grace was ideally suited to the job. She quickly grasped the varied needs of newcomers to the United States—from confronting basic problems of transportation, work, and housing, to negotiating the legal mazes involved in attaining citizenship and facing the court system. Although many social agencies provided services as charity, the league took a more "professional" approach, developing policies and mechanisms to integrate new Americans as a matter of simple justice. Grace Abbott's practical approach led to effective innovations, such as recruiting staff members who spoke the immigrants' native languages and setting up a greeting center opposite Union Station to aid immigrants who had just arrived in Chicago. Just as important, she was a staunch and vocal advocate, testifying before Congress against the literacy test that was designed to keep immigrants out. She also wrote *The Immigrant and the Community* (1917), which refuted popular misconceptions and proposed ways to improve immigrants' integration into American life.

Grace Abbott had a special interest in issues that concerned women. Through her work with the league and at Hull House, she became involved in the Chicago garment workers' strike in 1910-1911, where she learned of the economic exploitation of the women and children who made up half of the strikers. She backed the presidential campaign of Theodore Roosevelt in 1912, once he announced his support for woman suffrage, and continued her mother's tradition of working for suffrage herself. Soon after World War I broke out, she served as an American delegate to an International Congress of Women at The Hague (1915), a meeting which had been organized to protest the war and demand the alternative of continuous mediation by neutral countries. Although subjected to sexist ridicule, these women offered a feminist perspective on thinking about the world as a unified system. In 1921, Abbott participated in a conference sponsored by the League of Nations on international efforts to halt the illegal sale and transport of women and children.

Children's welfare also represented a major concern for Abbott. In 1912, her Hull

House friend and colleague Julia Lathrop had become the first director of the federal Children's Bureau, and, in 1917, Abbott joined her there to administer the 1916 Keating-Owen child labor law. When the Supreme Court ruled the legislation unconstitutional in 1918, she promptly began rallying women around the country to lobby Congress for a constitutional amendment on child labor (such an amendment was finally submitted to the states in 1924 but was never ratified). In 1918, she and Lathrop organized a successful national Conference on Standards of Child Welfare, which examined all aspects of children's lives, including health, education, labor, and home life. When Lathrop resigned from the Children's Bureau in 1921, Abbott was appointed to succeed her, just in time to set up the administration of the Sheppard-Towner Act.

This innovative law addressed the critical problem of maternal and infant mortality. It represented the first federal venture into social welfare legislation, appropriating $1.5 million in federal matching funds to enable states to set up educational health programs for mothers. Abbott used the same strategy as she had in administering the child labor law, working with state agencies to develop practical programs suited to local conditions. Not only did she and the bureau use the new law to distribute clearly worded pamphlets and films on pregnancy, childbirth, and child care throughout the country, but they also funded prenatal and well-baby examinations, the training and certification of nurse-midwives, and a special truck called the "Child-Welfare Special" for health check-ups in isolated rural areas. The program was immensely popular among women, some of whom obtained accurate information about caring for their health for the first time. It drew bitter attacks from the American Medical Association, however, and Congress allowed the program to lapse in 1929.

Abbott had favored Herbert Hoover's election in 1928, but soon opposed him over his plan to move the Children's Bureau from the Department of Labor to the Public Health Service; this would have seriously limited the bureau's authority. At the White House Conference on Child Health and Protection in 1930, Abbott and Hoover's respective supporters all but rioted over the proposed change; the bureau stayed where it was. While Abbott nominally retained control, she had incurred Hoover's lingering hostility and her precarious health (debilitating flare-ups of tuberculosis) limited her activity until the advent of the New Deal. She developed a good working relationship with Franklin D. Roosevelt's Secretary of Labor, Frances Perkins, eventually helping to draft the Social Security Act (1935) and the Fair Labor Standards Act (1938); the latter finally included effective child labor provisions. After resigning from the Children's Bureau in 1933, Abbott returned to Chicago, where she shared a house and editorial responsibilities with her sister, taught courses in public welfare at the University of Chicago, and compiled *The Child and the State* (1938). She also participated in the Pan-American Child Congress (1935) and an International Labor Organization conference (1937). Grace Abbott died of cancer in Chicago on June 19, 1939.

Summary

In many ways, Grace Abbott embodied what was best about Progressivism. She committed herself to protecting those too weak to help themselves, such as children, and to devising practical means to empower others, such as immigrants and mothers, who simply needed information and basic support to make their contribution to the common life of the nation. She had boundless faith in education, broadly construed, for herself and for others. She understood that all individuals need access to accurate information in order to control their own lives and that society as a whole must also have such access in order to ensure social justice. Providing people with the knowledge they needed remained a consistent theme in her life, whether in classrooms, in her writings, in international conferences, in translations of documents for immigrants, or in pamphlets on breast-feeding for new mothers. If the power of federal agencies was necessary to do the job, she was quite willing to use it.

At the same time, Abbott believed in the power of individuals working together to make a difference. Perhaps because of her remarkably cordial and productive relationship with her sister, she developed supportive relationships with women colleagues in the United States and around the world, mobilizing vast networks of women to work for issues that mattered to them. Although women in positions of power were still rare, she confidently maintained her feminist perspective in her work with both men and women. Most of all, she continued to strive for social justice her entire life.

Bibliography
Abbott, Grace. *The Child and the State.* 2 vols. Chicago: University of Chicago Press, 1938. Collection of documents, statutes, reports, and court rulings, with analytical introductory essays by Abbott; volume 1 on the legal status of children in families and on child labor conditions is especially helpful.

———. *The Immigrant and the Community.* Reprint. New York: Jerome S. Ozer, 1971. A facsimile reprint of Abbott's original edition, published in 1917. In a clear, personal style, supplemented by useful statistical tables, Abbott refutes popular misconceptions (that immigrants break the law more frequently than others, that they are political radicals) and offers dozens of practical suggestions to facilitate and improve immigrant participation in American life (for example, changing techniques for teaching English).

Bradbury, Dorothy E. *Five Decades of Action for Children: A History of the Children's Bureau.* Washington, D.C.: U.S. Department of Health, Education, and Welfare, Social Security Administration, Children's Bureau, 1962. Useful government publication that traces the Children's Bureau's policies, political problems, successes, and failures, written by an agency insider; approximately the first third deals with Abbott's tenure at the bureau.

Chambers, Clarke A. *Seedtime of Reform: American Social Service and Social Action, 1918-1933.* Minneapolis: University of Minnesota Press, 1963. Important revisionist account of the persistence of Progressivism in the 1920's and of how the actions and attitudes in this period laid the groundwork for the New Deal; very helpful in its detailed picture of the social and political environment in which Abbott worked.

Costin, Lela B. *Two Sisters for Social Justice: A Biography of Grace and Edith Abbott.*

Urbana: University of Illinois Press, 1983. Indispensable double biography that makes a strong case for the mutual influence of the two sisters and for their impact on education and policy; the topical, rather than chronological, organization is occasionally confusing.

Skocpol, Theda. *Protecting Soldiers and Mothers: The Political Origins of Social Policy in the United States.* Cambridge, Mass.: The Belknap Press of Harvard University Press, 1993. Not specifically about Abbott, but a thought-provoking analysis of the development of "maternalist" social policy; does an excellent job of demonstrating the powerful social networks among educated women and how these affected government policy, especially the Children's Bureau.

Susan Wladaver-Morgan

BELLA ABZUG

Born: July 24, 1920; New York, New York

Area of Achievement: Government and politics

Contribution: One of the most colorful and well-known members of Congress in the 1970's, Abzug has been an aggressive spokesperson for women's rights throughout her life.

Early Life

Born in New York City on July 24, 1920, the second daughter of Emanuel and Esther Savitzky, Bella Savitzky experienced neither great deprivation nor great prosperity in her childhood. Her father, an unsuccessful businessman whose shop failed in the 1920's and who had to turn to bookkeeping and selling insurance to support his family, died in the 1930's when Bella was just entering an all-girls high school in the west Bronx; her mother supported the family on the combination of his insurance money and her earnings as a cashier and saleswoman in local department stores.

What Bella's upbringing lacked in material wealth was, by all accounts, offset by her family's closeness and spiritual wealth. Yiddish and Russian folk songs were often sung at the Savitzky home, an apartment Bella shared with her sister, parents, and maternal grandmother, and one of her mother's bachelor brothers. From her family came her ethnic heritage in the Jewish faith. As a child Bella regularly attended the solemn services of the church; as a pre-teen she joined a Zionist pioneer youth group and collected money for the Zionist cause and dreamed of going to Palestine to help build and establish a Jewish homeland there during the 1930's.

In school Bella excelled. Elected as president of her high school class and later as student body president while at Hunter College, Bella also found time to teach Hebrew and Jewish history to the young on weekends and to march in protest against the spread of Nazism in Europe and against British and American neutrality in the Spanish Civil War.

Ironically, it was her faith that somewhat inadvertently led to the development of Bella Savitzky's commitment to feminism. As she later wrote in her 1972 autobiography, when she attended synagogue with her grandfather, she was offended "that women were consigned to the back rows of the balcony."

A dedicated activist by the time she received her B.A. degree from Hunter College in 1942, Bella entered Columbia University Law School already oriented toward a career in litigation work. In 1945, she received her LL.B. degree and joined a firm specializing in labor law, one of the most confrontational of all areas of the law and one whose practitioners were viewed with suspicion during the "red scare" days following World War II.

It was during her transition from college into the study and practice of law that Bella also embarked on other dimensions of her life important to her: her roles as wife and mother. In 1944, she married Maurice M. Abzug, a man she had met on a bus in Miami on the way to a concert performance by violinist Yehudi Menuhin. Together, the couple had two daughters: Eve Gail in 1949 and Isobel Jo in 1952.

Life's Work

Perhaps the term which best describes Bella Abzug's life is "activist." Tongue in cheek, she notes in her autobiography that her "family used to say, prophetically" that she was born "yelling." She has been yelling ever since for the causes to which she has been drawn.

In the early 1950's, while she was still a young attorney, Abzug became deeply involved in the Civil Rights movement. Indeed, while carrying her second child in 1952, she undertook to defend a black man in Mississippi accused of raping the white woman with whom he had been having an affair. Although she ultimately lost the case, Bella Abzug later noted that she was able to delay the man's execution for two years by appealing the conviction twice to the Supreme Court. These appeals were based on her arguments that her client had been unconstitutionally convicted by a jury from which black Americans were systematically excluded and that in being sentenced to death for a rape conviction—a sentence virtually never given to a white man for the same crime—he had unconstitutionally received a "cruel and unusual punishment." The arguments were nearly two decades ahead of their time; the Warren and Burger Courts would eventually accept both arguments in applying at the state level those provisions of the Bill of Rights guaranteeing a fair trial and prohibiting cruel and unusual punishment.

During the 1960's, Bella Abzug juggled the demands of her Manhattan legal practice with her growing interest in banning nuclear testing. She joined with women across the country to protest the resumption of nuclear tests, helped to found the Women's Strike for Peace organization, and often led that organization in its lobbying efforts before Congress and in its demonstrations in Washington, D.C., and New York between 1961 and 1970. After the signing of the Test Ban Treaty, she also helped to refocus the antinuclear movement into an antiwar movement as the United States became involved in the conflict in Vietnam.

By the late 1960's, Abzug's concerns about the war in Vietnam and the continuing decay of American cities drew her even further into the American political arena. She struggled to forge a broad, progressive coalition across party lines to address the concerns of the poor, ethnic minorities, and women's groups in shaping a new national agenda. The 1968 Democratic Party convention in Chicago, however, frustrated Abzug's efforts. Hubert Humphrey's nomination in Mayor Richard Daley's city seemingly signaled that insider politics and the old order were still in control of the national Democratic Party. Two years later, however, political opportunity beckoned in her own backyard.

During the 1960's, New York's Twentieth Congressional District, located along Manhattan's West Side, became a political haven for reformist Democrats, typified by William F. Ryan. First elected in 1960, Ryan was reelected to Congress throughout the decade despite his early opposition to the Vietnam War, his efforts to abolish the House Committee on Un-American Activities, and his embrace of many causes out-of-step with Washington's leadership at the time. Ryan's success, in turn, encouraged progressives in neighboring districts to challenge old line politicians backed by the Tammany Hall machine, including Leonard Farbstein in the adjacent Nineteenth District of lower Manhattan. Throughout the decade, however, these challengers failed. Then, in 1970, Farbstein confronted a new challenger: Abzug.

Running on her ties with labor to win union support and campaigning with glamorous celebrities such as Barbara Streisand to win over the Jewish vote from her opponent, Bella Abzug won the Democratic primary and comfortably won the 1970 general election. Moreover, once in Congress she rapidly championed progressive causes even more aggressively than Ryan. Unlike Ryan, she also challenged many of the conventions of the House—wearing her wide, trademark hats inside Congress in spite of requests made by the House Doorkeeper to remove them and addressing committee chairmen brusquely when disagreeing with them.

Abzug's career could have ended with that one term. Following the 1970 census, which cost New York one of its seats in the U.S. House of Representatives, the New York legislature reapportioned its congressional seats by essentially merging Abzug's district into Ryan's. Instead of accepting the outcome, Abzug took the offensive and challenged Ryan for the Democratic nomination for Congress in 1972. She lost the acrimoniously fought primary by a two-to-one margin, largely because of Ryan's longer years of service in Congress. Three months later, however, Ryan died, and Abzug was chosen by the party's district committee to represent the Democrats in a general election to replace him. During this election, she had to run against a Republican opponent and against Ryan's widow, who campaigned as a Liberal. Abzug won with an outright majority of 56 percent and two years later was reelected with a 79 percent majority.

Having achieved national celebrity and winning praise from mainstream Democrats for her tireless work on the Government Operations and Public Works committees on which she served, Abzug had perhaps as safe a seat as any in Congress. Nevertheless, she announced her decision to run for the Senate in 1976. Her subsequent career in politics was nearly as flamboyant and swift as her rise to national attention. She lost the 1976 Democratic primary for the Senate seat to Daniel Patrick Moynihan, failed the following year to win the New York mayoral primary against challenger Ed Koch, and ended her electoral career in 1978 by losing to her Republican opponent in the race to fill Koch's vacated seat representing New York's Eighteenth Congressional District, a district with a liberal but youthful, trendy, and Waspish constituency quite different from that of Abzug's former district and Bella Abzug herself.

Although they were the centerpiece of her life in public affairs, Bella Abzug's six years in Congress formed only a short period of that life. In Congress, she was a symbol for her time—an outspoken champion of feminism and a variety of other progressive causes. After leaving Congress, she continued her activism, serving in such posts as presiding officer of the National Commission on the Observance of International Women's Year and the National Women's Conference in 1977, acting as cochair of the President's National Advisory Council for Women in 1978, and serving subsequently as a cable television commentator, Fellow at Harvard University's Kennedy School, and a popular speaker throughout the country for more than a decade. The early 1990's likewise found her active on behalf of numerous causes, cochairing the Women's Environmental Development Organization in 1991, serving as a senior adviser to the United Nations Conference on the Environment and Development in 1992, and actively campaigning on behalf of David Dinkins' 1993 attempt for a second term as mayor of New York. In her work with the Women's Environmental Development Organization, Abzug joined Greenpeace in supporting a worldwide ban of chlorine-based chemicals because of their suspected link to breast cancer.

Summary

As a lawyer, a politician, and a leading civil rights and women's rights advocate, Bella Abzug has distinguished herself as one of the foremost woman activists of her time. As the chair and cofounder of the bipartisan National Women's Political Caucus (NWPC), Abzug joined leading activists such as Betty Friedan and Gloria Steinem in encouraging more women to run for elective office and in generating funding to help these women candidates achieve victories. As a regular columnist for *Ms.* magazine since 1979, Abzug has shaped public opinion on a variety of issues pertaining to the role of women in society. As a highly visible member of NOW and a staunch crusader for the passage of the Equal Rights Amendment, Abzug marched with other supporters in a variety of rallies and parades in order to generate greater attention and support for the amendment. Finally, at a time in her life when many of her contemporaries have chosen to relax in retirement, Abzug has continued to work on behalf of a number of social causes near to her heart, many of which focus on women's roles in preserving and protecting the environment. As she wrote in *Gender Gap: Bella Abzug's Guide to Political Power for American Women* (1984), women can either "learn to become political leaders and activists, or [they] can sit back and let a minority of men in government, backed by powerful money and military interests . . . try to run the whole world." Certainly the career of Bella Abzug has amply demonstrated her unwillingness to sit back and watch the world go by.

Bibliography
Abzug, Bella S. *Bella! Ms. Abzug Goes to Washington.* New York: Saturday Review Press, 1972. With an acknowledgement to her staff, Abzug's autobiography is built around a diary chronicling her first year in Washington, D.C. She combines a warm portrait of her family life with a vivid picture of the challenges she faced in Washington's male-dominated political arena and the in-your-face manner with which she responded to these challenges.
Abzug, Bella, with Mim Kelber. *Gender Gap: Bella Abzug's Guide to Political Power*

for American Women. Boston: Houghton Mifflin, 1984. Much more than a "how to" book for mobilizing American women to fight for true equality in American parties and politics, this book provides a clear exposition of citizen Abzug's lifelong political philosophy and fighter's disposition to translate that philosophy into practice.

Barone, Michael, Grant Ujifusa, and Douglas Matthews. *The Almanac of American Politics, 1974: The Senators, the Representatives—Their Records, States and Districts.* Boston: Gambit Press, 1973. The best source for background reading on the members of Congress, placed in the context of their political lives and the constituents who sent them there. This volume chronicles Congresswoman Abzug at the beginning of her second term.

Barone, Michael, and Grant Ujifusa. *The Almanac of American Politics, 1982: The President, the Senators, the Representatives, the Governors—Their Records, States and Districts.* Washington, D.C.: Barone & Company, 1982. A later version of this key reference work. The entries on Abzug are chiefly interesting for their account of her failed races for the Senate in 1976 and mayor of New York City the following year.

Ruben, Barbara. "Bella Abzug: Giving Women a Voice." *Environmental Action Magazine* 24 (Summer, 1992): 12-14. An interview with Abzug that provides insights into her activities on behalf of the environment and in the area of world affairs since her departure from Congress after being defeated for election to the Senate in 1976.

Witt, Linda, Karen M. Paget, and Glenna Matthews. *Running as a Woman: Gender and Power in American Politics.* New York: Free Press, 1993. A journalist, a political scientist, and a historian collaborated on this narrative overview of the experiences of female candidates in American politics. Although this work includes many references relating to Abzug's career, perhaps the most intriguing anecdote is the story of how Mayor John Lindsay of New York City told Abzug that she would be less critical of politicians if she tried being one herself. Lindsay's exasperated comment inspired Abzug to launch her own political career instead of remaining on the sidelines in supporting male candidates.

Joseph R. Rudolph, Jr.

ABIGAIL ADAMS

Born: November 22, 1744; Weymouth, Massachusetts
Died: October 28, 1818; Quincy, Massachusetts
Area of Achievement: Women's rights
Contribution: An early proponent of humane treatment and equal education for
women, Abigail Adams wrote eloquent, insightful letters which provide a detailed
social history of her era and her life with John Adams.

Early Life

Abigail Smith was one of four children born to William Smith, minister of North
Parish Congregational Church of Weymouth, and Elizabeth Quincy from nearby
Braintree, Massachusetts. Both parents were members of prominent New England
families of merchants, statesmen, and ministers. From her parents, Abigail learned a
conservative, rational Puritanism. She retained throughout her life a solid Christian
faith and shared with her Puritan forebears a belief in the fundamental depravity of
humankind. These religious convictions influenced her political opinions.

Observing her mother's example, Abigail learned her future duties as wife and
mother. Within her role as minister's wife, Elizabeth Smith provided relief for the
town's poor, nursed the town's sick, and presented herself as a model of wifely
behavior. She was nurturing and kind to her children.

In eighteenth century Massachusetts, education was prized. In government-
supported schools, boys studied Latin, Greek, French, mathematics, and literary arts
in preparation for higher education either at Harvard or abroad. Girls, however, were
educated almost exclusively at home, receiving only rudimentary training in reading
and writing; some remained illiterate. Instead, they learned domestic skills such as
sewing, fine needlework, and cooking, which were considered vital preparation for
marriage. Abigail received only informal home instruction yet shared with her sisters
the advantage of a keen intellect and unlimited access to her father's extensive library.

In her early adolescence, Abigail was encouraged in her studies by a young
watchmaker and scholar, Richard Cranch. Although self-educated, Cranch conveyed
his passion for scholarship to Abigail and to her sisters Mary and Elizabeth. It was
through Cranch, who wedded Mary, that Abigail met her future husband.

Abigail Smith proved a shrewd judge of character when at the age of nineteen she
married Harvard-educated lawyer John Adams. Although they were not social
equals—he was from a markedly less prominent family and practiced a profession that
was poorly regarded—the match proved exceedingly profitable and satisfying for
both parties. In John, Abigail found a man who appreciated and even encouraged her
forthrightness and her intellectual ability, while John in turn received emotional,
financial, and intellectual support from Abigail.

Life's Work

Abigail Adams is best known for her remarkably detailed, eloquent letters. Although many creative outlets were considered unsuitable for women to pursue, letter writing was a socially sanctioned literary art for women in the eighteenth century. Abigail, who felt compelled to write, naturally selected that medium.

During her first ten years of marriage, however, Abigail's letter writing was not prolific as she was kept extraordinarily busy with domestic affairs. Enduring five pregnancies in seven years, she also suffered the death of an infant daughter. In addition, she was plagued by several physical afflictions including frequent colds, rheumatism which caused acute swelling of joints, and insomnia.

During these early years, she moved her household several times to remain with John in his work. The turmoil of their lives as they uprooted their family paralleled the contemporary political events in which John played a leading role. This was a pattern they would repeat throughout his working life and would include residence in Boston, Philadelphia, New York, Paris, and London. Abigail demonstrated repeatedly that she was extraordinarily adaptable and found pleasure in observing foreign customs. She always, however, longed for the idealized pastoral life in Braintree that she had shared with John during their first few years of marriage.

In 1775, John embarked for Congress on the first of frequent extended absences from Abigail. With her husband away, Abigail weathered several personal tragedies, including a difficult pregnancy in 1777, during which she apparently suffered from toxemia and finally eclampsia, a condition that is usually fatal to the infant and often to the mother. A remarkable series of letters were written between John and Abigail during this period; in them, Abigail expressed loneliness and fear for her unborn child. The child, a girl, was indeed stillborn. John and Abigail's letters provide invaluable information on the social history of parent-and-child relationships.

The pattern of intimate and frequent letters between husband and wife continued over the next twenty-five years as John, an extraordinarily ambitious man, accepted political positions that removed him from home for periods often extending to years. While Abigail considered their separation as a patriotic sacrifice, she nevertheless frequently expressed her loneliness to John, imploring him to return home.

Because she was a married woman, Abigail was legally prevented from owning property in her own name. Notwithstanding, she repeatedly demonstrated her ingenuity and self-sufficiency. During their first ten years together, John's legal fees and the income from their farm supported the family. As events took him farther from home, his legal practice was largely abandoned and Abigail assumed most financial duties. She never welcomed the addition to her already burdensome domestic responsibilities, yet she consistently proved herself a competent manager. Abigail deplored debt and worked to ensure that her family avoided it. She successfully ran the farm for four years during which she was responsible for the odious chore of collecting rents from several tenants as well as supervising agricultural production. Scarcity of labor and acute inflation made the task a difficult one. After four years, she lessened her burden by renting the farm.

In 1778, Abigail began requesting luxury goods from John, who was then serving as a diplomat in France. She then profitably sold these items, which, because of war shortages and inflation, were scarce in Massachusetts. At the same time, Abigail also purchased land and speculated in currency. Through these endeavors, she kept her family solvent.

During the ten years in which she saw her husband only sporadically, Abigail expanded her literary interests, exploring, through John's guidance, political theory, biography, and history. She also wrote voluminously, to John and to other family members as well as to friends. It was during this period that Abigail wrote to John of her political views regarding women's roles in the new nation. Her famous letter of March 31, 1776, in which she requested John to "Remember the Ladies," has established Abigail's reputation as an early proponent of women's rights. In context, however, it is clear that Abigail wrote not of political rights but of women's legal rights, specifically those which guaranteed them protection from physical abuse. At the time, divorce, although allowed in a few extreme instances, was generally unavailable. In addition, women abrogated all rights to property ownership upon marriage, which in turn made them ineligible to vote because property ownership was a key qualification for voting.

Abigail also advocated equal education for women. She argued for equal education within the context of her perception of women's traditional domestic roles. The concept of "Republican Motherhood" held that because women taught the sons who were destined to become leaders, women had an important role in maintaining the existence of an informed citizenry capable of supporting a republican government. To teach their sons successfully, these women required equal education, which Abigail hoped would be supported by law.

Although she is now viewed as an early advocate for women's rights, Abigail Adams saw her own life as highly traditional. An adept manager of her family's resources, she nevertheless viewed her role as currency speculator, land purchaser, and farmer as aberrant and a patriotic sacrifice. She was comfortable only in her domestic role, and in that, as in all else, she excelled. Abigail was an affectionate mother and grandmother who lived to see her son John Quincy establish a successful diplomatic and political career. Several personal tragedies marred her happiness, including the death of her son Charles from alcoholism when he was thirty years old and her daughter Nabby's brutally painful mastectomy and subsequent death from breast cancer.

Until 1800, when John retired from government office, Abigail functioned at times as hostess during his several years as a diplomat, first in England, then in France. She also served two terms as the vice president's wife during the Washington Administration and finally as First Lady during her husband's presidency.

During the last eighteen years of her life she retired with her husband to Braintree, already renamed Quincy, and lived in relative domestic peace surrounded by children, grandchildren, sisters, nieces, and nephews. At the family's Quincy farm, Abigail pursued her lifelong hobby of gardening. Dying of typhoid fever in 1818, she was mourned by John, who, lamenting the loss of his "dearest friend," survived his wife by eight years.

Summary

Abigail Adams always functioned within the prescribed social roles for women of her time. She was an affectionate, protective mother who cared for her children physically and emotionally her entire life. She provided intellectual and emotional companionship as well as financial support for her brilliant but irascible husband John. Although Abigail for a time functioned as merchant, farmer, and speculator, she viewed these roles as a patriotic sacrifice on her part to support the political career of her husband.

While her own marriage provided her intellectual and emotional satisfaction, she condemned the tyranny of men over women and longed for legal protection for women. Women's education she hoped would one day rival that of men. She also yearned for the day when women could limit their number of children. Nevertheless, her life must be viewed within the context of her eighteenth century world, where she functioned primarily within the domestic sphere. She was not a public advocate for women's rights; the term "women's rights" was not even used in her time. Neither did she view her role within her marriage as less valuable than that of her husband. To Abigail and to John, marriage was a true partnership. She was a supremely shrewd, able woman who took every advantage available to her to expand her intellectual horizons and enjoyed a wide correspondence through her letters. In addition to insights which they provide into this remarkable woman's psyche, Abigail Adams' copious letters provide a detailed social history of her era as well as invaluable insights into the character of her husband John Adams and into those of several other political leaders, including her close friend Thomas Jefferson.

Bibliography

Adams, Abigail. *The Book of Abigail and John: Selected Letters of the Adams Family, 1762-1784*. Edited by L. H. Butterfield, Marc Friedlaender, and Mary-Jo Kline. Cambridge, Mass.: Harvard University Press, 1975. Because Abigail Adams' literary achievements were her eloquent, informative letters, particularly to her husband John, the letters in this volume are illuminating and interesting.

Akers, Charles W. *Abigail Adams: An American Woman*. Boston: Little, Brown, 1980. Written specifically for the college undergraduate and high school student, Akers' work is admirably detailed yet readable. Abigail's life is well grounded in historical context and the 192 pages of text are not formidable.

Gelles, Edith B. *Portia: The World of Abigail Adams*. Bloomington: Indiana University Press, 1992. This is the most insightful biography of Adams, viewing her not only as John's wife and John Quincy's mother but also within the context of her domestic and predominantly female world. Because it requires a knowledge of fundamental historical events, it should be read in conjunction with a broader history, such as Akers'. Includes an instructive introductory historiographic chapter, footnotes, bibliography, and chronology.

Levin, Phyllis Lee. *Abigail Adams: A Biography*. New York: St. Martin's Press, 1987. By far the most detailed biography of Adams; makes extensive use of the sources.

Unlike other Adams biographers, Levin provides ample discussion of Abigail's life during the years after John Adams' retirement, although she does so against the backdrop of John Quincy's career. Similarly Abigail's earlier life is viewed against John's career. Just shy of 500 pages, the work is footnoted, contains a bibliography, and provides a family tree.

Nagel, Paul C. *The Adams Women: Abigail and Louisa Adams, Their Sisters and Daughters.* New York: Oxford University Press, 1987. While not exclusively about Abigail Adams, Nagel's work is useful for placing her life within the context of her close female relations, including her sisters Mary and Elizabeth. Despite his admiration of her intellect, Nagel provides a portrait of Adams that is largely unsympathetic; she appears domineering and shrewish.

Withey, Lynne. *Dearest Friend: A Life of Abigail Adams.* New York: Free Press, 1981. Withey's biography is one of the less satisfying works on Adams because the author judges Abigail by twentieth century standards rather than understanding her within her historical context. Withey focuses extensively on Abigail's political views while paying scant attention to her more notable successes in her domestic roles, viewing Abigail as a "prisoner" in her world.

Mary E. Virginia

JANE ADDAMS

Born: September 6, 1860; Cedarville, Illinois
Died: May 21, 1935; Chicago, Illinois
Area of Achievement: Social reform
Contribution: The two major achievements of Addams' life were the founding of Hull House, a social settlement in Chicago, and the promotion of peace through her presidency and involvement with the Women's International League for Peace and Freedom.

Early Life

Jane Addams was born on September 6, 1860, in the small town of Cedarville in northern Illinois. She was the youngest child of eight and one of only four to reach adulthood. Her mother died before she was three years of age, and thus she was reared by her father, John Huy Addams, and his second wife, Anna Haldeman Addams. John Addams was a prosperous businessman in Cedarville, and Jane's early life was spent growing up comfortably in a rural community. Her father was well respected, having served as an Illinois state senator from 1854 to 1870. He was born a Quaker, although he did not practice, and he was an abolitionist and a good friend of Abraham Lincoln. Jane Addams cited her father as the major influence in her life, and he helped to shape her political views.

Jane Addams attended Rockford Seminary in Rockford, Illinois, from 1877 to 1881. She was very active in college life, serving as editor-in-chief of the school publication and valedictorian of her class. During the summer after graduation her father died, and his death was a tremendous loss for her. Determined to begin a career in medicine, Jane went to Philadelphia to study at the Woman's Medical College. She began her studies but fell ill from a spinal defect she had had since childhood. After her health improved, she decided to visit Europe to help regain her strength. She traveled abroad from 1883 to 1885. Throughout her travels, she was struck by the conditions of the poor. Upon her return, she was still searching for direction and purpose. She remained busy with philanthropic and business pursuits and spent time caring for her nieces and nephews.

In 1887, Jane Addams traveled to Europe once again, accompanied by her college friend Ellen Gates Starr. During their travels together, Addams continued to search for a purpose and for a way to bring help to the poor. The two travelers discovered Toynbee Hall on their visit to London, and it served as the model for their plans. Toynbee Hall was the first settlement house, a place where university students could learn about the plight of the poor at first hand and also work to improve life in the community. Addams brought the idea to Chicago, where she felt she could fulfill her life's work and help the poor.

Life's Work

Jane Addams, with the help of Ellen Gates Starr, opened Hull House on September 18, 1889. Hull House was the first settlement house in the Midwest. It was the former home of millionaire Charles Hull and was located on the near West Side of Chicago, which had become a neighborhood of poor immigrants. At the time that Addams appropriated it, it was dilapidated and in need of repairs.

Addams believed in living and working in the community. Hull House was a community center as well as the residence of those who worked there. The doors were never locked, and Hull House was open to all residents of the surrounding neighborhood. Addams identified herself simply as the "head resident," although over the years she gained national fame and was influential in shaping American social policy and social institutions.

Addams and Starr's earliest reform attempts were to bring art and literature to the slums as a way of brightening a drab existence. They quickly discovered that people had more immediate needs. The working-class neighbors of Hull House were in great need of food, clothing, and better housing. Viewing people's needs at first hand, Addams worked to change the larger social systems which seemed to ignore her neighbors. Continuing to offer social activities for area residents, Addams and her fellow workers at Hull House began to shift their attention to rooting out the causes of poverty and other social ills they witnessed. Thus, Hull House became famous for serving individuals, the neighborhood, and American society as a whole.

Hull House was a success from its earliest years. In the first year, fifty thousand people came to the house. From only two residents in the first year, the house grew to include other committed residents. By 1899, ten years after opening, there were twenty-five resident workers and numerous volunteers and community supporters.

Addams and her Hull House reformers were directly involved in developing the first organized kindergarten and in establishing social clubs, an employment bureau, adult education classes, a library, a theater, and an art gallery. These programs were developed at Hull House under the direct supervision of Addams at the same time that she was advocating social reform.

The efforts of Addams and Hull House residents focused primarily on two areas: problems affecting children and labor issues. In her book *The Spirit of Youth and the City Streets* (1909), she wrote about the problems of delinquency and that environment had a significant influence on youths. She argued that young people needed outlets for recreation and creativity. From the earliest years of Hull House, Addams focused on helping poor children. She was deeply concerned about the lack of activities for children and the limited space available for them to play. In 1892, the first public playground was created through her efforts.

Residents of Hull House became sorely aware of the terrible conditions many children suffered. Poor children were forced to endure twelve-hour workdays in dangerous factories. Florence Kelley, a resident of Hull House during the 1890's, enlisted the assistance of Jane Addams in addressing this problem. Joining with other labor organizers, they fought for and successfully gained legislation limiting child labor. In response to the maltreatment of delinquent youths, Hull House residents successfully argued for a separate justice system for juveniles. In 1899, state law created the first juvenile court in the nation.

Hull House was known for its efforts in organizing workers and supporting unions. In 1891, Addams founded the Jane Club, a social and support group for young factory girls. Over the years, the group organized and developed a boarding club in an adjacent building. Young working women lived cooperatively in the Jane Club, sharing responsibilities for cooking and cleaning. The club also served as a place for organizing women workers into labor unions.

Addams herself was very involved in the organization and support of unions. She believed that unions and organized labor would help create better economic conditions for all. In 1904, she was elected vice president of the National Women's Trade Union League. In addition to union organizing, she was deeply involved in city and national politics. In her early years at Hull House, she served on the Chicago Board of Education and throughout her years at Hull House pressured city officials for political reform.

As Addams gained national recognition, her political influence grew. A leading suffragist and officer of the National-American Woman Suffrage Association (NAWSA) from 1911 to 1914, Addams found little support for her views within the platforms of the two major political parties. In 1912, she publicly supported the new Progressive Party and its presidential candidate, Theodore Roosevelt. The party's platform included recommendations from the National Conference of Charities and Correction, a social work organization of which, in 1909, she was the first woman to be elected president. The Progressive Party platform articulated values and principles which Addams held dear. Her active support of the party included campaigning throughout the Midwest, in spite of the fact that as a woman, she herself could not yet vote.

Through their observations and reform programs, Addams and Hull House residents also influenced the academic realm of studying social problems. In 1895, the publication of *Hull-House Maps and Papers* introduced the practice of social research. This collection of essays was the first extensive survey done on urban social conditions and documented the living conditions of people in the surrounding community. The book was full of data used to highlight the needs of the neighborhood and supported Hull House reform efforts in demanding city services such as public playgrounds, public bathhouses, and trash removal. Addams helped develop formal education for social workers and reformers through her work as one of the founders of the Chicago School of Civics and Philanthropy. The school later became the School of Social Service Administration at the University of Chicago, known for its outstanding contributions to the field of sociology.

Until the outbreak of World War I, Jane Addams enjoyed great acclaim among the American people. As American neutrality gave way to the nation's entry into the war, Addams' pacifist opposition to the war put her at odds with public opinion and led to widespread criticism of her work. She advocated peace because she believed it was her social responsibility to oppose war and its ruthless destructiveness. In 1915, she helped to create the Women's International League for Peace and Freedom (WILPF).

She was elected as the organization's first president, a position she held until 1928. She was deeply hurt by the outcry against her pacifism and disappointed in the public's retreat from social reform. Throughout the 1920's, she spent much of her time traveling abroad working for the WILPF.

The economic despair of the 1930's made Jane Addams' message and work relevant again. Public opinion was once again supportive of her. In 1931, she won the Nobel Peace Prize for her tireless efforts on behalf of world peace; she shared the award with Nicholas Murray Butler. Her last years were spent writing, supporting the peace movement, and advocating further social reform. Her death on May 21, 1935, brought an outpouring of sadness and sympathy.

Summary

On many occasions throughout her life, Jane Addams was voted one of the most outstanding women of her time. She was revered for her work to improve life for the urban poor, even while she was criticized for her strong pacifist views. Jane Addams lived her life with a singleness of purpose, striving to make the world a better place in which to live, particularly for those who were powerless and impoverished. She was a member of the first generation of college-educated American women, and she demonstrated the breadth of influence and power a woman could achieve. She especially fought for the rights of children and women through labor organizing and political reform. For Jane Addams, her purpose at Hull House was to remove conflict in human relations. Believing war to be the epitome of human conflict, she directed her later efforts toward achieving world peace. Jane Addams serves as a powerful role model for women—as a social reformer, an organizer, an activist, and a supporter of world peace.

Bibliography

Addams, Jane. *Peace and Bread in Time of War*. New York: Macmillan, 1922. Reprint. New York: Garland, 1972. Written by Addams as an explanation of her pacifist beliefs, this book chronicles her work with the Women's International League for Peace and Freedom.

—————— . *Twenty Years at Hull-House*. New York: Macmillan, 1910. An autobiography, this book provides an in-depth look at the early years of Hull House from Jane Addams' perspective. It includes personal reminiscences of her childhood as well as her life at Hull House.

Davis, Allen F. *American Heroine: The Life and Legend of Jane Addams*. New York: Oxford University Press, 1973. A thorough biography of Addams, detailing her early life until her death. The approach is both sympathetic and analytical.

Levine, Daniel. *Jane Addams and the Liberal Tradition*. Madison: State Historical Society of Wisconsin, 1971. A biography with emphasis on the philosophies and ideas of Jane Addams.

Linn, James Weber. *Jane Addams: A Biography*. New York: D. Appleton-Century, 1935. An admiring biography written by Addams' nephew. Although it does not provide objective interpretation, the work is valuable for its wealth of detail regarding Addams' life.

Stroup, Herbert. *Social Welfare Pioneers.* Chicago: Nelson-Hall, 1986. A collection of biographies of the first social workers committed to social reform. The first chapter discusses Jane Addams' contributions to social welfare.

Tims, Margaret. *Jane Addams of Hull House, 1860-1935.* New York: Macmillan, 1961. Spanning all Addams' life, this book provides a general overview and is not as detailed as that of Linn.

Elizabeth A. Segal

ELIZABETH CABOT CARY AGASSIZ

Born: December 5, 1822; Boston, Massachusetts
Died: June 27, 1907; Arlington, Massachusetts
Area of Achievement: Education
Contribution: First president and cofounder of Radcliffe College, Agassiz helped create a college for women taught by the faculty of Harvard University.

Early Life

Elizabeth Cabot Cary was born December 5, 1822, in Boston, Massachusetts, to parents descended from families that had settled in New England during the seventeenth century. Her mother, Mary Ann Cushing Perkins Cary, was the daughter of Thomas Handasyd Perkins, one of the wealthiest Boston merchants. Her father, an unsuccessful lawyer, joined his father-in-law's firm in 1832, and later became an officer of a major Massachusetts cotton mill. Elizabeth and her four sisters and two brothers grew up in a home provided by their grandfather, with many cousins similar in age living nearby. Because her parents thought her health too delicate to allow her to attend school, she was educated at home by governesses.

Her world expanded after her oldest sister Mary Louise Cary married Cornelius Felton, professor of Greek at Harvard University. In 1849, Elizabeth went to live with them in Cambridge to help her sister during a pregnancy. While living with the Feltons, Elizabeth met Louis Agassiz, a world-renowned Swiss geologist and zoologist whose enthusiastic reception during a lecture tour in Boston in 1846 had convinced him to remain in the United States, accepting a position as professor of natural history at Harvard in 1848. Agassiz, whose first wife had died in Europe shortly after his arrival in the United States, frequented the house of his close friend, Cornelius Felton. It was during these visits that he and Elizabeth fell in love despite the fifteen-year difference in their ages. The two were married April 25, 1850. When Agassiz's three young children arrived from Europe, Elizabeth welcomed them and mothered them throughout her life. She had no children of her own.

Elizabeth Agassiz proved a valuable associate in her husband's scientific work. Despite her sheltered upbringing, she chose to accompany him on his collecting expeditions in the United States and Brazil and on a circumnavigation of South America. She took careful notes at her husband's lectures and kept a detailed diary of their travels that provided Louis Agassiz with the basis for much of what he published during their marriage. Elizabeth proved a graceful writer and authored two introductory volumes on marine biology. Although the title page of *A Journey in Brazil* (2 vols., 1867) reads "by Professor and Mrs. Louis Agassiz," the book is a revised version of the journal Elizabeth kept during their two-year collecting expedition on the Amazon River, with technical footnotes added by her husband.

To aid family finances strained by her husband's scientific expenditures, Elizabeth Agassiz ran a school for young girls from 1855 to 1863 in the family's Cambridge home. She supervised the entire operation and managed the finances while teaching

English composition and music appreciation. Elizabeth's stepson taught French and German while Louis Agassiz himself lectured on natural history. Other Harvard professors volunteered or were recruited to teach Greek, Latin, and mathematics. Elizabeth would later say the Agassiz School was the forerunner and inspiration for Radcliffe College.

After her husband's death on December 14, 1873, Elizabeth Agassiz devoted herself to collecting his materials and writing a biography, published as *Louis Agassiz: His Life and Correspondence* (2 vols., 1885).

Life's Work

Although fully engaged in writing her husband's biography, Elizabeth Agassiz joined a committee of women in February of 1879 who were attempting to open Harvard instruction to women. The cause of women's education would become her major interest for the rest of her life. The first impulse for the drive came from Arthur Gilman, a Cambridge resident and popular historian who did not want to send his college-aged daughter to a distant women's college. Although coeducation of men and women was common in the West, older Eastern colleges were exclusively male and the Harvard governing boards proved particularly resistant to assuming any educational responsibility for women. President Charles W. Eliot of Harvard had publicly expressed doubts on the value of higher education for women, but he eventually agreed not to oppose a plan to pay Harvard professors to repeat their courses for women, provided it was clear that Harvard had no direct responsibility.

On February 22, 1879, the committee with Elizabeth Agassiz at their head and Arthur Gilman serving as secretary, announced that several Harvard professors would offer course work at the undergraduate level in the fall to properly prepared women and sign certificates of accomplishment for those who passed. Women completing a four-year course of study would receive a certificate signed by all the professors testifying that they had successfully completed the work for a college degree.

Twenty-seven women passed the entrance exam that September and began classes in rooms rented in a private house. In 1880, forty-two women took twenty-seven classes taught by twenty-three members of the Harvard faculty, including several senior professors who found the extra income a useful addition to their skimpy academic salaries. Most students were commuters; many were daughters of Harvard faculty or came from Boston families long associated with the college. Agassiz and her committee arranged for others to board in Cambridge. Although Eliot insisted on a clear separation between the university and "The Society for the Collegiate Instruction of Women," as the organization was formally titled, most people referred to it as the "Harvard Annex."

The society was formally incorporated in 1882, allowing it to accept bequests from wills and to hold real estate. Agassiz took the presidency, Gilman continued as secretary, and a committee of Harvard faculty determined academic policy. Agassiz led the continual fund-raising needed to keep the operation going and served as diplomatic intermediary with Harvard officials. Her social connections with much of the wealth of Boston and her prestige as the widow of Louis Agassiz made her particularly effective in both roles.

"My object," she wrote in 1887 to Annie Nathan Meyer, who would play a comparable role in attaching Barnard College to Columbia University, "was to get the collegiate instruction for women, and at the same time conciliate both those who wished women to be immediately admitted to the classes with the young men and those who wished them never to be so admitted." Not even Agassiz's diplomatic skills could accomplish this task without stirring controversy.

With 263 students enrolled in 1893, the success of the Annex was evident. Nevertheless, the women still could not receive degrees upon completion of their four-year course, a situation that particularly hampered those seeking teaching positions. Every attempt to get Harvard degrees for the women failed. An offer by the Women's Education Association of Boston to raise an endowment of $250,000 if Harvard took over the Annex was rejected in 1893. Since Harvard adamantly refused to award diplomas to women, Agassiz's society itself would have to be empowered.

After lengthy negotiation with President Eliot, Elizabeth Agassiz reached what she believed was a workable compromise: The society would ask the Massachusetts legislature for authority to award degrees, the president and fellows of Harvard College would act as "Visitors" and approve all faculty appointments in the new college, diplomas would be countersigned by the president of Harvard, monetary affairs would be solely the responsibility of the new college. At Eliot's suggestion, the society was renamed Radcliffe College, honoring Ann Radcliffe, Harvard's first female benefactor.

Agassiz thought this a reasonable next step in her campaign to open Harvard education to women, but she came under fierce attack from women who believed she had not been aggressive enough and had settled for too little. The Women's Education Association withdrew its support for the endowment drive, causing it to collapse. Annex alumnae who had joined the drive hoping to secure Harvard degrees for their successors signed a petition protesting the compromise. The Association of Collegiate Alumnae, a national organization, hired lawyers to oppose the Radcliffe charter before the state legislature on the ground that its endowment, facilities, and ties with Harvard were too insecure to justify giving it degree-granting power. According to President Eliot, it was Elizabeth Agassiz's forceful and dignified defense of her institution that convinced the opposition to withdraw their objections. Radcliffe College was formally chartered March 23, 1894.

Agassiz became the first president of Radcliffe, continuing to lead in fund-raising as its land acquisition and building program expanded the physical presence of the college in Cambridge. New dormitories, a gymnasium, and laboratories testified to the permanency of Radcliffe. On Agassiz's eightieth birthday, her stepchildren and friends donated funds for a student activities building named Agassiz House in her honor. After failing to convince her associates in 1899 that it was time for her to retire, she accepted the office of honorary president. In 1903, she insisted on giving up even this symbolic office and was pleased that the choice of Le-

Baron Russell Briggs, Harvard's dean of faculty, as her successor brought the union of Harvard and Radcliffe one step closer.

In 1904, Agassiz suffered a stroke from which she only partially recovered. She later died after suffering a second stroke in 1907.

Summary

Elizabeth Agassiz was never a vocal feminist. She did not join the movement to secure the vote for women or any of the other causes that involved activist women of her generation. In her twenty-four years of campaigning to secure a Harvard education for women, Agassiz had to restrain ardent feminists who called for immediate admission to all Harvard classes and degree programs at the same time that she worked to overcome the resistance of men who considered the presence of women in the Harvard Yard to be unthinkable. The pattern of a coordinate women's college that Agassiz pioneered was imitated with variations at Columbia, Brown, and other Ivy League men's colleges.

Agassiz's persistent, patient pressure on Harvard, moving step by step toward greater equality, did not succeed fully in granting educational parity to women during her lifetime. Some additional progress was made when graduate courses and many upper-level undergraduate courses at Harvard were opened to women after 1894. It was not until 1943, when faced with empty classrooms as men went to war, that Harvard eliminated duplicate classes for women. Moreover, it was not until 1963 that separate Radcliffe degrees were abandoned and Harvard diplomas issued to women. It took seventy years after Harvard accepted responsibility for women's education for Agassiz's successors to achieve full equality. Their success rested on the foundations laid by her careful, conciliatory approach.

Bibliography

Horowitz, Helen Lefkowitz. *Alma Mater: Design and Experience in the Women's Colleges from their Nineteenth-Century Beginnings to the 1930s.* New York: Alfred A. Knopf, 1984. Describes how Agassiz's Radcliffe created a new pattern for women's colleges.

Kendall, Elaine. *"Peculiar Institutions": An Informal History of the Seven Sister Colleges.* New York: G. P. Putnam's Sons, 1976. An anecdotal history that focuses on personalities, the volume describes the way in which academic life and customs developed as Radcliffe succeeded.

King, Patricia M. "The Campaign for Higher Education for Women in Nineteenth Century Boston." *Proceedings of the Massachusetts Historical Society* 93 (1981): 59-80. Using primary sources, the author puts the work of Agassiz in the context of other efforts to achieve educational equality for women.

Lurie, Edward. *Louis Agassiz: A Life in Science.* Chicago: University of Chicago Press, 1960. Although somewhat dated in its interpretation, this detailed biography of Louis Agassiz's scientific achievements praises his wife for her important contributions to his work.

Paton, Lucy Allen. *Elizabeth Cary Agassiz: A Biography*. Boston: Houghton Mifflin, 1919. An older work that is still valuable. Extensive quotations from Elizabeth Agassiz's letters and diaries show her mind in action. Especially strong on her involvement with Radcliffe.

Tharp, Louise Hall. *Adventurous Alliance: The Story of the Agassiz Family of Boston*. Boston: Little, Brown, 1959. A well-written book bringing to life the personalities and struggles of Louis and Elizabeth Agassiz and their children.

Milton Berman

JOANNE AKALAITIS

Born: June 29, 1937; Cicero, Illinois

Area of Achievement: Theater and drama
Contribution: Akalaitis is one of the preeminent American theatrical directors of the late twentieth century. Unlike most directors on the commercial stage, she develops her productions using a collaborative method. Her work as a playwright and a director is considered eclectic and avant-garde.

Early Life

JoAnne Akalaitis was born and reared in a blue-collar suburb of Chicago. Her parents, Clement Akalaitis, a supervisor at General Electric, and Estelle, née Mattis, were of Lithuanian Roman Catholic ancestry. As a child, JoAnne Akalaitis attended Lithuanian school, where she appeared in many plays. Still, she did not pursue her interest in drama when she reached college, preferring instead to take a B.A. degree in philosophy from the University of Chicago in 1960. Akalaitis won a fellowship to pursue graduate studies in philosophy at Stanford University, but she eventually dropped out of that program and instead used the money to study at the Actor's Workshop in San Francisco. She met her future collaborators there and in workshops with the San Francisco Mime Troupe.

Eager to expand her theatrical experience, Akalaitis moved to New York in 1963 and to Paris in late 1964. In Paris, she collaborated with Lee Breuer and Ruth Maleczech, friends from San Francisco, on a production of *Play* by Samuel Beckett. Another participant in the project was Philip Glass, whom Akalaitis married on July 15, 1965.

In 1968, when her first child Juliet was six months old, Akalaitis joined Maleczech in studying for a month with Jerzy Grotowski, the leader of the movement of the "poor," or actor-centered, theater. This experience shaped the rest of Akalaitis' career. She came to the realization that the psychological motivation of a character must have a physical dimension or manifestation. Also, she came to believe that the actor was not just an interpreter of other people's art, but an artist in his or her own right, just as much as the playwright. She said, "I saw a whole development of Stanislavsky that involved the body, that involved my own personal history, and involved my value as an artist."

When she returned to New York, in late 1969, Akalaitis formed a theater collective with Maleczech, Breuer, Glass, and David Warrilow. During the troupe's rehearsals in 1970, which were held in Glass's beach house in Nova Scotia, Canada, Akalaitis was pregnant with her second child. At first, the men in the group expected her and Ruth Maleczech, who was also pregnant, to cook, clean, and care for the babies, in addition to rehearsing all day. She said, "We decided that the men had to wash the dishes and the company had to pay for the babysitter. And at that time, there was resistance to it. . . . [N]ow it's different, it's accepted."

Akalaitis' desire for the equitable distribution of housekeeping responsibilities continued to manifest itself as her career progressed. Though she and Glass divorced in 1974, they continued to share the upbringing of their children. "He does it three days and I do it three, then we alternate every other Saturday. Because he's involved in performing, I take care of the children when he's on tour, and he takes them when I'm on tour," she said in a 1976 interview.

It was Akalaitis who suggested that the new theater company take the name of a nearby Nova Scotian mining town, Mabou Mines. The troupe debuted its first play, Lee Breuer's *The Red Horse Animation*, at the Guggenheim Museum in New York City in November, 1970.

Life's Work

"I think all the people involved in the group really started their artistic lives—in a sense we were reborn—when Mabou Mines began," JoAnne Akalaitis later said about her work with the theatrical group. The group staged several "animations," works that could be considered performance art pieces, under Breuer's direction in the early 1970's.

When the Mabou Mines performed three plays by Samuel Beckett at the Theater for the New City Festival, their work caught the attention of New York's theater "establishment," and they were invited to play at Joseph Papp's Public Theater in 1976.

For her direction of her first production, *Cascando*, by Samuel Beckett, with the Mabou Mines company, Akalaitis won her first Obie Award for excellence in an off-Broadway production. From this point on, Akalaitis changed her focus from acting to directing. She went on to stage her own script, *Dressed Like an Egg*, based on the writings of the French novelist Colette, with Mabou Mines at the Public Theater in 1977. Akalaitis won her second Obie Award for this production.

In 1978, Akalaitis won a Guggenheim fellowship and used it to cowrite, design, and direct a play about Antarctica, called *Southern Exposure*, with Mabou Mines in 1979. This effort brought her a third Obie Award.

Her 1980 collaboration with Mabou Mines was called *Dead End Kids: A History of Nuclear Power*, about the dangers of atomic energy and weapons. It played at the Public Theater for more than two-hundred performances and also found success on tour at regional theaters around the country. The script was made into a film in 1986, which Akalaitis also directed.

Akalaitis won the Rosamond Gilder Award from the New Drama Forum and a Drama Desk Award for her 1981 direction of Franz Xaver Kroetz's *Request Concert*. Also in 1981, Akalaitis acted the role of Mrs. Lammle in the play *Dark Ride* by Len Jenkins.

Akalaitis directed a piece called *Red and Blue* by Michael Hurson in 1982. In 1983, she staged a multimedia production called *The Photographer* with music by her former husband Philip Glass at the Next Wave Festival at the Brooklyn Academy of Music.

Akalaitis staged two notable works in 1984. The first was *Through the Leaves* by Franz Xaver Kroetz. Ruth Maleczech and Frederick Neumann, her colleagues from Mabou Mines, won Obie Awards for their acting in this production. Akalaitis went on to direct an unconventional staging of Samuel Beckett's *Endgame* in Cambridge, Massachusetts, at the American Repertory Theater. Beckett became so upset when he learned that she had wavered from his exact stage directions that he threatened to go to court to stop the production. He finally allowed the show to go on, with the provision that his caveat denouncing the production be attached to every play program.

Akalaitis directed another iconoclastic production at the American Repertory Theater late in 1985, a new translation of Jean Genet's *The Balcony*. In 1986, she directed herself and Ruth Maleczech in *Help Wanted* by Franz Xaver Kroetz. In the same year, she traveled to the Mark Taper Forum in Los Angeles to create a work entitled *Green Card*, about the American immigrant experience—a play considered by many to contain the hallmarks of her work as a playwright.

In 1987, Akalaitis staged Georg Büchner's play *Leon and Lena* at the Guthrie Theatre in Minneapolis. She returned to that theater in 1989 to direct *The Screens* by Jean Genet.

She finally came to national prominence, however, when she was asked to direct William Shakespeare's *Cymbeline* at the New York Shakespeare Festival in the summer of 1989. In May of 1990, Joseph Papp invited her to become one of his four artistic associates. She accepted, and in 1991 directed Shakespeare's two part historical drama *Henry IV*.

In August of that year, Joseph Papp, who was suffering from cancer, resigned his post as artistic director of the New York Shakespeare Festival and named Akalaitis as his successor. Her tenure was brief and bitter. That fall, she conducted a town meeting of playwrights to discuss their concerns. She wanted to promote the works of new playwrights in spite of the severe budget cuts that wracked her organization.

In the spring of 1992, Akalaitis staged *'Tis Pity She's a Whore* (pr. 1629[?]-1633, pb. 1633) by John Ford. In December, she mounted Georg Büchner's *Woyzeck*. On March 13, 1993, the board of directors of the New York Shakespeare Festival suddenly fired Akalaitis and named African American playwright George C. Wolfe as her replacement. Akalaitis was given scarcely a week to clean out her desk.

She had planned to stage Shakespeare's *Henry VIII* that summer for the Festival. Instead she directed a Lincoln Center Theater Company production of a play by Jane Bowles called *In the Summer House*, which opened in August, 1993.

Apparently, Akalaitis' sudden dismissal was influenced by the savage reviews of her work written by *The New York Times* theater critic Frank Rich. Robert Brustein warned, in a 1993 article in the *New Republic*, that Rich and the Festival board of directors were, "still in the grip of Reagan-Bush conservatism, despite the recent change in administration, and a bottom-line mentality continues to rule our art." He called this movement New Aesthetic Populism, a "war on the arts" from the center.

Brustein stated that Rich exposed his "continuing indifference to art with any depth or daring. . . . It is bad enough for one newspaper to control the destiny of commercial production, but when a powerful critic begins to arbitrate the conduct of non-profit institutions, then a shudder passes through the entire theater community."

Akalaitis concurred with this opinion. "The center of this story is an agenda on the part of *The New York Times*. . . . In this case, it's not that the board [of directors] has a strong opinion—it has no opinion. It's waiting to be told what to think by the newspapers."

Brustein has predicted that Akalaitis will continue to be a strong artist who might be better suited to independence than the administrative duties inherent in running a large theater. Yet, he worries that there might not be anyplace left that she will want to work, given the conservative nature of the present climate of the cultural world.

Summary

Even Frank Rich, the theater critic whose brutal assaults on Akalaitis may have resulted in her downfall, admitted in 1981, "Almost single-handedly she is giving new life to the whole notion of political theater."

Her power grew with the nascent women's movement in the late 1960's and early 1970's. She began as a pregnant actress, demanding equality in housekeeping chores with her male counterparts. Even though she was a single mother, she continued in her career, growing more experienced and skilled as a theatrical director. Akalaitis remained true to her artistic vision, even when that meant she had to stand up to Samuel Beckett or to suffer a dismissal from the Public Theater that Robert Brustein described as "unusually brusque and humiliating."

Akalaitis has faced the practical problems of raising a family while working in the theater. She has struggled against sexism, anti-intellectualism, and political conservatism. Yet, Akalaitis has persisted, providing leadership in the theater world and maintaining her integrity in both her personal and professional life.

Bibliography

Brustein, Robert. "Akalaitis Axed." *New Republic* 208 (April 26, 1993): 29-31. Brustein writes a sympathetic interpretation of the events that led up to Akalaitis' dismissal from her post as artistic director of the New York Shakespeare Festival. He includes a review of the last production there under her tenure, a musical version of the play *Wings* by Arthur Kopit.

Kalb, Jonathan. "JoAnne Akalaitis." *Theater* 15 (Spring, 1984): 6-13. Kalb interviews Akalaitis on her directing theories. She discusses the projects she was involved in then, such as *Dead End Kids* and *Green Card*. She talks about the importance of her children to her work and the practical problems of being a working single mother.

Kenvin, Roger. "JoAnne Akalaitis." In *Notable Women in the American Theatre: A Biographical Dictionary*, edited by Alice M. Robinson, Vera Mowry Roberts, and Milly S. Barranger. New York: Greenwood Press, 1989. This is the most scholarly biographical article on Akalaitis available. Covers her career up to her directing debut at the New York Shakespeare Festival.

O'Quinn, Jim. "Change of Will." *American Theatre* 10 (May-June, 1993): 43. O'Quinn gives a factual interpretation of the events that led up to the firing of Akalaitis from the Public Theater. He summarizes Akalaitis' reaction to the event and the reactions of the American theater world.

Sommer, Sally R. "JoAnne Akalaitis." *The Drama Review* 20 (September, 1976): 3-16. Sommer interviewed Akalaitis for a special magazine issue subtitled "Actors and Acting." Akalaitis talks about her life as an actress in the collaborative environment of the Mabou Mines and addresses the problems of being a single mother working in the professional theater.

Irene E. McDermott

TOSHIKO AKIYOSHI

Born: December 12, 1929; Ryoyo, Manchuria, China

Area of Achievement: Music
Contribution: A composer, bandleader, and pianist who has significantly enriched jazz through a blend of Eastern and Western instruments, techniques, and textures. Akiyoshi has created an entire library of her own compositions and arrangements and has organized virtuoso jazz orchestras to play them, resulting in a series of unique recordings.

Early Life

Toshiko Akiyoshi was born in Ryoyo, Manchuria, in China, on December 12, 1929. The youngest of four daughters born to a Japanese textile and steel mill owner, Toshiko and her family moved back to Japan in 1946 in the wake of dangers posed by the incipient communist revolution.

She began her musical training at the age of six by studying classical piano. All of her musical schooling from kindergarten through high school was Westernized. The only association she had with Japanese music was through her family: One of her sisters was a student of traditional dance and her father was a student of the Noh play.

After World War II, when Akiyoshi was a teenager without any training in jazz or popular music, she went to work at a U.S. Army base in Tokyo playing piano in a dance band. During that time, she began to appreciate and learn the features of American jazz. She began her study of jazz by transcribing solos from records and then writing her own solos. Akiyoshi has considered herself to be a jazz musician ever since, influenced by bebop pianist Bud Powell and arranger Gil Evans, but also by other earlier jazz artists such as pianist/composer Duke Ellington.

Akiyoshi worked with a variety of jazz-influenced Japanese bands before forming her own quartet in 1951 that included renowned Japanese saxophonist Sadao Watanabe. Two years later, visiting pianist Oscar Peterson heard her playing in a Tokyo night club. He was so impressed with her playing that he invited her to record with his rhythm section and encouraged her to go to the United States. Her recording with Peterson led to a music scholarship in the United States.

Life's Work

Toshiko Akiyoshi studied music at the Berklee School of Music in Boston from 1956 to 1959. During her school years, and in subsequent years, she worked in Boston and New York as a jazz pianist for trios, small combos, and recording sessions. She also composed music for these groups. In 1959, Akiyoshi married saxophonist Charlie Mariano. For the next several years, they were coleaders of a jazz quartet. Their daughter, Michiru, was born a few years later, but their marriage ended by the mid-1960's. One of Akiyoshi's important formative experiences was a ten-month period between 1962 and 1963 when she performed with bassist Charles Mingus.

Years later she recorded an album entitled *Farewell to Mingus* (1980), a deeply felt tribute to him for the profound impact he had on her life and music during those critical early years.

Although the piano remained Akiyoshi's instrument for playing jazz, she grew more and more interested in music for larger groups. She once compared piano playing to painting in black and white and conducting a big band to painting in color. During the 1960's, Akiyoshi also became interested in composing for larger groups, but found it difficult to perform pieces without having such a group of her own. She began to doubt whether she could exist as a jazz musician because she believed that any real contribution she could make to the world of jazz had to be through writing. Her inspiration came from Duke Ellington, a composer who was proud of his heritage and whose music was influenced by his African roots. Ellington's example encouraged Akiyoshi to draw from her own roots. She wanted to give something back to jazz and was convinced that it had to be something created from her Japanese background and tradition. Finally in 1967, she organized a big band for a concert at Town Hall in New York. The band performed music which was all composed, arranged, and conducted by Akiyoshi. This group did not stay together for more performances because of the high cost of rehearsing a big band in New York. It was a frustrating as well as a productive time for Akiyoshi, and it was during this time that she met and married flute and saxophone player Lew Tabackin.

Writing and performing jazz as a woman and a foreigner have always been obstacles Toshiko Akiyoshi has to face in the male-dominated world of American jazz. But time after time, she has proven to be a competent and talented musician. In her album *Dedications* (1979), Akiyoshi pays tribute to several great jazz artists important in her own development, including pianist Bud Powell, whom she met on her first night in Boston. Powell later called her the best female piano player he had ever heard. His musical influence on Akiyoshi was so great that it took several years before reviewers stopped hearing echoes of his technique in her playing.

Akiyoshi and Tabackin moved to Los Angeles in 1972 and proceeded to form their own big band of studio musicians who performed and recorded together for a decade. Once they formed the band, Akiyoshi quickly excelled as a composer, writing several scores for the group in the big band tradition of Gil Evans and Thad Jones. Her innovative use of flutes and saxophones gave her band a distinctive sound, and the talented and enthusiastic players gave warmth to her strong and complex music. The band developed a unique style as Akiyoshi began to mix both Asian and American musical features and instruments.

In 1974, the band enjoyed its first success when RCA of Japan recorded and distributed their album *Kogun* in Japan. The album reached unexpected sales levels, selling more than twice as many records than the previous best-selling jazz record there. From this accomplishment, the band toured Japan and performed to sold-out concert halls. Back home in the United States, the band began to perform at concerts and festivals. By 1980, the Toshiko Akiyoshi/Lew Tabackin Big Band was one of the leading big bands in jazz.

During this period, Akiyoshi wrote a tragic tone poem about a Japanese fishing village destroyed by mercury poisoning. Large in scope and written in four parts, *Minamata* is a twenty-one-minute suite and ranks as one of Akiyoshi's greatest achievements. The first part, "Peaceful Village," features a long, droning chord that seems to make time go on and on until the listener feels that something must happen to break the spell. The opening of the next section, "Prosperity and Consequences," charges the air with excitement; its energetic melody, with its familiar jazz swing sound, builds up to the tragic outcome that follows. Finally, in the "Epilogue," a voice from a Noh actor and tsuzumi drums reflect the sad and horribly unexpected fate of the village. A grant from the National Endowment for the Arts enabled Akiyoshi to complete *Minamata* and gave her a chance to express her concerns and social consciousness through her music.

Akiyoshi has incorporated rich color, texture, and mood along with original techniques that blend Western jazz with Eastern instruments and themes in her compositional, arranging, and conducting styles. Not surprisingly, the Toshiko Akiyoshi/Lew Tabackin Big Band received numerous awards from *Down Beat* magazine and Grammy nominations. Despite this critical recognition, the band's records remained slow sellers in the United States—a fact Akiyoshi attributed to their record company's lack of interest in promoting or distributing their brand of new jazz.

In 1980, Akiyoshi and Tabackin moved back to New York where they formed a new big band and continued to perform regularly at concerts and festivals in the United States, Japan, and Europe. By 1985, they disbanded the group and Akiyoshi formed a new big band, Toshiko Akiyoshi's New York Jazz Orchestra, featuring Tabackin. As before, she continued to compose and arrange all the music performed by the orchestra. The orchestra released a recording of live music from a 1991 concert at Carnegie Hall commemorating Akiyoshi's thirty-five-year career as a leading jazz composer and pianist in the United States. Her main goal has been to create a library of original music, thus establishing a legacy in jazz history "that will be a little different from the mainstream of American tradition."

Summary

The appearance of Toshiko Akiyoshi on the American jazz scene has made an important difference in the way in which jazz is viewed by artists and audience alike. When Akiyoshi came to the United States to study music in the late 1950's, she was faced with three obstacles: She was not an American, she was not black, and she was not male. An American art form, jazz has been almost exclusively the domain of men. Many of the most notable jazz musicians have been African American, primarily because the roots of jazz are so firmly entrenched in African American culture. Nevertheless, when Akiyoshi began to play or conduct, her talent would brush aside these racial and gender barriers.

Although critics and audiences alike find Akiyoshi's performances as a jazz pianist competent and compelling, it is in her writing that her full musical talents flow and where she has made the greatest contribution. She introduced fresh ideas into a traditional format, the big band, particularly with her use of Eastern instruments and ideas. As an art form in which individual creative talents and improvisational techniques are pivotal elements, jazz has provided Akiyoshi an important outlet for expressing a musical vision informed by her own personal experience. Few jazz artists, male or female, have matched her accomplishments as evidenced in the works she has composed, arranged, conducted, and recorded.

Bibliography
Duncan, Amy. "How Toshiko Akiyoshi Finds Time for All That Jazz." *The Christian Science Monitor*, December 19, 1985, p. 1. A brief biographical sketch given shortly after the formation of Toshiko Akiyoshi's New York Jazz Orchestra. Discusses Akiyoshi's career, with particular focus on her work as a composer and an arranger and her collaborative efforts with her husband, Lew Tabackin.
Feather, Leonard. *The Jazz Years: Earwitness to an Era.* New York: Da Capo Press, 1987. A retrospective of Feather's associations and experiences with jazz artists, recording sessions, and concerts over several decades. The five sections— Beginnings, Transitions, Prejudices, Business and Pleasures, and Travels—cover the growth of jazz in America.
——————. *The Passion for Jazz.* New York: Horizon Press, 1980. A series of interviews and reminiscences that gives the reader inside knowledge of the world of jazz from talks with club owners and jazz artists to recent developments in such areas as big bands and the international scene.
Lyons, Leonard. *The 101 Best Jazz Albums.* New York: William Morrow, 1980. A collection of essays describing 101 jazz albums which the author feels are the best jazz recordings to date.
Lyons, Leonard, and Don Perlo. *Jazz Portraits.* New York: William Morrow, 1989. Personal, artistic, and historical facts about many famous and not so well known jazz artists give insight into people who have shaped an important American art form.
Seidel, Mitchell. "The Perils of Toshiko: Toshiko Akiyoshi." *Down Beat* 60 (February, 1993): 30-32. An interview with Akiyoshi shortly after the release of her orchestra's live album, *Carnegie Hall Concert* (1992). In addition to outlining her methods of composing and arranging music for the orchestra, Akiyoshi discusses prospects for improving the group's bookings in the wake of its new recording contract with Sony Music.
Stephen, Lynnea Y. "Toshiko Akiyoshi: Jazzing It up at Carnegie Hall." *Ms.* 3 (May-June, 1993): 82. Profile of Akiyoshi that provides an overview of her impressive career. She talks about her jazz beginnings in Japan as well as the implications of the twelve Grammy nominations she received in connection with her work with her various big bands and jazz orchestras.

Marilyn Kongslie

LOUISA MAY ALCOTT

Born: November 29, 1832; Germantown, Pennsylvania
Died: March 6, 1888; Boston, Massachusetts
Area of Achievement: Literature
Contribution: Assuming financial responsibility for the support of her family, Louisa May Alcott launched a literary career as a prolific writer of works for both adult and juvenile audiences. Her writing reveals the vitality of everyday life, with the family being her most frequent subject.

Early Life
Louisa May Alcott was devoted to her family throughout her life. Her father, Bronson Alcott, was an educator who struggled to earn a decent living for his family. Soon after Louisa's birth, her father moved the family to Boston. During the years preceding Louisa's success at writing, her family lived in poverty. This poverty forced the young Alcott daughters to work in order to contribute to the family funds. The family moved frequently, covering the areas from Boston to Concord. The four sisters, Anna, Louisa, Elizabeth, and Abba May, were reared by their father and their mother, Abigail (Abba) May.

As a result of their frequent relocations, the Alcotts came into contact with a variety of people. Through contact with Quaker neighbors, Louisa was exposed to Quaker notions of simplicity, which emphasized family relationships, rather than materialistic acquisitions. The Alcott family's admiration for this ideal of simplicity made their poverty more bearable. Louisa was also exposed to Transcendentalism by her father, a serious philosopher who believed that honesty, sincerity, unselfishness, and other spiritual characteristics were more important to acquire and practice than the material pursuit of wealth and comfort. Bronson Alcott launched a utopian communal experiment on a farm known as Fruitlands in Harvard, Massachusetts, where the girls maintained the family garden and worked in the barley fields. During this time, the family was influenced by their close proximity to the Shakers, who owned property in common and who worked together to complete tasks.

Because her father was interested in philosophy and education, Louisa and her family were acquainted with many of the great minds of the time. Bronson Alcott was a close friend of Ralph Waldo Emerson and Henry David Thoreau, and these men greatly influenced Louisa, who had little formal education. After Thoreau's death, Louisa wrote a poem, entitled "Thoreau's Flute," which was published in *Atlantic* in May, 1863.

In Concord, at the age of thirteen, Louisa began to write and produce little dramatic plays in the barn. At age sixteen, she decided to accept a job as teacher to Emerson's children so that she could contribute to her family's earnings. During these years of teaching, Louisa wrote stories for Ellen Emerson. These stories were later compiled into a book, entitled *Flower Fables*, published by George W. Briggs in 1855.

As a child, Louisa was deeply affected by contrabands, runaway slaves who had escaped from the South and fled to northern towns for protection. She was filled with compassion for the slaves and later wrote a poem for John Brown, the radical abolitionist who led the raid on Harpers Ferry. When the Civil War broke out, Louisa volunteered as a nurse and went to Georgetown Hospital in Washington, D.C. During her experiences in the hospital, she wrote a series of "Hospital Sketches" which were printed serially in *Commonwealth* and later published as a book in 1863. Her volunteer service as a nurse was terminated after only a month because Louisa came down with typhoid and had to return to Concord.

In 1865, Louisa sailed to Europe as a nurse and companion to a family friend's invalid daughter. During this year-long trip, Louisa met Ladislas Wisniewski, who became a close friend. Ladislas would later serve as the model for the character Laurie in *Little Women*.

Life's Work

A wide range of experiences gave Louisa May Alcott the opportunity to observe many different people. She knew farmers, Quakers, Shakers, and people of Boston society. She knew poverty, but she was also exposed to a rich intellectual world by her father, and by Emerson and Thoreau. Her travels to Europe gave her further perspectives on people, but when it came time to write, she wrote of what she knew best—her family.

Little Women, Alcott's most popular book, was published by Roberts Brothers in Boston. The book was published in two parts: part 1 (1868) and part 2 (1869). *Little Women* was Alcott's story of her life as one of four sisters. Family members and family friends were at the core of her writing. Daughters, mothers, and grandmothers across the country loved this book written by a female author who understood their experiences. With the success of *Little Women*, Alcott's works were in demand, and she wasted no time in producing more books.

In 1870, Alcott began work on *An Old-Fashioned Girl*, which was published in March of the same year. Many readers praised the story for offering an accurate picture of life in Boston society during that time period. Alcott's observations of life in Boston were particularly keen because she drew upon her own rural background to offer a point of comparison.

Alcott's next book, *Little Men*, was published in June, 1871. Although it was a fictional work, the book drew upon the real life experiences of Alcott's sister Anna, who reared two sons alone following her husband's death. Louisa May Alcott wrote *Little Men* in three weeks while staying at an apartment in Rome. Her description of the death of the character based on her brother-in-law John Pratt is a fine illustration of how she translated intimate personal experiences into literature.

Eight Cousins was written within six to eight weeks and was published in 1875. By this time, Alcott had been labeled as a writer for children, so when Henry James read a copy of this book, he was puzzled by its content. The satirical tone used in describing elders and social mysteries seemed out of place. Nevertheless, Alcott's many juvenile readers seemed eager to accept *Eight Cousins* as a mirror of reality.

The book's sequel, *Rose in Bloom* (1876), was written in three weeks while Alcott stayed at Orchard House in Concord. Just as *Eight Cousins* revealed something of Alcott's social theory, *Rose in Bloom* reflected her views on love and morality. In *Rose in Bloom*, Alcott combines reason with emotion in warning readers to look closely at potential marriage partners before commitment. She advises that no person is completely perfect; all humans have their flaws. The story of Rose and Mac is a rational approach to love and was written for a public that used common sense to control the extremes of romance.

Alcott abandoned her customary juvenile subject matter in 1877, when she wrote *A Modern Mephistopheles*, a story inspired by Goethe's Faust. Critics claimed that this novel of emotion was similar to the romances Alcott had written at age fifteen, but this story lacked the vitality of her earlier material. The book met with an indifferent reception and was called by some, "her middle-aged folly."

Louisa May Alcott went on to write additional stories, but they came out of a life that was increasingly more difficult. In her 1938 biography on Alcott, Katharine Anthony aptly described how Alcott translated her life into writing: "Out of such flights into loneliness, restlessness, and emptiness she made her rich, breathing, ardent stories of home." When Alcott's life was touched by the tragedy of losing family members and close family friends, she concealed her grief over their deaths and wrote cheerful, lively tales. Although she enjoyed literary celebrity and financial security as a result of her publications, Alcott suffered from a variety of illnesses during her later years. After visiting her dying father in Boston on March 4, 1888, she herself fell unconscious and died in her sleep two days later at the age of fifty-five.

Summary

Louisa May Alcott was a born storyteller who could deliver realistic plots and maintain a compelling point of view. She wrote of the life she saw in Boston and Concord and also offered simple reforms to improve American society. Honing her writing skills in her early sentimental stories and Gothic thrillers for magazine readers, she was most popular as a children's writer who captured family life during a particular time in history. Although many critics admired her skill in portraying affectionate and intelligent American families, some questioned her literary art. Some claimed she wrote of a simplicity that was common rather than intelligent; others claimed that her stories were too coldly rational, mercenary, and didactic. Nevertheless, admirers praised Alcott's importance as a writer of childhood tragedy and melodrama whose popularity with young readers stemmed from her ability to depict the ups and downs of childhood from a sympathetic point of view. Her stories were read widely by daughters, mothers, and grandmothers who admired Alcott's writing because they perceived themselves in her stories.

Alcott's concern for women went beyond her stories of family and relationships. With her interests in philanthropy, abolitionism, and other aspects of the reform movements that flourished during her era, Alcott was concerned with social issues. She was particularly interested in the right of women to work to support themselves economically. Having grown up in a family of poverty, she recognized the need for women to be respected in the work place. In the early years, Alcott concentrated her efforts in gaining recognition for women workers and in striving for economic equality for women.

Later, however, she became more active in her support of political rights for women. She edited a suffrage magazine and led a procession to gain delegates for woman suffrage. She also convinced her chief publisher, Thomas Niles, to publish a history of the suffrage movement. In addition, Alcott was interested in other reforms concerning education, temperance, housing, and prisons. Realizing that because she paid a poll-tax, she was entitled to vote, Alcott encouraged several other women to follow her example. Although she took a stance on these issues, her primary interest in life was storytelling. While instructing her readers on the nature of democracy, simplicity, and affection, Alcott also created stories that convey a strong and picturesque image of life in the United States during the late nineteenth century.

Bibliography

Alcott, Louisa May. *A Double Life: Newly Discovered Thrillers of Louisa May Alcott.* Edited by Madeleine B. Stern. Boston: Little, Brown, 1988. This book contains tales of mystery and melodrama that were published anonymously in weeklies before Alcott wrote her tales of social realism. These stories reveal a side of Alcott that is little known by the general public.

——————. *Louisa May Alcott: Selected Fiction.* Edited by Daniel Shealy, Madeleine B. Stern, and Joel Myerson. Boston: Little, Brown, 1990. A collection of stories that cover the romances Alcott wrote during her teens and the thrillers and Gothic novels she wrote before turning to realism. In these stories, Alcott's rebellious spirit is reflected as a supporter of abolition and women's rights.

——————. *The Selected Letters of Louisa May Alcott.* Edited by Joel Myerson and Daniel Shealy. Boston: Little, Brown, 1987. Many of Alcott's unpublished journals are housed in the Houghton Library at Harvard University. This book, however, offers a personal look at the experiences and responses that she wrote in letters to family members and friends throughout her life.

Anthony, Katharine S. *Louisa May Alcott.* New York: Alfred A. Knopf, 1938. Reprint. Westport, Conn.: Greenwood Press, 1977. Reveals the social influence of Alcott's writing as she kept alive the ideals of the Victorian period. Anthony's biography discusses the misrepresentation of Alcott by the literary world, which consistently categorizes her as a children's writer. Includes an excellent bibliography on Alcott and her entire family.

Elbert, Sarah. *A Hunger for Home: Louisa May Alcott and Little Women.* Philadelphia: Temple University Press, 1984. A feminist study of Alcott, this critical biography analyzes the connections between Alcott's family life and her work, and places Alcott squarely within the reform tradition of the nineteenth century and the debate over the proper role of women.

Meigs, Cornelia. *Invincible Louisa.* Boston: Little, Brown, 1933. This biography emphasizes Alcott's work with young people and her belief that children must have the opportunity to earn independence. Meigs also discusses Alcott's assistance to soldiers during the Civil War and her trip to Europe. Contains a fine chronology of Alcott's life.

Strickland, Charles. *Victorian Domesticity: Families in the Life and Art of Louisa May Alcott.* University: University of Alabama Press, 1985. Like the work by Elbert above, Strickland's study surveys the range of Alcott's ideas about domestic life and considers Alcott's literary treatment of women, families, and children within the various fictional forms in which she chose to work.

Linda J. Meyers

GRACIE ALLEN

Born: July 26, 1900; San Francisco, California
Died: August 27, 1964; Hollywood, California
Areas of Achievement: Theater and drama, radio, film, and television
Contribution: Gracie Allen was the first woman to star in a radio program and one of
the first woman comedians whose career successfully spanned vaudeville, films,
radio, and television.

Early Life

Grace Ethel Cecile Rosalie Allen was born in San Francisco, California, on July 26,
sometime around 1900. The year of her birth is recorded variously as 1895, 1902,
1905, and 1906. Her parents were Margaret Darragh Allen and George Allen, Sr.
Grace had three older sisters—Hazel, Bessie, and Pearl—and a brother, whose name
was George. The family lived at 668 Fourth Avenue, San Francisco. A well-known
minstrel and dance teacher, Grace's father left the family when she was about five
years old. Her mother was later remarried to a captain in the San Francisco police
department, Edward Pidgeon.

The theater was Grace's first interest and love. Her stage debut was at the age of
three or four in an act with her father and her sisters. When she was young, Grace spent
her free hours studying playbills and photos displayed at theater fronts and marquees,
and she dreamed of performing at San Francisco's Orpheum. She was so familiar with
the location of the city's theaters that her mother used to send her on errands, giving
directions to destinations by telling her which theater was nearby.

At age fourteen, Grace joined her sisters in a vaudeville act, singing and doing Irish
folk dances at venues in the San Francisco area on weekends and during school
vacations. After Grace finished her education at Star of the Sea Convent School, she
and her sisters took their act out of town, traveling on theater circuits across the
country. They eventually joined up with Larry Reilly & Company and began touring
on the East Coast. When her sisters tired of the stage life, they returned to San
Francisco, leaving Grace with the act in New York.

Grace left Larry Reilly shortly afterward and started attending secretarial school in
New York so that she would have a skill to support herself between theater jobs. She
was living and studying in New York for only a few months when her roommate
introduced her to George Burns—whose real name was actually Nathan Birnbaum—
and they began their lifelong association.

Life's Work

When Grace Allen's roommate introduced her to George Burns, Grace was looking
for a male partner to join her in an act she had planned. Burns and his partner at the
time were deciding to split up and launch separate acts. Although his partner could
sing well, the man spoke with a severe stutter. Because her act involved a lot of
dialogue, Grace chose to work with Burns.

In the early days of their partnership, the Burns and Allen team battled poverty. Because they could not afford the scenery for Grace's act, they began with an act Burns had written. They could not afford to rent a rehearsal hall, so they practiced in music publishers' officers on the pretext that they were going to use some of the songs from the publishers in their act. They scrambled for bookings and took anything that paid. Nearly all of their early work was done in the East on the Loew's circuit as a "disappointment act"—performing their own material to fill in for somebody who was unexpectedly unable to appear.

Grace's first vaudeville act with Burns was in 1923 at the Hill Street Theater in Newark, New Jersey. He was worried because she had done poorly in rehearsal, but once they were on stage, she was in her element. She was getting all the laughs for doing the straight lines, whereas Burns was getting none for telling the joke lines. He recognized Grace's talent and realized that making good use of it was the best thing he could do for their act. Between the first and second performance, he changed the act so that he played straight man and had Grace deliver his former lines. The audience's enthusiastic laughter told the pair they had made a wise move. The character of "Gracie" was born. By the end of their first month together, she was the star of the act, and she maintained that position for the nearly forty years that they performed together.

The character of Gracie was developed by the audiences' responses to how Grace delivered the lines that Burns wrote. Audiences enjoyed watching a female character who was not quite bright, one whose logic was comically misdirected. They wanted her to be ladylike, never sarcastic or rude, loud or flamboyant. It was easy for Grace to incorporate ladylike aspects into her character, but to excel at portraying a scatter-brained and somewhat dizzy character demanded a great deal of intelligence and talent.

After two years on the Loew's circuit, Burns and Allen received a contract on the Orpheum circuit and took their act to theaters in the West. On their schedule was a date at the Orpheum in San Francisco—the fulfillment of Grace's lifelong dream. She missed her San Francisco debut, however, because of an emergency appendectomy. Once she recovered from surgery, she and Burns finished their tour and returned to New York.

In New York, their professional partnership came under great strain. Burns had known for some time that he was in love with Grace Allen. She was genuinely fond of him, but she had a long-standing serious relationship with another man. The situation had become very painful for Burns, and he issued an ultimatum: marry him or they would have to break up the act. They were married on January 7, 1926, in Cleveland, Ohio.

Their career took off at about this time. In the six-year contract Burns and Allen signed with the Keith theaters tour, one of the terms was that they could accept other offers for several weeks each year. They took advantage of this to do tours in Europe. In 1929, during one of their European tours, they made their radio debut in England on the BBC. They were a big hit and accepted a twenty-week radio contract there.

In 1930 they began their film career. Their first film, a nine-minute adaptation of one of their vaudeville acts, was for Warner Bros. In 1931, Burns and Allen signed a contract with Paramount Studios, where they made numerous short films as well as several full-length motion pictures. During the fourteen years of her screen performances, "The Gracie Allen Murder Case" was the only film in which she appeared without her husband.

At about the same time that they began to make films together, Burns and Allen launched their American radio career. Eddie Cantor offered Allen a spot on his show. Burns was not included on this program, but soon the two of them were being booked on other shows. They were so well received that the Columbia Broadcasting System (CBS) radio network offered them a contract for their own program.

February 15, 1932, marked the beginning of the Burns and Allen radio show, which ran for eighteen years. The first few years they did flirtatious routines, but as they matured, they began doing domestic comedy, especially after they adopted a new format when they moved to the National Broadcasting Company radio network in 1945. Their performances nearly always included Gracie telling preposterous stories about some member of her huge imaginary family. Twice during her radio career, Allen carried off enormously successful publicity stunts. The first one occurred in 1933, when she involved the nation in helping her to search for an imaginary lost brother. The second stunt was her bid for the presidency in 1940 on the Surprise Party ticket.

In 1950, Burns and Allen moved from radio to television. Their transition was successful, and their domestic comedy show aired on CBS television. When it first began, *The George Burns and Gracie Allen Show* was produced as a half-hour live show in New York and was broadcast every other Thursday from 8:00 to 8:30 P.M. By the fall of 1952, the show became a weekly broadcast that originated as a filmed episode from a Hollywood television studio. Maintaining a highly realistic domestic setting throughout its eight-year run, the show eventually featured the couple's adopted son Ronnie playing himself. After Allen retired under doctor's orders to improve her health, Burns and the rest of the cast continued to appear in a substantially revised sitcom known as *The George Burns Show* that aired for a little more than six months between 1958 and 1959.

Through the years, Burns consistently credited his wife's comedic acting talent, her professionalism, and her off-stage personality for their successful career and happy private life.

Grace Allen was adamant that she was not a comedienne and did not play to an audience. She did not even really consider herself an actress who was performing a role. She believed in Gracie. Allen was convinced that if the situations and lines were not believable from Gracie's perspective, and that if she could not deliver them honestly from that perspective, the act just could not work.

Allen's portrayal of Gracie's unflagging cheerfulness and unfeigned conviction in the sensibility of her logic were so convincing that the public believed that Gracie was real. The line between Grace Allen and Gracie had dissolved. Her fans adored her.

Women understood her. Men believed they saw her personality in the women they knew and loved.

Other performers and those who were involved in Allen's career respected and delighted in her talent. They admired Allen for her personal integrity and professionalism. She never acknowledged her own talent and, in fact, thought that others were overgenerous in their estimation of it. She was diligent and reliable in preparing for performances. She treated all those involved in any of her projects with respect.

Grace Allen recognized the boundary that separated her life from that of her character. She worked hard to make Gracie a success, but she was also devoted to her large extended family and her two adopted children. Her home was her sanctuary. She maintained strong, lifelong friendships. Above all, she enjoyed and was grateful for the material gifts that her association with Gracie earned for her.

Summary

Grace Allen was a pioneer in the entertainment industry. She took full advantage of her ability to portray a zany character without resorting to mere parody. She dressed stylishly and delivered her lines with sincerity. She was able to make a successful transition from her career in vaudeville to new opportunities in radio, films, and television. The example she set for women comedians who followed her continues to be a major influence.

Much of her career spanned the years of world and national distress—the Great Depression and World War II. The warm and personable humor that was her trademark was especially well received during those years. Her name became a friendly colloquialism for any confused behavior.

Throughout her life, Grace Allen was a generous and loyal woman in her professional and personal relationships. She offered financial and emotional support to aging, ailing relatives and to down-on-their-luck associates. Her ability to portray a seemingly scatterbrained character with humor and respect served as an inspiration to many young female comedians who followed her, including Carol Burnett.

Bibliography

Blythe, Cheryl, and Susan Sackett. *Say Goodnight, Gracie!* New York: E. P. Dutton, 1986. Subtitled *The Story of Burns & Allen*, this book provides good insights into Grace Allen's relationships with other television cast members. Contains many comments by other celebrities and coworkers and an epilogue that discusses the cast members' lives after the show left the air. Includes an appendix with program vital statistics and one with episode synopses.

Burns, George. *Gracie: A Love Story.* New York: G. P. Putnam's Sons, 1988. Compared with the book listed below, this has more detailed, personal biographical information and is focused on Gracie. Written in a more mature, thoughtful style, yet very entertaining. Many personal photos and anecdotes which include their celebrity friends.

——————. *I Love Her, That's Why!* New York: Simon & Schuster, 1955. An entertaining autobiography filled with personal and publicity photos. Many anecdotes including other celebrities. Historical insights into the quirks and mechanics of vaudeville and the development of radio and television.

Martin, Linda, and Kerry Segrave. *Women in Comedy*. Secaucus, N.J.: Citadel Press, 1986. Gracie Allen is one of about fifty women discussed in this book which analyzes, from a moderate feminist perspective, the role of women in comedy. Quotes from various scripts and comic performances illustrate the changing perception of women's roles.

Wertheim, Arthur Frank. *Radio Comedy*. New York: Oxford University Press, 1979. This book offers an analysis of humor in the context of the times and discusses the evolution of radio comedy and its transition to television. Allen's timing and delivery are analyzed, using examples from scripts, comparing her vaudeville, radio, and television performances.

Marcella Joy

LAURIE ANDERSON

Born: June 5, 1947; Wayne, Illinois

Areas of Achievement: Performance art and music

Contribution: A leading figure in the field of performance art, Anderson's integration of contemporary musical themes and cultural issues popularized the idiom and attracted a larger audience to the genre, and as a result, she became one of the first women to be in the vanguard of the postmodern artistic movement.

Early Life

The second of eight children, Laurie Anderson was born on June 5, 1947, in Wayne, Illinois, an affluent town fifty miles outside of Chicago. Her mother and father, the owners of a profitable paint business, instilled in their children a love for music. At the age of five, Laurie began studying the classical violin and played in the family ensemble. Later she joined the Chicago Youth Symphony. Despite demonstrating her virtuosity, Laurie abandoned the violin at the age of sixteen to pursue other artistic goals.

At the age of nineteen, Laurie moved to New York City and enrolled in Barnard College in the fall of 1966. In 1969 she was graduated magna cum laude with a B.A. in art history. Following graduation, she enrolled in the Master of Fine Arts program at Columbia University. In 1972 she received an M.F.A. in sculpture, a field far distant from her initial college major, library science. She initially considered being a librarian because of her interest in language, an outgrowth of her family's practice of telling stories to pass the evening hours and the unusual fictional language her twin brothers developed. Laurie's love of words found expression in her sculptures and photographic projects. The year of her graduation from Columbia, Laurie exhibited the "Story Show" at the John Gibson Gallery in New York City. Combining photographs and textual material, the exhibit established a reputation for the recent graduate among artists in the city. In 1974, she accepted an invitation to participate in the touring group exhibition "Women Conceptual Artists."

Life's Work

By the mid-1970's, Laurie Anderson realized that her artistic projects increasingly focused on the importance of the human language. The textual material outweighed the visual and convinced her that she should return to her first love, words. Ironically, the instrument with which she chose to explore the subtleties of language was the instrument she abandoned more than a decade before, the violin. She returned to the violin more for its technical capabilities than for its ability to produce musical sounds. The sounds that Anderson wanted from the violin were words. She adapted the violin for this purpose by replacing the horsehair bow with a prerecorded audio tape and the strings with a tape head. Later she amended this version and remolded the violin so that a turntable sat on the base of the instrument, while she inserted a needle in the bow. The revamped violin now was capable of playing 45 rpm records. Anderson used the modified instrument to manipulate the words and phrases recorded on the record. Her bowing technique enabled her to transform phrases or to repeat words, forcing the audience to listen more carefully and discover the different levels/meanings that the artist produced.

While experimenting with her modified violin, Anderson listened to the works of minimalist composer Philip Glass and pop musician Captain Beefheart and read the works of avant-garde writer William S. Burroughs. These influences combined with the outdoor rock concerts of the counterculture movement of the late 1960's and early 1970's pulled her toward a by-product of the period, performance art. A multimedia genre, performance art began to appear in the SoHo District of New York City in the early 1970's. Sometimes labeled action art, the boundaries of the new genre were limited only by the imagination of the artist. Considered a nonserious art form or too extreme by the mass media, performance art rarely attracted an audience that extended beyond other performance artists. Anderson's first action art projects fell into this category.

Although her early performance projects attracted few members of the general public, they did create enthusiasm among the artist colony along the East Coast, including patrons of the art world. Grants from the New York State Council on the Arts, the National Endowment for the Arts, and private philanthropic organizations enabled Anderson to concentrate her energies on her art, rather than pursue employment opportunities to meet her financial needs. During this period, she listened more and more to avant-garde music and began to experiment with the use of music to create visual images in the minds of her audience.

By the mid-1970's, Anderson's interest in music began to appear in, and then dominate, her performance art. The mixing of pop music rhythms and video images in her work first appeared in 1975 with *Songs and Stories for the Insomniac*. The following year, she produced *Refried Beans for Instants*. The multimedia performances reached a peak in 1977, when she premiered *For Instants Part 5 (Songs for Lines/Songs for Waves)* at the Kitchen, a showcase for the avant-garde in the SoHo District. Using the strong bass line and percussion beat of rock as the musical underpinnings for her narrative, and video images on a large screen to reinforce the story line, Anderson's performance received enthusiastic reviews from art and music critics alike. Because of this response, she received invitations to perform her works throughout the United States and Europe. During this period, Anderson began to explore the meaning of modern America in a new work, *Americans on the Move*. Performed in 1979 at the Kitchen, the project increased her reputation as a leading figure in the field of performance art and as one of the few figures of that genre who could reach a more mainstream audience. Her mainstream appeal was demonstrated in 1981 when, with funds provided by the National Endowment for the Arts, Anderson released the single "O Superman." The song reached number two on England's pop charts and sold more than 800,000 copies. Because of this success, Warner Bros. Records signed her to an eight-album recording contract.

Her first recording for Warner Bros. appeared in 1982 and was entitled *Big Science*. Although the album included the song "O Superman," the record failed to match the earlier success her music had achieved in Europe. The recording was merely one part of a larger project that premiered the following year. An impressionistic profile of her country, the seven-hour epic *United States I-IV* premiered at the Brooklyn Academy of Music over a two-day span in early February of 1983. Divided into four parts— Transportation, Politics, Money, and Love—the multimedia performance included 1,200 photos, cartoons, and film sequences. A musical foundation consisting of altered violins, synthesizers, electronic keyboards, conventional instruments and Anderson's voice reinforced these vital images. Employing a vocoder, an electronic device which transformed her voice into a chord, and a Synclavier II, which played prerecorded conversations, Anderson's multilayered songs created new and unusual sounds for commonplace phrases. Although critics labeled her effort as overly ambitious, *United States I-IV* drew overflow audiences and acted as a catalyst for increased sales of her album, *Big Science*.

During the mid-1980's, Anderson concentrated her efforts on music compositions and recordings and less on performance projects. The theme of her music also changed. By the end of the decade, she had shifted the focus of her work from an exploration of being a modern American to expressing a concern for what it meant to be a woman in modern America. This concern was the focus of her 1989 release, *Strange Angels*. Unlike her previous Warner Bros. albums, *Strange Angels* became a best-seller and attracted a larger and more diverse audience than any of her earlier recordings or performance pieces. Five of the ten songs examined America from a woman's point of view. Using humor, irony, and literary metaphors, Anderson's recording became a successful vehicle to express her concerns and demonstrated her attraction for the sounds of the human language, especially the language of women. The success of *Strange Angels*, by the beginning of the 1990's, had established Anderson's reputation as an accomplished composer and performer. In 1994, Harper-Collins published a retrospective of her first twenty years as an artist, *Stories from the Nerve Bible: A Retrospective 1972-1992*.

Summary

Laurie Anderson's accomplishments in performance art and the recording industry are a product of her single-minded determination to explore all artistic avenues. Those avenues, however, were a by-product of the success of the emerging feminist movement of the 1960's and the counterculture movement of the same period. It is likely that if Anderson had attempted the same career a decade or two before, those artistic avenues would have been closed. Her success at maintaining her independence and artistic integrity would have been severely tested and probably compromised had it not been for the supportive environment created by the women's movement and the artist colony of the SoHo District of New York. Anderson arrived in New York when the definition of women's role in society was undergoing a dramatic reevaluation and when the cultural values of American society were openly challenged by her generation. These two events nurtured her creative impulses and encouraged her to explore a means of expression and communication that fell outside the mainstream of New York's art world. Her success at blending the visual and the literal through her music to create new mental images forced her audience to reimagine the world they found themselves in and to reexamine their position in that world. Anderson's success as an artist stemmed from her ability to imagine a different world, one that did not limit women's opportunities. In the process of creating that world for herself, she provided the opportunity for her sister artists to do the same.

Bibliography

Anderson, Laurie. *Stories from the Nerve Bible: A Retrospective 1972-1992.* New York: HarperCollins, 1994. As indicated by its subtitle, this work provides a retrospective of Anderson's career as performance artist/musician. Especially useful for its illustrations, providing an excellent visual perspective on Anderson's varied performances and techniques.

Berger, Maurice. *Endgame: Strategies of Postmodernist Performance.* New York: Hunter College Art Gallery, 1984. The introductory essay places Anderson's work in historical context and is followed by a profile of leading figures in the performance art world. Each profile includes excerpts from an interview that the author conducted earlier that year.

Furlong, William. *Laurie Anderson: An Interview.* London: Riverside Studio Publication, 1981. A transcript of an interview conducted with Anderson during one of her first European tours. The interview provides Anderson's insight into her early works, her growing interest in music, and comments on the beginnings of what would become *United States I-IV.*

Gordon, Mel. "Performance Artist/Art Performer: Laurie Anderson." In *Contemporary American Theatre.* New York: St. Martin's Press, 1991. In his assessment of twentieth century American drama, Gordon includes a chapter on Anderson's work and discusses how her multifaceted performances cut across genres to provide fresh inspiration within a theatrical format.

Howell, John. *Laurie Anderson.* New York: Thunder's Mouth Press, 1992. Part of a series on "American Originals," Howell's work provides a complete discography, filmography, videography, and musicography of Anderson's career. In addition, the book has a bibliographical reference list which is helpful for the researcher. Besides a discussion of Anderson's work, Howell includes a lengthy interview he conducted with the artist.

Kardon, Janet. *Laurie Anderson: Works from 1969 to 1983.* Philadelphia: University of Pennsylvania Press, 1983. Kardon provides an overview of Anderson's work through her first recording for Warner Bros. Records.

McCorduck, Pamela. "America's Multimediatrix." *Wired* 2 (March, 1994): 79-83. An interview with Anderson that provides perspective on her recent projects and explores the ways in which her access to high-tech multimedia equipment has revolutionized the creative process behind her music.

Nichols, Janet. *Women Music Makers: An Introduction to Women Composers.* New York: Walker, 1992. Describes the lives and accomplishments of ten women composers who challenged the gender barriers that threatened to silence their music. The profile of Laurie Anderson appears alongside sketches on Clara Schumann, Florence Price, Ethel Smyth, and others.

David O'Donald Cullen

MARIAN ANDERSON

Born: February 27, 1897; Philadelphia, Pennsylvania
Died: April 8, 1993; Portland, Oregon
Area of Achievement: Music
Contribution: Anderson was among the first black American singers to build a concert singing career and to achieve international acclaim. Her 1939 Easter Sunday concert on the steps of the Lincoln Memorial made her a symbol of the struggle for civil rights in America.

Early Life

Marian Anderson was born February 27, 1897, in Philadelphia, the oldest of John and Anna Anderson's three daughters. Young Marian enjoyed a happy childhood in a poor but racially integrated south Philadelphia neighborhood. She began singing when she was three, and at the age of six joined a children's choir at the Union Baptist Church. As a child, her deep, strong contralto voice began to emerge, and she showed such promise that she was invited to sing with the adult choir at age thirteen. She enthusiastically sang in both junior and senior choirs until she was twenty.

Life changed dramatically after Marian's father died when she was ten. The family moved in with her paternal grandparents, and her mother, despite her training as a schoolteacher, started work as a cleaning woman. Marian contributed the few dollars she earned by giving recitals locally.

Although she was naturally talented, Anderson recognized as a teenager that her voice lacked training, and she knew that if she were to have a career, she must begin professional studies. She attempted to enroll in a Philadelphia music school, but was rebuffed because of her race. Although she always regretted that she did not attend music school, she did study privately with several distinguished vocal teachers. The most influential was Giuseppe Boghetti, a noted Italian vocal coach who took few students. Anderson managed to arrange an audition with him, but she was unable to accept immediately his offer to teach her because she could not afford to pay for the lessons. Nevertheless, the congregation at the Union Baptist Church rallied to her support, staging a gala benefit concert that paid for her instruction with Boghetti.

Life's Work

Intent upon forging a career as a concert singer, Marian Anderson threw herself into her studies with Boghetti, training her voice and expanding her repertory beyond the hymns and spirituals she had grown up with to include classical French, Italian, and German songs. Her hard work paid off, and she developed a reputation in the black community in and around Philadelphia. She soon began to sing elsewhere on the East Coast and in the South, with engagements at black schools, churches, civic groups, and colleges. It was on these early southern tours with her manager and accompanist, Billy King, that she encountered the discrimination of Jim Crow legislation, which had established separate and inferior facilities for blacks, in train cars, waiting rooms, hotels, drinking fountains, even in entrances to public buildings. Although she had experienced prejudice before, she had come from an integrated neighborhood, and the discriminatory practices she found in the South came as a shock.

Anderson's steady concert schedule and the earnings that came with it allowed her, just before her twentieth birthday, to make a down payment on a small house for her mother and sisters. Eventually, she was able to support her mother, and later remembered that the proudest moment of her life was in telling Anna Anderson's employer that she would not be returning to work.

Among Anderson's early triumphs was a stunning victory in the National Music League's annual vocal competition. As winner, she sang with the New York Philharmonic in Manhattan's Lewisohn Stadium, and her appearance there in August of 1925 received glowing reviews in the New York press. Shortly thereafter she signed with the Judson management company. As her fame steadily increased, she received concert invitations from across the United States and Canada and began singing to increasingly integrated audiences.

Despite this fame, racial prejudice placed limitations upon black singers such as Anderson. Few had gone where Marian Anderson dreamed of going, and by 1929, with concert bookings dwindling, she felt that her career had reached a plateau. She looked to Europe for the opportunity to both perform and to master the German language so she could better sing the lieder, or art songs, of the German composers she loved. She financed a short stay in England herself, and in 1930 received a scholarship from the Julius Rosenwald fund to study in Berlin.

Her modest recitals in Berlin and Paris attracted the attention of a Swedish concert manager who believed that a black singer named Anderson would certainly be a success in Scandinavia. His prediction proved true—Scandinavian audiences welcomed Anderson warmly. Nevertheless, it was at a small Paris recital that she caught the attention of Sol Hurok, a powerful American impresario who proposed to represent her.

Hurok was able to present Anderson in premier concert venues, and during the 1930's she toured Europe and America extensively. Anderson developed a commanding stage presence—singing with her eyes closed and making few gestures, she radiated personal dignity and serenity. She always included spirituals on her program, insisting upon their value as concert pieces. In the 1930's, she started to receive international acclaim, gaining the respect not only of the public but also of other musicians. Her admirers included the Finnish composer Jean Sibelius, who dedicated his song "Solitude" to her, and the conductor Arturo Toscanini, who was widely reported to have told Anderson that "a voice like yours is heard once in a hundred years."

In spite of her international acclaim, Anderson still faced racial barriers at home. During Anderson's 1939 tour of the United States, Hurok was unable to rent Constitution Hall in Washington, D.C., after its owner, the Daughters of the American Revolution (DAR), claimed that all performance dates were taken. Citing racial discrimination, Hurok notified the press of the DAR's refusal, touching off a storm of controversy. Anderson, who herself learned the full details of the situation from the newspapers, routinely faced this kind of prejudice and initially treated the incident as another booking problem. She had no wish to engage in a public controversy.

The dispute, however, began to take on a life of its own. First Lady Eleanor Roosevelt resigned from the DAR in protest, and prominent concert artists canceled their appearances at Constitution Hall. The problem was brilliantly resolved when Secretary of the Interior Harold Ickes, at the urging of Eleanor Roosevelt, invited Anderson to give a free, open-air recital on the steps of the Lincoln Memorial on Easter Sunday. At first, she was reluctant to accept, but then realized that a greater principle was at stake. She later wrote that "I could see that my significance as an individual was small in this affair. I had become, whether I liked it or not, a symbol, representing my people. I had to appear." As Anderson walked onto the steps of the Lincoln Memorial, she faced an audience of more than 75,000 people of all races, who came to hear her sing patriotic numbers, spirituals, and Schubert's "Ave Maria." It was a triumphant occasion for Anderson, as it was for the struggle for civil rights in America.

Already well known, Anderson was catapulted to even greater fame by the controversy. Her concert schedule included ever more prestigious awards and engagements. Eleanor Roosevelt invited her to sing at the White House during a state visit of the king and queen of England. In March of 1941, Anderson became the second woman and the first black person to receive Philadelphia's prestigious Bok Award for 1940, a prize established by a local philanthropist to recognize the achievements of outstanding citizens of Philadelphia. Mindful of her own early struggles, she used the $10,000 prize money to establish the Marian Anderson Scholarship Fund to assist aspiring young vocalists.

Anderson's personal life changed as well, when she married Orpheus "King" Fisher. The prominent architect had courted Anderson, off and on, for nearly twenty years, and finally, in 1943, she consented to marry him. Together they made a home on a farm in rural Connecticut, which became a haven for her to return to after her extensive concert engagements.

Another historic event in Anderson's career occurred in 1955, when conductor Rudolf Bing invited her to make her debut at New York's Metropolitan Opera, as Ulrica in Giuseppe Verdi's *Un ballo in maschera* (1859). That occasion marked two firsts: Anderson's first opera appearance and the first time a black singer performed with the Metropolitan Opera.

Anderson continued to tour the globe throughout the 1950's and 1960's. She also channeled her energies into other activities, and for a year served as a delegate to the United Nations after being appointed by President Dwight D. Eisenhower in 1957. She sang at the presidential inaugurations of Eisenhower and John F. Kennedy, and was invited to sing at a special memorial service for Kennedy in December of 1963.

Among the many honors she received were more than thirty honorary doctoral degrees, many from the nation's most prestigious universities, numerous humanitarian awards, and two presidential medals. She was particularly appreciative of the 1939

Spingarn Medal she received from the National Association for the Advancement of Colored People (NAACP). Anderson made a point of accepting as many honors in person as her schedule allowed. In 1978, she received one of the five inaugural Kennedy Center Honors awards for lifetime achievement in the arts.

Anderson retired from performing in 1965. She devoted her later years to her husband and home, and to charity work, quietly supporting civil rights causes and helping young singers. She occasionally appeared on the stage in the 1970's as a reader in Aaron Copland's *Lincoln Portrait* (1942). Her final days were spent with her nephew, James DePriest, one of America's foremost conductors. She died of congestive heart failure on April 8, 1993, at the age of 96.

Summary

Marian Anderson is most often remembered for the 1939 Lincoln Memorial concert which made her, however reluctantly, a symbol of the struggle for civil rights and equality in the United States. Yet she is also remembered as a tremendously gifted contralto who, through much hard work and determination, rose from humble circumstances and overcame pervasive racial prejudice to build a distinguished international singing career.

She was always conscious that she was a pioneer. Combining extraordinary hard work and immense personal dignity, she strove to set the kind of example that would both inspire young African Americans and change racist thinking. She was deeply committed to equal rights for all people, but was never militant or political in the struggle. Rather than engage in a fight, Anderson always chose to live above racism, to meet it with quiet dignity and determination, and to lead the way along a higher path.

Anderson was inspirational to Americans of all races, but was particularly influential for the generations of African American singers who followed her. Leontyne Price and Jessye Norman, who enjoy distinguished operatic careers, both point to her as an important early influence and role model. After Anderson's death, Price paid tribute to the great contralto, noting that "Her example of professionalism, uncompromising standards, overcoming obstacles, persistence, resiliency and undaunted spirit inspired me to believe that I could achieve goals that otherwise would have been unthought of."

Bibliography
Anderson, Marian. *My Lord, What a Morning*. Madison: University of Wisconsin Press, 1992. Anderson's autobiography, originally published in 1956, chronicles the singer's life and career up to her debut with the Metropolitan Opera in 1955. The book, like its author, is characteristically reticent and humble, but provides invaluable insight into Anderson's character. An excellent introduction by Nellie Y. McKay places Anderson's life and achievements into the historical perspective of twentieth century America.
Newman, Shirlee P. *Marian Anderson: Lady from Philadelphia*. Philadelphia: West-

minster Press, 1965. This biography, intended for young readers, covers Anderson's life and career up to her retirement from the concert stage in 1966. Anderson cooperated with author Shirlee P. Newman, granting interviews and contributing a short prefatory note.

Sims, Janet L. *Marian Anderson: An Annotated Bibliography and Discography.* Westport, Conn.: Greenwood Press, 1981. A very useful source for research on Anderson, containing more than 1,300 annotated entries subdivided into three main sections: Personal Data, Career Activities, and Awards and Honors. Though it concentrates on newspapers, books, magazines, there is also a listing of manuscript and archival holdings relating to Marian Anderson and a complete listing of her recorded works.

Tedards, Anne. *Marian Anderson.* New York: Chelsea House, 1988. Also intended for young readers, Tedards' biography of the singer is one of the few published books that deals with Anderson's activities after her retirement from the concert stage and is richly illustrated with photographs from Anderson's career and personal life.

Vehanen, Kosti. *Marian Anderson: A Portrait.* New York: Whittlesey House, 1941. Reprint. Westport, Conn.: Greenwood Press, 1970. Vehanen, a noted Finnish pianist, became Anderson's accompanist for her 1931 concert tour of Scandinavia, and worked with her until the mid-1940's. His memoir of their years mainly discusses their experiences touring together in Europe, the United States and South America.

Catherine Udall Turley

MAYA ANGELOU

Born: April 4, 1928; St. Louis, Missouri

Area of Achievement: Literature
Contribution: Best known for her poetry and autobiographical works, Angelou has
had a multifaceted career, enjoying success as a dancer, actress, and teacher.

Early Life

Maya Angelou was born Marguerite Annie Johnson in St. Louis, Missouri, in 1928
to Vivian Baxter and Bailey Johnson. Following her parents' divorce, Angelou and her
brother were sent to live with their paternal grandmother, Annie Henderson, in
Stamps, a poor rural section of Arkansas. Angelou's grandmother, whom she called
"Momma," was the stable force in Angelou's early life. Annie Henderson was a
strong, religious woman who made sure that the family went to church regularly.
Religion and spiritual music were important factors in the Johnson family life.
Angelou also enjoyed a close relationship with her brother Bailey, who gave her the
name "Maya." Angelou and her brother lived with their grandmother and Uncle Willie
in the rear of the Johnson store, which Annie Henderson had owned for twenty-five
years. Because the store was the center of activity for the black community, Angelou
saw at first hand the indignities that black residents suffered as a result of the
prejudices of the white community in Stamps.

Angelou was a victim of violence at an early age. During one of her visits to her
mother in St. Louis, Angelou was raped by a friend of her mother. When her mother's
brothers found out about the rape, they killed the man responsible. Believing that she
had caused the man's death by speaking his name, Angelou refused to speak for five
years following these traumatic events. With the encouragement of Mrs. Flowers, an
educated black woman from Stamps, Angelou regained her speech. Under Mrs.
Flowers' further guidance, Angelou began to read the works of William Shakespeare,
Edgar Allan Poe, and Paul Laurence Dunbar.

After graduating at the top of her eighth grade class in Stamps, Angelou and her
brother continued their education in California. While still in high school, she worked
as the first black woman streetcar conductor in San Francisco. At the age of sixteen
and unmarried, she gave birth to her son, Guy Johnson. To support herself and Guy,
she took jobs as a waitress, cook, and nightclub singer. In 1950, she married Tosh
Angelos, a former sailor of Greek ancestry, but they were divorced after a few years.
(Angelou's surname was derived from that of her former husband.)

Angelou continued her early interest in music and dance by studying with Martha
Graham. She went on to tour twenty-two countries during 1954 and 1955 as the
premier dancer in *Porgy and Bess*. Her travels with the cast took her to Italy, France,
Greece, Yugoslavia, and Egypt. During the late 1950's, Angelou and Guy lived in a
houseboat commune in California, where they went barefoot, wore jeans, and let their
hair grow long. These experiences brought Angelou into contact with a variety of

people from different countries and of different races.

As Angelou became interested in a writing career, she moved to New York in 1958 and joined the Harlem Writers Guild. In addition to working on her writing, she starred in the New York production of Jean Genet's *The Blacks* (1960) with Godfrey Cambridge and collaborated with Cambridge to produce, direct, and star in *Cabaret for Freedom* (1960).

In 1960, Angelou and Guy moved to Cairo, Egypt, with a South African freedom fighter, Vusumzi Make. In Egypt, she served as an editor for *Arab Observer*, an English-language newspaper. Two years later, she and Guy moved to the West African nation of Ghana, where she worked for three years as a writer, as an assistant administrator for the University of Ghana, and as a feature editor for *African Review*.

Life's Work

In the first volume of her autobiography, *I Know Why the Caged Bird Sings* (1970), Maya Angelou shares her experience of growing up as a poor black female in the segregated rural South. Throughout her career she has continued to draw on her own experiences as the subject matter for her work. She has published four more volumes of her personal narrative showing how she was able to overcome obstacles posed by her race and gender to achieve success in many areas. In *Gather Together in My Name* (1974), Angelou writes about a difficult period in her life, a time when she was forced to work at menial jobs to support herself and her son. In *Singin' and Swingin' and Gettin' Merry Like Christmas* (1976), Angelou describes her life as a dancer and actress, including her travels with the cast of *Porgy and Bess*. The next two volumes, *The Heart of a Woman* (1981) and *All God's Children Need Traveling Shoes* (1986), follow the rise of her career.

Angelou's early exposure to spirituals and gospel music influenced her poetry. This poetry reveals a woman whose faith has sustained her in difficult times, and the rhythm of gospel music finds its way into her poetry. She has published several volumes of poetry: *Just Give Me a Cool Drink of Water 'fore I Diiie* (1971), which earned a Pulitzer Prize nomination; *Oh Pray My Wings Are Gonna Fit Me Well* (1975), whose title came from a nineteenth century spiritual; *And Still I Rise* (1978); *Shaker, Why Don't You Sing?* (1983); *Now Sheba Sings the Song* (1987); and *I Shall Not Be Moved* (1990).

Her firsthand knowledge of the harmful effects of racism led her to become a political activist, working for civil rights and for a wider understanding of the African American culture. In the 1960's, at the request of Martin Luther King, Jr., Angelou served as the northern coordinator of the Southern Christian Leadership Conference. Her knowledge of the traditions and culture of black society went beyond political activism as Angelou worked to share this culture with a wider audience. She produced *Blacks, Blues, Black* (1968) for National Educational Television. This ten-part series explored African traditions in American life. Other television credits that deal with African American culture include *Assignment America* (1975), *The Legacy* (1976), *The Inheritors* (1976), and *Trying to Make It Home* (1988).

The diversity of her experiences and considerable talents have led her into the fields of dance, theater, and film. As an actress, she is probably best known for her portrayal of Kunta Kinte's grandmother in the television production of Alex Haley's *Roots* (1977). She played the role of the grandmother in the 1993 television film, *There Are No Children Here*. In addition to her acting career, she has produced and directed for the stage and screen. She also wrote the screenplays for *Georgia, Georgia* (1972) and *All Day Long* (1974), and collaborated on the teleplay for *Sister, Sister* (1982).

In recognition of Angelou's many accomplishments she has been awarded a variety of honors. *Ladies' Home Journal* named her "Woman of the Year in Communications" in 1976. She holds honorary doctorates from the University of Arkansas, Claremont College Graduate School, Ohio State University, Atlanta University, Wheaton College, Occidental College, Columbia College, Kean College, Smith College, Mills College, Lawrence University, and Wake Forest University and others. At the request of President Bill Clinton, Angelou wrote and delivered the commemorative poem at his inauguration on January 20, 1993. This poem, "On the Pulse of Morning," was later published by Random House. Angelou holds a lifetime appointment as Reynolds Professor of American Studies at Wake Forest University in North Carolina.

Summary

In the first volume of her autobiography, *I Know Why the Caged Bird Sings*, Maya Angelou evokes an authentic portrait of what it was like to be black, poor, and female in the segregated South during the 1930's. As she relates her personal narrative, she reveals herself as a strong, determined black woman who can overcome adversities and emerge triumphant. Through this work and others, Angelou has provided a role model for other black women who struggle to support their children, while maintaining a positive outlook on life. As she reveals the problems and challenges she has faced, she casts light on the lives of other black people, providing an insight into the quality of their lives. As she has matured as a writer, Angelou has extended that insight to include all persons, regardless of race or color.

In stressing the theme of triumph of the human spirit, Angelou urges others to rise above their defeats. Her philosophy is, "You may encounter many defeats, but you must not be defeated." The power of Angelou's personal narrative impacts the lives of other women who follow her. Her works have earned praise for their candor in revealing the struggles, challenges, and triumphs that are her life. In showing how she overcame obstacles, she has served as a role model for other women. In her personal appearances and in her written work, Angelou shows herself to be a joyful, warm, articulate, and strong woman who writes about the challenges of the real world.

Bibliography

Braxton, Joanne M. *Black Women Writing Autobiography: A Tradition Within a Tradition*. Philadelphia: Temple University Press, 1989. Discusses how Angelou employs the image of the protecting mother as a primary archetype within her work. Traces Angelou's development of themes common to black female autobiography:

the centrality of the family, the challenges of child rearing and single parenthood, and the burden of overcoming negative stereotypes of African American women.

Cudjoe, Selwyn. "Maya Angelou and the Autobiographical Statement." In *Black Women Writers (1950-1980)*, edited by Mari Evans. Garden City, N.Y.: Anchor Press, 1983. Cudjoe discusses the importance of Angelou's biographical work, arguing that she represents "the condition of Afro-American womanhood in her quest for understanding and love rather than for bitterness and despair." Cudjoe stresses that by telling the story of her own life in *I Know Why the Caged Bird Sings*, Angelou has shown the reader what it means to be a black female in America.

Elliott, Jeffrey M., ed. *Conversations with Maya Angelou*. Jackson: University Press of Mississippi, 1989. Part of the University Press of Mississippi's ongoing Literary Conversations series, this work is a collection of more than thirty interviews with Angelou that originally appeared in various magazines and newspapers, accompanied by a chronology of her life. Provides a multifaceted perspective on the creative issues that have informed Angelou's work as an autobiographer and a poet.

Lupton, Mary Jane. "Singing the Black Mother: Maya Angelou and Autobiographical Continuity." *Black American Literature Forum* 24 (Summer, 1990): 257-275. A scholarly assessment of Angelou's literary contributions to the field of autobiography, placing her within the rich context of African American narratives.

O'Neale, Sondra. "Reconstruction of the Composite Self: New Images of Black Women in Maya Angelou's Continuing Autobiography." In *Black Women Writers (1950-1980)*, edited by Mari Evans. Garden City, N.Y.: Anchor Press, 1983. O'Neale argues that Angelou's primary contribution to the canon of African American literature lies in her realistic portrayal of the lives of black people, especially black women. O'Neale goes on to demonstrate the ways in which Angelou successfully destroys many of the stereotypes of black women.

Tate, Claudia, ed. *Black Women Writers at Work*. New York: Continuum, 1983. In this collection of interviews, Tate explores the personal lives and works of such contemporary African American writers as Gwendolyn Brooks, Alice Walker, and Toni Morrison. In her interview, Angelou discusses the importance of black role models.

Judith Barton Williamson

SUSAN B. ANTHONY

Born: February 15, 1820; Adams, Massachusetts
Died: March 13, 1906; Rochester, New York
Area of Achievement: Women's rights
Contribution: A leading organizer of the early woman suffrage movement, Anthony dedicated her life to the achievement of full political emancipation for women.

Early Life

Susan Brownell Anthony was born on February 15, 1820, on a farm in northwestern Massachusetts in the heart of the Berkshire Hills. Her father Daniel was a fifth-generation Quaker who married Lucy Read, a Baptist whose family property bordered the Anthony farm. Daniel's prosperity as the owner of a small cotton mill came to the attention of a New York investor who invited Daniel to build a system of related mills in and around Battenville in upstate New York.

A former schoolteacher himself, Daniel Anthony considered the instruction of his daughters to be essential to provide them with the means to support themselves if necessary. After hearing that they were not receiving the same level of instruction as male students at Battenville's district school, he organized a home school for the girls as well as evening classes for his factory employees. Serving as the school's first instructor, he eventually hired a full-time teacher. Soon Susan herself began to teach at the school. Profits from the mills allowed Susan to attend a Quaker women's seminary near Philadelphia in 1837, but financial setbacks forced her to return home in the spring of 1838.

The family business was bankrupted by the economic panic of 1837. All of their property was seized by creditors to be auctioned to pay business debts. Susan had accepted a teaching position and used her salary to help purchase some of their belongings, but it was her uncle Joshua Read who came to bid on many of the family's possessions.

After teaching at a Quaker boarding school in New Rochelle, at various schools near Battenville, and as a governess for a family in Albany, Susan came home in 1845 to help her family move west to Rochester, New York. The following year, with the help of Joshua Read, Susan was appointed to serve as girls' headmistress at the Canajoharie Academy, a private school in upstate New York. Socializing with many non-Quakers, Susan abandoned her Quaker speech and plain dresses, indulged a newfound taste for fashion, and learned to dance at parties. At the same time, Susan became interested in more serious pursuits. She took up the cause of temperance, becoming president of the town's Daughters of Temperance society, organizing various fund-raisers, and giving her first public speech—an activity considered unusual for a woman. Letters from home and visits by her father exposed Susan to ideas associated with the more radical antislavery movement. Her father's insurance business required more of his attention, and after he invited her to come home to take charge of the family farm, Susan resigned her post and returned to Rochester in 1849.

Life's Work

Susan B. Anthony's return to Rochester marked a new chapter in her life. In addition to their support for temperance, the Anthony family was part of a growing body of liberal Quakers in Rochester who were dedicated to the antislavery cause. Anthony's father hosted prominent abolitionist leaders and eventually became involved in the local network of sympathizers who provided sanctuary for fugitive slaves.

Anthony's interest in women's rights developed only gradually. While she was still in Canajoharie, her parents and her youngest sister Mary had attended a women's rights meeting held in Rochester on the heels of the 1848 Seneca Falls Convention. At the time, Anthony scoffed at her family's involvement in such a radical cause, but her involvement in reform work in Rochester brought her into contact with many of the Seneca Falls activists. After inviting Anthony to attend an antislavery lecture in Seneca Falls in 1851, journalist Amelia Bloomer introduced Anthony to Elizabeth Cady Stanton. This meeting marked the beginning of a long and fruitful association between two women who became leading figures of the suffrage movement.

Her association with Stanton brought about a gradual conversion of Anthony's convictions regarding suffrage, but one noteworthy incident served as a catalyst for Anthony's increased public activism on women's issues. As a delegate to a state temperance convention in 1852, Anthony was seated separately with other women in attendance. Rising to join the discussion, Anthony was admonished by the convention chairman for her presumption in seeking to address a mixed audience in public. Indignant at this disregard for their opinions, Anthony and several women delegates stormed out of the meeting. Arranging her own meeting in a nearby church that evening, Anthony convinced a sympathetic audience to help her form the Woman's State Temperance Society, where their views and their efforts would not be slighted. Calling for a convention later that spring, Anthony persuaded Stanton to give the keynote address while Anthony busied herself with organizing the convention, coordinating regional lecturers, and raising funds for the society. The following year, men were granted voting privileges in the society, and when Stanton was defeated for reelection as president by a coalition of conservative members, Anthony and Stanton resigned from the organization in protest.

Never discouraged, Anthony traveled throughout New York to meet with the local temperance societies she had recently organized. She was shocked to find that many had disbanded because their married women members lacked the time and independent income to support efforts which their husbands found to be frivolous. Anthony and Stanton saw that this situation could not be changed unless legislation was passed to ensure a married woman's right to hold and dispose of her own property and funds. Anthony canvassed the state, gathering signatures on a petition for such reform, and Stanton delivered a stirring address to the legislature, but their demands were rejected. Anthony redoubled her efforts to generate public support, eventually using funds from a wealthy philanthropist to mount a wider campaign that brought her in contact with a larger network of women activists. After seven years of labor,

Anthony's efforts were at last rewarded when the New York state legislature passed the Married Women's Property Bill in 1860.

During these campaigns, Anthony also spoke out in favor of abolition. A staunch supporter of this cause from the 1850's through the Civil War, she found it increasingly difficult to tolerate male abolitionists' blindness to the cause of women's rights. To her, it was incomprehensible that men who fought against the inhumanity of a black slave's bondage to a white master could not see the similar unfairness of a married woman's bondage to the will of her husband.

Eager to resume the drive for woman suffrage at the war's end, Anthony helped organize the American Equal Rights Association in 1866 to work for the passage of an amendment guaranteeing universal suffrage. It soon became apparent that many abolitionist allies were willing to support only black male suffrage. Many of these former allies believed that combining the two suffrage causes would present the Republican Party with insurmountable opposition to the full liberation of blacks and threaten what was thought to be "the Negro's hour"; these arguments seemed to belittle the courageous public activism of many women abolitionists. Once the Fourteenth and Fifteenth Amendments were ratified with wording that failed to protect voting rights for all, it became clear to Anthony that if women were to win additional rights, they would have to fight for these rights themselves.

Disputes within the Equal Rights Association led Anthony and Stanton to organize the National Woman Suffrage Association (NWSA) in 1869. Limiting its voting membership to women and pledging its support to the passage of a national woman's suffrage amendment, this new organization alienated many conservative reformers of both sexes, who believed that state-based suffrage was a more acceptable and achievable goal. These conservatives, led by Lucy Stone and other prominent Boston suffragists, formed a rival organization called the American Woman Suffrage Association (AWSA). Despite this schism within the movement, activists from both organizations worked to expand woman suffrage and were gratified by the extension of full suffrage rights in the territories of Wyoming and Utah by 1870, in the state of Colorado in 1893, and in the state of Idaho in 1896.

In a bold bid to test her opinion that the postwar amendments guaranteed suffrage rights to all citizens, Anthony registered to vote and cast her ballot in the 1872 presidential election. After being arrested for voting illegally (which her action had been deliberately calculated to provoke), she was convicted by a hostile judge without a poll of jury members and was fined. Procedural inconsistencies in her case prevented her from appealing to the Supreme Court, but Anthony's lecture tour while awaiting trial and her conduct during the trial did solicit widespread sympathy for the suffrage cause.

Determined to focus her entire energy toward achieving suffrage as the pivotal right that would allow women to secure all other civil rights, Anthony spent the final decades of her life recruiting new supporters to the cause. As a second generation of suffragists came under her tutelage, Anthony was able to shift many of the arduous organizational duties to them and turn her attention to chronicling the history of the movement. The younger workers helped bring about the merger of the two suffrage associations as the National-American Woman Suffrage Association (NAWSA) in 1889. As Stanton became more involved in issues beyond suffrage, Anthony was elected to succeed her as president of the NAWSA in 1892 and served in this capacity until 1900. Her support of the movement continued until her death in 1906.

Summary

Susan B. Anthony did not live to see her dream of full voting rights for women become reality with the passage of the Nineteenth Amendment in 1920, but the organizational groundwork she had established directly contributed to this victory. An extremely practical woman whose single-minded quest for equality was informed by natural rights philosophy as well as her Quaker values, Anthony persuaded her admirers and detractors to reconsider the role of women in American society. Encouraged by her family to cultivate personal independence and financial self-sufficiency, Anthony was able to pursue a wide range of activities that had been considered undesirable for a woman to engage in, since they were deemed to be outside woman's proper domestic sphere. Her unmarried status gave her certain legal privileges, including the ability to take on financial responsibilities denied to those suffrage leaders who were married. Despite severe ridicule and derision of her efforts, Anthony dedicated more than fifty years of her life to honing her skills as an organizer, as a shrewd crafter of alliances, and as a tireless campaigner and lecturer—skills that helped her educate women about the importance of claiming their individual political rights and of working together for the collective good of their sisters at home and abroad.

Bibliography

Anthony, Katharine. *Susan B. Anthony: Her Personal History and Her Era.* Garden City, N.Y.: Doubleday, 1954. A thorough early biography, with much attention given to Anthony's family background as well as her personal relationships with the leading figures in the battle for woman suffrage.

Barry, Kathleen. *Susan B. Anthony: A Biography of a Singular Feminist.* New York: New York University Press, 1988. As indicated in the subtitle, this work takes a decidedly feminist perspective on Anthony as a woman and as a reformer. While some of its claims regarding Anthony's psychological character cannot be fully substantiated, this account offers important insights into the woman behind the movement.

DuBois, Ellen Carol, ed. *Elizabeth Cady Stanton, Susan B. Anthony: Correspondence, Writing, Speeches.* New York: Schocken Books, 1981. A collection of primary sources related to Anthony and Stanton. Each of the three main sections contains useful editorial introductions which place these women's political philosophies and reform activities within the context of their times.

Flexner, Eleanor. *Century of Struggle: The Woman's Rights Movement in the United States.* Rev. ed. Cambridge, Mass.: The Belknap Press of Harvard University Press,

1975. Revised and updated since its 1959 original edition, this overview of the women's rights movement has been acclaimed for its scholarly insights into the intellectual origins of American feminism.

Gurko, Miriam. *The Ladies of Seneca Falls: The Birth of the Woman's Rights Movement*. New York: Macmillan, 1974. A collective biography of the leading figures in the suffrage movement, including Anthony. Though somewhat dated in its approach, this work is useful for its thumbnail sketches of the historical impact of these women.

Scott, Anne Firor. *Natural Allies: Women's Associations in American History*. Urbana: University of Illinois Press, 1991. Though Anthony and the NWSA receive only brief coverage here, this survey of women's associations provides an informative context for understanding the suffrage movement as part of a larger pattern of social activism by women.

Wendy Sacket

VIRGINIA APGAR

Born: June 7, 1909; Westfield, New Jersey
Died: August 7, 1974; New York, New York
Area of Achievement: Medicine
Contribution: Noted for contributions in anesthesiology, public health, genetics, and
   basic research, Virginia Apgar is best remembered for the Apgar Newborn Scoring
   System, a system of health evaluation which has saved the lives of countless infants
   worldwide.

Early Life

Virginia Apgar was born in Westfield, New Jersey, in 1909. She may have become
interested in science through the influence of her father, who built a telescope and
experimented with radio waves and electricity in his basement laboratory. She never
knew what caused her to go into medicine, but by the time she went to college, Apgar
knew she wanted to be a doctor. At Mount Holyoke College, she relied on scholarships
and several jobs, including one in the zoology laboratory, to support herself. After she
completed her bachelor's degree in 1929, Apgar entered the College of Physicians and
Surgeons at Columbia University in September. The stock market crashed that
October, and Apgar had to borrow money during the Great Depression to continue her
education. She owed nearly $4,000 (a considerable sum in those days) when she
graduated in 1933, but finished fourth in her class.

Columbia awarded her a coveted surgical internship, but she was advised not to
continue in surgery, since she had to support herself at a time when even male
surgeons were having difficulty in establishing themselves in New York City. Apgar
decided to enter anesthesia, which was considered a more suitable field for a woman
at the time. Although anesthesia was considered a nurse's job, surgeons were beginning to acknowledge that surgical advances were dependent on advances in anesthesia. Many of these same medical professionals believed that women physicians were
ideally suited to develop the field of medical anesthesiology. Apgar completed her
surgical internship in 1935 and spent the next two years in an anesthesiology resi-
dency program at Columbia, at the University of Wisconsin in Madison, and at
Bellevue Hospital in New York.

Life's Work

In 1938, Virginia Apgar was named as director of the division of anesthesia at
Columbia. She worked hard to overcome formidable problems in staff recruitment, an
overwhelming workload, resistance from surgeons who refused to accept anesthesiologists as their equals, and an inadequate salary. (Physician anesthetists were not
permitted to charge professional fees.) She was the only staff member in the division
until 1940. By 1945, however, more anesthetics were administered by physicians than
by nurses, and by 1948, there were eighteen residents in the program. (The number of
nurse anesthetists on staff decreased from fourteen in 1937 to four in 1948.) Apgar's

workload improved when many physicians returned from World War II to enter anesthesiology. Apgar often came into conflict with older surgeons who were accustomed to giving nurse anesthetists orders, but eventually she was able to win over the younger surgeons. The problem with getting satisfactory financial compensation was resolved only after Apgar threatened to resign in 1940 and a separate budget for the anesthesia division was funded in 1941.

By 1946, anesthesia was becoming recognized as a specialty on a national level. There was a move at Columbia to establish a physician-only department, separate from surgery, with a strong research program. Apgar expected to be made chair of this new department. In 1949, however, a Bellevue anesthesiologist with a research background replaced her as head of the division. Six months later, when the division was made a department, Apgar was appointed professor, making her the first female full professor at Columbia University.

Freed from administration of the department, Apgar moved on to obstetric anesthesia, where she made her greatest contribution. Before her development of the Apgar score, there was no standard evaluation of the transition of the newborn to life outside the uterus. The initial examination of the infant at birth was often haphazard and disorganized, since obstetricians often devoted most of their attention to mothers. In response to a medical student's question about evaluating the newborn at the time of delivery, Apgar developed her scoring system in 1949. She listed five categories— heart rate, respiratory effort, muscle tone, reflex irritability, and color—that should be assessed at one minute after birth to indicate the need for resuscitation. (Eventually, the score would be repeated at five and ten minutes after birth to evaluate the baby's response to resuscitation.) Each category was to be scored as 0, 1, or 2 points and then added for a total score for the baby. A score between 7 and 10 indicated that the newborn was in satisfactory condition; a score between 4 and 7 indicated the need for further observation and possible intervention; and a score of less than 4 alerted the staff to the need for immediate intervention, with concerns about the survival of the infant. The score was first published in 1953 and was eventually adopted throughout the world.

Apgar had always appreciated the need for research, but her heavy clinical workload and administrative duties had left her little time to pursue her interest in this area. With the development of new technology to measure blood gases, pH levels, and blood levels, she was able to collaborate with Duncan Holaday, an anesthesiologist-researcher, and L. Stanley James, a pediatrician, to study the effects of labor and delivery and maternal anesthetics on the baby's condition, using the Apgar score as a standard evaluation. Low Apgar scores noted in babies with poorly oxygenated blood (hypoxia) or pH imbalanced blood (acidosis) could alert attending physicians that these conditions should be promptly treated. During her studies, Apgar was the first person to catheterize the umbilical artery of the newborn, a procedure that became an essential component of neonatal care. In their studies of the effects on the newborn of anesthetics given to the mother during labor, Apgar and her coworkers discovered that cyclopropane gas, which had been considered a harmless anesthetic, markedly depressed the newborn. After reviewing the data, Apgar is said to have remarked, "There goes my favorite gas." The obstetrical use of cyclopropane declined dramatically after the research was published. Another Apgar study with significant implications for neonatal care was a collaborative research project, involving twelve institutions and 17,221 infants. It determined, unequivocally, that the Apgar score, especially as assessed at five minutes after birth, was a good predictor of neonatal survival and neurologic development.

Apgar assisted in the education of more than 250 physicians in anesthesiology, and her ideas inspired both practice and research. Her motto was "Do what is right and do it now." She always admitted her mistakes—at a time when errors were usually denied—and her constant encouragement, her honesty, and her humility enabled students to accept criticism without being offended.

After a distinguished career of thirty years at Columbia-Presbyterian Medical Center, Apgar decided to improve her knowledge of statistics related to research, and she left anesthesiology to earn a master of public health degree from The Johns Hopkins University School of Hygiene and Public Health. She considered her pursuit of this degree at the age of fifty to be her most significant decision. It changed her whole life, and she never regretted it.

In 1959, Apgar was persuaded to join the National Foundation-March of Dimes, where she headed the division on congenital malformations from 1959 to 1967 and directed the foundation's basic research program from 1969 to 1972. This period was a critical time in the foundation's history, when the focus of its mission was being diverted from preventing poliomyelitis to the prevention of all birth defects. From 1973 until the time of her death, Apgar served as the foundation's vice president for medical affairs. As principal fund-raiser, she increased the foundation's annual income from $19 million in 1959 to $46 million in 1974, helping to fund research into the many causes of birth defects as well as their prevention and treatment. As comfortable with the public as she was with her medical colleagues, Apgar made frequent public talks and coauthored a book for parents about birth defects, *Is My Baby All Right?* (1972). During this time, she also served as a research fellow in medicine at The Johns Hopkins University and a clinical professor of pediatrics at Cornell University Medical College, where she was the first physician in North America to have an appointment that included teratology (birth defects) as a subspecialty.

In recognition of her important scientific contributions, Apgar received many honors. The American Academy of Pediatrics named a prestigious award for her and the American Society of Anesthesiologists presented her with the Ralph Waters Medal. In 1973, she was awarded the Gold Medal of Columbia University for special service to medicine. Her undergraduate alma mater, Mount Holyoke College, named an academic chair in her honor. In addition, Apgar received four honorary degrees and was honored by *Ladies' Home Journal* as Woman of the Year in 1973.

Determined to dedicate herself to her career, Apgar remained single. Her private life was full and rewarding—she was a gifted musician, an avid gardener, an aviator, a photographer, and a philatelist. Apgar was also an untiring student: When she died in 1974 at age sixty-five, she was commuting from her March of Dimes work in New York to The Johns Hopkins University in Baltimore to study genetics.

Summary

During her career, Virginia Apgar received international recognition for her pioneering work in anesthesiology, neonatology, and teratology. She probably did more to improve the health of mothers and infants than anyone during the twentieth century. Modern obstetricians, pediatricians, and nurses include the Apgar score—a scientifically validated standard for evaluating the newborn—in their vocabulary as a result of her concern for babies during the critical first few moments after birth. As a professor of anesthesiology at the Columbia-Presbyterian Medical Center for more than twenty years, Apgar assisted in the delivery of more than 17,000 babies. Apgar's research laid the foundation for the development of perinatology, and countless infant deaths have been prevented because of her work. She was a wonderful teacher, and her ideas inspired much productive research.

When she could not become a surgeon because she was a woman, Apgar became an anesthesiologist. When she could not become department chair, Apgar entered obstetrical anesthesia. When she believed there was no room for her to advance at Columbia-Presbyterian Medical Center, Apgar became enormously successful in preventing birth defects and developing the field of teratology. While not publicly supportive of women's liberation, Apgar was outraged at the restrictions facing women. Nevertheless, she believed there were ample opportunities, particularly within various medical fields, for both men and women who were willing to overcome their limitations. She considered women more competitive, more rational, more sincere, and stronger than men. She took advantage of every available opportunity, made an incalculable contribution to society, created a marvelous career, and served as a role model for women everywhere.

Bibliography

Apgar, Virginia, and Joan Beck. *Is My Baby All Right?: A Guide to Birth Defects*. New York: Trident Press, 1972. A book written to answer the questions of parents and other lay people, in nontechnical terms, about birth defects. There are interesting details of Apgar's life in the preface and "About the Authors" section.

Calmes, Selma. "Virginia Apgar: a Woman Physician's Career in a Developing Specialty." *Journal of the American Medical Women's Association* 39 (November-December, 1984): 184-188. The best source of information about Virginia Apgar's early life and career at Columbia University. The article's wealth of detail comes from its author's skillful use of such primary sources as Apgar's diary, letters, and reports.

Diamonstein, Barbaralee. *Open Secrets: Ninety-four Women in Touch with Our Time*. New York: Viking Press, 1972. An entertaining interview with Apgar that reveals her delightful sense of humor and opinions on a great many topics.

Kass-Simon, G., and Patricia Farnes, eds. *Women of Science: Righting the Record.* Bloomington: Indiana University Press, 1990. Contains only a brief paragraph about Apgar, but the preface and introduction give valuable feminist insights into the context in which women scientists have worked and the obstacles they have had to overcome.

Mitford, Jessica. *The American Way of Birth.* New York: E. P. Dutton, 1992. Mitford's work provides little direct coverage of Apgar's life, yet it does give a historical overview of the changing attitudes toward childbirth that have prevailed from medieval times through the twentieth century and their impact on American obstetrical medicine. Although her acerbic comments fall short of a purely objective history, Mitford does provide a context for understanding modern obstetrical practices as well as childbirth alternatives, such as delivery by licensed nurse midwives and lay midwives.

Vare, Ethlie Ann, and Greg Ptacek. *Mothers of Invention: From the Bra to the Bomb— Forgotten Women and Their Unforgettable Ideas.* New York: William Morrow, 1988. Although this work is primarily devoted to women inventors in other fields of study, it does include a sketch on Apgar that provides details of her research as well as her fund-raising efforts on behalf of the National Foundation-March of Dimes.

Edna B. Quinn

DIANE ARBUS

Born: March 14, 1923; New York, New York
Died: July 26, 1971; New York, New York
Area of Achievement: Photography
Contribution: A pivotal figure in contemporary documentary photography, Diane Arbus created startling images of dwarfs, twins, transvestites, and physically deformed individuals that were always controversial and often misunderstood.

Early Life

Diane Nemerov was born to a wealthy family in New York City. Her father, David Nemerov, owned a fashionable Fifth Avenue department store called Russeks, which his wife's family had founded. Diane attended Ethical Culture and Fieldston schools, which were considered to be progressive institutions. At school, Arbus exhibited much creativity, particularly in art class, where she sketched, painted in oils, sculpted, and made collages.

When she was thirteen she met Allan Arbus, a copy boy in her father's department store and an aspiring actor. They fell madly in love, and for the next four years carried on a passionate courtship with clandestine meetings, secret phone calls, rendezvous in Central Park, and hand-delivered letters. Aside from her brother, Howard, with whom Diane always shared a close relationship, Allan became the most important person in Diane's life.

Under Allan's influence, Diane began creating her own style and look. In her parents' home she had been taught that hairiness, menstruation, and body odors made one "impure." Rebelling against her parents' preoccupation with cleanliness, Diane always believed in female naturalness. She could understand neither why women were kept in a state of innocence about their bodies nor why they were denied their sensuality. In time Diane chose to wear no deodorant. As she grew older, people—particularly men—would comment in embarrassed tones about her body odor. Nevertheless, she always carried herself proudly, ignoring their comments.

In 1941, when Diane was eighteen, she and Allan Arbus were married. Three years later she bore a daughter, whom she named Doon. It was during this period that she began to express an interest in photography. When her husband returned from the army, where he was trained as a photographer, he finally decided to go into fashion photography, with Diane as his partner. The couple had dabbled in this work briefly in 1941 and had been rather successful, although neither of them had any interest in fashion. Her father asked Diane and her husband to take advertising photographs for his store, and in the beginning of their career, Diane and Allan worked only inside the photography studio at Russeks. The couple collaborated as photographers for almost twenty years, eventually producing fashion photographs for *Harper's Bazaar*. Despite her early efforts, Diane once said that she did not begin photographing seriously until she was thirty-eight years old. Before that she had spent her time learning to be a good wife and mother.

Life's Work

Between 1955 and 1957, Diane Arbus studied photography under Lisette Model, the most famous teacher of photography in the country at the time. Model taught Arbus everything she knew and encouraged her pupil to concentrate on personal photographs and to develop further what Model recognized as a uniquely incisive documentary eye. Soon after Arbus began her studies with Model, she began to devote herself fully to documenting transvestites, twins, midgets, and asylum inmates, as well as various other people on the streets and in their homes. Model knew that Arbus was fragile as a person but strong as an artist. She also understood that Arbus needed to shoot photographs in order to relieve her mind of the faces and specters that were haunting it. Through some mysterious, unconscious force, Arbus was beginning to create in her photographs a kind of art that would be both a release and a vindication of her life, and Model more than anyone understood this.

Arbus later commented to friends that her desire to be daring originated in an overly protective, overly organized childhood in which she broke the monotony and defied the security of home by being naughty. What she rebelled against in her childhood was not the restrictions, however, but the loss of reality imposed by her sheltered life. She was determined to reveal what others had been taught to turn their backs on. As she had rejected her family values, she rejected fashion and went on to look for experiences less fictitious, more factual, and also to respond to a growing sense of self-awareness.

In 1965, three of Arbus' earliest photographs were included in a show at the Museum of Modern Art called "Recent Acquisitions," along with the work of two other influential new photographers, Garry Winogrand and Lee Friedlander. Her images, which stripped away all artiness and evoked powerful emotions, were described as direct and primitive. These were photographs to which the public was not accustomed. Arbus' focus had sharpened and her vision and her discomfort had become more pronounced. The electronic flash and the square format she was using gave her more control and outlined her subjects in nightmarish detail. Her camera was described as an x-ray machine that in an uncanny way could capture what her subject was feeling.

Arbus questioned why ugliness, deviations, and flaws were so unacceptable. She depicted her subjects with a stark directness beyond value judgments. For her, existence was amoral. Later in her career, still pursuing what was specifically different, she began to photograph ordinary people out of an awareness of the gap between intention and effect. She believed that because people are not content with the exterior they are given, they create an entirely new set of peculiarities in an effort to project a different image. Thus, while each person is unique, most want to be unique in another way. Arbus photographed the resulting collision of interests. Some efforts to change were more obvious than others: men dressing like women, and vice versa. Others were less drastic, such as middle-aged women dressing like teenagers. There were also the costumes that identified one person with another, as in the case of twins, or with a cause, as in the case of the protesters, or those who disguise identity with masks.

In not attaching values, in not seeking out people for their physical distinctions alone, but for their uniqueness in the context of their whole being, Arbus was not exploitive. She had a tremendous ability to empathize, which allowed her subjects to trust her. Despite her empathy, she realized that "It's impossible to get out of your skin into somebody else's. . . . That somebody else's tragedy is not the same as your own." Her empathy was always balanced by her sense of herself as a photographer, her desire not to avoid the facts. She was simultaneously detached and intimate. While she was empathetic, she realized that the camera would be clinical. The resulting photograph would combine her ideas, the subjects' responses to her, and the camera's indiscriminate record.

Arbus' approach to photography was as radical as her subject matter. Her sources were not confined to the conventional history of photography. She was influenced in part by the snapshot and news photography and detested the photographs of those she believed were too self-consciously aware of themselves as artists, such as Edward Weston, Ansel Adams, and Harry Callahan. The photographers she most respected were those who understood darkness, particularly Weegee (Arthur Fellig), Gyula Halasz Brassai, and William Brandt.

"New Documents," the photography exhibit at the Museum of Modern Art, which opened March 6, 1967, was probably the high point of Arbus' life. It introduced Arbus' work to the world. Although the show received mixed reviews from critics, the photographic community's response was notably silent. When her portrait of identical twins appeared in the exhibit, the twins' parents protested that the image was a distortion and tried to stop the picture from being reproduced elsewhere because they thought their daughters would be exploited. Eventually "The Twins" became Arbus' most famous photograph—her trademark—and was reproduced on posters, her book cover, and even inspired Stanley Kubrick in his 1980 horror film, *The Shining*.

Arbus rarely exhibited or published her noncommercial photographs. She was so secretive about her work that even her closest friends and her children were unfamiliar with the entire body of her work. In 1970, Arbus made a limited portfolio containing ten photographs, but by then she had established an international reputation as one of the pioneers of the "new" documentary style. Her work was often compared with that of August Sander, whose "Men Without Muscles" expressed similar concerns, although in a seemingly less unmerciful manner.

In July of 1971, Arbus took her own life in Greenwich Village, New York. Her brother, poet Howard Nemerov, gave the eulogy at her funeral and later wrote a poem for his sister entitled "To D—Dead by Her Own Hand," which has since been reprinted extensively.

Summary

Toward the end of her short but intense career (ten productive years as a photographer), Diane Arbus was regarded as a consummate professional. Her images, mainly of people, appeared to many as metaphors for the uneasy dislocations of a society at war with itself and others. Since her suicide in 1971, her life and work have undergone increased scrutiny. To some extent this increased interest is attributable to the upsurge of interest that often occurs after an artist's death and also to society's tendency to assume that a woman artist's suicide vindicates that assumption that women are too delicate for the demands of artistic creation. Her death brought even more attention to her name and photographs. In the following year, Arbus became the first American photographer to be represented at the Venice Biennale. A major retrospective at the Museum of Modern Art, New York, in 1972, which traveled throughout the United States and Canada, was viewed by more than 7.25 million people. The next year, a Japanese retrospective traveled through Western Europe and the Western Pacific.

Arbus was very proud of her work. In her short span of years as a photographer, she changed the way photographers saw the world. She knew that she had succeeded at carving out territory of her own, and no one could enter without reckoning with what she had done. She believed that there were things which nobody would photograph unless she photographed them.

Bibliography
Arbus, Diane. *Diane Arbus: Magazine Work.* Edited by Doon Arbus and Marvin Israel. Millerton, N.Y.: Aperture, 1984. In the years since its publication, this monograph has remained the foundation for all critical assessments of Arbus' life and work. As a collection of some of her best work and a clue to her intentions, the book is a roughly chronological record of her magazine work. Numerous reproductions and bibliography.

——————. "The Vertical Journey: Six Movements of a Moment Within the Heart of the City." *Esquire* 54 (July, 1960): 102-107. The photographs in this piece, accompanied by terse captions by Arbus herself, established her both as a professional photographer and also a talented writer.

Bosworth, Patricia. *Diane Arbus: A Biography.* New York: Alfred A. Knopf, 1984. In this insightful book, the author follows Arbus' progress as a photographer and discusses her influences. Through the voices of her friends and colleagues, her mother, sister, and brother, Bosworth charts the dangerous and ultimately fatal course of Arbus' struggle to confront the fears and anguish that pursued her throughout her life. Notes and sources included.

Tucker, Anne. *The Woman's Eye.* New York: Alfred A. Knopf, 1973. In this work devoted to the most prominent female photographers of the time, the author discusses Arbus' early years of rebellion through her mature work, stressing her radical approach to documentary photography. Contains numerous reproductions.

Walsh, George, Colin Naylor, and Michael Held, eds. *Contemporary Photographers.* New York: St. Martin's Press, 1982. A biographical collection of essays on photographers. The section devoted to Arbus discusses the photographer's major preoccupations, her early career, and her contributions to the field of documentary photography. Includes list of individual and group exhibitions and a bibliography of primary and secondary material.

Genevieve Slomski

ELIZABETH ARDEN

Born: December 31, 1884; Woodbridge, Ontario, Canada
Died: October 18, 1966; New York, New York
Area of Achievement: Business
Contribution: An entrepreneur who founded Elizabeth Arden, Inc., a multimillion dollar international cosmetics and beauty salon business, Arden is considered one of the individuals responsible for the creation of the cosmetics industry.

Early Life

Elizabeth Arden was born Florence Nightingale Graham in Woodbridge, near Toronto, Ontario, Canada. Since throughout Arden's life she looked much younger than her chronological years, her age was a very sensitive issue. Consequently, the year of her birth has been reported as ranging anywhere from 1878 to 1890, but 1884 was the official date provided by a company spokesman at the time of her death.

Named for her mother's idol, young Florence was the fourth of five children and the third of four daughters of William and Susan Tadd Graham. Susan Tadd came from a wealthy Scottish family who disapproved of her interest in William. The only way that the couple could marry was to elope to Canada on the money that William got for winning a horse race and selling the horse. Their dreams of wealth and opportunity never materialized and they became poor tenant farmers.

Florence's childhood was difficult and complicated by the family's poverty. Her mother, who died of tuberculosis when Florence was only five years old, secured an allowance from a wealthy aunt in England to pay for the children's education. When the aunt died, Florence was forced to leave high school. She tried a semester of nursing school, but found that she did not have the stomach for taking care of sick people. A diligent worker who was unable to find a career that she really enjoyed, Florence drifted through a series of jobs—cashier, stenographer, bank teller, dental assistant, and so on.

An attractive petite redhead with sparkling blue eyes and beautiful skin, Florence had no desire to settle down and marry. Instead, influenced by the hard life that she had seen her mother endure, she expressed a desire to be the richest woman in the world. Against the wishes of her father, she followed her only brother, William, to live in New York in 1908.

Life's Work

One of Florence Graham's first jobs in New York was as a clerk at Elizabeth Adair's beauty salon. Ever ambitious and eager to better herself, Florence convinced her boss to teach her the art of giving facials. Because make-up was associated with the theater and consequently was not worn by respectable women at this time, good skin care was the only way that a woman could maintain a youthful appearance. Affluent women came in as often as once a week for facial treatments. Florence's large hands were well suited to this task, and she soon acquired a large following of customers.

Not content to work for someone else, in 1909 Florence joined forces with Elizabeth Hubbard, a manufacturer of a line of skin care products. Using Hubbard's products and Florence's facial techniques, they opened their salon, "Mrs. Elizabeth Hubbard's" on Fifth Avenue. Deciding on the name was only the first of many skirmishes between the two strong-willed entrepreneurs, and Hubbard soon left to open her own salon two doors down the street.

Since Florence had paid the rent out of her facial tips, she remained at the old salon. Needing a new name for her business, she decided to keep as much of the expensive gold lettering on the window as possible. So the "Mrs. Elizabeth" stayed and she added the last name "Arden" from one of her favorite poems by Alfred, Lord Tennyson—*Enoch Arden* (1864). From this point on Florence Nightingale Graham was on her way to becoming Elizabeth Arden.

She displayed an innate sense of marketing savvy and an understanding of her targeted customers' needs. Borrowing $6,000 from her brother William, she used the loan to create a luxurious ambiance for her salon that would attract the type of affluent woman she wanted as her customer. On the front of the salon, she installed what was to become her trademark at all of her locations for the next fifty years—a bright red door with an elegant brass nameplate. The inside of the salon was decorated with oriental rugs, pink damask, French antique furniture, and Venetian glass chandeliers. Giving facials by day and doing her own cleaning by night, she repaid her brother's loan in six months. Her timing for this type of business was perfect. The suffrage movement was crusading to give women more freedom through the right to vote, and in 1912, *Vogue* magazine endorsed a discreet application of make-up to improve a lady's appearance. Arden capitalized on these trends by creating and perfecting subtle powders and rouges that she applied to her clients for special social events. By 1914, she was successful enough to place advertisements in the newspaper announcing her availability for services as Miss Elizabeth Arden.

Never afraid to take chances and believing that one had to spend money to make money, Arden sought a bank loan to establish a second salon in Washington, D.C. On an ocean voyage to France to study the European competition, she became friendly with Thomas Jenkins Lewis, the bank official who had processed this loan. More out of loneliness than passionate love, the two eventually married on November 29, 1915, after Lewis enlisted in the army. Arden, ever more involved in business than her personal life, took one hour off from work and returned to the salon to finish her workday after the ceremony.

Learning from the Europeans, Arden set out to upgrade her line by hiring chemists to analyze and improve upon the products she brought back. The result was the first fluffy product that could truly be called a "cream"—Cream Amoretta. She also introduced Ardena skin tonic and promoted the use of mascara and eye shadow by American women.

The outbreak of World War I and the freer social climate for women brought many changes to Arden's business. Fleeing the Germans, Helena Rubinstein left Paris and brought her salon and cosmetics business to New York. The two strong-willed women, actually quite alike in personality, would be lifelong competitors and business adversaries. As the country approached the Roaring Twenties, improving on one's appearance with make-up even during the day was becoming socially acceptable for respectable women in the larger cities.

After the armistice was signed, Arden hired two people who would change the direction of her business forever. Her recently divorced younger sister, Gladys, was badly in need of money. She refused Arden's offer of support, however, preferring a job instead. Arden's husband, Tom, had recently returned from serving three years in the army and was having difficulty finding a job. From the beginning, both Gladys and Tom recognized the potential of expanding the sale of Arden's cosmetic products into smaller cities across the country, but Arden resisted. She was more comfortable catering to the elite in the salon and treatment business that she knew so well than she was in mass merchandising. Eventually, Tom and Gladys prevailed. Gladys traveled across the United States with a team of young saleswomen, demonstrating products. Tom remained in New York to handle the manufacturing and business side of the enterprise. The expansion was a huge success and orders came in a rapid pace. Lewis and Arden agreed that the quality image of the line was vital because it allowed a higher profit margin. Since their products were targeted at women in the top income bracket, only prestigious stores were allowed to sell Arden products. Soon the wholesale business expanded to Europe, and Arden was selling products in elite stores such as Harrod's and the Galeries Lafayette. In 1920, Arden sent Gladys to Paris to open a new salon, which was soon followed by one in London. In 1925, the business was grossing two million dollars per year. By 1929, it was grossing eight million dollars, approximately half of it from the wholesale division managed by Arden's husband, who was never allowed to own stock in the company.

While the cosmetics business was one of the few industries to successfully survive the Depression, the Arden-Lewis partnership did not. Arden's marriage to Tom Lewis had deteriorated into little more than a business partnership. By 1935, her husband's infidelities led Arden to file for an uncontested divorce on the grounds of mental cruelty. In spite of the significant contribution he had made to the success of the business, Lewis received only a $25,000 settlement in return for an agreement not to work in the cosmetics industry for five years. In his own way, Lewis got even with Arden. Five years after their divorce he went to work for her strongest rival, Helena Rubinstein. During that same time period, Arden fired five managers who were hired to replace Tom and her company lost $500,000.

It was after her divorce that a friend, Sam Riddle, introduced Arden to what would be the second passion in her life in addition to her business—horse racing. Since her childhood on the farm in Ontario, Arden had always loved horses. At last she had the money to buy them. In addition to the personal pleasure that owning and racing thoroughbreds gave her, Arden enjoyed a new ability to socialize with the moneyed elite, a group that had invited her to their fund-raising events in New York but never into their inner social circle.

Arden pampered her horses in much the same way she pampered her customers.

Horses were rubbed down with her Ardena Cream. Stables were kept scrupulously clean, and employees who did not adhere to her strict directions for the care of the animals were frequently fired. Her Lexington, Kentucky, stable produced the 1947 Kentucky Derby winner, Jet Pilot.

While her business thrived, her personal life did not. A second marriage in 1942 to Russian émigré Prince Michael Evlanoff ended in divorce after only thirteen months. When she converted her Maine vacation home into a beauty and health spa called Maine Chance, it was so successful that she opened a second location in 1947 near Phoenix, Arizona, for the winter season.

She devoted the remainder of her life to developing new beauty products and expanding her worldwide network of salons, working until she was in her eighties. Her business success, however, translated into personal loneliness, and in her later years she invited her divorced niece, Patricia Young, to live with her. At the time of her death from a heart attack on October 18, 1966, Arden was the sole owner of more than fifty salons and a multimillion dollar cosmetics business that manufactured more than three hundred products.

Because Arden had failed to make provisions that would shield her estate from the $37 million tax burden after her death, Elizabeth Arden, Inc., had to be sold to settle the estate, the bulk of which was distributed to her niece Patricia, her sister Gladys, and several loyal longtime employees. Pharmaceutical giant Eli Lilly purchased the corporation and attempted to direct the product lines more toward younger consumers. In August of 1989, the company was sold to Unilever, which successfully launched the corporation's first new fragrance line since 1930. The fragrance was named Red Door in honor of Arden's salon trademark.

Summary

Elizabeth Arden was a true entrepreneur who was responsible not only for the success of her multimillion dollar business but also for much of the growth of the entire cosmetics industry. Although she capitalized on a certain image of femininity, Arden never accepted the idea that her gender should limit her ability to run her own business. She had the ability to capitalize on business trends and the insight to take advantage of changing social mores. She was a true innovator and risk-taker who introduced countless new products to American women and was also the first to market a line of fragrances for men. Although her success in business came at considerable cost and loneliness in her personal life, she did achieve her childhood dream of becoming an extremely wealthy woman.

Bibliography
Lewis, Alfred Allan, and Constance Woodworth. *Miss Elizabeth Arden*. New York: Coward, McCann & Geoghegan, 1972. This illustrated book is full of interesting anecdotes and material about Arden's life and career. It is particularly useful in providing complete information about her later years which is not available in many sources.

Rice, Faye. "Elizabeth Arden: Profiting by Perseverance." *Fortune* 125 (January 27, 1992): 84. This article updates what happened to Arden's business after her death.

Rogers, Agnes. *Women Are Here to Stay.* New York: Harper and Brothers, 1949. Although this volume contains minimal information on Arden, it features many photographs of her and profiles her rivalry with Helena Rubinstein.

Shuker, Nancy. *Elizabeth Arden: Cosmetics Entrepreneur.* Englewood Cliffs, N.J.: Silver Burdett, 1989. This juvenile biography, part of the publisher's American Dream series, provides an ample overview of Arden's career with special attention given to her struggle to establish herself in the growing American cosmetics industry.

Carol P. Harvey

HANNAH ARENDT

Born: October 14, 1906; Hanover, Germany
Died: December 4, 1975; New York, New York
Areas of Achievement: Philosophy and social science
Contribution: One of the most challenging political philosophers of the twentieth century, Arendt adopted an Aristotelian approach to explore the origins of totalitarianism, the structure of human consciousness, and the nature of violence and evil.

Early Life
Hannah Arendt was the only child of Paul and Martha (Cohn) Arendt, a German-Jewish couple who lived in Hanover. Arendt's father was an engineer and the family moved to the town of Königsberg, the former capital of East Prussia, where the young Hannah grew up. She attended the University of Königsberg shortly after World War I, receiving a bachelor's degree from that institution in 1924. Later that same year, she began postgraduate study with the existentialist philosopher Martin Heidegger at the University of Marburg. Arendt met Hans Jonas (her future colleague at the New School for Social Research) when she and Jonas were the only two Jewish students to enroll in a New Testament seminar offered at Marburg by the biblical scholar Rudolf Bultmann.

Arendt's education continued at the University of Heidelberg where she studied philosophy under Karl Jaspers. During her years at Heidelberg, Arendt began to be influenced by Jasper's Christian existential philosophy and his view that each individual is ultimately responsible for his or her own actions. In 1928, when Arendt was only twenty-two years old, the University of Heidelberg granted Arendt a doctorate. In the following year, her dissertation was published as *Der Liebesbegriff bei Augustin* (1929; *The Idea of Love in St. Augustine*). In September of 1929, Arendt married the young Jewish philosopher Günther Stern, whom she had met in 1925 during her postgraduate training in Marburg.

As the National Socialist movement (the Nazis) began to gain power in Germany, Arendt felt that her Jewish heritage was placing her in increasing danger. She fled to Paris in 1933, and began to work for Youth Aliyah, a relief organization that attempted to find homes in Palestine for Jewish orphans. Her relationship with Stern began to deteriorate during the 1930's, and the couple obtained a divorce in France in 1937. Arendt's activity in relief work continued, however, until 1940, when she married Heinrich Blücher, a professor of philosophy. Blücher was to remain one of Arendt's most important mentors during the course of their thirty-year marriage.

In 1941, France was invaded by the Nazis, forcing Arendt and Blücher to move to the United States. From 1944 until 1946, Arendt performed humanitarian work for the Conference on Jewish Relations in New York City. At the same time, she worked to preserve the writings of several Jewish authors, many of whose works had been suppressed by the Nazis during World War II. In 1946, Arendt assumed the position of chief editor for Schocken Books, remaining at that post until 1948. She applied for

American citizenship in 1950, and was granted full citizenship during the following year.

Life's Work

Hannah Arendt began to draw the attention of international scholars in 1951 with the publication of her first major book, *The Origins of Totalitarianism*. In this work, Arendt suggested that the roots of both communism and National Socialism could be traced not only to the imperialism of the nineteenth century but also to the anti-Semitism rampant throughout Europe at that time. Arendt's thesis initially met with mixed reviews. Many scholars praised the extensive research that was reflected in *The Origins of Totalitarianism* and concurred with its view that the rise of modern dictatorships resulted from the collapse of the nation-state. Nevertheless, many critics also rejected Arendt's view that anti-Semitism had been a decisive factor in shaping all forms of totalitarianism in the twentieth century. Arendt was criticized for taking too personal a view of modern history and for failing to be objective in her interpretation of events. Since the original publication of *The Origins of Totalitarianism*, however, Arendt's central thesis has gained considerable academic support.

In 1958, Arendt's Walgreen lectures delivered at the University of Chicago were published as *The Human Condition*. With its groundbreaking distinction between work, labor, and activity, and its optimistic view that political activity can enhance civilization, this book improved Arendt's reputation as a scholar. One of Arendt's most influential works, *The Human Condition* uses an Aristotelian approach to address issues of concern in modern society. Nevertheless, several critics found the book's prose style to be extremely dense, even awkward. Arendt's literary style continued to be criticized following the publication of several of her later works.

Arendt became the first woman to hold the rank of full professor at Princeton University when she accepted the position of visiting professor of politics in 1959. Soon after, her major study of modern society and its values, *Between Past and Future* (1961), was published. In this work, Arendt argued that by rejecting both tradition and authority modern society had deprived itself of the basis for establishing generally approved standards of behavior. Her view that moral relativism had left the twentieth century without a shared system of values was to be echoed repeatedly in the decades that followed.

In 1963, Arendt completed the work that was to reach her largest general audience. *Eichmann in Jerusalem: A Report on the Banality of Evil* began as a series of articles for *The New Yorker* magazine. Adolf Eichmann, a leading official of the Nazis, had been captured in Argentina by agents of the Israeli intelligence service in May of 1960. His war crimes trial in Israel attracted international attention and inspired *The New Yorker* to send Arendt to Jerusalem for her perspectives on the trial.

Coining the phrase "the banality of evil," Arendt characterized Eichmann, not as a Nazi fanatic, but merely as an officious bureaucrat whose personal ambition had caused him to be responsible for horrific actions. Unlike the prison guards and the executioners who took an active role in exterminating the Jews, Eichmann was (in

Arendt's view) little more than a "paper shuffler" whose duties had resulted in unimaginable suffering. The Nazi regime, Arendt continued, did not arise because of the fanaticism of a few of its leaders but because of a collapse of conscience throughout Europe. Jewish leaders themselves, Arendt contended, were not wholly guiltless in permitting the Holocaust to occur. To imply that one person was single-handedly responsible for the murder of millions was to attribute more power to him than any individual can possibly have. Finally, Arendt's book criticized the Israeli government for its conduct of the trial.

With the publication of *Eichmann in Jerusalem*, Arendt found herself once again on the defensive for her views. While many scholars had regarded her interpretation of history as excessively Zionist in *The Origins of Totalitarianism*, there were some critics who now accused her of being anti-Semitic for criticizing the Israeli court in *Eichmann in Jerusalem*. Despite years of service to Jewish relief organizations, Arendt found her book condemned by the Jewish humanitarian league B'nai B'rith ("Sons of the Covenant") as a "distortion" of history.

Despite this criticism, Arendt's academic career continued to prosper. In the same year that *Eichmann in Jerusalem* was published, Arendt accepted a professorship from the highly prestigious Committee on Social Thought at the University of Chicago. *On Revolution* (1963), a philosophical and political comparison of the French and American revolutions, was also released at this time. In 1967, Arendt left Chicago to begin teaching at the New School for Social Research in New York City. During that same year, Arendt was the only nonspecialist invited to speak at Harvard University at a conference commemorating the fiftieth anniversary of the Russian Revolution.

Arendt's collection of intellectual profiles, *Men in Dark Times*, appeared in 1968. Despite the title of that work, its most influential essays were those that dealt with women, including the German socialist leader Rosa Luxemburg and the Danish author Isak Dinesen. *On Violence*, Arendt's philosophical essay dealing with the use of force in society, was published in 1970.

That same year Arendt's second husband, Heinrich Blücher, died. Although Arendt mentioned to friends at the time that she would not be able to continue her work without Blücher, she soon occupied herself with several major projects. *The Jew as Pariah: Jewish Identity and Politics in the Modern Age* (1978) helped to restore Arendt's tarnished reputation in the Jewish community. *The Life of the Mind* (1978) was envisioned as a three-volume work, only about half of which was ever completed. In this massive study Arendt attempted to explore what she regarded as the three major activities of human consciousness: thought, will, and judgment. Both *The Jew as Pariah* and the completed portions of *The Life of the Mind* were published posthumously.

Hannah Arendt died suddenly in New York on December 4, 1975, the victim of an apparent heart attack. Four days later, Arendt was eulogized at Riverside Memorial Chapel in New York City by Hans Jonas, her longtime friend and colleague at the New School for Social Research, and the novelist and essayist Mary McCarthy, who served as Arendt's literary executor.

Summary

Hannah Arendt's political philosophy resulted from the union of three independent strands in her intellectual training: Arendt's Jewish heritage led her to seek philosophical explanations for human suffering and exposed her to the threat of anti-Semitic totalitarianism; her familiarity with the existential philosophy of Heidegger, Jaspers, and Bultmann encouraged her to develop an emphasis upon individual responsibility; and her study of the Greek and Roman classics led her to adopt the methods of classical philosophy in her study of the problems afflicting modern society.

Criticized both for excessive Zionism and anti-Semitism in her writing, Arendt was, in the end, an original thinker who resisted all categorization. Her rigorous philosophical analysis of political issues and, in the last decade of her life, of human consciousness itself made her works among the most influential texts in political philosophy to be written since World War II. Running counter to the pessimistic tone found in a great deal of modern scholarship, Arendt viewed political life as a potentially heroic activity that is fully in keeping with the highest values of Western culture.

Bibliography

Canovan, Margaret. *The Political Thought of Hannah Arendt.* New York: Harcourt Brace Jovanovich, 1974. Arguing that Arendt's works are more useful for their general interpretation than their specific solutions to problems, Canovan sees Arendt as challenging the basic assumptions of modern thought. Canovan also concludes that Arendt's view of politics was "romantic."

Glazer, Nathan. "Hannah Arendt's America." *Commentary* 60 (September, 1975): 61-67. This article, written for the general reader, argues that Arendt's interpretation of European fascism is correct but that her attempts to see parallels between prewar Germany and postwar America are generally misleading.

Jonas, Hans. "Hannah Arendt." *Social Research* 43 (Spring, 1976): 3-5. A reprint of the eulogy delivered by Jonas at Riverside Memorial Chapel in New York City on December 8, 1975. It provides a fascinating personal assessment of Arendt's importance by a colleague who knew her well.

Parekh, Bhikhu C. *Hannah Arendt and the Search for a New Political Philosophy.* London: Macmillan, 1981. This challenging analysis of Arendt's philosophy explores how she sought to reconcile an Aristotelian world view with the existentialism of Jaspers and others. Parekh argues that Arendt's most original contribution to modern thought was her integration of politics into the general conception of "culture."

Social Research. 44 (Spring, 1977). This entire issue was devoted to articles dealing with various aspects of Arendt's thought and its impact. Twelve scholars contributed to this special issue, including Robert Nisbet on Arendt and the American Revolution, Elisabeth Young-Bruehl on Arendt's story-telling, Erich Heller on Arendt as a critic of literature, and Hans Morgenthau on Arendt and totalitarianism.

Whitfield, Stephen J. *Into the Dark: Hannah Arendt and Totalitarianism.* Philadelphia: Temple University Press, 1980. The most thorough analysis of the issues raised by Arendt's *The Origins of Totalitarianism*, this book also contains extensive notes and an excellent bibliography.

Young-Bruehl, Elisabeth. *Hannah Arendt, For Love of the World.* New Haven, Conn.: Yale University Press, 1982. The best biography available of Arendt's intellectual and personal life. Highly readable, it also contains a useful analysis of Arendt's philosophical works and a few rarely available examples of poetry by Arendt.

Jeffrey L. Buller

LILLIAN HARDIN ARMSTRONG

Born: February 3, 1902; Memphis, Tennessee
Died: August 27, 1971; Chicago, Illinois
Area of Achievement: Music
Contribution: At a time when few female jazz musicians were well known and highly respected, Lillian Hardin Armstrong was in great demand as a pianist for the best bands in jazz. She was responsible for advising and motivating her husband, Louis Armstrong, who became the most successful jazz musician of his era as a direct result of her coaching.

Early Life

Lillian Hardin was born on February 3, 1902, into a family in Memphis, Tennessee, that had a great appreciation for music. Her father died when she was two years old, and she was reared by her mother. The family owned a pump organ, and Lillian was playing the instrument almost as soon as she could walk, aided by a cousin who worked the organ pedals that she was unable to reach. When she was six, she began to take piano lessons from one of her grade school teachers, and it was not long before she was playing both at school and at church.

While she was still in grade school, Lillian began to attend Mrs. Hook's School of Music, from which she was graduated at age eleven. When she was fifteen, she began to attend Fisk University in Nashville, Tennessee, as a music major, but she was not to complete her studies there. In 1918, her mother and stepfather moved from Memphis to Chicago, Illinois, and Lillian went there during her summer vacation.

During the summer of 1918, Lillian spent much of her time buying sheet music and learning the popular songs of the day. One day, she went into Jones's Music Store on State Street in Chicago and asked to be allowed to play some music before she bought it. She was permitted to do so, and her playing impressed the store's demonstrator, who offered her a job as a demonstrator on the spot. She accepted the position and went to work playing sheet music for potential customers for a salary of three dollars a week. Lillian's mother was horrified that her daughter would work at all, and was particularly upset that she would work for such a low wage. Lillian was excellent at her job, however, and before long she was making eight dollars a week.

One of the things she liked about her work was that she sometimes heard the best pianists of the time, who would come in to try out the latest music. On one occasion, she heard Jelly Roll Morton, the great pianist and composer who always claimed that he had invented jazz. Lillian was thrilled with his playing. Later, she said, "In no time at all, he had the piano rockin', and he played so heavy . . . the goose pimples were just stickin' out all over me . . . after that I played just as hard as I could. . . . Until this day I am still a heavy piano player."

Life's Work

Mrs. Jones, the owner of Jones's Music, was involved in booking bands in Chicago, and she brought the New Orleans Creole Jazz Band to town to play an engagement at a Chinese restaurant. The band had no pianist at the time, and Jones suggested that Lillian Hardin should audition for the job. Hardin only needed to hear the first tune the band played, "Livery Stable Blues," to realize that this was the kind of music she wanted to play. She tried out for the job, asking before she played with the band where the music was and what key the first song would be in. She was somewhat surprised when she was told that the band did not use written music and never worried about such things as keys. She was instructed, "When the leader gives two knocks, you start playing." Hardin must have played well; she was hired on the spot in spite of the fact that a number of male pianists had also auditioned.

Hardin avoided telling her mother that she had gone to work for a jazz band, but her mother found out when a friend of hers told her that she had seen her daughter in a cabaret. Hardin's budding career was in danger of being cut short by her mother's objections, but Hardin begged to be allowed to continue playing with the band. The two finally agreed that Hardin would continue to play but that her mother would pick her up at the end of each engagement. It was embarrassing for Hardin, but at least it allowed her to keep doing what she cared about more than anything else.

From that point on, Lillian Hardin never had any trouble finding work as a pianist. Although she was not a gifted soloist, she developed a reputation as a capable pianist who could be counted on to back up soloists and provide an appropriate harmonic background She was also popular because she was a trained musician who could read music well, could write out parts, and understood musical theory and harmony. Although such skills are taken for granted in the modern era, they were unusual at that time. The average jazz musician of the 1920's learned to play by imitating others and could not read music at all.

Hardin went on to work in a number of bands. In 1921, she was asked to play with Joe "King" Oliver's Creole Jazz Band. Oliver was considered the finest jazz cornetist/trumpeter of the time, and his band was one of the best. He had just arrived in Chicago from his native New Orleans, which he had left because he had realized that the larger city would offer him more musical opportunities. When the Creole Jazz Band traveled to San Francisco for a six-month stay, Hardin decided to leave California early and return to Chicago. She played there at the Dreamland club with a band led by violinist Mae Brady, but she rejoined King Oliver's band in 1922, after he had returned to Chicago.

In 1922, Oliver decided that he wanted a second cornetist in his band, and he sent for the best cornetist he knew: Louis Armstrong. Oliver and Armstrong had been close friends in New Orleans, and Oliver had served as Armstrong's mentor, helping him find work and encouraging him in his playing. Oliver knew, however, that Armstrong was a far better player than he himself was, so he was careful to control what Armstrong played. He made certain that Armstrong stayed in the background.

Oliver and the other members of the band had talked about "Little Louie" frequently before he arrived; all of them were pleased that he would be playing with them. After hearing all the stories about Armstrong, Hardin had high expectations of him. She was severely disappointed that "Little Louie" was overweight, dressed poorly, and wore his hair in bangs. She was also disappointed in his playing, because he spent most of his time in the shadow of Oliver, played many phrases in unison with Oliver, and suppressed his own musical creativity. One night, however, Oliver told Hardin that Armstrong was actually a far better player than he was. He said, "But as long as I got him with me, he won't be able to get ahead of me. I'll still be king."

The Creole Jazz Band went on to become a sensation in Chicago. Oliver's band had been popular before, but now all the best players came regularly to hear it. Oliver and Armstrong began to play more and more complicated lines in unison, amazing the listeners. The combination of Oliver's musical direction and good playing and Armstrong's superb playing made the band unique.

Hardin began to pay more attention to Armstrong, and the two spent more time together. For his part, Armstrong appreciated the fact that Hardin, unlike most pianists, played four solid beats to the bar, providing a rhythmic foundation that was ideal for his New Orleans style of playing. Hardin, who was far better educated than Armstrong and much more sophisticated, began to act as his new mentor. She helped him pick out clothes, shared her knowledge of theory and harmony with him, rehearsed with him often, and introduced him to classical music.

In 1923, after making a tour of the Midwest, the King Oliver Creole Jazz Band went to Richmond, Indiana, where the group recorded thirty-seven pieces for four different record labels in a single day. There were many difficulties during the course of the recording, and every member of the band except Hardin was nervous. They had no need to be, however, since the music they recorded that day made history. Those recordings are still studied extensively by jazz critics and enjoyed by aficionados.

In 1924, Lillian Hardin married Louis Armstrong, and "Miss Lil," as she liked to be called, began to urge Armstrong to step out of Oliver's shadow. Armstrong was becoming frustrated in his limited role in the band, but he did not want to hurt Oliver's feelings. Lil told Louis that she did not want to be married to a second trumpet player. When he told her he could not "quit Mr. Joe," Lil said, "Well, it's Mr. Joe or me." Lil got her way.

Armstrong left Oliver and became the first trumpeter for the Ollie Powers band, while Lil stayed in the Oliver band. Soon afterward, Lil and Louis left for New York, where Louis joined Fletcher Henderson's big band. Henderson's band was the perfect place for Louis Armstrong, who ultimately changed the band's style single-handedly, but there was no place there for Lil Hardin Armstrong, since Henderson himself played the piano. She decided to return to Chicago, where she formed her own band, Lil's Hot Shots. After spending fourteen months with Henderson's band, Louis Armstrong went back to Chicago, where he played first trumpet in his wife's band. The band was successful, and Armstrong also played with the band of Erskine Tate, where he was allowed to sing as well as play the trumpet. As a result of their financial success, the Armstrongs were able to buy a home in Chicago.

Armstrong went on to form his own group, the Hot Five, which featured Lil Hardin Armstrong on piano, Edward "Kid" Ory on trombone, Johnny St. Cyr on banjo, and

Johnny Dodds on clarinet. The Hot Five and other groups led by Louis Armstrong and including Lil Hardin Armstrong made numerous recordings that are among the most famous in jazz history. The recordings of the Hot Five and the Hot Seven are particularly prized by lovers of early jazz. Lil Hardin Armstrong contributed not only by providing a solid rhythmic background for Louis Armstrong but also by writing out arrangements for the band and contributing her own compositions. On occasion, she also sang vocal duets with her husband, and her smooth, clear voice provided the perfect musical foil for his rich, gravelly one. In addition, Lil often took charge of booking the various Armstrong bands.

Louis Armstrong and Lil Hardin Armstrong were divorced in 1938, but they remained on good terms in spite of the fact that a music publishing company refused to give her credit for some of the songs she had written while she and Louis had been married. Louis Armstrong went on to become the best-known musician in the history of jazz, and Lil Hardin Armstrong went on to play with virtually all the best jazz musicians of her time. She played for a time with the superb trumpeter Freddy Keppard, and she led many bands over the years, including a sixteen-piece band featuring trumpeter Jonah Jones and the band she called Lil Armstrong and Her Swing Band, which featured trumpeter Joe Thomas, clarinetist Buster Bailey, and tenor saxophonist Chu Berry.

During the 1930's, Lil Hardin Armstrong studied at the Chicago College of Music. After she received a teacher's certificate from that institution, she went on to study at the New York College of Music, which issued her a postgraduate diploma. After spending a few years in New York, Armstrong returned to Chicago, where she lived for the rest of her life in the house that she and Louis had bought. She remained active as a performer and composer, and she spent the rest of her time sewing and studying photography.

Louis Armstrong died on July 6, 1971, in his home in Corona, New York. On August 27, a memorial concert for Louis Armstrong took place at the Civic Center Plaza in Chicago. Lil Hardin Armstrong was a featured performer at that concert. She was playing the "St. Louis Blues" on the televised program when she died of a massive heart attack.

Summary

It never occurred to Lillian Hardin Armstrong that she would not be successful in her chosen field. She was utterly self-confident, partly because it was her nature to be so and partly because she knew that very few jazz musicians of her era were as well trained as she was. Although she was not an outstanding soloist and did not become a star, she was a successful pianist, composer, bandleader, singer, and businesswoman. Armstrong served as an example to other women by demonstrating that it was possible to succeed in a business that was male dominated, and at times she helped other female jazz musicians find work. In the 1930's, for example, she formed an all-female band. One of Lil Hardin Armstrong's most important achievements was her guidance of Louis Armstrong, who was as unsure of himself in his personal life and in business as he was self-assured and gifted in his playing. Without the advice and the prodding of Lillian Hardin Armstrong, Louis Armstrong would never have achieved the success he did ultimately achieve, and the world of jazz would have lost its first superstar.

Bibliography

Dahl, Linda. *Stormy Weather: The Music and Lives of a Century of Jazzwomen.* New York: Pantheon Books, 1984. Lillian Hardin Armstrong is discussed in some detail in chapter 2, "First Ladies of Early Jazz." The rest of the chapter also sheds light on the era during which Armstrong established herself as a force to be reckoned with in jazz. Armstrong is also discussed briefly at various points throughout the book. Indexed and illustrated. Contains a discography and a bibliography.

Handy, D. Antoinette. "Lillian ('Lil') Hardin Armstrong." In *Black Women in American Bands and Orchestras.* Metuchen, N.J.: Scarecrow Press, 1981. This extremely brief entry is useful in that it lists a number of the artists with whom Armstrong recorded.

Jones, Max, and John Chilton. *Louis: The Louis Armstrong Story, 1900-1971.* Boston: Little, Brown, 1971. This useful and well-organized biography discusses Lil Hardin Armstrong at various points, but the most informative section is the chapter "Miss Lil," which discusses Lil's first meeting with Louis Armstrong and her subsequent influence on his career. Indexed and illustrated.

Schuller, Gunther. *Early Jazz: Its Roots and Musical Development.* New York: Oxford University Press, 1968. Although his book does not discuss the work of Lil Armstrong at length, Schuller does provide informed criticism of her playing at various points. This book contains the most significant musical analysis available of early jazz. Indexed.

Unterbrink, Mary. "Lil Hardin Armstrong." In *Jazz Women at the Keyboard.* Jefferson, N.C.: McFarland, 1983. This essay is the best single source of written information about Lil Hardin Armstrong. Highly recommended.

Shawn Woodyard

DOROTHY ARZNER

Born: January 3, 1897; San Francisco, California
Died: October 1, 1979; La Quinta, California
Area of Achievement: Film
Contribution: An exception within the Hollywood film industry, Arzner was the major woman film director of the Hollywood studio system from the late 1920's through the early 1940's.

Early Life

Although she was born in San Francisco, Dorothy Arzner grew up around the film stars, directors, and stage personalities who gathered at her father's well-known Hollywood restaurant, the Hoffman Cafe. D. W. Griffith, Charlie Chaplin, Eric von Stroheim, Hal Roach, and Mack Sennett among others met at the round table Louis Arzner's café featured for its show business guests. When asked later in life about her early years in Hollywood's film colony, Arzner remarked that it was a wonder that she went into films at all since she spent her youth being terrified by actors who were always tossing her up into the air.

After graduating from the Westlake School, Dorothy entered the University of Southern California, where she planned to study medicine. During World War I, she volunteered as an ambulance driver, an experience, among others, that deterred her from further medical studies.

The Hollywood studios expanded after the war and demand for workers rose dramatically as a result of the devastating flu epidemic of 1918. In 1919, Dorothy Arzner, who had never expected to work in the motion picture business, went to Famous Players-Lasky (later Paramount Studios) looking for a job, and she was hired as a $15-per-week script typist. Shortly after her arrival, she was made script supervisor. Arzner later confided that her work in the script department taught her the basics of film structure.

Soon Arzner began training as an assistant cutter responsible for splicing and assembling motion picture film negatives into a unified work. By 1921, she had moved to a Paramount subsidiary, Realart Studios, as chief editor. During the next year she cut more than fifty films and trained other editors. In 1922, she went back to Paramount to work on Fred Niblo's *Blood and Sand*, a vehicle starring Rudolph Valentino for which she earned her first credit. Next, James Cruze took her on location as the editor for his epic western, *The Covered Wagon*. By the mid-1920's, Arzner had a reputation as one of the best cutters in the business. She also began to write scenarios, some of which were filmed by Paramount's best directors. Impatient to begin her own career as a director, Arzner threatened to leave Paramount, but she was placated when the studio gave her her first directing assignment. She brought *Fashions for Women* (1927) in under budget and ahead of deadline, completing her apprenticeship and opening a position for herself as a director within the Hollywood studio system.

Life's Work

Capitalizing on the success of her first film, Dorothy Arzner secured her place at Paramount by making two more silent comedies in 1927. *Ten Modern Commandments* starred Esther Ralston, who had been acclaimed for her role in *Fashions for Women*, and *Get Your Man* featured the "it" girl, Clara Bow. Next she was asked to direct Paramount's first sound film, *Manhattan Cocktail* (1928). That she was chosen suggests that either Arzner was highly regarded as a professional and therefore capable of tackling the new technology or that she was expendable and could be blamed if the film failed. She made her first talking picture in 1929, a remake of *Wild Party*, a silent film she had edited in 1923. Again, the film starred Clara Bow and launched the career of Fredric March, who had appeared in the stage version from which the film was adapted. Through the years, Arzner became known as something of a career maker and was responsible for directing films which established a number of actors who later became major Hollywood stars.

Dorothy Arzner was very busy during the early 1930's. In 1930, three of her films were released by Paramount: *Sarah and Son*, *Anybody's Woman*, and an episode for a compilation film *Paramount on Parade*. In addition, Arzner worked on two more films: *Behind the Makeup*, which she codirected with Robert Milton, and *Charming Sinners*, which she completed for the same director. *Sarah and Son* was the first film that was scripted by playwright and screenwriter Zoë Akins—with whom Arzner was to work later—and it made Ruth Chatterton into an international star. A smash hit at the box office, *Sarah and Son* established Arzner as one of Paramount's most sought-after directors. When *Anybody's Woman* also became a hit, Arzner remarked that the studio would give her anything she wanted. She next directed *Honor Among Lovers* (1931), which featured Ginger Rogers in one of her earliest roles and advanced the rising careers of Fredric March and Claudette Colbert. In a somewhat daring move, Arzner ended the film with Colbert's heroine running off to take a world cruise with her boss (March) before she had divorced her first husband. It is a mark of Arzner's success that the studio did not interfere with the film's ending. Her next film was a far more typical "woman's picture." Despite its script by Zoë Akins, Arzner's *Working Girls* (1931) did not do well at the box office and became her least successful film of the 1930's. In 1932, she made *Merrily We Go to Hell*, her last film for Paramount. A bittersweet comedy, the film has received critical attention, especially for the ingenuity and courage of its central female character as played by Sylvia Sidney. In spite of the film's success, Arzner left Paramount to work as an independent director and moved from studio to studio for the rest of her professional career.

The first film that Arzner made as a freelance director was *Christopher Strong* (1933), which was scripted by Zoë Akins and shot at RKO for producer David O. Selznick. The story goes that Arzner rescued her leading lady, Katharine Hepburn, from a jungle picture by literally bringing her down out of a tree. *Christopher Strong* became one of Arzner's most famous films, and Hepburn's performance as a head-strong woman aviator helped boost her fledgling career. The critics were largely complimentary, and studio executive Samuel Goldwyn admired the film so much that he hired Arzner to make an adaptation of Émile Zola's novel *Nana*, which was released in 1934. The film was designed to launch the career of the Russian actress, Anna Sten, who Goldwyn hoped would rival Greta Garbo. Moving over to Columbia Pictures, Arzner made *Craig's Wife* (1936), a film based on the well-known play by George Kelly, whose niece Grace eventually became a film star herself. *Craig's Wife* starred Rosalind Russell, who received an Oscar nomination for her portrayal of an obsessive housewife. Joan Crawford was sufficiently impressed by the film, or at least by Russell's Oscar nomination, that she took the lead in Arzner's next film, *The Bride Wore Red* (1937), which was shot at Metro-Goldwyn-Mayer (MGM) with a screenplay by Tess Slesinger from a Ferenc Molnár play. Arzner disliked the superficiality of the film's plot, but she became a lifelong friend of Crawford.

Although she did not know it at the time, Arzner was to direct only two more pictures. The first, *Dance, Girl, Dance* (1940), adapted from a Vicki Baum story by Tess Slesinger, once again helped to advance the careers of its principal actors: Maureen O'Hara and Lucille Ball. Subsequently, it also generated a sizable body of critical commentary, particularly for its feminist perspectives. During the early part of World War II, Arzner made some training films for the Women's Army Corps (WACs). In 1943, however, she returned to Columbia to make her final film, a war picture starring Merle Oberon as a member of the Norwegian underground entitled *First Comes Courage*.

At this time a serious illness forced Arzner to take a temporary leave from directing; eventually, her retirement became permanent. Nevertheless, Dorothy Arzner did not entirely leave filmmaking. She established the first filmmaking course at the Pasadena Playhouse and taught film at the University of California at Los Angeles (UCLA) for four years during the 1960's. She also shot some fifty Pepsi commercials for television during Joan Crawford's association with that company. Arzner was the first woman member of the Directors Guild of America (DGA); at a Guild tribute in 1975, her former student Francis Ford Coppola attested to her influence on his directing career. In 1979, Dorothy Arzner died at the age of eighty-two at La Quinta, near Palm Springs, California, where she had spent the last years of her life.

Summary

Dorothy Arzner was the only major woman director during the Golden Age of Hollywood and as such occupies a unique position in film studies and a central one for feminist film criticism. Although Arzner denied any overtly feminist intentions in her cinema and often talked of herself as just one of the "boys" who made motion pictures at the studios, her films are increasingly read as promoting opposition to the dominant male-centered, or patriarchal, ideology of American studio films. As interest in gender studies has grown, increasingly Arzner's work has been examined as well for its possible lesbian content. There is still controversy over whether her films developed a fuller expression of gay sexuality than was otherwise occasionally available in other films of the period.

Regardless of Arzner's own sexual orientation, her films are receiving increasing attention from both film scholars and the general public alike. She has become recognized as one of the best American directors of the 1930's, and her films are being revived around the world. It is a recognition that might have come sooner had she not cut short her career in the mid-1940's. Not only are her films praised for their overall quality, but Arzner herself is being acknowledged for the careers she helped to launch or further. Not just another marginal Hollywood professional, Dorothy Arzner has begun to be considered a major directing talent, one significant enough to rank with her male counterparts as a cocreator of the classic Hollywood cinema of the interwar years.

Bibliography
Doty, Alexander. "Whose Text Is It Anyway?: Queer Cultures, Queer Auteurs, and Queer Authorship." *Quarterly Review of Film and Video* 15 (November, 1993): 41-54. Doty examines Arzner's films along with those of her contemporary, director George Cukor. Doty attempts to demonstrate that these works, although made for straight audiences, were subtly influenced by the directors' sexual identities as a lesbian and a homosexual.
Heck-Rabi, Louise. "Dorothy Arzner: An Image of Independence." In *Women Film-makers: A Critical Reception.* Metuchen, N.J.: Scarecrow Press, 1984. Heck-Rabi's chapter on Arzner places her within the context of Hollywood's "boom" years. Surveys film critics' assessments of Arzner's career, discusses the revival of interest in her work during the 1970's, and includes a filmography of motion pictures directed by Arzner.
Houston, Beverle. "Missing in Action: Notes on Dorothy Arzner." *Wide Angle* 6, no. 3 (1984): 24-31. This essay introduces Arzner's work and examines four of her films to judge how effectively they violate the specular practices of classic Hollywood films.
Johnston, Claire, ed. *The Work of Dorothy Arzner: Towards a Feminist Cinema.* London: British Film Institute, 1975. This first short monograph on Arzner contains critical essays, an interview with Dorothy Arzner, and a comprehensive filmography.
Kort, Melissa Sue. "'Spectacular Spinelessness': The Men in Dorothy Arzner's Films." In *Men by Women,* edited by Janet Todd. New York: Holmes & Meier, 1981. The author argues that it is not the weakness of the men but the strength of the women in her films which marginalizes the male in her narratives.
Lesage, Julia. "The Hegemonic Female Fantasy in *An Unknown Woman* and *Craig's Wife.*" *Film Reader* 5 (1982): 83-94. According to Lesage, the countervailing tendencies in Arzner's *Craig's Wife* attack the hegemonic female fantasies promoted by Hollywood—fantasies that flattened out contradictions in women's lives and promoted conventional solutions to women's issues.
Mayne, Judith. *Directed by Dorothy Arzner.* Bloomington: Indiana University Press, 1994. Based on research in archival collections at the University of California at Los Angeles, this book-length work is more properly a critical study of

Arzner's career than a definitive biography. Mayne explores the connections between Arzner's provocative depiction of women in her films and her identity as a lesbian at a time when such an identity was commonly repressed and ignored.

——————. "Female Authorship Reconsidered." In *The Woman at the Keyhole: Feminism and Women's Cinema.* Bloomington: Indiana University Press, 1990. Mayne raises questions about how overtly Arzner's life and films can be read as raising lesbian issues. Considers whether her films present anything more sustained or developed than the occasional lesbian images that have routinely appeared in other Hollywood films.

Charles L. P. Silet

MARY KAY ASH

Born: May 12, 1915 (?); Hot Wells, Texas

Area of Achievement: Business and industry

Contribution: As founder and chairman emeritus of Mary Kay Cosmetics, a Fortune 500 company based on direct sales by women who demonstrate beauty products in homes, Mary Kay Ash is famous for her motivational techniques, including awarding pink Cadillacs as prizes.

Early Life

Born in Hot Wells, Texas, a small town twenty-five miles from Houston, Mary Kathlyn Wagner was the youngest of four children of Edward Alexander and Lula Vember (Hastings) Wagner. The family owned a hotel where Lula Wagner's good cooking attracted customers. Edward Wagner fell ill with tuberculosis, spent three years in a sanitarium, and returned home an invalid. The Wagners sold the hotel and moved to Houston, where Lula leased and managed a café Washington Avenue. Lula put in fourteen-hour days as cook and manager, so it became seven-year-old Mary Kay's job to clean, cook, and care for her dad. Mary Kay also learned to take the streetcar downtown to shop for her own clothes. Her persuasive powers as a business executive grew out of her youthful experiences trying to convince salespeople that she had the money and authorization from her mother.

Lula Wagner's loving encouragement and her exemplary work ethic inspired Mary Kay to excel. In addition to achieving excellent grades in school, Mary Kay sold the most tickets for her school's May Fete. She learned to type fast enough to win a class trophy, won honors on the debate team, and gave speeches that earned recognition for her as the second best speaker in Texas. Mary Kay applied her sales skills to her extracurricular activities as well, earning distinction as a top seller of Girl Scout cookies.

One of Mary Kay's closest competitors was her friend Dorothy Zapp, who was rich, smart, and capable. Mary Kay continually aspired to outdo Dorothy when it came to selling school tickets or achieving high grades. The Zapp family appreciated Mary Kay for her persistence and intelligence and included her in their family vacations and Christmas parties. Dorothy and Mary Kay shared joys, sorrows, and secrets. Eventually, their lives began to follow separate paths when Dorothy went off to college, a luxury that Mary Kay's family could not afford during the Depression.

After condensing four years of studies into three, Mary Kay was graduated from Reagan High School at the age of seventeen. After graduation, she was married to Ben Rogers. Rogers was a musician who played guitar with the Hawaiian Strummers, a band that was featured on a local radio program. With the arrival of the couple's three children, he took a day job at a gas station and played music at night.

Pressured by the tough economic times and her compulsion to work, Mary Kay began to sell children's books for the Child Psychology Bookshelf. Ida Blake, a company saleswoman, encouraged Mary Kay and taught her to drive a car, enabling her to sell books throughout Houston. When Ben lost his job at the gas station, the couple began to work together selling cookware, but were forced to abandon the venture because of poor sales during the continuing economic depression. In 1939, Mary Kay began to work part-time for Stanley Home Products.

Like her own future company, Stanley Home Products conducted direct sales parties at people's homes. Mary Kay was not successful at first. Realizing she had a lot to learn, she borrowed twelve dollars to attend the company's annual convention in Dallas. Motivated by the recognition given to the company's leading salesperson— in this case, a crown and alligator handbag awarded to a woman—Mary Kay resolved to be next year's winner, a resolve she announced to the president of the company. Taking steps to ensure her success, Mary Kay attended a demonstration conducted by the current winner, took nineteen pages of notes, and memorized the woman's sales pitch. Mary Kay's determination and hard work put her at the top of sales the next year. Instead of winning the coveted alligator purse, however, she was given a flounder light, a light used by fishermen.

Such lack of consideration embittered Mary Kay as she labored to succeed in the male-dominated world of sales. Nevertheless, she managed to rise above these slights to pursue her career goals while still caring for her family. During World War II, her husband joined the Army and was sent abroad. Fortunately, Mary Kay's sales career as a Stanley dealer was flourishing and provided the family with a steady income.

In 1942, she decided to pursue her dream to become a medical doctor. Since married women were not supposed to take places from men, Mary Kay posed as an unmarried coed and enrolled in premedical courses at the University of Houston. A woman dean called her in to discuss the results of a three-day aptitude test and informed her that she had tested higher in marketing and sales than in science. That news plus the prospect of making a ten-year commitment to become a doctor on top of her heavy workload as wife, mother, and saleswoman persuaded Mary Kay to drop out of college and work full-time for Stanley instead. Shortly thereafter, her husband was mustered out of the Army and informed Mary Kay that he had met another woman and wanted a divorce after eleven years of marriage.

Life's Work

The postwar years marked a new chapter in Mary Kay Rogers' life. As a young career woman and a divorced parent, she had little time to wallow in pity since her children depended on her for their emotional and financial support. She joined what her mother described as the "Five O'Clock Club," rising at 5 A.M. to plan her household chores and the day's three sales parties. Her children were also involved and learned to package her products, keep accounts, and do household chores. As her income rose, Mary Kay hired a housekeeper. After being named a manager at Stanley and moving to Dallas, Mary Kay thought she would continue to progress within the company hierarchy. Instead, she encountered a glass ceiling—a variety of gender-based barriers that hindered her advancement at Stanley.

In 1952, she transferred to World Gift Company in Houston, where she became a top saleswoman, then an area manager, and finally a training director. In this capacity, she visited forty-three states and traveled three weeks out of every month. As she rose through the ranks, she faced discrimination. A male assistant, whom she had trained, was named as her boss and given twice her salary. Another incident involved an efficiency expert who told Mary Kay she had too much power. Eventually, the company decided to transfer her every six months. In 1963, she voluntarily retired from the company.

After leaving World Gift Company, Mary Kay decided to write her memoirs. While reviewing her business experiences, she wrote down her ideas for a dream company. In her ideal company, the Golden Rule would be practiced. Above all, the company would be sympathetic to the concerns of working women and especially to those of working mothers. All she needed was a product, and she remembered an invention she had been introduced to by the daughter of a deceased tanner of hides—homemade cosmetics. She had been using these cosmetics, in spite of their smell, since 1952, and she bought the formulas for them in 1963.

Mary Kay began preparations to launch her new company. A month before Mary Kay Cosmetics was scheduled to open, her second husband of several years died of a heart attack. An executive in the vitamin industry, he was to be in charge of the new company's finances and administration. The crisis caused by his death was overcome when her youngest son Richard agreed to take over the financial end of the company. Against the advice of her lawyer and accountant, Mary Kay opened her company on September 13, 1963, backed by her life savings of $5,000.

The first year of retail sales, amounting to nearly $200,000, were encouraging to the beginning staff of nine sales representatives. Eventually, the company established certain guidelines for sales. Independent salespeople, known as beauty consultants, were encouraged to purchase a makeup case containing the company's products, to make extensive telephone contacts among their friends and neighbors, to organize intimate home-based parties demonstrating the products, and to sell the makeup for twice what they paid for it. Each time a consultant recruited additional sales representatives, she was awarded a percentage of their sales forever. No cap was placed on the consultants' earnings. As their sales increased, consultants advanced through the ranks to sales director and eventually to national sales director. The company placed particular emphasis on individual recognition, providing bonuses and prizes in the form of jewelry, fur coats, and complimentary Cadillacs and sponsoring annual sales conventions to highlight the success of each sales representative.

The business skyrocketed and the company went public in 1968. From 1973 to 1983, the company's stock price rose by 670 percent. Between 1984 and 1985, however, the company's growth slowed, and Mary Kay and Richard decided to buy back publicly held stock and become a family-owned business again. Initially, all three of Mary Kay's children worked for her company, although her oldest daughter Marilyn left after four years because of an injured back.

Mary Kay married businessman Melville Jerome Ash in 1966. Their marriage was happy, and they built a large $4 million circular house in Dallas. Mel was popular with the staff at Mary Kay Cosmetics, even though he tried to get Mary to spend less time at the office. He died of cancer in 1980.

By the early 1990's, Mary Kay Cosmetics was operating in nineteen countries and was included on the Fortune 500 list of the largest industrial companies in America. Of its estimated 350,000 beauty consultants, some fifteen percent work abroad. Four subsidiaries were established in Australia, Canada, Argentina, and Germany, and the company's worldwide wholesale sales were estimated at $609 million in 1992.

In 1993, Mary Kay dedicated the Mary Kay Museum, which exhibits thirty years of the company's history. In that year she received the Dallas Mother of the Year Award and the Outstanding Texas Citizen Award from the Exchange Clubs. In 1990 she won the Woman of Achievement Award from the General Federation of Women's Clubs. She has appeared on most of the prominent television talk shows and *60 Minutes*. In 1987, she received the Churchwoman of the Year Award from Religious Heritage of America. She is especially proud of the Horatio Alger Distinguished American Citizen Award she received from Norman Vincent Peale, and she serves on the Horatio Alger Association Board of Directors. A major philanthropist, she supports many causes such as the Prestonwood Baptist Church and cancer research. She is the author of two books: her autobiography and a best-selling book containing her management philosophy.

Summary

Despite criticism of her emphasis on a rather traditional image of women, Mary Kay Ash considers herself a feminist with a difference. She built her dream company by offering women opportunities for financial independence, career advancement, and personal fulfillment. On the way up, employees gain recognition and are feted at an annual seminar. By the 1990's, there were four separate seminars held consecutively to accommodate 35,000 consultants over a two-week period each July in Dallas. Mary Kay focuses her efforts on motivating her salespeople, building up their self-confidence by recognizing their improved personal appearance and sales. In addition to providing financial incentives, Mary Kay gives them praise, applause, personal notes and calls. Her consultants idolize her.

Mary Kay has created an egalitarian culture as she promised. In 1993 Mary Kay Cosmetics was listed for the second time among *The 100 Best Companies to Work for in America*. There are about 2,000 male sales representatives and a line of men's skin care products has been introduced. There is no glass ceiling, no loss of commissions if one moves, no favoritism, ageism, racism or sexism. Personal testimonies from those who have gained riches beyond their dreams come from blacks, farm wives, and elderly. Most employees are part-timers, who can set their own hours for working.

Bibliography
Ash, Mary Kay. *Mary Kay*. New York: Harper & Row, 1981. An autobiography that
    is the basis for secondary works on Ash and Mary Kay Cosmetics. The book reveals

her analytical mind, which was able to work out principles for personal and corporate success in the midst of setbacks, frustrations, discrimination against women, divorce, child-rearing, and housework.

——————— . *Mary Kay on People Management.* New York: Warner Books, 1984. This *New York Times* best-seller emphasizes recognition as the most powerful of all motivators. She underscores the importance of the Golden Rule and that businesses should be more like families and "praise people to success."

Cohen, Sherry Suib. *Tender Power.* Reading, Mass.: Addison-Wesley, 1989. The author believes that women can revolutionize corporate structure through "tender power" by creating a nurturing, cooperative business environment emphasizing peer recognition. As the president and chief operating officer of Mary Kay Cosmetics, Dick Bartlett championed the concept of tender power, and Mary Kay Ash is cited as an example of the concept in action.

Farnham, Alan. "Mary Kay's Lessons in Leadership." *Fortune* 128 (September 20, 1993): 68-77. An article that focuses on the power of recognition and other motivational techniques as displayed at the company's annual seminar in Dallas. Provides a snapshot overview of the corporate structure and describes the support role assigned to husbands whose wives work for the company. Illustrated.

Rosenfield, Paul. "The Beautiful Make-Up of Mary Kay," *The Saturday Evening Post* 253 (October, 1981): 58-63, 106-107. A cheerful, upbeat review that provides a summary of Ash's achievements and a snapshot overview of her company and its corporate structure.

Rozakis, Laurie. *Mary Kay.* Vero Beach, Fla.: Rourke Enterprises, 1993. An entry in the publisher's Made in America series, this biography is directed at juvenile readers and provides a concise introduction to Ash's life and career, highlighting her struggle to achieve.

Virginia W. Leonard

GERTRUDE ATHERTON

Born: October 30, 1857; San Francisco, California
Died: June 14, 1948; San Francisco, California
Area of Achievement: Literature
Contribution: A prolific writer known for her California themes, Atherton produced
several popular novels featuring strong-willed female protagonists.

Early Life
Gertrude Franklin Horn was born on October 30, 1857, in San Francisco, where she would die more than ninety years later. Although California was the focus of many of her more than fifty books (mostly novels) and numerous essays and newspaper columns, and though she often proclaimed herself a proud daughter of that state, she found California provincial; she thus traveled the globe, residing for extended periods of time in New York City, Europe, the West Indies, and Havana, Cuba. Her restless spirit stemmed at least in part from her turbulent childhood. Her father, Thomas L. Horn, was a native of Connecticut who migrated to San Francisco, where he established a cigar and tobacco business; her mother, Gertrude Franklin, was a native of New Orleans. Before Gertrude reached age three, her parents divorced, and she and her mother lived for a time with her maternal grandparents, Stephen and Eliza Franklin, at their ranch near San Jose, California. In 1865, Gertrude's mother married John Frederick Uhlhorn, a wealthy Easterner whom young Gertrude despised. After he attempted suicide in 1870, her stepfather left the family, and Gertrude and her mother once again lived with her grandfather, whom Gertrude admired and who engendered in her an enduring love of literature.

In her autobiography *Adventures of a Novelist* (1932), Gertrude remarked that as a child she determined to be as different—as independent-minded—as possible. To her teachers, family members, and most everyone else who knew her, she was not only different but difficult: haughty, short-tempered, and rebellious. Her supreme act of rebellion against her mother was to elope, in 1876, with George Atherton. The twenty-four-year-old son of a wealthy California land baron and his Chilean wife, George had been her mother's suitor before falling in love with Gertrude. The marriage, however, was an unhappy one; George had no interest in literature, and his mother (with whom they resided) was domineering. Gertrude bore two children (the first of whom died of diphtheria in 1882), but motherhood and domestic life did not appeal to her. Against fierce opposition from her husband, she wrote her first novel, "The Randolphs of Redwoods" (1882), which was serialized anonymously in the *Argonaut*, a San Francisco weekly, and later was published in book form under the title *A Daughter of the Vine* (1899). Sexually suggestive scenes in the novel brought her notoriety, which further alienated her from her husband and his family. In 1887, George Atherton died, freeing Gertrude to pursue her own path in life, the path of the writer.

Life's Work

Shortly after her husband's death, Gertrude Atherton placed her daughter under the care of her mother and moved to New York City, a major center of cultural and literary activity, hoping to find a publisher for her new novel, *What Dreams May Come.* Meanwhile, she wrote a weekly column, "Letter from New York," for the *Argonaut,* keeping her fellow Californians abreast of New York's social and cultural life.

What Dreams May Come, which deals with the theme of reincarnation, was published in 1888; it sold well but was largely ignored by the critics. In 1889, she published *Hermia Suydam,* which she composed during her first few months in New York City, the story's setting. Atherton once remarked that she wrote this tale of an unmarried woman's amorous adventures out of a spirit of mischief, to rile conservative-minded critics. She achieved that objective: The book caused an uproar and was harshly condemned for being immoral and prurient; some critics even suggested that its author had a diseased mind. Disappointed but not defeated, Gertrude set sail for Europe in 1889.

Ironically, it was while in Europe that Atherton decided to become a novelist and social historian of her native California, for Europeans at this time were fascinated by the American Wild West. She wrote *Los Cerritos* (1890), her first California novel, while staying at a French convent. Returning to California in 1890 following the death of her grandfather, Atherton was determined to capitalize on the rich history of Old California, which had hardly been tapped by other writers; she visited many of its historic missions and interviewed the local inhabitants in order to gather material for her fiction. In 1891, she published a series of stories on California, an important essay titled "The Literary Development of California" in *Cosmopolitan Magazine,* and a weekly column titled "Woman in Her Variety" for the *San Francisco Examiner.* To the dismay of many women readers of her column, Atherton as often disparaged as championed her sex. This period also marked the beginning of one of the more interesting chapters in her remarkable life: her friendship with Ambrose Bierce, the *San Francisco Examiner*'s most influential—and acerbic—critic.

Bierce, who verbally flayed many women writers (including Charlotte Perkins Gilman) in the weekly "Prattle" column he wrote for the *San Francisco Examiner,* developed a great respect for Atherton and assumed the role of her mentor. When she published *The Doomswoman* (serialized in 1892, then published as a volume in 1893), Bierce lavished praise upon it, giving a boost to her career. In *The Doomswoman,* a tragic love story in the vein of William Shakespeare's *Romeo and Juliet,* Atherton continued her literary explorations of California's past, focusing in this case on the conflict between the state's traditional (Mexican) and modern (Anglo-American) cultures. Atherton found much to admire in the Mexican heritage, but she shared Bierce's belief that Anglo-Americans possessed a superior culture and were destined to dominate the state.

In 1892, shortly after *The Doomswoman* first appeared, Atherton returned to New York City, where she churned out journalistic pieces to earn money. During her stay, she completed the manuscript of one of her most ambitious novels, *Patience*

Sparhawk and Her Times, a sensationalistic drama about a woman who is accused of murdering her husband. As preparation for writing the book, Gertrude attended a murder trial and even sat in the electric chair at Sing Sing prison. Failing to find a New York publisher for the novel, the nomadic Atherton moved once again, to England in 1895.

Her four years in England were very productive. In addition to publishing *Patience Sparhawk and Her Times* (1897), she published five other novels. In *The Californians* (1898), Atherton examined her native state not with romantic nostalgia but with disillusionment. In *American Wives and English Husbands* (1898), she explored the "international theme" on which Henry James had so successfully capitalized. This novel received high praise from critics and earned for her the celebrity status that she had been seeking for more than a decade.

Atherton returned to the United States in 1899 with the idea of writing a novel that would critique the nation's political and social life. Settling in Washington, D.C., to gather material and generate ideas for her planned book, she attended debates in Congress, interviewed politicians, and even managed to secure for herself an invitation to the White House, where she met President William McKinley. The novel that she produced, *Senator North* (1900), focuses on the congressional debates that had preceded the outbreak of the Spanish-American War (of 1898); it projects the jingoistic mood of the country at the time. Unfortunately, it also clearly projects Atherton's aristocratic disdain for democracy and her deep racial prejudice.

After completing *Senator North*, Atherton passionately undertook writing a fictionalized biography of her favorite American historical figure, Alexander Hamilton. She conducted part of the research for the book in the West Indies, where Hamilton was born. *The Conqueror* (1902) glorifies Hamilton and debunks the reputation of his adversary, Thomas Jefferson. Critics gave the book mixed reviews, but it was a commercial success, earning for Atherton fame in the United States equal to that she enjoyed in Europe.

From 1903 to 1910, Atherton continued to publish prolifically and shuttled between residences in San Francisco, where she was honored as a celebrated author, and Munich, Germany. Most of her early personal correspondence and other private papers were lost in the San Francisco earthquake and fire of 1906. Though she continued to distance herself from organized feminism, she did write a play, later published as a novel, supporting the women's suffrage movement, *Julia France and Her Times* (1912).

When World War I broke out, Atherton went to Europe as a news correspondent for *The New York Times*. Though her commitment to charity work temporarily interrupted her fiction writing, she wrote two novels dealing with the conflict, the more interesting of which is *The White Morning* (1918); the book fantasizes a revolt of German women against the kaiser.

When the war ended, Atherton, who was in her sixties, felt depressed and listless; she therefore underwent Steinach treatment, radioactive stimulation of the ovaries that supposedly could "reactivate" aging women. She claimed that the controversial treatment had a miraculous effect on her, and she returned with renewed vigor to her writing. The next novel she wrote, *Black Oxen* (1923), is a tale about an elderly woman's successful "reactivation"; it was a best-seller (and, like several other of her novels, was made into a film).

Atherton lived out most of the final two decades of her life in San Francisco, where she presided over its branch of the International Association of Poets, Playwrights, Editors, Essayists, and Novelists (PEN). In 1935, she hosted the famous expatriate American writer Gertrude Stein, whom she had met in Paris in 1925. Age did not slow Atherton: she published an autobiography, several more novels with women rebels as the central characters, a collection of essays, and two histories of San Francisco. In 1938, she was elected a member of the prestigious National Institute of Arts and Letters; in 1947, the year before her death, she was awarded the Gold Medal from the city of San Francisco.

Summary

During the 1890's and early decades of the twentieth century, Gertrude Atherton was regarded by many eminent writers and critics as one of the ablest women authors in the United States. Her reputation as a fiction writer, however, has faded over the years, and she has been overshadowed by several of her contemporaries, most notably Edith Wharton, Kate Chopin, and Charlotte Perkins Gilman. Nevertheless, her chronicles of California were pioneering works, earning for her a firm place in that state's literary and social history. Although she refused to ally herself with and even often disparaged feminists of her era, she endorsed a view of women that rejected social and cultural stereotypes. At a time when women were expected to be polite, diffident, and satisfied with domestic life, Atherton produced a series of strong-willed, independent-minded heroines who challenged the gender role assigned them by patriarchal Victorian culture—just as she challenged that role in her own free-spirited life. Atherton's faults, especially her racial and class prejudices, cannot be ignored, but neither can the fact that thousands of women readers have felt inspired and empowered by her novels and essays.

Bibliography

Atherton, Gertrude. *Adventures of a Novelist.* New York: Liveright, 1932. Written when she was in her seventies, Atherton's autobiography is not always trustworthy, and there are significant omissions; it nevertheless contains a rich store of information about her life and is filled with amusing anecdotes and sketches of her contemporaries.

Bradley, Jennifer. "Woman at the Golden Gate: The Last Works of Gertrude Atherton." *Women's Studies* 12, no. 1 (1986): 17-30. Focuses on Atherton's literary productions during the 1930's and 1940's, when Atherton's continuing preoccupation with California history led some critics to complain that she was trapped in the past.

Forrey, Carolyn. "Gertrude Atherton and the New Woman." *California Historical*

Quarterly 55 (Fall, 1976): 194-209. Forrey offers an intelligent and thorough analysis of the heroines of Atherton's major fictions. She argues that though Atherton sought to promote the emancipation of women, she never freed herself from a romantic attachment to and dependence on men.

Leider, Emily Wortis. *California's Daughter: Gertrude Atherton and Her Times.* Stanford, Calif.: Stanford University Press, 1991. An excellent critical biography of Atherton; Leider clearly admires but does not idolize her subject. The book includes a thorough chronology of Atherton's life and writings, as well as a group of interesting photographs.

McClure, Charlotte S. *Gertrude Atherton.* Boston: Twayne, 1979. Though superseded by Leider's book (above), this is a reliable study of Atherton's life and major writings, with a useful bibliography of primary and secondary works.

Lawrence J. Oliver

MARGARET ATWOOD

Born: November 18, 1939; Ottawa, Ontario, Canada

Area of Achievement: Literature
Contribution: Noted for her witty analysis of modern life, Atwood has become a major figure in North American literature. Her many books of fiction and poetry are widely discussed in relation to both Canadian nationalism and the women's movement.

Early Life
Margaret Eleanor Atwood was born in Ottawa during the early weeks of World War II. Her father, Carl Edward Atwood, was an entomologist who spent long periods in the forests of northern Quebec and Ontario; her mother, born Margaret Dorothy Killam, shared his Nova Scotian ancestry and his love of the "bush" country. The family wintered in Ottawa, then in Sault Ste. Marie and Toronto; but they spent the rest of each year in the bush, leaving the war behind. Margaret grew up in relative isolation and wrote to amuse herself. Her older brother, Harold, was born in 1937; her younger sister, Ruth, in 1951.

Margaret was finally able to attend classes for the full school year when her father joined the faculty at the University of Toronto in 1951. She entered Leaside High School in 1952, in the five-year Latin course for college-bound students, and became involved in groups like the United Nations Club. At sixteen, she began writing stories for the school magazine. Entering Victoria College at the University of Toronto in 1957, she found herself in an intensely literary environment. The college principal, Northrop Frye, was winning international fame for his *Anatomy of Criticism* (1957), which made bold claims for the role of myth in literature. His brilliant protégé, the poet Jay Macpherson, joined the faculty that same year and shared her collection of Canadian literature with promising writers such as Atwood and Dennis Lee. Frye and Macpherson told their students that Canadian literature was finally coming of age. The Canada Council was created in 1957 to provide economic stimulus for the arts.

In 1961, as she was graduating, Atwood won the college award in poetry for her chapbook *Double Persephone*. She was tempted to run off to Europe and write, but following her teachers' advice, Atwood went to Harvard University with a Woodrow Wilson Fellowship. During the next decade she moved in and out of academia. She earned a master's degree in 1962 and then entered the doctoral program at Harvard. Later, she returned to Toronto for a year and wrote the unpublished novel "Up in the Air So Blue" while working for a market research company. Atwood spent a year teaching at the University of British Columbia, where she completed a new book of poetry, *The Circle Game* (1966), and began a novel about a young woman working for a market research company. Returning to Harvard, she began a dissertation on the literary romances of H. Rider Haggard and completed the novel about the market researcher, later published as *The Edible Woman* (1969). Atwood never finished the dissertation, but the essays in *Second Words: Selected Critical Prose* (1982) leave no doubt that she would have become a leading scholar and critic had she had not achieved such ready success as a poet and novelist.

Life's Work

In 1967, Margaret Atwood became the youngest Canadian ever to receive the Governor-General's Award for Poetry, previously won by Macpherson in 1959. In the exuberance of Canada's centennial, there was a new spirit of nationalism in the arts, and Atwood's voice was heard increasingly. She left Harvard that year and accepted the first in a series of teaching positions that included year posts at four Canadian universities. She won the Centennial Commission Poetry Competition with her third book of poetry, *The Animals in That Country* (1968), and wrote *The Journals of Susanna Moodie* (1970) as a personal response to Canada's first woman writer. She came to think of survival as the central concern, not only of this nineteenth century pioneer, but of Canadians generally and especially Canadian women. She developed her thoughts in *Survival: A Thematic Guide to Canadian Literature* (1972), which grew out of her teaching notes. Her second published novel, *Surfacing* (1972), treated the theme of survival in the wilderness settings of her childhood, pitting north against south, forest against city, Canada against the United States, woman against man. The critical acclaim came fast and fervently. Canada's leading novelist, Margaret Laurence, said the novel was "so striking that I become evangelical about it." Canadian readers spoke about "the two Margarets."

Atwood's early fame brought a certain notoriety. Some male reviewers confused her with the Medusa figures in her poetry, especially in the "Circe/Mud Poems" from *You Are Happy* (1974). When this Medusa figure showed up as a character in a short story, and just happened to be named Atwood, the real Atwood asked the publisher to remove the work from circulation. Her actions led to unpleasant countercharges, in a closely knit world where readers often thought they knew the original models on which literary characters were based. Nevertheless, her activism led to her involvement in the newly formed Writers' Union of Canada, which she served as vice president. She became active in various organizations dedicated to helping writers in need, including Amnesty International, the Canadian Civil Liberties Association, and P.E.N. International in Canada.

Atwood is most famous for her fiction. Her first two novels followed the romance conventions she had researched for her dissertation, with heroines on personal quests of mythic dimensions, but showed an eye for detail and a wicked wit. In *Lady Oracle* (1976), she took the romance form to its limits with the story of a successful hack who tries to live a life of romance but gets caught in everyday realities. In her next novels, Atwood became increasingly political and realistic. *Life Before Man* (1979) looks at the three sides of a romantic triangle and provides Atwood's most fully realized male character. *Bodily Harm* (1981) tells the stories of two Canadian women caught up in revolution on a small Caribbean island. *The Handmaid's Tale* (1985) is set in a postrevolutionary society, ruled by the religious right, where talk about "women's rights" is tantamount to subversion. *Cat's Eye* (1989) is a retrospective novel, a semiautobiographical account of a painter getting ready for a one-woman show and realizing to what a large extent her art is based on early memories. *The Robber Bride* (1993) returns to the multiple points of view in *Life Before Man*; telling the stories of three women who have been hurt by the same man-eater over the course of three decades. Atwood's stories have been collected in three volumes: *Dancing Girls and Other Stories* (1977), *Bluebeard's Egg* (1983), and *Wilderness Tips* (1991). Some have autobiographical details—the poignant "Unearthing Suite" from *Bluebeard's Egg* is about aging parents much like Atwood's own. Despite these similarities, Atwood bristles at suggestions that she or anyone else is one of the characters. "If the characters were all me," she told students in Arizona, "I'd have to have a really exaggerated case of multiple personality—especially for the male characters."

Meanwhile, Atwood has produced a steady stream of experimental poems, including those in *Selected Poems* (1976) and *Selected Poems II: Poems Selected and New, 1976-1986* (1986). Some have disturbing images of victimization; others offer the possibility of change or give voice to those who have been silenced. *Good Bones* (1992) includes a set of prose poems spoken by the three pariahs in fairy tales: the ugly sister, the wicked witch, and the evil stepmother, all eager to tell their stories. Atwood has also written children's books, beginning with *Up in a Tree* (1978), and television dramas for the Canadian Broadcasting Corporation. Two of her novels have been made into films, and other novels have been optioned for film adaptation. The film version of *Surfacing* (1980) suffered from a low budget and weak screenplay; the film version of *The Handmaid's Tale* (1990), with a screenplay by Harold Pinter, brought Atwood's imagination to a large audience.

Atwood received an honorary doctorate from Trent University in 1973 and many more degrees since then. She has held visiting appointments at universities in the United States and Australia and has received such honors as the Ida Nudel Humanitarian Award from the Canadian Jewish Congress in 1986, the American Humanist of the Year Award in 1987, and the Commonwealth Literature Prize in 1987. Two national magazines, *Ms.* in the United States and *Chatelaine* in Canada, have named her Woman of the Year. She was made a Companion of the Order of Canada in 1981 and a Fellow of the Royal Society of Canada in 1987.

Atwood met the American writer James Polk during her first year at Harvard and married him in 1967. Although he shared her interest in Canadian culture and even entered Canadian politics, the marriage did not last. After their divorce in 1973, she bought a farm in Alliston, Ontario. She moved there with the novelist Graeme Gibson, whom she had met in 1970. They never married—for tax reasons, according to Atwood—but have stayed together ever since. Their one child, Eleanor Jess Atwood Gibson, was born in 1976.

Summary

When Margaret Atwood entered Leaside High, the school handbook listed five careers for women: nurse, stewardess, teacher, secretary, and home economist. Journalism had few opportunities for women beyond the ladies' page; fiction was not a viable profession in Canada, where a popular novel might sell a few thousand copies. Atwood chose home economics and represented her school in a Miss Homemaker contest, but she eventually resolved to become a writer. That she succeeded so quickly and completely was a sign that conditions for women writers were improving; it was also testimony to her creativity, intelligence, and strength of character. With her success, she felt obliged to promote Canadian writing, especially by women. She once said she lent her name to Canadian causes and women's concerns, very much as she gave blood, because it was helpful and not because she enjoyed it; one exception may be *The CanLit Foodbook: From Pen to Palate, a Collection of Tasty Literary Fare* (1987), a recipe book she edited as an inspired fund-raiser. She has also met her obligations as a public figure speaking for women, Canada, and the arts.

Atwood has made a strong impression on many readers. The city of Toronto will never look quite the same to those who find themselves in the parks and restaurants that Atwood describes—and she feeds her characters well. The experience of being modern—and especially of being a modern woman in a crassly commercial world, counting calories and divorced friends—will always seem different to those who have been touched by her writing.

Bibliography
Atwood, Margaret Eleanor. *Margaret Atwood: Conversations.* Edited by Earl G. Ingersoll. Princeton, N.J.: Ontario Review Press, 1990. A valuable, often amusing collection of twenty-one interviews with Atwood. There is an index of names and titles mentioned in the interviews.
McCombs, Judith, ed. *Critical Essays on Margaret Atwood.* Boston: G. K. Hall, 1988. A collection of early reviews and criticism of Atwood's poetry and prose, with contributions by such famous Canadian writers as Margaret Laurence. Contains a bibliography of Atwood's publications through 1986.
McCombs, Judith, and Carole L. Palmer. *Margaret Atwood: A Reference Guide.* Boston: G. K. Hall, 1991. A comprehensive and fully annotated bibliography of popular and scholarly writing about Atwood from 1962 to 1988—there are more than two hundred entries for 1985 alone—with an author index and a useful subject index. The introductory essay charts the progress of Atwood's reputation and is followed by a list of her publications to 1990.
Rosenberg, Jerome H. *Margaret Atwood.* Boston: Twayne, 1984. An overview of Atwood's creative output through the 1970's, written with Atwood's cooperation and quoting from her manuscripts. The author is an American sympathetic to the problems of writers in an emergent literary culture such as Canada's; his last chapter provides information on Atwood's early skirmishes in the Canadian press, including the controversy over her approach to Canadian literature. Includes a chronology and an annotated bibliography of primary and secondary sources.
VanSpanckeren, Kathryn, and Jan Garden Castro, eds. *Margaret Atwood: Vision and Forms.* Carbondale: Southern Illinois University Press, 1988. A collection of

original essays on Atwood's work, published in the Ad feminam series of feminist criticism. The book includes a chronology and the transcript of Atwood's lively responses to students at the University of Tampa, who ask about her reading and writing habits and her politics.

Woodcock, George. *Introducing Margaret Atwood's Surfacing: A Reader's Guide.* Toronto: ECW Press, 1990. A good introduction to one of Atwood's most powerful novels, written by an influential Canadian critic and including a brief chronology. The chapter on Atwood's critical reception rightly stresses the connections between her poetry and fiction.

Thomas Willard

LAUREN BACALL

Born: September 16, 1924; New York, New York

Areas of Achievement: Film and theater
Contribution: A major performing artist since her screen debut in 1944, Bacall continues to appear in major stage, television, and film roles. The endurance of her popularity and critical acclaim are a testament to Bacall's perseverance and dedicated professionalism.

Early Life

Lauren Bacall was born Betty Joan Perske in New York City on September 16, 1924. Her father, William Perske, was a medical supplies salesman, and her mother, Natalie, was the child of Romanian Jewish immigrants whose name Weinstein-Bacal was shortened to Weinstein at Ellis Island.

The Perske marriage was unhappy; when Betty was six, her parents were divorced. By the time she was eight, her father had disappeared from her life, and Natalie and Betty, her only child, adopted the name Bacal. Like her own mother, who had been widowed at age fifty-three, Natalie carried on a family tradition of strong, independent women; throughout Betty's life, she was a bastion of love and support.

Concerned about Betty's care after school, Natalie, with financial help from her two attorney brothers, sent Betty to a private boarding school not far from New York City in Tarrytown. Although Bacall missed her mother, these were idyllic years. Highland Manor had a beautiful rural campus and Betty danced, sang, and acted in the weekly dramatic programs.

When Betty graduated from Highland Manor grade school at age eleven, her mother decided to move in with Betty's grandmother and uncle for financial reasons and decided that Betty should attend Julia Richman, a Manhattan public high school. Betty's life with her mother, grandmother, and Uncle Charlie was warm and loving and filled with good humor. Charlie Weinstein was assistant corporation counsel for the City of New York under Mayor Fiorello La Guardia, and his influence planted the seeds of political awareness in Betty's later life. He urged Betty to read *The New York Times* and provided her with the memorable experience of seeing her hero, Franklin Delano Roosevelt, at Madison Square Garden.

An unenthusiastic high school student, Bacall would cut classes to watch Bette Davis films. Her main loves were her dance classes and her Saturday mornings at the New York School of the Theatre. Told she had the "wrong feet" for dancing, Betty focused entirely on her acting and, with the financial help of her uncles, enrolled in American Academy of Dramatic Arts, a respected, rigorous school. Although she passed her final performance and was recommended for a second year, she could no longer afford to attend and was told that no scholarships were awarded to women. Upset, but with characteristic determination, she added a second "l" to her last name for greater ease in pronunciation and, between stints as a fashion model, ushered in

Broadway theaters and sold *Actor's Cue* in front of Sardi's during lunch, hoping to make her face known. Rarely shy about approaching celebrities, Betty met and befriended a number of established actors, directors, and producers. Her assiduity paid off and Bacall made her Broadway debut at age seventeen as a walk-on in the short-lived play *Johnny 2 x 4* (1941). Shortly thereafter, she approached playwright George S. Kaufman in the lobby of the Lyceum Theatre and landed a speaking part in a pre-Broadway failure, *Franklin Street* (1942). Through a friend's connections, Bacall began modeling for *Harper's Bazaar* in November, 1942, and by March, 1943, she was featured on the cover.

Life's Work

Struck by Betty Bacall's photograph on the *Harper's Bazaar* cover, Hollywood producer Howard Hawks invited her to Hollywood for a screen test. The test confirmed her rare photogenic qualities, and Bacall signed a seven-year contract with Hawks and his partner Charlie Feldman. Although Hawks supported Bacall's refusal to fix her teeth or change the shape of her eyebrows, he did convince her to change her name from Betty to Lauren, to become "mysterious" by talking little, and to deepen her voice to its trademark, husky pitch.

The famous "whistle" scene in the screen test for the 1944 film *To Have and Have Not* confirmed her star quality, and she was cast as the female lead. Unbearably nervous about the making of her first film, Betty devised a trick where, whenever she felt an attack of nerves, she would lower her chin and lift her eyes. Dubbed "The Look," it embodied the sultry, defiant, sexually charged screen persona of Lauren Bacall that would be her hallmark throughout the mid-1940's.

Lauren Bacall was an overnight sensation in *To Have and Have Not*. The critics used superlatives, praising her as "a find," and author James Agee described her as having "a fierce female shrewdness and a special sweet-sourness." Bacall was thrilled but miserable at the same time. During the filming of *To Have and Have Not*, she and costar Humphrey Bogart fell in love. Hawks was jealous and ordered her to stop seeing Bogart. Bacall's mother was opposed to the relationship, too. Bogart was twenty-five years older, a heavy drinker, and was still married to his third wife, a jealous alcoholic. When the filming was completed, Bacall and Bogart had no excuse for meeting, and Bogart was reluctant to abandon a sick wife. Except for an exchange of love letters, they had little contact with each other for the next several months.

Bacall was ecstatic when she learned that she was to repeat a tough girl role opposite Bogart in the 1946 film adaptation of Raymond Chandler's *The Big Sleep*. Both on-screen and offscreen the romance escalated, and in May, 1945, Lauren Bacall and Humphrey Bogart were married.

Immediately following the making of *The Big Sleep* but prior to its release, Bacall starred in *Confidential Agent* (1945), her first attempt to make a film without the guidance of Hawks and Bogart. Miscast and poorly directed, her reputation as an overnight sensation plummeted. Her acting was criticized as "wooden" and one-dimensional. The release of *The Big Sleep* the following spring restored her in the critics' eyes and once again she received high praise, but never to the extent of her first film.

These ups and downs were upsetting to Bacall but her role as Bogart's wife took precedence over her career. The marriage also gave her the financial freedom to turn down roles. Hurt by her experience in making *Confidential Agent*, Bacall was determined to pick only those roles which suited her. After several suspensions without pay, Bacall accepted a sexy, sultry role opposite Bogart in *Dark Passage* (1947). Reviews were mixed, the most positive describing her as a "sharp-eyed, knows what she wants girl." This directness offscreen had caused her difficulty during the filming of the picture when she disagreed with the quality of the cinematography and was forced to apologize. Her last film with Bogart, *Key Largo* (1948), marked a change in Bacall's film persona and the critics were impressed with her unaffected style in her solemn portrayal of a war widow.

Bacall and Bogart's marriage became the symbol for domestic tranquillity and a pleasing contrast to the typical Hollywood relationship. Bacall gave birth to two children: a son, Steven (named in honor of Bogart's character in *To Have and Have Not*), in 1949, and a daughter, Leslie, in 1952. Between her pregnancies, Bacall made two unremarkable films; she also satisfied her need for independence by buying her contract from Jack Warner. After leaving Warner Bros., Bacall made several films, including the memorable *How to Marry a Millionaire* (1953), which established her as a fine comic.

Throughout this period, Bacall became increasingly involved in politics. She and Bogart joined the Committee for the First Amendment, a group of actors that sent a delegation to Washington, D.C., to protest the political probes into the motion picture industry by the House Committee on Un-American Activities. Attracted to Adlai Stevenson's political views, intelligence, and humor, Bacall was active in Stevenson's campaign for president in 1952. She was a dogged political worker and friend and continued in the 1960's to campaign for other liberal Democrats such as John and Robert Kennedy and Eugene McCarthy.

Bacall further established both her comedic talents and dedicated professionalism in the 1957 film *Designing Women*. During the filming, Bogart was struggling with terminal cancer and died just prior to the film's release in 1957. Devastated by the death of her beloved husband and by her subsequent ill-fated romance with singer and family friend Frank Sinatra, Bacall moved to England two years later. She hoped the change would help her escape the constrictions of a life in Hollywood defined by her identity as Bogart's widow.

After a mild success in a British film, *Flame Over India* (1959), she again moved, this time to New York, to star in the Broadway production, *Goodbye Charlie* (1959). The critics agreed that Bacall had made a successful transition from screen to Broadway. *Goodbye Charlie* confirmed her comedic talents and was the first in a series of Broadway triumphs.

In 1961, she married actor Jason Robards, Jr., and later gave birth to their son Sam. The marriage ended in divorce in 1969. In spite of her troubled personal life, Bacall continued to make films, and in 1966, returned to the stage with rave reviews in *Cactus Flower*. In 1970, Bacall received the Tony Award for Best Actress in a Musical for her singing, dancing, acting role in *Applause*; in 1981, she won again for *Woman of the Year*. Her role in the 1985 London production of *Sweet Bird of Youth* was acclaimed, but the United States production never made it to Broadway.

Throughout the years Bacall has maintained a reputation as a reliable, dedicated performer with numerous appearances on television and radio and has continued to make major films, as recently as 1993. Bacall has received many awards, including the 1980 American Book Award for her autobiography *By Myself* (1979); in 1990, the George Eastman Award for distinguished contribution to the Art of Film; in 1991, the American Cinema Award and the Merit of Achievement Award; and, in 1992, the D. W. Griffith Career Achievement Award from the National Board of Review.

Summary

Lauren Bacall's worldly wise screen personality, as created by Howard Hawks, had little to do with the real Betty Bacall, a naïve and innocent eighteen-year-old. At the same time, Hawks did capture an independence and resiliency of character that would serve Bacall well over the next five decades. Her early roles capitalized on her youth and beauty, yet she brought an intelligence to the screen that transcended a host of Hollywood stereotypes of women. During an era when most women were forced to choose between career and family, Bacall negotiated a successful balance of the two. Recognizing the importance of establishing her own identity as a performer, she was careful in her selection of roles, stretching and challenging her talents at every opportunity and refusing to be typecast. At a time in her life when most glamorous actresses seem to dread the onset of middle age, Bacall embarked on a highly successful stage career. She has managed to resist most of the stereotypes and pitfalls of being a celebrity, scoffing at the youth obsession that pushes her colleagues into face lifts and other indignities and ignoring insensitive critics who pan her acting because she has chosen to age naturally. Bacall has eschewed attempts to capitalize on her marriage to Bogart; although she has narrated a documentary on his life, she refuses to authorize any films portraying their private life and their careers. Drawing upon a tradition of strong women in her own family and among her acting contemporaries, Bacall has proved the power that women can assume through independence, integrity, and endurance.

Bibliography

Bacall, Lauren. *Lauren Bacall By Myself*. New York: Alfred A. Knopf, 1979. This well-written autobiography won the American Book Award in 1980. Summing up her life and career with humor and insight, she manages to avoid a sentimental and self-congratulatory style. Bacall pays homage to her devoted mother and family and relates some honest details about her two marriages.

Buckley, Michael. "Lauren Bacall." *Films in Review* 43 (May-June, 1992): 152-153. A retrospective on Bacall's career written after she received a career achievement award from the National Board of Review. Covers her film debut, at age nineteen, in *To Have and Have Not* all the way through her work opposite Gregory Peck in the cable television film *Painting Churches* (1993), directed by Arthur Penn.

Haskell, Molly. *From Reverence to Rape: The Treatment of Women in the Movies.* New York: Holt, Rinehart and Winston, 1974. Though Bacall received sporadic and brief coverage here, she is placed in the context of films and female contemporaries in the 1940's and 1950's.

Hepburn, Katharine. *The Making of The African Queen: Or, How I Went to Africa with Bogart, Bacall, and Huston and Almost Lost My Mind.* New York: Alfred A. Knopf, 1987. In this memoir about the filming of *The African Queen,* Hepburn provides vivid recollections of her adventures on location in the Congo and Uganda. Among her many anecdotes are intimate observations of the relationship between Bogart and Bacall, whose successful Hollywood marriage stood in striking contrast to Hepburn's own clandestine relationship with Spencer Tracy.

Quirk, Lawrence J. *Lauren Bacall: Her Films and Career.* Secaucus, N.J.: Citadel Press, 1986. The book contains a wonderful collection of film stills, publicity photos, and personal photographs. The author has a chatty, dramatic style both in his delineation of Bacall and the making of her films from *To Have and Have Not* in 1944 to *Health* in 1982.

Royce, Brenda Scott. *Lauren Bacall: A Bio-Bibliography.* Westport, Conn.: Greenwood Press, 1992. A comprehensive 283-page volume that chronicles Bacall's life in a variety of ways. Fascinating and well written, includes a short biography accompanied by a detailed chronology. The work gives a detailed description of every Bacall film, providing brief annotations of critical reviews and interesting, sometimes gossipy notes about the making of the film. Also included are a home video guide and a list of films she refused. Bacall's television, radio, and stage appearances are described in similar detail, as are her recordings, awards, nominations, and honors. The forty-page annotated bibliography is an exhaustive account of Bacall's life through news items and journal articles. The appendix lists her advertising affiliations and gives fan club information.

Susan Chainey

JOAN BAEZ

Born: January 9, 1941; Staten Island, New York

Areas of Achievement: Music and peace advocacy
Contribution: After achieving great success as a folksinger, Baez used her considerable influence to support causes ranging from civil rights to global peace, becoming
an icon for the disaffected generation of the 1960's.

Early Life
Joan Chandos Baez was born in Staten Island, New York, on January 9, 1941, the
second child of a physics professor and his Scottish-born wife. Her father, Albert
Baez, was born in Mexico and brought up in Brooklyn, New York. The son of a
Methodist minister, Albert Baez devoted his life to science. During the 1940's, when
he was working in the defense industry in Buffalo, New York, Dr. Baez started to
attend Quaker meetings with his family. After making a commitment to pacifism, he
accepted a position as professor at the University of Redlands in California for half
the pay he had been earning and never again worked at a defense-related job. Joan's
mother, Joan Bridge Baez, devoted herself to homemaking and the care of her three
daughters during the many moves demanded by her husband's academic career. Mrs.
Baez had a genius for comforting young Joan, who felt she never fit in with others.
   The Baez family spent a year in Iraq when Joan was ten. She reacted with horror to
the poverty and brutality she saw in the streets of Baghdad, a formative experience
which probably helped shape her social conscience. After two difficult weeks of trying
to adjust to a French-English Catholic school, Joan was permitted to remain at home
for the year. Secure in the Baez household, Joan baked cakes, studied insects, made
drawings for a biology professor, and enjoyed a burst of creativity.
   Joan attended high school in Palo Alto, California, when her father accepted a post
at Stanford University. It was there that she acquired her first guitar and taught herself
to play "House of the Rising Sun." There, too, she started her career in social activism,
gaining local notoriety by refusing to evacuate the high school during a bomb drill.
At sixteen, she met Ira Sandperl at a Quaker meeting. More than fifteen years older
than Joan, Sandperl was an activist for nonviolence who was greatly influenced by
the writings of Mohandas K. Gandhi. Joan and Sandperl developed an enduring
friendship based on their profound commitment to social justice.
   After high school, Joan moved with her family to Boston. She briefly attended the
Fine Arts School of Drama at Boston University and sang in coffeehouses around
Harvard Square, where her ethereal soprano voice and simple style soon gained popularity. She met Manny Greenfield, a Boston impresario who managed her career for
many years. After a second appearance at the Newport Folk Festival in Rhode Island
in 1960, she made her first recording for Vanguard Records, titled simply, *Joan Baez*.
The album was an immediate success. In early 1961, a national concert tour drew
capacity crowds and critical raves. Barely twenty, Joan Baez was a national celebrity.

Life's Work

Joan Baez accepted fame on her own terms, as she had won it. Throughout the early 1960's, she turned down offers for concert engagements that would have netted huge amounts of money. She refused nightclub engagements, Hollywood offers, and roles in Broadway musicals. There was a quality of both innocence and arrogance in her style; a slender girl with long, black hair, Baez confronted her audience with nothing but a guitar and a haunting soprano that moved listeners to wild applause. She sang ballads, blues, spirituals, and folk songs from all over the world, as well as topical songs on brotherhood and disarmament that spoke for themselves.

Even more than the music, Baez was interested in establishing a relationship with her audience. By the end of 1963, she had become involved in a variety of protest causes demanding social change. She sang at black colleges in the South and was highly visible at the important landmarks of the Civil Rights movement: Selma, Montgomery, and Birmingham, Alabama. She sang at the Lincoln Memorial beside Martin Luther King, Jr., during the March on Washington in 1963. Baez was also active in the antiwar movement and refused to pay the sixty percent of her income tax that she estimated went for defense. With her mother, she went to jail for participating in a draft resistance protest at the Oakland Military Induction Center.

Baez settled in California in 1961, first in the Big Sur area and then in Carmel Valley. She took part in the free speech movement at the University of California, Berkeley, in the fall of 1964 with Ira Sandperl, who was then working at a bookstore in Palo Alto. A few months later, Baez and Sandperl developed the idea for the Institute for the Study of Nonviolence, which Baez established in an old adobe school she bought in 1965 in Carmel Valley, near her house. During the first four years of the Institute's existence, Baez studied and acted as a teacher's aide to Sandperl. Speakers, scholars, and activists came from all over the world to study and teach. Followers of Martin Luther King, Jr., attended for a time, and young men from nearby Fort Ord came to learn how to leave the army. Each seminar began with ten or twenty minutes of silence, and one day a week silence lasted for the whole afternoon. The members' primary task was to study the concept, theory, and application of nonviolence in all its aspects, from personal relationships to the international struggle against oppression. Baez gave about twenty concerts a year, many of them benefits for nursery schools, Quaker meetings, or peace groups. During these years, she earned vast sums on record royalties and donated much of this money to support nonviolent activities around the country.

In 1967, Baez met David Harris at the Santa Rita Rehabilitation Center, where she was being detained for civil disobedience. A leader in the movement against the draft, he shared Baez's commitment to nonviolence. After her release, she went on the road with Harris and Sandperl, singing and speaking out against the war in Vietnam. Along the way, Baez and Harris decided to get married. By the time they found a pacifist minister and flew all the wedding guests to New York, Baez was suffering from psychosomatic stomach ailments that often plagued her under stress. The incident was perhaps an inauspicious omen for the marriage that *Time* magazine called the "Marriage of the Century" but that lasted only three years. Harris was found guilty of refusing induction into the armed services and went to jail in July, 1969. During his incarceration, Baez worked on a film, bore their son, Gabe, and traveled. When he was released, Harris returned home to his wife and son, but the arrangement was stifling for Baez. Accustomed to complete independence, she could no longer be a wife.

In 1970, Baez recorded a landmark album with Vanguard, *The First Ten Years*, which was on the charts for many months. In 1971, she recorded *Blessed Are . . .*, the first album to include a number of her own songs. Shortly thereafter, she parted company with Vanguard and signed with A&M Records, a larger and more prestigious company that allowed her a certain artistic license. The first two releases with A&M were political: *Come from the Shadows* (1972) and *Where Are You Now, My Son?* (1973), based on her controversial peace mission to Hanoi during the Christmas season of 1972. Although the albums sold fairly well, the political climate that responded to Baez was beginning to change.

By 1972, the Institute for the Study of Nonviolence no longer stimulated her, and Baez became involved in working for Amnesty International. This new challenge led to her meetings with and demonstrations on behalf of Soviet dissidents Andrei Sakharov and Anatoly Shcharansky, as well as the Mothers of the Disappeared in Chile and Argentina.

Baez decided to record an album that was nonpolitical in 1975. The album went gold and Baez realized that *Diamonds and Rust* was one of the best albums she had ever made. She went on tour and released an album of that tour in 1976, titled *From Every Stage*. At about this time, Baez began to have trouble with her voice and acquired a voice coach, Robert Bernard. She left A&M and signed with Portrait, a move she later considered a mistake. Her first two albums with the new recording label sold badly, and by the end of the decade Baez slowly and painfully realized that she was no longer in tune with public taste.

As her musical career foundered during the 1980's, Baez seriously considered giving it up but ultimately decided to make some important changes to attract new listeners. She sought the help of a new manager and settled on Mark Spector, who signed her with Virgin Records. Her 1992 release, *Play Me Backwards*, was her first album with a major label in more than ten years. The album was warmly greeted by critics and sold well. It was contemporary and sophisticated, with acoustic guitar, electric bass, and percussion backing Baez on songs written by Janis Ian, Mary-Chapin Carpenter, and Baez herself. She went on tour after the release, singing her new songs as well as familiar ones. She has successfully bridged generations: Her old fans continue to adore her, and she continues to attract new ones.

Summary

In her lifetime, Joan Baez not only experienced the tumultuous years of the 1960's, when the United States was undergoing profound social changes; her actions helped shape them. She was a beacon of her generation, swept by a spirit of rebellion after the complacency of the conservative Eisenhower years. Giving concerts, providing seed money, participating in protests, and going to jail for her beliefs, Baez attracted wide public attention for the causes she supported. She did this while creating beautiful, haunting music in the popular folk idiom of the day.

Although she was considered radical during the years of her greatest influence, her views reflected the values taught to her by her parents: a Quaker commitment to peace and a profound belief in the equality of all people, regardless of their color. Many of her views on civil rights have since been enacted into law, and she was one of the leaders of the protest against the war in Vietnam, later considered a grave mistake by the mainstream public. Amnesty International, one of the many once obscure organizations she publicized, now has strong international backing.

Baez has said that she has no interest in feminism as such, but her public stance, at a time when social movements were led primarily by men, provided a model for women in demonstrating the ways in which they might wield power.

Bibliography

Baez, Joan. *And a Voice to Sing With.* New York: Summit Books, 1987. A memoir of Baez's life from childhood to the early 1980's. Richly detailed and beautifully illustrated with photos and her own sketches, it also provides a social history of the 1960's. Essential reading for anyone interested in understanding the personal life behind the public figure.

Bernikow, Louise. "The Ballad of Joan Baez." *Lear's* 6 (April, 1993): 70-75, 106. Berkinow interviews Baez, who talks about the resumption of her career and what it involved, and the sources of her new songs. Portrays a mature artist who keeps refining her work.

Didion, Joan. *Slouching Towards Bethlehem.* New York: Farrar, Straus & Giroux, 1968. A perceptive collection of essays on the social climate in California during the 1960's. One chapter, titled "Where the Kissing Never Stops," gives a detailed description of the daily agenda of Baez's Institute for the Study of Nonviolence.

Dubois, Fletcher Ranney. *A Troubadour as Teacher, the Concert as Classroom?* Frankfurt-am-Main: Haag & Herchen, 1985. This unique study analyzes Baez's use of her music as a means to educate and motivate her audiences in nonviolence, and considers how successful she was.

Garza, Hedda. *Joan Baez.* New York: Chelsea House, 1991. This volume, one in the Hispanics of Achievement series, discusses Baez's identity with her Spanish heritage and the prejudice she faced as a child because of her dark skin. The focus is on Baez's work as a social activist.

Sheila Golburgh Johnson

JOSEPHINE BAKER

Born: June 3, 1906; St. Louis, Missouri
Died: April 10, 1975; Paris, France
Areas of Achievement: Dance, theater, and civil rights
Contribution: The first international black woman superstar, Baker achieved phenomenal success as a singer and dancer; offstage, she worked for international peace and civil rights.

Early Life

Born Freda J. McDonald on June 3, 1906, and reared in the black ghetto of St. Louis, Josephine Baker had a difficult childhood. Her mother, Carrie McDonald, was adopted by parents descended from Apalachee Indians and South Carolina slaves. Carrie McDonald was not married to the man she identified as Josephine's father: Eddie Carson, an itinerant street musician of Spanish ancestry. Soon after the birth of Josephine's brother Richard, fathered by another man, McDonald married Arthur Martin and had two more children.

Nicknamed Tumpy, Josephine lived with her grandmother and great-aunt much of the time. When she occasionally attended school, she battled with authority figures because she did not like being told what to do. At the age of eight, she was sent to live with employers who abused her: One scalded her with boiling water as punishment; another made sexual advances. Because her stepfather seldom worked, she had to scavenge food in markets and sell coal found along the railroad. Besides suffering this poverty, Josephine saw at first hand evidence of racism which left permanent emotional scars. When she was eleven, she allegedly witnessed the terrifying race riots that began in East St. Louis, in which white mobs killed an estimated one hundred African Americans, looted their businesses, and burned their homes. Josephine thought she saw God's vision in the smoke of this apocalyptic scene. Still other images haunted her: a family friend's face shot off, a pregnant woman cut open, a corpse strung up a telegraph pole. Fifteen hundred African Americans fled across the St. Louis bridge. She told an interviewer almost fifty years later that she had been running ever since.

Other childhood experiences influenced her life's work. Hearing spirituals sung in church and listening to ragtime, jazz, and blues by street and club musicians shaped Josephine's love of singing and dancing. She learned of the theater through accounts in newspapers, which her stepfather used to paper the walls of their home. To escape this poverty-stricken, unhappy home, she married Willie Wells when she was thirteen years old; she divorced him after a few months. When given the opportunity to perform a comedy dance at a theater, she quickly discovered that the same comic faces and eye-crossing that so upset her teachers made her a hit with audiences. After two weeks at the theater, she left St. Louis with the Dixie Steppers touring group, advertised as "The Best Colored Stock Company Before the Public, All Glittering New Except Its Fame." Like most black shows of the time, it combined vaudeville, minstrelsy, and folk music and dance. At the age of fifteen, she married Willie Baker. Although they soon separated, she kept his name professionally the rest of her life. When the touring group disbanded in Philadelphia in 1921, Baker bought a one-way ticket to New York City to make her dream of performing on Broadway a reality.

Life's Work

Upon her arrival in New York City, Josephine Baker lied about her age to be hired as a dresser for *Shuffle Along* (1921), a theatrical show with music and lyrics by noted black songwriters and performers Eubie Blake and Noble Sissle. Not content to be merely a dresser for other performers, she learned songs and dances from the show and soon had the opportunity to fill in for a chorus girl. As the comic at the end of the chorus line, she was soon making $30 a week and capturing the audience's attention. She had been rejected as a chorus girl when the show appeared in Philadelphia because she was too young; however, she recalled that the reasons were that she was too thin, small, and dark. Once in New York, she advanced quickly. By 1924, Baker was earning $125 a week with star billing in Blake and Sissle's Broadway show *Chocolate Dandies*.

Despite being Broadway's highest-paid chorus girl, Baker considered Paris her big break in show business. At nineteen, Baker was performing in the all-black Paris show, *La Revue nègre*, having been hired at $250 a week by Caroline Dudley Reagan, a wealthy white Chicago socialite backing the show. A new Josephine Baker personality emerged at this point. She posed nude for the show's program cover and poster, then consented to dance and sing in the nude. For her famous, wildly erotic *Danse Sauvage*, she and her male partner danced wearing only ankle and wrist bracelets and feathered loin cloths. She also triumphed on the show's tour throughout Europe, with audiences and theater critics approving enthusiastically of her frenzied, rhythmic movements and beautiful dark body. She had transformed herself from the comic to the exotic. She later took the Folies-Bergère by storm with her celebrated rubber banana skirt, evoking endless jokes about its phallic symbolism.

Linked romantically to many men, notably novelist Georges Simenon, she began a relationship with Pepito Abatino, who managed her career for the next decade. She opened her own cabaret, Chez Josephine, and made both recordings and silent films in the late 1920's. Having toured Europe and South America, she returned to Paris in 1930 to enjoy her greatest fame: making the sound films *Zou-Zou* (1934) and *Princesse Tam-Tam* (1935), performing on stage, and recording songs. She expected similar popular acceptance when she returned to the United States in 1935 as the first black woman to star in the Ziegfeld Follies, receiving $1,500 a week and equal billing with Fannie Brice. The trip was disastrous: She was turned away from a New York hotel, despite reservations; she got a cool reception to her performances; and she ended her relationship with Abatino, who died of cancer after he returned alone to Paris. America's rejection was an especially rude awakening, but she returned to the country which had always warmly embraced her and continued her successful career in Paris.

Baker made a new beginning in her private life as well. In 1937, she married Jean Lion, a Jewish businessman, and renounced her American citizenship to become a naturalized Frenchwoman. Ill-matched with different interests and separate schedules, Baker and Lion were soon estranged and later divorced. Baker's life took an intriguing turn in 1940 when she assisted the French Resistance, led by Charles de Gaulle, who later became president of France. On one trip, she carried military intelligence secrets copied in invisible ink over her music; on another, she hid messages by pinning them to her underwear. Throughout North Africa and the Middle East she entertained troops and gave benefit concerts. After the liberation of Buchenwald concentration camp, she sang for the former inmates. Plagued with recurring illness, she made no records from 1944 to 1949 and seldom performed in public during this period.

While convalescing, she fell in love with Jo Bouillon, her orchestra leader, and they married in 1947. Making still another attempt to win American audiences' approval, Baker began a tour of the United States in 1951. She insisted on performing before racially mixed audiences and was backed by a racially mixed orchestra. When she opened at a Miami nightclub with sold-out performances, she was introduced by the legendary singer Sophie Tucker and sang in English, French, Spanish, and Portuguese. Despite lingering racism in cities such as Atlanta, where hotels refused to accommodate her, she had won acceptance from American audiences at last.

Returning home, she and Bouillon, as well as other family members, worked to make their Renaissance château estate, Les Milandes, into a tourist attraction, with a hotel, nightclub, and restaurant. The venture failed eventually, and the estate was sold in 1968. Despite her feisty determination to stay on the property, she was physically evicted early one morning in 1969. Photographers she had called to record her degradation dutifully captured this sad picture of poverty: The onetime glamorous superstar was now an aging woman, sitting barefoot on the back steps near a pile of garbage and wearing her nightgown, robe, shower cap, and shawl. After a brief hospitalization, the resilient Baker soon bounced back. She performed in Paris, and, when she appeared in Monte Carlo, Princess Grace and Prince Rainier of Monaco came to the rescue of the homeless Baker and her dozen children, providing them with a home.

These dozen children, her Rainbow Tribe, exemplified her strong belief in international peace and harmony. Having survived an unhappy childhood and having endured several miscarriages, Baker was determined to have a happy family. In 1953, she and Bouillon adopted the first two of their twelve children of different races, nationalities, and religions. Baker believed that if the world's children could live together harmoniously, so could adults. Despite her commitment to her family, however, she turned to others to bring up the children and left for speaking and performance engagements to make enough money to support them and their large estate. Marital differences led to estrangement between Baker and Bouillon; they chose to live apart after 1960.

Baker's comeback ability epitomized her last years. In 1961, she proudly received the Legion of Honor medal for her service to the French Resistance. In the United States, she enjoyed successful Carnegie Hall concerts, perhaps easing the pain of previous rejection by American audiences, and she shared her concert proceeds with civil rights organizations. At the March on Washington, on August 28, 1963, she spoke of her dream of equality for black Americans. Wearing her Women's Auxiliary of the French Air Force uniform, she stood in front of the Lincoln Memorial and told the crowd of more than 200,000 how moved she was to see so many unified in a common dream and that victory was at hand. While Martin Luther King, Jr.'s "I Have a Dream" speech is most vividly remembered, commentators praised Baker's remarks. Although she had little direct involvement in the Civil Rights movement as a result of living in France, Baker was a staunch advocate of racial equality, proven by her European marriages, her Rainbow Tribe, and her demands for nondiscriminatory ticket sales and racially mixed bands whenever she performed. Her 1973 Carnegie Hall career retrospective was enthusiastically received. She entered in pink ostrich feathers and sequins, and her finale included Bob Dylan's "The Times They Are A-Changin'."

In April of 1975, Baker, almost sixty-nine, returned to the Paris stage. She dressed in a sequined body stocking that revealed an incredibly youthful figure. To celebrate fifty years of performing in Paris, she was honored at a gala affair with Princess Grace and other celebrities. Three days after her triumphant opening night, she died in her sleep of a cerebral hemorrhage. Twenty thousand mourners paid their final respects to her on April 15, 1975, at a state funeral.

Summary

Josephine Baker's bold dancing and dramatic freedom with her body captured the hedonism of Paris in the 1920's; her innovative, provocative dancing led to daring new trends in music and dance. She inspired many visual artists to portray her; her provocative image was captured in many famous drawings typifying Art Deco style. Her unique look and lavish outfits influenced women's fashions as well. American expatriate writers such as Ernest Hemingway, F. Scott Fitzgerald, and Gertrude Stein were so impressed with Baker's flamboyant performances and dynamic personality that they portrayed her in their works. (Baker is immortalized, for example, in Fitzgerald's popular 1931 short story, "Babylon Revisited.") Baker thrived in Europe, unfettered by the restrictions of racial prejudice that prevented her from achieving acclaim in America. Perhaps her professional longevity of half a century can be attributed to her multiple personalities: the comic, the exotic, the heroine, the Earth Mother, the reformer. As the first black international superstar, Baker achieved more than rags-to-riches success; she became the grande dame of the Paris theater, charming audiences and inspiring freethinking women.

Bibliography

Baker, Jean-Claude, and Chris Chase. *Josephine: The Hungry Heart.* New York: Random House, 1993. This biography, written by a man who was informally adopted by Baker during her years in Paris, is a bracingly honest yet loving attempt to filter through the many falsehoods and legends in order to uncover the real story of Baker's life. Provides a more accurate account of her origins, early life, and the development of her career.

Baker, Josephine, and Jo Bouillon. *Josephine*. Translated by Mariana Fitzpatrick. New York: Harper & Row, 1977. Baker's fourth husband bases this affectionate biography on a draft autobiography Baker left at her death. He portrays her as endearing, yet difficult, in her generosity and flamboyance.

Hammond, Bryan, and Patrick O'Connor. *Josephine Baker*. London: Jonathan Cape, 1988. This definitive biography, richly illustrated with more than three hundred photographs and other memorabilia, chronicles Baker's life and lists a comprehensive bibliography and complete discography.

Haney, Lynn. *Naked at the Feast: A Biography of Josephine Baker*. New York: Dodd, Mead, 1981. Though criticized for her gossip-columnist tone, ungraceful style, and creative license, Haney depicts Baker's glittering world of Paris music halls and conveys her sincere concern about social issues.

Papich, Stephen. *Remembering Josephine Baker*. Indianapolis: Bobbs-Merrill, 1976. A choreographer/producer, Papich presents a sympathetic but not thoroughly researched portrait based on anecdotes and memorabilia to document Baker's lavish lifestyle.

Rose, Phyllis. *Jazz Cleopatra: Josephine Baker in Her Time*. New York: Doubleday, 1989. Rose's scholarly study integrates Baker's celebrity into the era's historical, cultural, social, and literary events. A helpful bibliography categorizes books on Baker, dance, black American culture, and Americans in 1920's Paris.

Laura M. Zaidman

EMILY GREENE BALCH

Born: January 8, 1867; Jamaica Plain, Massachusetts
Died: January 9, 1961; Cambridge, Massachusetts
Areas of Achievement: Peace advocacy, social reform, women's rights, and economics
Contribution: A scholar, antiwar activist, social reformer, and women's rights advocate, Balch won the Nobel Peace Prize for her lifelong efforts to promote alternatives to war.

Early Life

Emily Greene Balch was born on January 8, 1867, in Jamaica Plain, Massachusetts, a small community near Boston and Wellesley. Her parents, Francis V. Balch and Ellen Noyes Balch, were progressive Unitarians who reared their five daughters and one son to be independent thinkers. Her father was a Harvard graduate and attorney; her mother taught school prior to her marriage. The large, close Balch household included grandparents, unmarried aunts, and Irish domestics who helped with the children. Emily later described her father as a caring, gentle man and her mother, who died when Emily was seventeen, as quick tempered but loving.

Emily was a successful student at Miss Catherine Ireland's School in Boston, where she was further encouraged to develop a strong, independent mind. She then studied philosophy, languages, and economics at Bryn Mawr College, becoming a member of the very first graduating class in 1889. It was at Bryn Mawr that her lifelong interest in economics took root. A bright but modest student, she earned Bryn Mawr's first European Fellowship given to exceptional graduates for travel and study abroad. Her studies in Paris at the Sorbonne from 1890 to 1891 led to her first publication, *Public Assistance of the Poor in France* (1893).

Economic and social problems were primary concerns for Emily throughout her life. After returning from the Sorbonne, she began work with the Boston Children's Aid Society. At the same time, along with other Progressive Era reformers, she became active in the Boston Settlement House movement. Although she believed her social work experience was useful, Balch became convinced that college teaching would be a better way for her to have an influence. With help from her father she pursued graduate work at Harvard University, the University of Chicago, and the University of Berlin. In 1896, she began teaching economics and sociology at Wellesley College, where she remained until 1919.

Life's Work

At Wellesley, Emily Balch refused to limit herself to academic work alone. In addition to teaching and doing research, she became involved in a variety of social causes. She served on the first commission on minimum wages for women in the United States, became cofounder and president of the Boston Women's Trade Union League, supported striking workers, advocated immigrant rights, promoted various child-welfare reforms, and served on Massachusetts commissions on industrial education and on the Boston city planning board. She regularly spoke out against racial discrimination and class exploitation. Having declared herself a socialist in 1906, she and a friend organized a socialist conference in 1907.

In spite of her controversial extracurricular activities, Balch was promoted and appointed chair of the department of economics and sociology at Wellesley in 1913. Her 1910 study of European immigration, *Our Slavic Fellow Citizens*, had established her as a distinguished scholar. Balch's study was based on her travels in Europe, where she lived with and observed various families, and her interviews with immigrants to the United States. The work gave evidence of the research style, based on direct observation, that was to characterize Balch's scholarship for the rest of her life.

Throughout 1914 and 1915, Balch began working closely with other Americans who actively opposed the war in Europe. She had been a pacifist since the Spanish-American War, but the prospect of American involvement in a worldwide conflict compelled her to become a leader in the women's antiwar movement. Especially important was her work with the Women's Peace Party, which in 1919 became the Women's International League for Peace and Freedom (WILPF). Balch also helped coordinate efforts among other antiwar groups, having the unusual capacity to get along well with more conservative groups as well as radical young activists.

In addition to opposing war, Balch opposed conscription as a violation of civil rights and worked on behalf of conscientious objectors. She also opposed espionage legislation, which she considered unconstitutional, expressing her views in publications such as *The Nation*. In 1915, she joined the American delegation to the International Congress of Women at The Hague, which was an effort to bring about peace through mediation. As part of that effort, she traveled to Russia and the Scandinavian countries and met with various world leaders, including President Woodrow Wilson. In 1916, she participated in the International Committee on Mediation in Stockholm, a venture supported by industrialist Henry Ford.

These efforts to bring about an early peace, to prevent the United States from joining the war, and to create new methods for avoiding war did not succeed. Balch's outspoken activism also convinced Wellesley's trustees not to renew her contract in 1919. Unemployed but undeterred, she began a new career as a full-time antiwar activist.

Balch did not contest Wellesley's decision, acknowledging that she had knowingly taken risks by engaging in controversial activities. She also acknowledged that she was no longer comfortable with socialism. Because her opposition to war was based on religious convictions, she found greater compatibility between her beliefs and those of the Quaker faith, with its devotion to pacifism and cooperation. In 1921, Balch renounced socialism and joined the Society of Friends.

In the meantime, she had begun work as full-time paid international secretary-treasurer for the WILPF, setting up and managing its headquarters in Geneva from 1919 until 1922. Under her leadership the organization's primary goal was to study the causes of war. In its early years it also attempted to influence development of the new League of Nations by lobbying for greater diversity in its membership and more democracy in its governing processes. The WILPF was one of the first organizations to point out weaknesses that eventually contributed to the League's failure. Also under Balch's leadership, the WILPF criticized those provisions of the Versailles Treaty that it feared would cause another world war.

Ill health prompted Balch to resign from her paid position with the WILPF in 1922, but she continued to serve as an extremely active volunteer leader for the organization's American and international sections. In 1931, she succeeded Jane Addams as president of the American section; in 1937, Balch was appointed honorary president of the international section. More important than her titles, however, were the responsibilities she assumed for the sake of world peace. In addition to her research excursions and her writing, she helped organize international peace conferences and peace education programs, including summer peace schools for young people, and organized WILPF chapters around the world.

In 1926, Balch and five other women traveled to Haiti to investigate the impact of U.S. Marines, there since 1915. Their findings, written up mostly by Balch in *Occupied Haiti* (1927), recommended withdrawal of American forces and return of independent government to Haitians. In 1930, President Herbert Hoover mandated a similar official study and concluded, as WILPF had, that Haiti's government needed to be returned to Haitians.

Along with her colleagues, Balch worked hard to promote passage of the 1928 Kellogg-Briand Pact to outlaw war. In response to opponents' criticism of the pact's idealism and lack of enforcement provisions, Balch and other supporters argued that there should be laws against war for the same reason there should be laws against murder and theft, even though laws themselves cannot fully prevent those crimes. To prevent wars, nations had to understand their causes and work toward prevention. Making aggression among nations illegal was only one essential step in a complex, long-term process.

Balch believed that in order to prevent war it was critical for nations, regions, and international organizations to devise alternative methods for resolving disputes. One method she advocated was use of collective economic sanctions against belligerent nations. Another alternative she supported was use of mediation by third parties. Nevertheless, she was not an idealist nor was she an absolute pacifist. Faced with Hitler's threat, she supported U.S. involvement in World War II. At the same time, Balch continued to work with the WILPF to encourage the development of lasting global peace. She was also an outspoken critic of the government's unfair treatment of Japanese Americans, who had been denied their political rights and forcibly moved to relocation camps. During the Cold War, Balch did not condemn communism as an ideology, yet she did condemn any nation's tendency toward expansion.

In 1946, Balch was awarded the Nobel Peace Prize, sharing that honor with John R. Mott of the Student Christian Movement. Although she was not at all wealthy, she donated the prize money to the WILPF. She was the second woman to receive the prize; Jane Addams, her friend and colleague in the international pacifist movement, received the prize in 1931. Both women had devoted their lives to a variety of social, economic, and political causes. Balch had worked especially hard to organize women for the purpose of opposing war. She was honored by the WILPF on the occasion of her ninetieth birthday in 1957 for her efforts to promote global peace—efforts that continued to inspire others long after her death in 1961.

Summary

Emily Greene Balch held a prominent position among Progressive Era antiwar women and men, influencing the ideas and activities of scholars, community activists and politicians. She inspired students and colleagues at the beginning of the twentieth century and her writings are still powerful at the end of the century. She struggled with and wrote about many of the most troubling twentieth century questions: those relating to immigration and racism, intervention and militarism, individual freedom and national security, women's rights and economic justice.

Among Balch's greatest contributions was her clearly expressed conviction that not only politicians and military leaders but also scholars and community activists need to resist the tendency to accept violence as an appropriate response to conflict. Balch saw how dangerous that tendency was during the World War and Cold War eras; it continues to be a problem.

Bibliography

Alonso, Harriet Hyman. *Peace as a Women's Issue: A History of the U.S. Movement for World Peace and Women's Rights.* Syracuse, N.Y.: Syracuse University Press, 1993. This study of American peace movements puts Balch's work into context and includes an analysis of her work as both peace activist and women's rights advocate.

Balch, Emily Greene. *Our Slavic Fellow Citizens.* Reprint. New York: Arno Press, 1969. Written originally as a series of articles, this volume exemplifies Balch's thorough scholarship based on both research about and visits with Slavic families. Its purpose was to influence American immigration policy.

Bussey, Gertrude Carman, and Margaret Tims. *Women's International League for Peace and Freedom, 1915-1965.* London: Allen & Unwin, 1965. A history of the first fifty years of accomplishments made by the organization that became the primary focus of Balch's efforts in pursuit of global peace. Provides an excellent chronology of the actions initiated by the WILPF and its leaders in response to critical international events during this period.

Laszlo, Erwin, and Jong Youl Yoo, eds. *World Encyclopedia of Peace.* 4 vols. Oxford, England: Pergamon Press, 1986. A useful resource of information on individual peace activists and organizations that have been central to the movement for global peace. Includes biographical sketch on Balch as well as information on the WILPF and other organizations associated with Balch. Volume 4 contains a bibliography as well as name and subject indexes.

Randall, Mercedes M., ed. *Beyond Nationalism: The Social Thought of Emily Greene Balch.* New York: Twayne, 1972. A small but important book that lists all of Balch's writings, summarizes some of them and excerpts others.

——————— . *Improper Bostonian: Emily Greene Balch.* New York: Twayne, 1964. The first full-length biography of Balch, written by one of her most devoted antiwar colleagues. Based on private papers, diaries, and correspondence that Balch entrusted to Randall.

Susan MacFarland

LUCILLE BALL

Born: August 6, 1911; Jamestown, New York
Died: April 26, 1989; Los Angeles, California
Areas of Achievement: Film and television
Contribution: Starring in the television series *I Love Lucy* during the 1950's, Lucille
Ball established herself as one of that medium's most popular comedic actresses.

Early Life

Lucille Désirée Ball was born August 6, 1911, in the small town of Celoron, New York, a suburb of Jamestown. Her father, Henry Durrell Ball, was a telephone lineman for the Bell Company, while her mother, Désirée (DeDe) Hunt, was often described as a lively and energetic young woman. Henry Ball's job required frequent transfers, and within three years after her birth, Lucille had moved from Jamestown to Anaconda, Montana, and then to Wyandotte, Michigan. While DeDe Ball was pregnant with her second child, Frederick, Henry Ball contracted typhoid fever and died in February, 1915.

At least one biographer has suggested that the grief associated with the loss of her father drove Lucille into playacting. Whether true or not, Ball's recollections of early childhood were, for the most part, happy. She and her brother lived with doting grandparents and a strong, independent mother. Her grandfather, Fred Hunt, was an eccentric socialist who enjoyed the theater. He frequently took the family to local vaudeville shows and encouraged young Lucy to take part in both her own and school plays.

At the age of fifteen, Lucy dropped out of high school, and with her mother's approval, enrolled in the John Murray Anderson/Robert Milton School of the Theater in New York City. Among her fellow students was Bette Davis. At this stage in Ball's life, she was hopelessly beyond her element. Nervous and shy in a large city she hated, Ball lasted only six weeks at the school and returned to Celoron.

Ball later returned to New York and, despite a bout with potentially crippling rheumatoid arthritis, worked as a model with dress designer Hattie Carnegie. Her only significant success came when she was chosen by Liggett and Myers to promote cigarettes as "the Chesterfield Girl." Ball's entrance into the film industry came about fortuitously, when she accidentally ran into Sylvia Hahlo, a local theatrical agent, while walking up Broadway one day. Hahlo informed Ball of an opportunity to appear in the new Eddie Cantor film, *Roman Scandals* (1933), produced by Samuel Goldwyn. Ball auditioned and was hired as one of the twelve "Goldwyn Girls." It was a small part, that of a slave girl, and it would be many years after her work in B-pictures before she would achieve celebrity status, but Lucille Ball had found Hollywood.

Life's Work

During Lucille Ball's first years in Hollywood, she progressed from bit parts to featured roles, though rarely in major films. Indeed, over time Ball became known as a "Queen of the B's." Despite her talent, it was quite possible that Ball might never have progressed beyond that level had she not met Cuban vocalist and bandleader Desi Arnaz.

Arnaz was born in 1917, in Cuba, where his father was mayor of Santiago, an important seaport city. The Arnaz family was wealthy, and Desi was reared in relative luxury until the political revolution of 1933. Following his father's imprisonment, Desi Arnaz and his family fled to the United States. Desi worked his way through numerous menial jobs (including one in which he cleaned bird cages) before joining bandleader Xavier Cugat as a vocalist. In 1939, he came to Hollywood. It was on the set of RKO Studios, during the filming of *Too Many Girls* (1940), that Ball and Arnaz met; they were married on November 30, 1940.

The Ball-Arnaz marriage was tempestuous, to say the least. The two were from vastly different cultures and backgrounds. Unlike her television personality, Ball was conservative in nature and uncomfortable when not among friends. Arnaz had a more outgoing personality, with a fondness for both liquor and women.

Following his army service, Arnaz and Ball established as their home a five-acre site in Chatsworth, California, which they called "Desilu." The same appellation would later be applied to the studio they established. The early years of their marriage were marked by long periods of separation as their careers progressed in different directions. By the late 1940's, Ball had become established as a bonafide star, but she rarely appeared in roles which showcased the full range of her comedic talents. As an "aging" star in her thirties, she was constantly in danger of early replacement by up-and-coming younger actresses. Arnaz, meanwhile, was frequently on the road with his band, only rarely seeing Lucille. Both wanted children and a stable family life, but found this goal impossible to achieve while they were apart.

In 1948, Columbia Broadcasting System (CBS) decided to produce a situation comedy on radio called "My Favorite Husband." The premise of the show was that the housewife would be a scatterbrained, clumsy type who constantly would find herself in trouble. Ball was signed for the part and immediately established herself in the role. The series ran until March, 1951, by which time Ball was recognized as an astute, if sometimes abrasive, actress in the area of physical comedy. By that time, Ball and Arnaz had made the jump into television.

In 1950, CBS decided to develop a television series based on Ball's radio performance. Ball pressured the studio to cast Arnaz in the role of husband, a suggestion that met with strong opposition. Though Ball and Arnaz had appeared together on the Ed Wynn show in December, 1949, the network's major objection was the belief the public would not accept a Latin bandleader as her husband. Ball's answer was direct: "We ARE married!" To overcome the network's reservations, Ball suggested that she and Arnaz embark on a personal summer tour to highlight their act. In June, 1950, they premiered successfully in Chicago, proving their point. To compound their happiness, it became apparent Lucille was pregnant. It was also during this period that the couple formed Desilu Productions, parent company for their studios.

With success came tragedy. In July, Ball suffered a miscarriage. After a period of recuperation, she and Arnaz returned to the stage with their act. The success of the tour finally convinced CBS to go ahead with a series, and in early 1951, preparations began. Ironically, Lucille again became pregnant, delivering a healthy girl, Lucie Arnaz, in July.

Disagreements over the nature of the filming convinced Ball and Arnaz to purchase and develop their own studios. One of the most significant changes was their decision to use 35mm film, rather than the lesser quality kinescope medium, to record the show. In addition to providing working conditions more familiar to Ball and Arnaz and allowing them to work in Hollywood instead of producing live shows in New York, the use of 35mm film enabled the preservation of the earliest shows for posterity. William Frawley and Vivian Vance were added to the cast, and the first filming of the *I Love Lucy* series took place on September 8, 1951.

I Love Lucy ran from October 15, 1951, the first televised show, to September 24, 1961. The original first-run episodes lasted for six years, with primetime reruns and numerous "specials" aired through 1961. At its peak, it was the highest rated show on television. One of the best-known episodes involved the birth of Little Ricky Ricardo—an episode that aired on the same night that Ball gave birth to her real son. Sadly, the marriage between Ball and Arnaz barely survived the end of the series. The day after the final show was filmed in March of 1960, Ball filed for divorce. Despite the end of their marriage, Ball and Arnaz never lost their love and respect for each other.

Following the demise of their series, Ball purchased Arnaz's shares of Desilu Productions in 1962, becoming the first woman to head a Hollywood studio since Mary Pickford many years before. After her subsequent marriage to comedian Gary Morton, Ball named him vice president of the studios. Although Arnaz possessed a wealth of business acumen and made most of the financial and production decisions connected with founding and expanding the Desilu studios—facts rarely recognized by those familiar only with his typecast acting role on *I Love Lucy*—Ball continued to maintain the quality of programming associated with the studio. Although high-budget shows such as *Mission: Impossible* and *Star Trek* escalated costs to the studio, the quality of the studio's output remained high throughout the years of Ball's tenure as president.

Ball began a role on her own television series in 1962, *The Lucy Show*. The premise of the show, which also included Vivian Vance, was Ball as a widow with two children. Rather than Arnaz as the foil, Gale Gordon played the long-suffering male. Despite what eventually became a tiring plot, the show remained popular for much of its twelve-year run (including title and character changes), at one point being the highest rated show on television.

Desilu Productions was sold to the large Gulf + Western Industries in 1967, severing Ball's connection with the company. Despite her wealth, Ball was uncomfortable with the idea of retiring from show business. The film production of *Mame* (1974) was designed as a starring vehicle to revive Ball's film career, but it was a critical and financial disappointment. Ball continued to work sporadically on television, appearing in specials and even making an attempt at a new series in 1986. Sadly, an aging Ball found it difficult to attempt the kind of "serious" physical comedy at which she had once excelled, and she recognized that to do so would result in a caricature of herself. The sitcom, *Life with Lucy*, was canceled soon after its debut.

In December of 1986, Arnaz died after a lengthy battle against cancer; Ball was one of the last people to speak with him. In May, 1988, Ball suffered a stroke, becoming partially paralyzed. Continuing her recuperation, she developed heart problems. After undergoing heart surgery, she died suddenly on April 25, 1989.

Summary

When *I Love Lucy* premiered during the 1951-1952 television season, only fifteen million television sets were to be found in American homes. Three years later, that number had doubled. In that time, Lucille Ball had become established as the most popular female comedian on television, and arguably the most popular female practitioner of physical comedy in the first half-century of prime-time television. Ball was not herself an inherently funny person; she looked at acting as a serious profession and "worked" at physical comedy. Yet Ball had an inherent ability to observe a situation and, by exaggeration of normal behavior, could present a routine which struck an observer with comedic overtones. It was a rare performer who could do so, while at the same time retaining the situation as one which was within the realm of possibility.

There is no question Ball had her faults and her detractors. At times, she exhibited anger and pettiness. Nevertheless, Ball could also recognize ability in those with whom she worked, and she felt secure enough in her position to allow her staff to do the jobs for which they were hired. Despite her well-publicized battles with Arnaz, she always recognized his importance to their careers, and Arnaz in turn never failed to give Ball credit where deserved. Most important perhaps, Ball recognized the importance of hard work in attaining success in one's career, and she was always willing to give help to aspiring performers who exhibited this character.

Bibliography
Andrews, Bart. *Lucy & Ricky & Fred & Ethel*. New York: E. P. Dutton, 1976. An outstanding biography of the characters from *I Love Lucy*. Included is a description of each individual show and special from the series. The volume provides a concise description of the lives and careers of both Frawley and Vance. An updated, revised edition was published in 1985.
Arnaz, Desi. *A Book*. New York: William Morrow, 1976. In his autobiography, Arnaz provides an interesting inside look at Lucille Ball and their lives together. Despite their tumultuous marriage, the couple remained on cordial terms after their divorce.
Higham, Charles. *Lucy: The Life of Lucille Ball*. New York: St. Martin's Press, 1986. A well-written biography of Ball with strong emphasis on her early life prior to breaking into film. Contains good description of the first years of the *I Love Lucy* series.

Morella, Joe, and Edward Epstein. *Forever Lucy: The Life of Lucille Ball.* Secaucus,
N.J.: Lyle Stuart, 1986. Not as detailed as some other biographies, but still an
excellent study of Ball and Arnaz. Portions of the book cover the lives of their
children and the effects of events associated with the parents on their own lives.

Sanders, Covne Steven, and Tom Gilbert. *Desilu.* New York: William Morrow, 1993.
Perhaps the most complete of the Arnaz-Ball biographies. A well-written, detailed
study of Arnaz and Ball's lives and careers until their deaths in 1986 and 1989,
respectively. Some illustrations, and numerous quotes from contemporaries are
included. Little is found on careers of *I Love Lucy* costars Frawley and Vance.

Richard Adler

ANNE BANCROFT

Born: September 17, 1931; New York, New York

Areas of Achievement: Film and theater
Contribution: A successful contemporary actor, both on stage and in film, Anne Bancroft has developed women characters of depth, complexity, and variety.

Early Life

Anne Bancroft was born Anna Maria Louisa Italiano on September 17, 1931, in the Bronx borough of New York City. Her father, Michael Italiano, was a cutter in Manhattan's garment district. Her mother, Mildred DiNapoli Italiano, known as Milly, took up work outside the home when Michael was laid off during the late Depression years. Milly landed a job as switchboard operator at the main branch of Macy's department store, and she remained at her job even when her husband once again found work.

Bancroft had an older sister, Joanne, and a younger sister, Phyllis. The three girls stayed with their grandmother when their parents worked. According to biographer William Holtzman, the Italiano family was large and close, and Bancroft was reared as "a good girl from a good family." Her mother, the disciplinarian of the family, was strict but fair, though sometimes a bit unpredictable. For example, Bancroft was allowed to take tap-dancing lessons, but when her mother noticed that Bancroft was losing weight, the lessons were discontinued.

Bancroft attended Christopher Columbus High School, a large public high school where she participated in drama and developed a keen interest in science. Though Bancroft was torn between science and drama, a number of influences, including a high school boyfriend and her mother, led Bancroft to study acting at the American Academy of Dramatic Arts in New York. Her mother paid the tuition, and the entire Italiano family took pride in and supported Bancroft's acting career.

Bancroft later chose her stage name from a list of preapproved names given to her by Darryl Zanuck of Twentieth Century-Fox, but her acting debut was under the name Anne Marno, a name she chose, in part, because it had an echo of her Italian heritage. As Anne Marno, she performed at Studio One in its 1950 production of Ivan Turgenev's *The Torrents of Spring* (1872). On Monday night, April 17, 1950, Anne Marno performed her role as Gemma and then returned home to face what were probably her toughest critics. When she arrived, she found a simple sign on the front door: "Welcome Home Star!" Inside, she was met by a capacity crowd of applauding relatives and other friends. Anne was deeply moved by her opening-night reception. Her career had begun.

Life's Work

Anne Bancroft's acting career began slowly, in a series of unmemorable television roles and in a brief marriage, that she later regretted, to Martin A. May (1954-1958).

But in 1958, when she earned the stage role of Gittel Mosca in playwright William Gibson's *Two for the Seesaw*, her acting career was on its way. As Gittel, Bancroft costarred with experienced actor Henry Fonda and played a Bronx dancer who falls in love with a married Midwestern lawyer; her performance earned for Bancroft her first Tony Award. The play, staged at the Booth Theatre, ran for 750 performances. By the end of the season, Bancroft had also won a Theatre World Award and the Drama Critics' Poll Award.

In 1959, Bancroft created another sensation in a quite different role, that of Annie Sullivan, Helen Keller's teacher, in William Gibson's *The Miracle Worker*. Bancroft spent weeks studying and preparing for the role—working with children at New York City's Institute of Physical Medicine and Rehabilitation and simulating blindness in herself. On opening night, Bancroft and Patty Duke (as Helen Keller) received round after round of applause and earned rave reviews from theater critics. For her performance in the play, which ran for 700 performances, Bancroft won her second Tony Award and a New York Drama Critics Circle Award. During the course of the stage production, Bancroft and Duke were privileged to attend Helen Keller's eightieth birthday party. In 1962, Bancroft and Duke were reunited to star in the film version of *The Miracle Worker*, for which Bancroft won an Academy Award for best actress and Duke won an Academy Award for best supporting actress in 1963.

Bancroft's performance as Courage in a 1963 production of Bertolt Brecht's *Mother Courage and Her Children* (1941) received mixed reviews, but the role itself once again showed Bancroft's great breadth and versatility as an actor. After the show closed in less than seven weeks, Bancroft turned her attention to film. Three of Bancroft's particularly strong film roles from this period include *The Pumpkin Eater* (1964), *The Slender Thread* (1965), and *Seven Women* (1966). In *The Pumpkin Eater*, a British film production, Bancroft plays an insecure wife in a performance so convincing that she won not only the 1964 best actress award for the Cannes Festival but also the Best Foreign Actress Award from the British Academy and her second Oscar nomination. In *The Slender Thread*, Bancroft plays a suicidal housewife who has overdosed on sleeping pills and calls a young student volunteer at a crisis clinic in Seattle. In *Seven Women*, the last feature film directed by John Ford, Bancroft plays a tough-minded, blunt doctor who saves a group of "proper" women missionaries at a Chinese mission that is overrun by Mongolian bandits.

During the early 1960's, Bancroft was also moving into her second marriage, this time to actor and producer Mel Brooks. Bancroft met Brooks on February 5, 1961, in New York City at a theater where Bancroft was performing. In August of 1964, they were married, much to the astonishment of social columnists, who found the serious Bancroft and the comedic Brooks an unlikely couple. During the course of their marriage, both of their careers continued to flourish.

In 1967, Bancroft performed in two memorable vehicles: on Broadway in a revival of Lillian Hellman's *The Little Foxes* and on film in *The Graduate*. In *The Little Foxes*, Bancroft played the ruthless Regina Giddens in the story of a greedy and heartless Southern family. The stage role of Regina had originally been played by Tallulah

Bankhead, and the 1941 film role had been played by Bette Davis. Bancroft imprinted a new style on the part, playing Regina with utter coldness, and received good reviews. The show played for sixty performances at the Vivian Beaumont theater and then moved to the Ethel Barrymore Theater for an additional forty performances. In *The Graduate*, Bancroft played the predatory Mrs. Robinson opposite the young Dustin Hoffman. Her seduction of the young male protagonist—a role that would hardly draw attention if the genders of the characters were reversed—made the film quite controversial. One critic even referred to Bancroft's character as a "grotesque." Despite the controversy, the film was well received. For her performance, Bancroft received a Golden Globe Award and another nomination for an Oscar.

Bancroft began the 1970's in a television presentation, *Annie: The Woman in the Life of Man*. As the only woman in the cast, Bancroft played a variety of different women in a series of comic, dramatic, and musical sketches. The feature received rave reviews, and Bancroft received an Emmy Award for best actress in a musical special. Throughout the decade, she continued her work on stage and in films. In 1977, Bancroft again played two strong female leads, one in the stage production of *Golda* and the other in the film *The Turning Point*. In *Golda*, another creation of William Gibson, Bancroft played the Israeli political figure Golda Meir. The play received mixed reviews, but Bancroft's performance was praised. In *The Turning Point*, Bancroft plays a prima ballerina who bypasses marriage for her career. Shirley MacLaine plays a suburban housewife who admits that she may have made a mistake in choosing marriage. Bancroft's role in the film marked a turning point of its own in exemplifying Hollywood's belated acknowledgment of changes wrought by the women's movement.

Bancroft ushered in a new decade by writing and directing the film *Fatso* (1980). The film, however, was panned because the tone was ambivalent. Audiences could not decide whether to laugh or cry. Throughout the 1980's, Bancroft turned her attention from stage to film, performing a variety of roles—as Mrs. Kendal in *The Elephant Man* (1980), as Anna Bronski (opposite her husband Mel Brooks) in a 1983 remake of the 1942 classic film *To Be or Not To Be*, as Estelle Rolfe in *Garbo Talks* (1984), as Sister Miriam Ruth in *Agnes of God* (1985), as Thelma Cates in *'night, Mother* (1986), as Helen Hanff in *84 Charing Cross Road* (1987), as Ma in *Torch Song Trilogy* (1988), and as Meredith Perlestein in *Bert Rigby, You're a Fool* (1989). A high point in this series of films was *84 Charing Cross Road*, in which Bancroft plays opposite Anthony Hopkins, as Frank Doel, in a twenty-year love story between two people who never meet. For her performance, Bancroft received an award for Best Actress from the British Academy. She continued to work as an actor and director in the 1990's.

Summary

Anne Bancroft began and sustains a dramatic career of noteworthy complexity. In the early years of her career, when critics distinguished "movie stars," such as Marilyn Monroe, Lana Turner, and Kim Novak, from "serious-artist actresses," such as

Shelley Winters and Joanne Woodward, Bancroft was placed easily within the latter category. She combined talent with education, studying both acting and specific parts, most notably for her part of Annie Sullivan in *The Miracle Worker*. She has demonstrated the versatility and maturity to play a variety of roles involving strong, credible, complex women, such as Annie Sullivan and Golda Meir. In her psychological profiles of troubled wives, such as in *The Pumpkin Eater*, and of strong mothers, such as in *'night Mother* and *Torch Song Trilogy*, she has brought sensitivity and understanding to the parts. Unlike actors who have made their mark in drama by doing one thing well, Bancroft has taken risks, explored new territory, and mastered many diverse roles. Some of the characters have struggled for simple survival, but many of the women characters of Bancroft's career are autonomous, with great inner strength to meet the difficulties of living.

Bibliography
Haskell, Molly. *From Reverence to Rape: The Treatment of Women in the Movies*. 2d ed. Chicago: University of Chicago Press, 1987. This 425-page analysis of American cinema explores women's film roles from a feminist perspective. The book, which includes illustrations and an index, does much to illuminate Bancroft's career in both film and theater roles.
Holtzman, William. *Seesaw: A Dual Biography of Anne Bancroft and Mel Brooks*. Garden City, N.Y.: Doubleday, 1979. Holtzman's dual biography begins on February 5, 1961, with a vignette of the first meeting between Mel Brooks and Anne Bancroft. The book, containing illustrations and an index, treats both actors' careers in a thorough manner.
Loney, Glenn. *20th Century Theatre*. 2 vols. New York: Facts on File, 1983. This 525-page, illustrated work contains chronological information about debuts, births, deaths, premieres, and other career accomplishments of twentieth century theater actors in the United States and England. An index, at the end of the second volume, makes the clips accessible.
Simon, John. *Movies into Film: Film Criticism, 1967-1970*. New York: Dial Press, 1971. Simon's exploration of films integrates cultural and sociological views of American film in the late 1960's. Though the book does not focus on Bancroft, it explores her role in *The Graduate* in chapter 3, "The Youth Film." Simon contends that in the late 1960's the youth film was emerging as a somewhat ineffective genre.
Stott, William, and Jane Stott. *On Broadway*. Austin: University of Texas Press, 1978. An entertaining look at Broadway performances, with performance photographs by Fred Fehl, this 420-page book contains photographs (black and white) and a discussion narrated by playwright William Gibson of the production of *The Miracle Worker*.

Carol Franks

TALLULAH BANKHEAD

Born: January 31 or February 12, 1902; Huntsville, Alabama
Died: December 12, 1968; New York, New York
Areas of Achievement: Film and theater
Contribution: A stage, film, and radio personality in the United States and England, Bankhead was instrumental in shifting stage images of women from the demure to the uninhibited.

Early Life
Tallulah Brockman Bankhead was born sometime between January 31 and February 12, 1902, in Huntsville, Alabama, the second daughter of William Brockman Bankhead and Adelaide (Ada) Eugenia Sledge Bankhead. Though some sources cite January 31 as Tallulah's birthday and 1903 as her birth year, it is more likely that she was born on February 12, 1902, as determined by a letter written by a local clergyman, than on January 31, her parents' anniversary. A few days after Tallulah's birth, her mother died of blood poisoning. As a result, Tallulah and her sister Eugenia were reared by their father, their paternal grandparents, and their Aunt Louise. When Tallulah and Eugenia were twelve and thirteen years old, respectively, William Bankhead remarried. Tallulah, who disliked her father's new wife, lived in a sixth-floor apartment with her grandparents, Senator John Hollis Bankhead, (Captain John) and his wife, the first Tallulah Brockman Bankhead, while Eugenia lived on the seventh floor with her father and his new wife, the twenty-five-year-old Florence McGuire. The Bankheads, a political family, divided their time between Washington, D.C., and Jasper, Alabama.

Although Tallulah learned the niceties of polite society, she was ambivalent about their practice, even as a child. She had frequent temper tantrums in front of almost anyone but her father, and she delighted—at least once—in singing off-color songs for her father and his friends. Both Tallulah and Eugenia adored their father, but various accounts of Bankhead family life suggest that he often drank too much, became melancholy, then morose, then suicidal. During these times, he grieved the death of his young wife. Tallulah's antics often cheered her father. She was outgoing, unlike Eugenia, and enjoyed entertaining others. She wanted to be an actor.

In 1917, her chance came when she sent a photograph and application to a contest in *Picture Play Magazine*. The contest promised an opportunity in drama in New York to the top twelve winners. Tallulah's photograph appeared among the winning photographs, but her application had been lost, so the picture was labeled "The Mystery Woman." With the help of their congressional letterhead stationery, the Bankhead family convinced *Picture Play Magazine* that the fifteen-year-old Tallulah, who had dressed herself up to look much older, was the mystery woman. Tallulah's father disapproved of his youthful daughter going to New York to pursue drama. Nevertheless, when Captain John offered to fund the trip for both Tallulah and her Aunt Louise, who agreed to act as a chaperone, William Bankhead gave his consent.

Life's Work

A versatile performer, Tallulah Bankhead had at least three distinct phases in her acting career. The first of these, in British drama, got underway in 1923. Between her 1918 Broadway debut in a minor role in *Squab Farm* and 1922, Bankhead performed in a number of mediocre plays in New York. Her first major break came when Charles Cochran, a British producer, saw her perform and arranged for her move to England where she was featured with Gerald du Maurier in Hubert Parson's *The Dancers* (1923). Bankhead was an overnight sensation, and the show ran for 346 performances. She was both popular and famous, particularly with her large following of fashionable young people. During her eight years in England, she performed in sixteen plays.

Despite Bankhead's success and popularity in England, she eventually returned to the United States, undoubtedly drawn by the lure of even bigger money in motion pictures. After making a series of unmemorable films for Paramount Studios, Bankhead decided to leave the film industry and return to the stage. Paramount, with considerable relief, agreed with her decision.

Paramount's relief stemmed from its inability to mold Bankhead into the image it wanted. In 1932, a particularly uncomfortable situation arose for Paramount when the Hays Office, the film industry's self-regulatory commission, censored Bankhead for "verbal turpitude." Their action was in response to a magazine interview in which Bankhead claimed she was able to start a love affair "with any man an hour after meeting him." The Hays Office urged all major magazines and newspapers to suppress Bankhead's comment, and all involved in the interview were rebuked.

In 1933, Bankhead produced and acted in the Broadway play *Forsaking All Others*. Playing the jilted bride Mary Clay, Bankhead received largely bad reviews, but, according to one biographer, the audiences adored Bankhead, especially groups of young working-class women in Boston, Providence, and New York. These women purchased tickets in the cheap balcony section, loudly cheered Bankhead's entrance, and raucously hissed at the faithless bridegroom.

Throughout her half-century career, Bankhead supported herself well with her talent and her notoriety. In general, Bankhead was taken more seriously in England than she was in the United States. Nevertheless, in the United States, Bankhead had a number of outstanding performances throughout her stage, film, and radio career. Among her finest were *The Little Foxes* (1939), *The Skin of Our Teeth* (1942), *Lifeboat* (1944), *Private Lives* (1948), and *The Big Show*, a radio show that she hosted in the late 1940's. In Lillian Hellman's *The Little Foxes*, the story of the greed and heartlessness of a Southern family, Bankhead played the ruthless Regina Giddens. Critics praised Bankhead's performance, several calling it the finest of her career. One critic said her portrayal of Regina was "honest, merciless and completely understanding." The play ran for 410 performances.

In Thornton Wilder's *The Skin of Our Teeth*, Bankhead, as the maid Sabrina, stole the show. Again, critics called Bankhead's performance brilliant. Unlike the critics, however, the audiences were often displeased with the play. They found the destruction of the "fourth wall" in theater, that between the actors and the audience, unsettling. *The Skin of Our Teeth* not only broke that wall down, but, as one critic put it, it did so "boisterously, loudly, violently," frequently reminding the audience that these were actors in a play. At every performance, some people left after the first act. Still, *The Skin of Our Teeth* had a forty-five-week run and won a Pulitzer Prize. *The New York Times* called Bankhead's performance "magnificent."

In Alfred Hitchcock's film *Lifeboat*, Bankhead played the part of Connie Porter, the only survivor who could communicate with the Nazi on board the lifeboat. Bankhead's performance earned her the New York Critics' citation as the year's Best Actress. In Noel Coward's *Private Lives*, Bankhead played Amanda Prynne, a minor role that Bankhead relished. Again, the reviews were excellent. One critic said in praising Bankhead that Bankhead managed to take a "trivial part in a trivial play and transform it." The show ran thirty-one weeks and returned the production costs five times over. In the late 1940's, Bankhead began hosting *The Big Show* on radio. This series marked her shift to a career as a stage, film, and radio personality. On the show, she insulted her guests, and her catch-phrase "Hello, Daahlings!" became nationally known.

Alcohol and drug abuse increasingly plagued Bankhead. She continued performing on stage until 1964, when she appeared in her last performance, as a sort of parody of herself, in Tennessee Williams' *The Milk Train Doesn't Stop Here Anymore*. Bankhead played Flora Goforth, a rich, aging woman intrigued with a handsome, no-good poet. The show failed.

Despite her failures, Bankhead's name still had appeal. She had become one of those personalities known by one name. Her best-selling autobiography, *Tallulah* (1952), was serialized in thirty American newspapers. She knew that her life's story was marketable. She joked that her necessities were "bourbon, cigarettes, and a comb," and, in fact, her water glass on *The Merv Griffin Show* was filled with bourbon. Bankhead was further reduced from actor to personality during a nasty public trial in which Evyleen Cronin, Bankhead's "wardrobe mistress," was accused of bilking Bankhead out of at least $10,000 by tampering with checks. During the trial, the public learned of Bankhead's temper, her use of cocaine and marijuana, her lewd language, and her young lovers.

By 1960, Bankhead had difficulty getting and keeping a household staff. Her days were filled with viewing soap operas, drinking, and taking drugs. Lapsing into unconsciousness while holding lit cigarettes, Bankhead started several fires, once setting her dog on fire. She was diagnosed with emphysema and began to have drug-related psychotic episodes. The scandals increased, while her career opportunities decreased.

Bankhead's autobiography ends with a passage from Edna St. Vincent Millay, a stanza that Bankhead calls her "plight," her "philosophy": "My candle burns at both ends;/ It will not last the night;/ But ah, my foes, and oh, my friends,/ It gives a lovely light." Bankhead's life ended in New York City's St. Luke's Hospital in 1968, where she died of pneumonia.

Summary
Tallulah Bankhead had a significant stage career, both in England and in the United States. She also left her imprint on U.S. film and radio and on the Hays Office. She had incredible appeal during her early career, particularly to young audiences in England and in the United States. Above all, however, Bankhead was a career woman, supporting herself and others for most of her life. She was instrumental in the expansion of stage "types" for women actors from the demure and helpless to the sophisticated, jaded, and flashy. Her major roles became benchmarks against which later actors were judged. Drama critic Helen Ormsbee contends, in *Backstage with Actors* (1970), that Bankhead brought a particular type of imagination to her performances. Through her acting, Ormsbee concludes, Bankhead extended the "reality of a scene beyond the limits of the stage setting," making the space off stage exist in the story, "just out of view."

Bibliography
Bankhead, Tallulah. *Tallulah: My Autobiography*. New York: Harper & Brothers, 1952. Dedicated to her father, Bankhead's best-selling autobiography focuses on specific events that influenced her life. The tone is warm and humorous, outrageous, and scurrilous. According to biographer Lee Israel, parts of the book were tested in court, so Bankhead's accounts are probably accurate. Illustrated and indexed.
Hewitt, Barnard. *Theatre U.S.A.: 1665 to 1957*. New York: McGraw-Hill, 1959. In Hewitt's history of drama in the United States, he studies patterns of change within drama, production, and the theater building itself. The 528-page book, containing both illustrations and an index, includes analysis of Bankhead in Lillian Hellman's *The Little Foxes* and Thornton Wilder's *The Skin of Our Teeth*.
Israel, Lee. *Miss Tallulah Bankhead*. New York: G. P. Putnam's Sons, 1972. Israel's biography of Bankhead covers Bankhead's life and career in a loosely chronological fashion. The book convincingly sketches Bankhead more as a personality than as a great actor. Contains illustrations and an index.
Loney, Glenn. *20th Century Theatre*. 2 vols. New York: Facts on File, 1983. This illustrated work contains chronological information about debuts, births, deaths, and dramatic premieres of twentieth century theater actors in the United States and England. Includes a useful index to newspaper and magazine reviews and other sources.
Ormsbee, Helen. *Backstage with Actors: From the Time of Shakespeare to the Present Day*. Freeport, N.Y.: Books for Libraries Press, 1970. Tracing the history of drama, Ormsbee explores the move from stage to motion pictures and radio. Although the book is not specifically about Bankhead, her career is discussed and evaluated. The book contains illustrations, an index, and a prologue.

Carol Franks

DJUNA BARNES

Born: June 12, 1892; Cornwall-on-Hudson, New York
Died: June 18, 1982; New York, New York
Area of Achievement: Literature
Contribution: A noted member of the American expatriate community in Paris, Djuna Barnes wrote a highly influential experimental novel and pioneered the treatment of lesbianism in literature.

Early Life

Djuna Chappell Barnes was born to an eccentric, bohemian family in the New York community of Cornwall-on-Hudson in 1892. Her mother, Elizabeth Chappell Barnes, was English and her father, Wald Barnes, American. Wald Barnes (a name he adopted in preference over his given name, Henry Budington) pursued many cultural interests, but does not seem to have been successful in any of them. He does, however, seem to have had an overwhelming and largely negative influence upon his daughter. There is indirect but compelling evidence of an incestuous relationship. Djuna Barnes takes up the theme of father-daughter incest repeatedly in her work, although usually obliquely. Whatever the physical or psychological reality of what took place, Djuna was evidently presented by her father in 1910 to a man far older than she was—Percy Faulkner, the brother of the woman destined to become Wald Barnes's second wife. Djuna's relationship with Faulkner seems to have been both informal and brief.

Barnes had been educated at home. Some time after 1910 she moved to New York City, where she studied art at the Pratt Institute and the Art Students' League. Barnes showed promise as both writer and artist: By the time she was twenty-one, she was producing articles and illustrations for New York City newspapers. Within a few years, she was able to earn a good living writing for these papers and for such magazines as *Harper's*. Besides reporting on local events, she interviewed a number of personalities, many of them long since forgotten, and turned out stylized, satirical sketches reminiscent of English artist Aubrey Beardsley.

In 1915, Barnes moved to Greenwich Village, a bohemian section of New York City synonymous with the newest ideas and trends in society and the arts. Her first "book," a pamphlet entitled *The Book of Repulsive Women*, also appeared in 1915. It consisted of a handful of poems and drawings and announced another theme that was to dominate her work, lesbianism.

Although she began to take many women lovers during this period, Barnes's sexual allegiance had not shifted entirely to women. About 1916, she was married to fellow writer Courtenay Lemon. This marriage may have been as informal as her first relationship with Percy Faulkner; in any case, she and Lemon had separated by 1919. Sometime that year or the next she left for Europe and, except for brief trips home, remained there until 1940. During those twenty years she produced a number of works, including a novel that would come to be regarded as one of the most important American literary works of the century.

Life's Work

Once in Europe, Djuna Barnes was commissioned to write various celebrity profiles and subsequently lived in both Paris, France, and Berlin, Germany. Among the figures she interviewed was Irish writer James Joyce, author of the novel *Ulysses* (1922), destined to become the most influential English-language work of the century. Barnes admired Joyce immensely, and declared after reading *Ulysses* that she would never write again. Nevertheless, she soon published her first substantial work, entitled simply *A Book* (1923).

A Book consisted of stories, plays, poems, and drawings. The stories were the most important components of the work; many subsequently appeared—usually in re-worked versions—in the collections *A Night Among the Horses* (1929) and *Spillwax* (1962). In style they are unexceptional, but in their subject matter—individuals cast adrift from ties of class or country—they are very much products of their time.

Barnes's next two works exhibited greater innovation: *A Ladies' Almanack* (1928, identified only as being "Written & Illustrated by a Lady of Fashion") and the novel *Ryder* (also 1928). *A Ladies' Almanack* is a short, mock-Elizabethan work that defies easy classification. Arranged in twelve sections, one for each month of the year, it is actually a gentle satire on the lesbian community of Paris. Those who were familiar with the community would be expected to recognize the real figures behind such characters as Evangeline Musset and Daisy Downpour.

Because of its sexual and scatological content, *A Ladies' Almanack* was privately printed in Dijon, France. *Ryder* was published openly in New York, but in a censored version that omitted several passages and drawings. *Ryder* is far longer and more stylistically complex than anything else Barnes had previously written. It draws on her painful and convoluted family history and clearly illustrates Barnes's interest in the intense literary experimentation that was going on around her.

The novel's central character, Wendell Ryder, has a wife and a mistress and children by each. The two families live an unconventional life together in one house, with the children being kept from school and Ryder finding himself chronically unable to choose between the two women who share his household. *Ryder* is an amalgam of styles and influences, ranging from the King James Version of the Bible to such English writers as Geoffrey Chaucer and Laurence Sterne. Despite its dark undercurrents, *Ryder* is light and airy in tone, if perhaps forbidding in its display of archaic language. Its risqué reputation made it a best-seller for a short time, although in later years it has been read mainly as a precursor to Barnes's greater and more accessible novel, *Nightwood* (1936).

Ryder was dedicated to "T.W." The initials belonged to Thelma Wood, Barnes's lover for a number of years and, next to her father, the most influential person in her life. Wood had been born in Missouri and was a gifted artist and sculptor. She and Barnes had met early in the 1920's and became a familiar, strikingly elegant couple in the expatriate community. They maintained an often-strained relationship for about a decade.

If in one sense *Ryder* is "about" Barnes's family, then *Nightwood* is "about" her relationship with Thelma Wood. *Nightwood* is set for the most part in Paris. Its eight sections revolve around the tangled lives of a group of expatriates, chief among them Robin Vote, a young American woman who seems to live beyond the categories— right, wrong, waking, sleeping, animal, human, and so on—that rule the others' existence. Another American, Nora Flood, has an intense affair with Robin, but loses her to Jenny Petherbridge. In her distress, Nora seeks out the bizarre Dr. Matthew O'Connor, an unlicensed physician whose long, drunken soliloquies on love and the night form the heart of the novel. O'Connor, who made his first appearance in *Ryder*, is Barnes's most brilliantly conceived character. A homosexual and transvestite, he is able, like the mythological Greek character Tiresias, to experience both the male and female sides of existence.

Barnes's British editor, poet T. S. Eliot, thought very highly of *Nightwood* and wrote an introduction comparing its mood to that of Elizabethan tragedy. The novel was published in London in 1936 and in New York City in 1937. The reviews were mixed, but sophisticated readers and other writers were as enthusiastic as Eliot, and the book has remained in print ever since.

Barnes had worked on the manuscript of *Nightwood* on a visit to Morocco in 1933 and had finished it in England. She returned to France in 1939, only to flee to the United States in 1940 with the approach of war. She eventually took an apartment in her old haunt of Greenwich Village—an apartment she would keep for more than four decades, gaining the reputation of a recluse. She had complained of exhaustion after completing *Nightwood*, and it is hard to escape the conclusion that she had put a lifetime of painful experience into its composition.

Barnes did have in her a third major work: *The Antiphon* (1958), a play on which she labored for years. It treats a family strikingly similar to the one in *Ryder*, but from a tragic point of view. Its three acts take place on the same day in ruined Burley Hall, in which the aged Augusta and her daughter and three sons reenact the disintegration of their family.

The Antiphon is a dense and stylistically forbidding work. Part of its difficulty stems from the fact that T. S. Eliot insisted on extensive cuts before its publication. The result was tighter, but more obscure. It received its world premiere in Stockholm, Sweden, in 1961 (where one of its translators was United Nations Secretary-General Dag Hammarskjöld), but has rarely been performed since.

Barnes's last years were often difficult. She had no regular income and subsisted for the most part on gifts from a small band of friends and admirers, including Irish-born author and Nobel laureate Samuel Beckett. She rarely left her apartment, and seems to have gone for months at a time without speaking to anyone.

Barnes continued to write, but published very little. She resisted efforts to collect her early journalism, declaring it undeserving, and scorned those of her contemporaries who produced their memoirs. Almost everything she wished to be remembered for—*Spillway*, *Nightwood*, and *The Antiphon*—appeared in her *Selected Writings* in 1962, to respectful reviews. A small renewal of interest came with the publication of two late poems, "Quarry" and "The Walking Mort," in *The New Yorker* in 1969 and

1971 respectively. In their brief compass, these dense, dark poems are among her very best works.

Barnes died a few days past her ninetieth birthday in 1982 after a short confinement to a nursing home.

Summary

Djuna Barnes's novel *Nightwood* has come to be regarded as one of the most important American novels of the twentieth century. Its highly poetic yet precise language, its rejection of realism, and its darkly comic vision rank it with such masterpieces as William Faulkner's *The Sound and the Fury* (1929) and Vladimir Nabokov's *Lolita* (1955). Although it has never achieved great popularity, it has had a continuing impact upon Barnes's colleagues, influencing such American writers as Faulkner, Anaïs Nin, John Hawkes, and Thomas Pynchon, and such British novelists as Lawrence Durrell.

Barnes's body of work is also important as a pioneering, if highly ambivalent, depiction of lesbianism in literature. As announced in *The Book of Repulsive Women* and *A Ladies' Almanack* and developed most fully in *Nightwood*, Barnes's treatment of lesbianism is far from being a didactic endorsement of a particular way of life. *Nightwood* is not a celebration of lesbianism, but a monument to the anguish of all love. Barnes herself stood aside from all movements, holding out little hope for the improvement of man's or woman's lot. She scoffed at the idea of women's liberation, and declared, in reference to a key relationship in her life, that she was not a lesbian but had simply loved Thelma Wood.

Bibliography

Barnes, Djuna. *Interviews*. Edited by Alyce Barry. Washington, D.C.: Sun & Moon Press, 1985. A collection of forty-one interviews written between 1913 and 1931, accompanied by Barnes's original illustrations. Subjects range from Diamond Jim Brady to James Joyce. Taken in total, a useful memoir of the period in which Barnes developed as a writer.

Broe, Mary Lynn, ed. *Silence and Power: A Reevaluation of Djuna Barnes*. Carbondale: Southern Illinois University Press, 1991. An invaluable compilation of essays about Barnes's work, supplemented with photographs and drawings, many of the latter by Barnes herself. Some strictly biographical material appears in a series of "Reminiscences."

Field, Andrew. *Djuna: The Formidable Miss Barnes*. Austin: University of Texas Press, 1985. A revised and corrected version of the biography that first appeared in 1983. Criticized for its idiosyncratic arrangement and lack of notes, it is still a lively and admiring work. Photographs, extensive bibliography.

O'Neal, Hank. *"Life Is Painful, Nasty & Short . . . In My Case It Has Only Been Painful & Nasty": Djuna Barnes, 1978-1981: An Informal Memoir*. New York: Paragon House, 1990. Memoir by an admirer who handled many of Barnes's literary and financial affairs near the end of her life. A series of portraits from the

1950's by Barnes's friend Berenice Abbott appears in an appendix.

Scott, James B. *Djuna Barnes*. Boston: Twayne, 1976. Thorough study of Barnes's work in an accessible format. Most biographical material appears in the opening chapter, "Early Life." Written before Andrew Field revealed the more controversial aspects of Barnes's life. Chronology, bibliography.

Grove Koger

ETHEL BARRYMORE

Born: August 16, 1879; Philadelphia, Pennsylvania
Died: June 18, 1959; Beverly Hills, California
Area of Achievement: Theater and drama
Contribution: One of the most distinguished actresses in American and British theater, Barrymore not only performed in classic plays but also created memorable roles in plays written specifically for her.

Early Life

Ethel Mae Blythe was born on August 16, 1879, in a house leased by her grandmother, the actress-manager Louisa Drew, the same house in which Ethel's brother Lionel had been born in April of the preceding year. The youngest in their family, their brother John, was born three years after Ethel, in a nearby leased residence. All three children grew up in Philadelphia, raised largely by their grandmother because their parents, Georgiana Drew and Maurice Blythe (who, along with his children, took Barrymore as his stage name), were often on tour, being distinguished performers themselves. Because of their parents' successful careers, the children came in contact with other great actors; later, Ethel was to say that the two people who most influenced her, because of their strength of character, were her grandmother, Louisa Drew, and the illustrious Polish actress Helena Modjeska.

After Ethel's mother became a convert to Catholicism, Ethel was sent to a convent school, where she received most of her education. When Ethel was thirteen, her mother died of a lung infection; six months later, her father remarried, and Ethel, unhappy at this new arrangement, begged her grandmother for a part in her touring company production of Richard Sheridan's *The Rivals* (1775). Secretly, Ethel had planned to be a concert pianist, but since no money was forthcoming for her future training, she chose the most familiar path—the theater. Her two brothers also had never intended to be actors: John hoped to be an artist; Lionel, a composer. They all had to earn a living and so drifted into a profession that would later make all three of them famous.

By 1895, Ethel, who had acted first in her grandmother's company and subsequently, when her grandmother fell ill, found work taking small parts on Broadway, was offered a role in a play starring William Gillette, one of America's leading actors. *Secret Service*, also written by Gillette, was to open in London at the Adelphi Theater in May of 1895, and Ethel jumped at the chance to perform. She quickly found favor with English audiences, and her social life also blossomed. Her uncle, John Drew, an enormously popular actor in London, furnished her with letters of introduction to such eminences as actress Ellen Terry, actor Sir Henry Irving, painter James Whistler, and author Henry James. Irving's son, Laurence, fell madly in love with Ethel and proposed marriage, as did the young Winston Churchill. Ethel, who at eighteen had become a great beauty, began to set the style in looks, dress, and manner; women even copied the way she wore her hair. Although she enjoyed her social success in London, she dreamed of conquering the New York theater and so returned in 1901 to star in Clyde Fitch's *Captain Jinks of the Horse Marines*, which marked the turning point of her career.

Life's Work

After 1901, Charles Frohman, America's leading theatrical producer, began to feature Ethel Barrymore in gossamer, forgettable comedies which she made successful because of her charm and her ability. Barrymore, however, wanted to match her mother's reputation by acting in the classics; above all, she wished to be taken seriously as an actress. To that end, and with Frohman's permission, since she was under contract to him, she chose the role of Nora in a 1905 production of Henrik Ibsen's *A Doll's House* (1879), which opened in Chicago shortly after her father's death. (Following a mental breakdown, Maurice Barrymore had been confined in a sanatorium since 1902). Ethel persuaded her brother John to play the role of the dying Dr. Rank, who is in love with Nora; the experience proved to everyone that John had finally arrived as an actor. Nevertheless, when Ethel brought the production to New York, the critics were lukewarm in their praise and audiences were also disappointed. Accustomed to seeing Ethel in effervescent pieces, theatergoers expected her to go on playing variations on her charming self. Mainly concerned with box-office profits, Frohman advised her against acting "heavy" roles in the future, and Ethel, who was understandably concerned about her career, never again undertook an Ibsen play.

On Christmas Day, 1905, Ethel opened at the Criterion Theatre in New York with James Barrie's *Alice-Sit-by-the-Fire*, winning the role over America's favorite Peter Pan, Maude Adams. The importance of the event was underscored by the appearance of all three Barrymores in the play, Ethel being instrumental in finding work for her brothers whenever possible. The role she played, that of a sexually experienced woman with three children, again displeased the critics, who had praised her rare and radiant "girlhood." Nevertheless, female theatergoers cheered her on, and their approval helped to make the play a success. When the play went on tour, Ethel realized that Lionel was very unhappy with an acting career and generously gave him enough money to go off to Paris where he could study and compose, as he had dreamed of doing. John also left to appear in another production, and eventually Ethel closed the play.

In 1907, Ethel, again wishing to appear in a serious play, chose John Galsworthy's *The Silver Box* (1906). It was an unusual role for her, that of a humble charwoman unjustly accused of stealing a box who suffers punishment because of the law's inequity. The critics were overwhelmed by her performance even as they were taken aback by her drab appearance: it was difficult for her public to accept her as an actress when they were forever expecting a personality. The next year, Ethel married millionaire playboy Samuel Colt, by whom she was to have three children: Samuel, Ethel, and John. The day after her honeymoon, Ethel went on tour in 1908 with a Somerset Maugham comedy, *Lady Frederick* (1907), determined that it would be possible to maintain both her marriage and her career. (The couple eventually proved incompatible, and Ethel received a divorce in 1921.)

A 1911 production of Arthur Pinero's play about an unhappy marriage, *Mid-Channel* (1909), next occupied Ethel, and again she was roundly applauded for her skill. In 1912, she broke new ground by appearing in a one-act play by James Barrie, *The Twelve-Pound Look* (1910), in vaudeville. In those days, vaudeville was not the rather tawdry kind of entertainment it was later to become: fine actors, singers, and dancers were proud to appear, and well-known playwrights were happy to write short pieces for the performers. Barrie's play attracted Ethel because it was the story of a woman who, having left her husband, struck out on her own and supported herself as a typist because, although her husband was rich, he was so pompous, insensitive and overbearing that she could not be happy with him. When she left, the woman led him to believe that she was interested in another man; it is only when they meet accidentally years later that her husband, divorced and remarried, learns the truth about her feelings—and about himself. It is a charming comedy, very feminist in its outlook, and Ethel took it on tour several times in her later career.

During the years between 1913 and 1915, Ethel drifted to Hollywood to make silent films, all unmemorable and poorly produced. She disliked the medium, and even years later, when it served her talents more successfully, she was never happy in it. In 1922, at age forty-three, she again tackled a problem play: Gerhart Hauptmann's *Rose Bernd* (1903), the tragedy of a servant woman who strangles her illegitimate child. The critic Alexander Woolcott gave Ethel high marks for her performance, but the part was evidently too raw for her public and it was not a success. Next, she decided that she had to prove herself by acting in a Shakespeare play and unwisely opted for *Romeo and Juliet*. Ethel was then too old and too overweight for the role of Juliet, and her performance was dismissed with a rancor hard to understand for one who had been the critics' darling for so long.

To counterbalance the poor reviews, Ethel appeared in a 1923 production of Alfred Sutro's *The Laughing Lady* (1922), a comedy which enjoyed a great success. Later in 1923, she combined her gift for comedy with her desire to perform in a classic: Acting with her uncle John Drew as Sir Peter, Ethel played a role her mother had made famous, Lady Teazle in Richard Sheridan's *The School for Scandal* (1777). The role proved one of the major triumphs of her career. In 1924, she joined actor-manager Walter Hampden, who had inaugurated a Shakespeare season in New York, playing Ophelia to his Hamlet and Portia to his Shylock (*The Merchant of Venice*) to good reviews. Then came Ethel's artistic and commercial success in Somerset Maugham's *The Constant Wife*, which opened in Cleveland in 1926, enjoyed a long run in New York, and toured throughout the country for two solid years. Maugham was to say later that her performance was responsible for making him enough money to build his villa in southern France.

At the end of the tour in 1928, she opened in Gregorio Martinez Sierra's play, *The Kingdom of God*, in the role of a nun who spans half a century of life in a convent. The contrast between the sophisticated heroine of Maugham's comedy and the dedicated religious of Sierra's play brought home to the critics just how enormous

Ethel's versatility was. The occasion was a special one because at the opening, the brothers Shubert, Broadway's best-known producers, named their theater on 47th Street the Ethel Barrymore Theater in her honor.

After the eighty-week tour of *The Kingdom of God* was over, Ethel was lured to Hollywood in 1932 to make her first talking picture. Brothers Lionel and John played Rasputin and the Prince-assassin, respectively, while Ethel took the role of the Czarina in *Rasputin and the Empress* (1933). It was the only time the three of them appeared in a film together. The next few years Ethel toured (in the United States and in England) in *The Twelve-Pound Look* and *The Constant Wife*, then returned to New York in 1938 as an aging matriarch in the theatrical adaptation of Mazo de la Roche's 1929 novel *Whiteoaks of Jalna*. In 1940, she appeared in another of her impressive roles, that of the schoolteacher in Emlyn Williams' *The Corn Is Green* (1938), and after its Broadway run toured with it for four years. Halfway through her tour, she received news of John's death on May 29, 1942. She went on that night anyway, even though she had been shattered by the news. She returned to Broadway in 1944 in Franz Werfel's *Embezzled Heaven*, playing the part of a deeply religious though ignorant servant woman, and again was much praised for her work. Her last stage appearance came in 1945 again as a nun in Philip Barry's *The Joyous Season* (1934), which toured but never opened in New York as the producers had small hope for its commercial success.

Increasing weariness and ill-health compelled her to return to Hollywood, where the climate was kinder. She appeared in a film starring Cary Grant, *None But the Lonely Heart* (1944), playing the part of a tired old Cockney. Her film performance earned for her an Academy Award. For the next several years she appeared in various pictures, most of them negligible except for *Kind Lady* in 1951, which starred an actor worthy of her, Maurice Evans. In 1954, when she finished her penultimate film, *Young at Heart*, Lionel died, and she said in an interview that she was forced to look back over their lives and think of what she and her brothers had wanted to achieve, but did not. She died peacefully in 1959, surrounded by her friends.

Summary

Ethel Barrymore established her reputation as a great lady of the theater in the United States and abroad while struggling against the typecasting that occurred as a result of her popularity. She aspired to act in roles in classic dramatic works, but was initially discouraged from playing such roles because audiences found her more believable in lighthearted comedic roles. Barrymore eventually found a larger scope for her talents, and the parts she played most effectively reflected her true character. Whether she was a patient nun, a clever wife tolerant of her husband's faults, a professional woman learning to be independent, or a humble servant bringing dignity to her surroundings, Ethel Barrymore established a stage and screen persona that reflected her innate grace and her strength of spirit.

Throughout the years, Barrymore overcame many adversities in her pursuit of an acting career. Proud of her family's rich acting tradition, Barrymore sought certain acting opportunities that would further the careers of her brothers and look after their interests even though they often disappointed her. She had hoped to find happiness in marriage, but chose a husband who neither understood nor appreciated her desire to act. Although her innate pride and her generosity to members of her family placed her in precarious financial situations over the years, Barrymore was rescued from difficult straits by the contributions that Katharine Hepburn and other acting colleagues made to the Ethel Barrymore Fund, established in her honor in 1956. This concrete proof of the love and admiration of her peers was a fitting testimony to Barrymore's achievements.

Bibliography
Atkinson, Brooks. *Broadway*. New York: Macmillan, 1970. This collection of essays on the theater by Atkinson, drama critic of the *New York Times* from 1925 to 1955, contains his evaluations of actors, writers, and producers during those years. There is a fine study of "The Royal Family" in which he traces the Drew-Barrymore heritage and discusses in detail the strong and weak points of Ethel Barrymore's art. Several photographs of her in her varied roles give an idea of her range.
Auster, Albert. *Actresses and Suffragists: Women in the American Theatre, 1890-1920*. New York: Praeger, 1984. A useful study of female performers, with attention to such actresses as Louisa Drew, Ethel's grandmother, who was outstanding not only for her acting but also for her unusually efficient management of her own acting company.
Barrymore, Ethel. *Memories: An Autobiography*. New York: Harper & Brothers, 1955. Ethel's reminiscences, told with wit and charm. Omitting much of her private life and personal sorrows, it is very much a public book and concentrates largely on the days when she was the toast of English society and the darling of the American theater. Ethel herself said that she had planned to call the book *So Many Tears* but felt that to do so would necessitate revealing facts she preferred to keep to herself.
Ferber, Edna, and George S. Kaufman. *The Royal Family*. Garden City, N.Y.: Doubleday, 1928. First produced at the Selwyn Theater, New York, in 1927, this comedy deals with three generations of actors, members of a famous family. Though thinly disguised, two of the fictional Cavendishes are unmistakable portraits of John and Ethel Barrymore. The latter was so incensed by the play that she refused to speak to the authors thereafter. The play was later made into a film starring Ina Claire and Fredric March.
Green, Abel, and Joe Laurie, Jr. *Show Biz: From Vaude to Video*. New York: Henry Holt, 1951. A collection of reviews, comments, and observations by reporters of *Variety*. The authors provide a valuable compendium of what was happening in the New York theater from 1905 to 1950. For example, Ethel Barrymore's Juliet is contrasted with that of Jane Cowl, who starred in the Shakespeare tragedy the same year and who proved far more effective in the role than Barrymore.
Peters, Margot. *The House of Barrymore*. New York: Alfred A. Knopf, 1990. The best

book ever written on Ethel and all the Barrymores. Extensively researched, Peters' biography benefited from the cooperation of Spencer Berger, a Barrymore devotee who supplied the author with tapes, letters, remembered conversations, and information never before revealed. What is particularly valuable about the book, besides its index and notes, is the collection of photographs, both personal and professional, and the listing of all performances, both on stage and in film, of the three Barrymores.

Mildred C. Kuner

CLARA BARTON

Born: December 25, 1821; North Oxford, Massachusetts
Died: April 12, 1912; Glen Echo, Maryland
Areas of Achievement: Education, nursing, and social reform
Contribution: After half a lifetime devoted to humanitarian pursuits, Barton became the key figure in establishing the American Red Cross.

Early Life

Clarissa Harlowe Barton (known as Clara) was influenced by her parents' liberal political attitudes. The youngest child, Clara had identity problems which worsened when she showed interests in academic and other pursuits considered masculine. Farm work and nursing relatives who were ill, however, led her increasingly to connect approval and praise to helping others.

In 1836, Barton began teaching school. She was a gifted teacher who chose to enforce discipline through kindness and persuasion at a time when physical force was the standard. During the next decade, Barton developed quite a reputation as she moved from town to town, taming obstreperous students and leaving for another challenge. As she gained self-confidence, she began to have an active social life, though she never married. Tired of teaching and concerned that her own education was inadequate, she enrolled at the Clinton Liberal Institute in Clinton, New York, at the end of 1850. She studied for a year, but as an older student, she felt out of place and made few friends.

Unable to afford more school and unwilling to be dependent on her family, Barton went to live with friends in New Jersey. In 1852, she convinced authorities to offer free public education by allowing her to open a free school. Although she was initially unpaid, Barton eventually made the school such a success that she was offered a salary and the opportunity to expand her program. As the school grew, however, the school board decided that a man should be placed in charge and paid more than any women involved. Frustrated and angry, Barton moved to Washington, D.C., in search of new opportunities in 1854.

She found work as a clerk in the Patent Office, where the commissioner was willing to give women positions. For several years Barton made good money and earned respect for her efficiency despite the resentment of her male colleagues. Shifting political fortunes forced Barton to leave her post in 1857. For three years, she lived at home in Massachusetts before returning to the Patent Office in 1860.

Life's Work

With the outbreak of the Civil War in 1861, Clara Barton began the humanitarian work that would occupy the rest of her life. Federal troops were arriving in Washington without baggage or food. She began to gather and distribute supplies to ease their distress. Her efforts quickly grew to include battlefield assistance in helping the wounded at the beginning of the war. Because the military had badly underestimated medical needs, Barton's individual effort gathering supplies and caring for the wounded at battles such as Fredericksburg proved immensely valuable. By the end of 1862, however, the army was becoming better organized and the work of amateurs was no longer significant. Barton also had problems getting official support and recognition because, unlike Barton, most volunteers were more harm than help. The army could not accept one volunteer while denying others. Barton, as she often did, became defensive, taking every rebuke, regardless of the source, personally.

After the war, Barton undertook a project to identify missing soldiers and inform their families of their fates. Her efforts included a trip to Andersonville prison where, with the help of a former inmate who had kept the death roll, Barton supervised the identification and marking of some 13,000 graves. Despite some success, Barton's work in tracing missing soldiers resulted in identification of less than ten percent of the missing. During her pursuit of these activities, Barton confronted two difficulties of a sort typical of her career. One problem arose because the army was also attempting to find missing soldiers. Barton sought sole control of the whole effort, but this control was not granted and she feuded with the officer in charge. Barton possessed a zeal for efficiency that made her reluctant to share responsibility or credit. This attitude prevented her from delegating authority and provoked hostility among many people who actually wanted to help her. The second problem was a result of poor accounting. She could not provide details of expenses, leaving herself open to charges of malfeasance. Although she was always more interested in field work than administration, Barton was unwilling to share power with someone who would handle paperwork. She paid little attention to tracking the disbursement of donated funds and poured her own limited resources into her projects even though she could produce no receipts. There is no evidence that she sought personal gain. Nevertheless, her poor accounting resulted in repeated complaints that ultimately came back to haunt her during her work with the Red Cross.

Barton's involvement with the Red Cross began in Europe, where she met some of the organization's leaders and learned that the United States had not ratified the Treaty of Geneva (1864) that had created the organization. Barton was invited to assist in the work of the International Red Cross during the Franco-Prussian War of 1870-1871. Her experiences gave her a new perspective on the suffering of civilians during war—she had worked almost entirely on behalf of soldiers in the Civil War. Friendship with Grand Duchess Louise of Baden, a Red Cross leader, resulted in Barton working six months in Strasbourg. She was convinced of the value of the Red Cross and determined that supporting self-help was better than handouts. She held these convictions the rest of her life.

In 1872, Barton returned to the United States, after suffering a nervous breakdown that some regarded as partially psychosomatic. Retiring from public life to stay in a sanatorium eventually improved her health. In 1877, she decided to form an American Red Cross society to gather funds to help victims of the Russo-Turkish War. She received permission from the International Red Cross, and began a campaign to secure American ratification of the Treaty of Geneva. U.S. government officials, however, insisted that since the country observed the tenets of the treaty, there was no reason for a formal alliance.

Barton lobbied diligently for ratification. She sought help from friends in Washington, D.C., cultivated the press, and relied upon her friendship with members of the Grand Army of the Republic, a Civil War veterans group that had honored her. To increase awareness of the work of the Red Cross, Barton made peacetime disaster relief a priority. Progress was slow, but the treaty was ratified in 1882. Her group was officially recognized by the government, paving the way for it to be associated with the International Red Cross. This recognition helped Barton launch her next campaign: to make the American Association of the Red Cross the central relief agency in the United States.

The 1880's and 1890's were times of heroic effort for Barton. Her labor was certainly greatly increased by her refusal to yield any share of control, and, during the decades of her presidency, she and the Red Cross were essentially synonymous. She wanted the national agency to be the center of a network of state groups, but she was frequently drawn away from organizing to oversee field work and was hampered by continual shortages of funds. She also spent much of 1883 running a women's prison at the request of Benjamin Butler, the former Union general who had become governor of Massachusetts. Assisting Butler with his political problems concerning the funding of the progressive prison, Barton established that the costs were mostly appropriate, despite sloppy administrative work. Unfortunately, her efforts on Butler's behalf diverted Barton's attention from the urgent demands of Red Cross work.

For the rest of her life, however, Barton devoted herself almost exclusively to Red Cross work. She traveled, seeking funds and public support—sometimes for herself as well as her cause—and attended annual meetings of the International Red Cross, where she was accepted as a delegate when no other woman was even allowed on the convention floor. She was a hero to feminists, whose cause she supported, although never so vigorously as to cause hostility toward the Red Cross. Field work continued to beckon, including relief efforts in the wake of floods in the Ohio and Mississippi River valleys in 1884 and an earthquake in Charleston, South Carolina, in 1886. She allowed the head of the New Orleans chapter to lead an effort in a yellow fever epidemic around Jacksonville, Florida, only to find that the nurses he took resembled camp followers more than care-givers. This incident confirmed her determination to do everything herself.

Barton received praise from the press for relief efforts in the wake of the 1889 Johnstown flood, but she was later greatly criticized for not keeping track of expenditures. Some of the expenses appear to have been inappropriate, though not fraudulent, but her lack of receipts made defense against such criticism almost impossible. Barton hoped to parlay the Johnstown success into government funding for the Red Cross as the official agency for coordinating wartime relief. This effort stalled, however, and she turned her attention to efforts to alleviate a Russian famine.

By the mid-1890's, relief funds were at a low ebb and criticism of her poor accounting hampered the activities of both the American and international organizations. Although Barton was in her seventies and her energy was beginning to decline, she repudiated every criticism, attacked critics, and continued. In 1896, she went to Turkey to aid Armenians suffering from Turkish atrocities. She secured permission from the Turkish sultan to send Dr. Julian Hubbell, one of her most loyal collaborators, into Armenia, where he had significant success.

Back in the United States, she found appeals from Cuban civilians suffering in the struggle against Spain. Since the United States government wanted to keep out of the situation, little was being done to provide relief. Eventually, Barton went to survey the situation with a committee of relief agencies. When the head of another agency criticized her work and tried to supplant her, Barton returned to the United States and got her rival discredited. By the time she returned to Cuba, however, the Spanish-American War had begun. The New York Red Cross chapter, which, along with several others, had been acting almost autonomously, provided necessary assistance to stateside military hospitals, and the California chapter sent aid to the Pacific front in the Philippines. Barton headed for Cuba, eventually leaving without official sanction. Although intending to help civilians, her team stumbled into a battle fought by the Rough Riders. To her delight, Barton found herself nursing soldiers again. Important work with civilians followed, and the Red Cross proved its value.

The organization's efforts during the Spanish-American War and its aftermath did lead to legislation granting a federal charter to the American Red Cross in 1900. In the end, however, this success was also Barton's downfall. Concerned that donations were in decline, some members of the Red Cross organized independent efforts during Barton's absence and were reluctant to relinquish control to her. The crisis came after a hurricane in Galveston, Texas, in September of 1900. Barton launched relief efforts without consulting the organization's new board of directors, and her bookkeeping was so lackadaisical that the national treasurer resigned rather than defend her expenditures. The struggle went on for several years, becoming more acrimonious because Barton came to regard her critics as personal foes. Finally, Barton was forced to resign all ties to the Red Cross in 1904. She did retain quarters at a house in Maryland that had been built largely with her own money and had served as Red Cross headquarters during the final years of her presidency. Continuing to support public health efforts and the woman's rights movement, Barton alternated living in Maryland and in North Oxford, Massachusetts, until her death in 1912.

Summary

Clara Barton established the American Red Cross almost singlehandedly. Earlier efforts to do so had failed, and the nation lacked a major disaster relief agency. Rival organizations did arise, but most were launched later in imitation of Barton's efforts. Barton's prodigious labor and self-sacrifice on behalf of establishing the American Red Cross ultimately earned for her the recognition she desired, yet she never allowed her ego to prevent her from giving unstintingly of her work and wealth to those who needed help.

That ego did, however, cause problems. The combination of childhood insecurity and individual success in the Civil War rendered Barton incapable of working equally with others. She preferred to work with trusted aides who deferred to her authority, and she seemed to interpret any initiative outside her control as a personal affront. This caused Barton much disquiet and slowed the growth of the Red Cross. Although most if not all the charges made against her personally were without merit, it cannot be denied that had she shared leadership with someone who was willing to do the vital paperwork much more progress could have been made. Furthermore, Barton's reputation would not have been sullied. Nevertheless, her crusading spirit on behalf of nursing reform created for Barton an impressive legacy.

Bibliography
Barton, Clara. *The Story of My Childhood.* Reprint. New York: Arno Press, 1980. Although it was intended to be the first chapter of an autobiography and hence covers only Barton's first years, this work is a valuable source given the influence of her childhood on her character.
Barton, William E. *The Life of Clara Barton.* 2 vols. Boston: Houghton Mifflin, 1922. An old-fashioned and uncritical biography, but filled with details and information often missing in modern studies.
Dulles, Foster Rhea. *The American Red Cross.* New York: Harper and Brothers, 1950. Written by an excellent historian, this valuable work provides background on Barton and her work with the Red Cross.
Oates, Stephen B. *A Woman of Valor: Clara Barton and the Civil War.* New York: Free Press, 1994. Best known for his biographies of Abraham Lincoln, Oates provides a vivid account of Clara Barton's early career during the Civil War years. While revealing Barton's drive to succeed and her skill in generating public support for her relief efforts, Oates's detailed narrative also sheds light on her difficult personality and strained emotional life, thus providing a welcome corrective to older, less critical accounts.
Pryor, Elizabeth B. *Clara Barton: Professional Angel.* Philadelphia: University of Pennsylvania, 1987. Although informed by the author's research into numerous primary sources, this biography suffers somewhat from a lack of critical distance in its approach, as suggested by its subtitle.
Ross, Ishbel. *Angel of the Battlefield: The Life of Clara Barton.* New York: Harper and Brothers, 1956. A reasonable biography, though somewhat dated. Like most of the work on Barton, this volume is adulatory in its approach.

Fred R. van Hartesveldt

KATHARINE LEE BATES

Born: August 12, 1859; Falmouth, Massachusetts
Died: March 28, 1929; Wellesley, Massachusetts
Areas of Achievement: Education and literature
Contribution: Although she edited critical editions of many literary classics, compiled collections of children's folk and fairy tales, translated ancient Spanish and Icelandic legends and ballads, and authored textbooks on English literature and history that are still in use, Katharine Lee Bates is best remembered for her own poetry—especially "America the Beautiful."

Early Life

Katharine Lee Bates was born on August 12, 1859, in Falmouth, Massachusetts to William Bates and his wife, Cornelia Frances Lee Bates. William Bates had been graduated from Middlebury College in Vermont, where his father had been president, before entering Andover Theological Seminary. After teaching for two years, he accepted a call to his first parish in Uxbridge, where he met and married Cornelia, a graduate of Mount Holyoke College who was also a schoolteacher. The couple settled in Northbridge, rearing their two sons and their daughter Jane before moving to Falmouth, where William had accepted a call to be the town's Congregational minister in 1858. Located on Cape Cod between Buzzards Bay and Nantucket Sound in the heart of New England's historic whaling district, Falmouth had been settled two centuries earlier by Quakers dedicated to the ideals of religious tolerance and freedom.

Within a month of young Katie's birth, her father was dead of a spinal tumor. Her mother Cornelia supplemented her widow's pension from the Massachusetts Congregational Society by raising and selling garden produce, eggs, and poultry and by sewing. Her sons picked cranberries, drove cows, fished for herring to sell as bait, and sold muskrat skins. The entire family did piecework by tying tags produced locally by the Dennison Manufacturing Company. Although her family struggled in near poverty, Katharine was surrounded by the warmth and love of her mother, who worked hard to educate her children. Eventually, Cornelia was called to care for her invalid sister Catherine, who lived in Grantville near the town of Wellesley. Eager to begin a new life, Cornelia Bates and her children moved from Falmouth to a house in Grantville generously provided for them by her sister's friends.

Life's Work

The year that Katharine Bates and her family moved to Grantville also marked the founding of Wellesley College in the adjoining town of Wellesley. Katharine learned of the plans for the college from her ailing aunt. Dedicated to higher education for women, the school was to be built on land surrounding Lake Waban owned by Henry Fowle Durant and his wife. The Durants had originally intended to give the property to their son, who had died. After learning of these plans, Katharine began to consider the possibility of attending the new college. Finishing her studies at Needham High School, Katharine moved with her family to Newtonville in 1874 after her aunt's death and entered Newton High School as a postgraduate student and teacher in preparation for attending Wellesley. In 1876, Katharine was accepted as a member of Wellesley's second graduating class and began an academic affiliation that was to last for more than forty years.

The college's Latin motto, translated as "Not to be ministered unto, but to minister," was especially suited to the career interests of a minister's daughter and granddaughter. Bates embarked on her Wellesley career with great enthusiasm, taking part readily in a scheduled curriculum that included varied course work as well as boating, calisthenics, and miscellaneous housework assigned for an hour a day. Amidst the wild natural beauty of the Massachusetts lake country so celebrated by Henry David Thoreau, academic study could go forward in its most idealized form. From the beginning of Bates's studies at Wellesley, the Browning Room served as a source of comfort and inspiration, a welcome haven from classes and a respite from her studies. She enjoyed browsing through the manuscripts and letters of Elizabeth Barrett Browning while relaxing in a comfortable, homelike atmosphere.

While she was still a student, Bates began to exert her lifelong influence on the college. Elected by her classmates to serve as a member of the first Committee of Five, Bates helped fashion the class constitution. Soon, her classmates chose her to be their perpetual president. The class of 1880 went on to organize the college's first glee club and its first boating crews. When summer vacation arrived, Bates confided to her friends that she longed for rest and would dread the return to study and writing. Yet she did return, fulfilling her own calling to become an educator.

In 1880, Katharine Lee Bates was graduated from Wellesley College after completing a double specialization in Greek and English. As Class Day poet, she was granted the opportunity to read some of her poetry, written in the style of New England poets such as Henry Wadsworth Longfellow and incorporating the rhythmic verse style and long lines favored by the English poet Algernon Swinburne. In the autumn of that year, Bates accepted a teaching position at Natick High School; she moved to Dana Hall to teach, beginning in 1881. Three years later, she was offered a post in the English department at Wellesley.

During her long teaching career, Bates introduced many innovations in the education of women and established a model of scholarship that was admired by her students and colleagues alike. In 1890, she was appointed to serve as chair of the English department, a post she retained until her retirement in 1925. Aside from study and lecture trips in the western United States and several trips to England and the European continent, Bates remained in Wellesley. It was during one of these lecture trips that Bates was inspired to write her famous poem. During the summer of 1893, Bates visited the World's Columbian Exhibition in Chicago on her way to lecture at a special session held at Colorado College. Bates was deeply impressed by the majestic architecture of the exhibition halls, whose pure white color gave the fairgrounds the nickname of the "White City." During her stay in Colorado, Bates took a journey to the summit of Pikes Peak. The view of the vast landscape spread out below her inspired Bates to write a poem in her personal journal that eventually became known as "America the Beautiful." The poem was not published until July 4, 1895, when it appeared in a periodical called *The Congregationalist*. Bates received so many suggestions from readers who had seen the poem that she rewrote various sections and submitted her revised version for publication in the *Boston Evening Transcript* in November of 1904. The poem became immensely popular, and the National Federation of Music Clubs sponsored a contest in 1926 to find an appropriate musical setting for the poem. Soon, a movement began to lobby for the song's adoption as the national anthem; although it was not selected, "America the Beautiful" eventually became widely accepted as one of the nation's best-known and best-loved songs.

Despite her popularity as the author of "America the Beautiful," Bates remained dedicated to her primary career as an educator. Since her life at the college was full with the duties of both administrator and educator, Bates welcomed the domestic assistance of her sister Jane, who took on the role of typist, cook, and housekeeper, and the scholarly assistance of her mother, who worked at translating literature and folklore from Spanish into English. Bates's home served as a gathering place for students and faculty members, and she entertained distinguished guests ranging from Matthew Arnold and William Butler Yeats to Vachel Lindsay, Carl Sandburg, and Robert Frost. Women writers such as Julia Ward Howe, Amy Lowell, and Sara Teasdale were also among Bates's guests. After her retirement from active teaching in 1925, Bates worked on a collection of poems published as *The Pilgrim Ship* (1926) and submitted articles and book reviews to various periodicals. Suffering from various illnesses during her later years, Bates was particularly saddened by the death of her sister Jane in 1928. Katharine Bates died of pneumonia at her home in Wellesley in 1929 at the age of sixty-nine.

Summary

During her lifetime, Katharine Bates established a solid scholarly reputation with the publication of more than forty volumes of work, including poetry, literary histories and anthologies, critical editions of literary classics, English translations of Spanish and Icelandic legends and ballads, as well as children's literature based on other legends and folktales. She was a dedicated educator whose efforts spanned a period when the pursuit of higher education by young women became more common than it had been during Bates's own adolescence. Her contribution to the education of numerous young women during her years at Wellesley was honored on the occasion of her retirement, when the college awarded her an honorary doctorate. Despite these achievements, Bates's most memorable work remains her poem "America the Beautiful," a heartfelt anthem that celebrates the soul of the country she loved and the ideals it embodies.

Bibliography
Bates, Katharine Lee. *America the Beautiful*. Illustrated by Neil Waldman. New York:

Atheneum, 1993. Bates's most famous poem, "America the Beautiful," serves as the text for this picture book, published in honor of the poem's centennial anniversary. Waldman's full-color, double-page paintings illustrate the various images evoked by Bates in the poem.

——————. *The English Religious Drama.* Reprint. Port Washington, N.Y.: Kennikat Press, 1966. Originally published in 1893, this text was based on Bates's studies at Oxford. The work established Bates's scholarly reputation and is still considered an excellent academic source on its subject.

——————. *The Retinue and Other Poems.* New York: E. P. Dutton, 1918. One of six collections of poetry, including one consisting of poems written under the pseudonym "James Lincoln," published by Bates during her lifetime. This small volume contains eighty-one poems, most of which were written during World War I.

Burgess, Dorothy Whittemore Bates. *Dream and Deed: The Story of Katharine Lee Bates.* Norman: University of Oklahoma Press, 1952. Burgess, the daughter of Bates's brother Arthur, provides a comprehensive chronological study of the educator and poet. Understandably adulatory in tone, this biography contains useful information on Bates's family background and makes liberal use of quotations from Bates's personal papers, allowing the subject to speak for herself.

Drury, Michael. "Why She Wrote America's Favorite Song." *Reader's Digest* 143 (July, 1993): 90-93. This article, which originally appeared in *Woman's Day* magazine in January of 1976, contains a tribute to Bates in the form of a recollection of the trip to Colorado that inspired "America the Beautiful." Reveals Bates's self-effacing modesty in the face of the poem's widespread popularity and her open-handed generosity in sharing the poem with its many fans.

Herst, Herman, Jr. "What the Country Is All About." *Stamps* 24 (December 12, 1992): 344. In the course of his personal commentary on the U.S. Postal Service's decision to issue a commemorative stamp of rock 'n' roll star Elvis Presley instead of honoring the accomplishment of Bates, whom he believes is a more worthy subject for such an honor, Herst provides a brief profile of Bates and makes a strong argument for her significance in encouraging a healthy spirit of patriotism among the American people.

Myers, Elizabeth P. *Katharine Lee Bates: Girl Poet.* Indianapolis: Bobbs-Merrill, 1961. Written for young readers, this juvenile biography of Bates provides lightly fictionalized adaptations of anecdotes taken from the personal diaries Bates began in her childhood and continued to keep throughout her life.

Betsey Pender

AMY MARCY BEACH

Born: September 5, 1867; Henniker, New Hampshire
Died: December 27, 1944; New York, New York
Area of Achievement: Music
Contribution: Amy Beach was the first American woman to achieve international fame as a composer, and the first major American composer, man or woman, to be trained entirely in the United States. She was, besides, a virtuoso pianist.

Early Life

Amy Marcy Cheney was born on September 5, 1867. Her father, Charles Abbott Cheney, was a graduate of both Philips Exeter Academy and Bates College. Though engaged in the manufacture, importation, and sale of paper, Charles Cheney had a lifelong interest in mathematics and literature. Amy's mother, Clara Imogene Marcy Cheney, came from a distinguished family, and pursued a hobby of music with considerable zeal and talent.

Amy was an only child. Her parents quickly recognized that she had unusual intellectual and musical talents. She mastered her alphabet at seventeen months and read easily at three years. She could carry a tune at the age of one and could improvise harmonies to her mother's melodies at age two. Endowed with absolute pitch, the small child would correct her elders if they started a tune in the wrong key.

Amy's parents followed two principles. On the one hand, they encouraged her to cultivate her remarkable gifts; fortunately Clara Beach was herself a sufficiently expert musician to supervise Amy's training through early childhood. On the other hand, they never allowed their daughter to know how precocious she was; by the time Amy realized that most children could not play full-scale sonatas on the piano or compose waltzes in their heads, she had developed the personality of a normal, well-balanced child. She also had sufficient discipline to improve her playing while pursuing a complete course of education in one of the best private schools in the Boston area, where her family had moved in 1870. At seven, she performed in public for the first time. On her program were works by Ludwig van Beethoven, Frédéric Chopin, and, as would so often be the case for almost seventy years thereafter, herself.

Amy did not go to Europe either for piano lessons or lessons in composition. She had six years of lessons with Boston's two preeminent piano pedagogues, Johann Ernest Perabo and Carl Baermann—each thoroughly trained by Europe's best. Although she studied composition for only one year, her mentor, William Junius Hill, was also eminently qualified. What is truly remarkable is that, other than this brief training, she was entirely self-taught in composition, working out elaborate systems for studying works of the great masters and translating Hector Berlioz's classic book on orchestration into English.

By the 1870's, the educated classes of Boston and surrounding communities had taken a passionate interest in performing music in secular and religious choral societies, in marching and concert bands, in amateur and professional orchestras, and in church. Above all, there was the piano, found in almost every parlor of the prosperous classes, with serious young men as well as young women learning to play it, often quite proficiently. Growing up in Boston, Amy Marcy Cheney was surrounded by good music, much to her pleasure and instruction. In 1880, the eccentric millionaire Henry Lee Higginson founded the Boston Symphony Orchestra. Meanwhile, the Cheney family continued to relish literary as well as musical culture. The old "Autocrat of the Breakfast Table," Oliver Wendell Holmes, Sr., was one of the family's friends. In 1906, Amy composed a cantata to the text of his favorite among his own poems, "The Chambered Nautilus."

Amy Marcy Cheney married Dr. Henry Harris Aubrey Beach on December 2, 1885, less than three months after her eighteenth birthday. The marriage was unusual, since Dr. Beach was more than twice the age of his bride. Unusual or not, the union had the full blessing of Mr. and Mrs. Cheney. The wedding ceremony, performed by the Reverend Phillips Brooks, took place in the ornately Romanesque Trinity Episcopal Church in Copley Square, designed by the acclaimed architect Henry Hobson Richardson shortly before his death. The Beaches settled into a comfortable, useful, and busy existence at 28 Commonwealth Avenue in Boston, at the center of Brahmin high culture. Besides being a leader in his medical profession, Dr. Beach knew and loved music. He encouraged his gifted young wife to continue composing.

Her marriage probably curtailed Amy Beach's career as a virtuoso pianist, for during her twenty-five years of marriage she performed in public only on special occasions, and never took the long concert trips characteristic of virtuoso performers. During their marriage, the Beaches remained childless, and their ample wealth allowed Amy to entrust most domestic duties to her servants, leaving her free to pursue her musical interests. She pleased her husband and herself with an outpouring of compositions in virtually every musical form. For the rest of her long life, the composer-pianist styled herself, "Mrs. H. H. A. Beach"; that is how her name appeared in concert programs, on her published compositions, in her occasional published writings, and in essays about her in musical journals.

Life's Work

Amy Cheney had started both aspects of her public musical career, performance and composition, before her marriage to Dr. Beach. She first performed with a symphony orchestra at the age of sixteen. A year later she performed Felix Mendelssohn's Piano Concerto No. 1 with the Theodore Thomas Orchestra, and shortly before her marriage she made her debut with the Boston Symphony Orchestra under Wilhelm Gericke, playing Chopin's Second Piano Concerto. In 1885, she also published her *Four Songs*, op.1.

In 1886, within the first year of her marriage, she composed an ambitious Mass in E-flat Major, for four solo singers, a large chorus, symphony orchestra, and organ. Although the work breaks no new paths in its musical language, it does display Amy Beach's mastery of the expressive styles of her age and exhibits both beauty and originality in setting the familiar words of the Latin ordinary. Amy Beach's Mass, which requires more than an hour to perform, cannot be used in the routine services of the church; like the *Missa Solemnis* (1823) of Beethoven or the *Messa da requiem* (1874) of Giuseppe Verdi, it is intended for concert performance. Later, Beach wrote many anthems, cantatas, and settings of the service, but she never again composed a work as grand or ambitious as her Mass, perhaps because she realized that few musical organizations had the resources to perform such a work.

The critical success of her Mass, several songs, and solo piano pieces led many American musicians and critics to hail Amy Beach as the nation's foremost woman composer when she was barely twenty-five years old. Her reputation led to a commission from the Women's Committee for the Chicago World's Fair and Columbian Exposition, to compose a work to celebrate the opening of the Women's Building, the first of its kind, at the fair in May, 1893. Beach fulfilled this commission with her *Festival Jubilate*, op. 17, a setting of Psalm 100 for large chorus and orchestra. In 1893, she also completed a short, highly effective Romance for Violin and Piano, dedicated to the brilliant American violin virtuoso, Maud Powell. Powell and Beach performed the piece at the Exposition and, at the urgent request of their audience, performed it again. A few years later the Belgian Eugène Ysaÿe, one of the world's foremost violinists, added her Sonata for Violin and Piano (1896) to his repertoire. The fame of America's foremost woman composer had reached Europe.

The year 1896 also saw Amy Beach complete her *Gaelic* Symphony, op. 32, which was first performed by the Boston Symphony Orchestra conducted by Emil Paur. The symphony had its champions, but there were some critics who thought it less than fully successful. While opinion remains divided on its merits nearly one hundred years since its debut, it is evident that Beach's only symphony was an imposing achievement: cogently organized, richly orchestrated, and full of melody and excitement.

More successful with contemporary audiences was her only Piano Concerto (1900) dedicated to the celebrated virtuoso Teresa Carreño, but played more often and perhaps to greater effect by Beach herself. As with her *Gaelic* Symphony and Mass, Beach's concerto demonstrated her ability to handle large and complex musical forms with skill and gusto. Increasingly, however, her most effective works seemed to be in smaller forms, especially solo piano works, songs for voice and piano, and varied works for small instrumental and vocal ensembles.

The death of her husband in 1910 proved a major turning point in the life of Amy Beach. She arranged for her first European tour and spent the next four years performing in Europe. Orchestras, audiences, and critics accepted her as a major composer and piano virtuoso. The outbreak of World War I in 1914 abruptly halted her tour. Beach returned to the United States to live in New York which, she recognized, had become the musically most exciting city in the United States. She took up residence at the American Women's Club and also maintained summer homes on Cape Cod and in her native New Hampshire.

Beginning in 1921, Amy Beach became a frequent resident at the McDowell summer colony for artists in Peterborough, New Hampshire. Through her activities at the colony and through her frequent performances, she kept in touch with old friends, among the finest musicians and writers of the United States, and befriended many new ones. At the MacDowell colony, she was famous for winning far more than her share of the games of skill played after working hours. Once, the American violinist Albert Spalding visited the colony to perform Beethoven's *Kreutzer* Sonata, but had forgotten to bring the piano score. Beach played it with him flawlessly, entirely from memory.

Amy Beach continued to compose and perform until well into her seventies. She died in her New York apartment in 1944.

Summary

Before Amy Beach, no woman had appeared in the front rank of American composers. Her example undoubtedly inspired other women, and she helped as much as any male in her generation to win worldwide appreciation for serious music composed in the United States. In more than five decades of composing, she produced more than two hundred pieces—some short and relatively easy, others complex and demanding—in virtually every serious musical form. Her songs were most widely performed during her life; she had an exceptional gift for setting words. She was also an expert and popular performer throughout her career and one of those immensely gifted people who offered encouragement and advice to fellow artists, literary as well as musical. She was a beloved and unique figure in the cultural life of the nation from 1885 to her death in 1944.

Bibliography

Beach, Mrs. H. H. A. *The Life and Music of Amy Beach: The First Woman Composer of America*. Pacific, Mo.: Creative Keyboard Publications, 1992. This collection of musical scores of many of Beach's piano compositions includes a sixteen-page biographical sketch with informative details on Beach's life and work.

Benninghoff, Susan R. "A Woman's Classics." *The Washington Post*, October 3, 1984, p. B7. As part of an article spotlighting a planned performance of Beach's Mass in E-flat, Benninghoff provides a capsule biography of Beach's life and explains the resurgent interest in Beach's work.

Block, Adrienne Fried. "Amy Marcy (Cheney) Beach." In *The New Grove Dictionary of American Music*, edited by H. Wiley Hitchcock and Stanley Sadie. 4 vols. New York: Grove's Dictionaries of Music, 1986. Though brief, this sketch benefits from Block's deep knowledge of her subject and contains a catalog of Beach's compositions that is almost as complete as the one by Myrna Eden listed below.

_____ . "On Beach's Variations on Balkan Themes, op. 60." *American Music* 11 (Fall, 1993): 368-371. Block, a noted scholar of Beach's work, takes issue with assertions made by E. Douglas Bomberger in his musical analysis of "Variations on Balkan Themes" contained in the article listed below.

Bomberger, E. Douglas. "Motivic Development in Amy Beach's Variations on Balkan Themes, op. 60." *American Music* 10 (Fall, 1992): 326-347. This article illuminates Beach's breadth of culture as well as her compositional skill by analyzing her use of Balkan folk songs in a piece which she first composed for piano in 1904, revised for orchestra in 1936, and revised later for two pianos in 1942.

Eden, Myrna G. *Energy and Individuality in the Art of Anna Huntington, Sculptor and Amy Beach, Composer.* Metuchen, N.J.: Scarecrow Press, 1987. Myrna Eden's comparison of two outstanding female artists illuminates both brilliantly, especially as regards their place in the high culture—"the cultivated tradition"—of their times. Eden's chapter titles encapsulate her sensitive and technically expert analysis: "Spiritual Life," "Moral Earnestness," "Symbolic Expression," and "Folklore and History." The book contains a complete catalog of Beach's works and a discography of recordings available through 1987.

Hughes, Rupert. *Contemporary American Composers.* Boston: Page, 1900. Although long out of print, this work reflects the high standing Amy Beach enjoyed among her peers, men as well as women, at a relatively early stage in her career.

Robert McColley

MARY BEARD

Born: August 5, 1876; Indianapolis, Indiana
Died: August 14, 1958; Phoenix, Arizona
Areas of Achievement: Historiography and social reform
Contribution: An engaged, creative intellectual, Beard demonstrated—through her historical research and her writings—women's vital contributions to civilization.

Early Life

Born during the centennial year of the Declaration of Independence, Mary Ritter was the eldest daughter in a family of six children, all raised in the upper-middle-class comforts of their Indianapolis, Indiana, home. Eli Foster Ritter, Mary's father, was a successful lawyer, a Republican, and a devout Methodist. Her mother, née Narcissa Lockwood, came from a strong southern Protestant background. Better educated than most women of her time, Narcissa had graduated from a female academy to work as a schoolteacher. Daughter Mary initially followed much the same course. She left Indianapolis for nearby Greencastle, in 1894, to enter DePauw University. There, she concentrated her studies in the fields of government (political science), literature, and language. Graduating in 1897, she spent the next three years teaching German in an Indianapolis high school, until 1900 and her marriage and subsequent forty-eight-year partnership with Charles Austin Beard.

Little direct knowledge remains of Mary Ritter's early life, or for that matter about any of her private life. She and husband, Charles, who became one of the country's most influential—and controversial—historians, ironically determined to leave no documents regarding their private affairs. To the consternation of other historians, Mary Beard faithfully executed that wish after her husband's death. The Beards chose to let the world's remembrances of them emanate from their writings and other intellectual activities.

In 1897, Charles Beard had begun studies abroad at the University of Oxford. Following their marriage, the Beards lived in England for two years, first in Oxford, where Charles was instrumental in founding the "free university," Ruskin Hall, and then in Manchester, where Mary was deeply moved by the appalling conditions of working-class life.

While in England, Mary came under the influence of American feminist Charlotte Perkins Gilman through reading her book *Women and Economics* (1898), a denunciation of regnant gender roles. Almost simultaneously, Mary was inspired by the militant British suffragette Emmeline Pankhurst to whom Mary attributed her own lifelong interest in the plight of female workers. Both Mary and Charles came to believe that the assemblage of facts, mere learning, was worthless unless it was dedicated to the task of freeing the world; this philosophy coalesced during the years while the young couple were living in England. Mary, in any event, had begun studiously reading history and, tentatively, had begun writing it as well. Writing history, both she and Charles agreed, could also change history.

Life's Work

While her husband Charles studied and then taught history and political science at Columbia University from 1900 to 1915, distinguishing himself not only by the fecundity of his work but also by its arresting quality—his *An Economic Interpretation of the Constitution of the United States* (1913) quite notably—Mary Beard was preoccupied with children and family. As her children matured and she was freed from some of these responsibilities, Mary resumed her activism in 1910, first with women's suffrage organizations and then with the New York Women's Trade Union League. Like many women of the Progressive Era, she devoted her attention to a variety of reform issues. Involvement with additional suffragist groups followed later. These causes, which obviously had carried over with full, if delayed, intensity, were continuations of the profound concerns fostered during her sojourn in England. Her efforts involved stints of politicking, picketing, and then editing and writing. The first of her joint works with Charles, *American Citizenship*, appeared in 1914; her solo works from this period include *Women's Work in Municipalities* (1915) and *A Short History of the American Labor Movement* (1920). Throughout these activities, however, manifesting her characteristic singularity, she publicly eschewed identification with any professional "guild," a modestly contemptuous term for the male mandarinate dominating the historical and other professions. Mary Beard was a self-styled "student and writer," a description that subsequently never varied.

The Beards' joint authorship from the early 1920's until the 1940's was remarkable not only for its quantity but also for its quality and its influence. Their *History of the United States* appeared in 1921, *The Rise of American Civilization* (2 volumes) in 1927, *The Making of American Civilization* in 1937, *America in Midpassage* (2 volumes) in 1939, *The American Spirit* in 1942, and *A Basic History of the United States* in 1944. Almost universally, the historical profession treated these joint works as if they were solely Charles Beard's. Feminists were virtually alone in reacting against this treatment, noting that if nothing else, it violated a basic professional canon: accuracy. Charles Beard himself emphasized that the works were coauthored, and ample evidence later confirmed that Mary Beard had been responsible for the pair's decision to include the vital role of women in the events chronicled in these publications.

In those writings that were singularly hers, Mary Beard sought to recover what to her was the distinctive and monumentally important role of women in the development of world civilization. In addition to her numerous articles, Mary Beard's two major works stand out for their novelty, vigor, and eventual influence: *On Understanding Women* (1931), and *Woman as Force in History* (1946). Recognizing her failure to breach the walls of male-dominated historiography, if only because the reading and professional communities saluted her husband while failing even to touch their hats for her, she published her basic positions, though with different materials, in each of these works.

It was Mary Beard's belief that when sufficient evidence was collected, women would be shown to have played a role in the history of civilization not only equal to men's but also different from men's. Each work was something of a cri de coeur for research on women's history, and as much as anyone else she would eventually be credited by later historians such as Nancy Cott, Ann Lane, Gerda Lerner, Bonnie Smith, and Barbara Turoff as the founder of twentieth century women's studies.

To the dismay of her feminist friends and admirers, however, Beard quarreled with their strategy of seeking to compete equally with men. That approach, she believed, crippled women's capacity to make distinctive contributions to their societies. Indeed, it was she who attacked the theory that women historically had been oppressed or victimized by men. Because of their intensive political, institutional, and legal research, many historiographers had in fact lent credence to this dogma, but Beard argued that unquestioning acceptance of this notion of completely subjugated women obscured the true historical significance of women's roles. Although Western law clearly had subordinated women, she denied that law as codified by men had accurately reflected practice. Despite legal disabilities, women had been and continued to be major contributors to all civilization, more so, in Beard's view, than was indicated by the preemptive claims of men.

Feminine contributions, too, extended well beyond women's mere existence, their giving birth to and raising children. In what she described as the "long history," Mary Beard contraverted assertions drawn by others from Thomas Carlyle and Karl Marx that had "shot women into the lumber room of the past." Rather, she cited the dicta of enlightened male historians such as Germany's Oswald Spengler to the effect that while Man made history, Women were history. Women had exercised seminal influences in launching civilization, in laying the foundations of social organization, in elevating men from their normally bestial conditions (resulting in the traditional worship of women as goddesses), in building the great states of the West (even through women's participation in battle), and—in the long view—in governing them. Not until eighteenth century commercial and political revolutions, according to Mary Beard, did women lose their historical eminence to parliaments of men. Even so, in the post-Enlightenment world of social philosophies, women continued to dominate and guide the great intellectual salons.

Mary Beard was frequently criticized for the awkwardness of her prose, and to some critics her work seemed strained as she ransacked classical and early modern history for women to exemplify her thesis. Nevertheless, both before and after her death in 1958, she provoked intense curiosity among both sexes about women's place in the past, thereby initiating greater interest in women's roles in the present as well as in the future.

Summary

Mary Beard helped pioneer the historical investigation of women that ultimately inspired the women's studies programs of the 1970's and 1980's. By the 1990's, Beard clearly had inspired a substantial number of feminist scholars who, having read her work in graduate schools, had themselves become productive scholars. Ann Lane, who became professor of history and director of women's studies at Colgate

University, was one, along with Gerda Lerner, Bonnie Smith, and Nancy Cott— feminist scholars whom Beard's writing inspired and provided with intellectual direction. The same inspiration also moved Barbara Kivel Turoff, author of a study on Mary Beard, to observe that by 1978 a Beard renaissance was underway, testimony being Mount Holyoke College's Berkshire Conference, a scholarly gathering dedicated to Beard and the lasting significance of her work.

Yet, Mary Beard's writings only partially represented the range of her activities. True to her craft, she pioneered attempts to found her principles upon documents that filled the vast gaps that had obscured a clear understanding of women's place in history. Acting on the initiatives of Rosika Schwimmer, a Hungarian-born feminist, Beard took a leading role in the World Center for Women's Archives in 1935, which in time expanded to encompass the Sophia Smith Collection at Smith College and Radcliffe College's Schlesinger Library. Beard's perception of these documentary collections on women was not as antiquarian landfills, but more ambitiously as centers of an educational revolution and as reserves that all women might utilize better to inform their public protests and extend their social leadership. The Women's Archives failed in 1940. Its purpose was soon revitalized, however, and its resources recovered by a rising generation of scholars whose specialty was the women's history Beard founded and by the new generation of feminists who were already deriving instruction and inspiration from Mary Beard's work only a few years after her death in 1958.

Bibliography

Beard, Mary R. *Woman as Force in History: A Study in Traditions and Realities.* New York: Macmillan, 1946. Reprint. New York: Octagon Books, 1981. In this work, covering the period from classical times to the twentieth century, Beard takes issue with feminists, denying women's historical "subjugation" by men. Although her writing is frequently dense and repetitive, Beard's main thrusts are quite clear. She sees no reason from her evidence why women should be assigned inferior roles in history, and more than implies that their contributions were generally unique and often superior to men's. Brief annotated bibliography and useful index.

Cott, Nancy F., ed. *A Woman Making History: Mary Ritter Beard Through Her Letters.* New Haven, Conn.: Yale University Press, 1991. An important work considering the paucity of personal documentation on both Beards. Informative introduction by Cott along with her enlightening contextual comment on letters. Mary's admirable spirit and principles shine in many places. Detailed notes to pages; locations to sources and letters; pertinent select bibliography and valuable index. A splendid complement to Beard's formal writing.

Lane, Ann J., ed. *Mary Ritter Beard: A Sourcebook.* New York: Schocken Books, 1977. A well-selected collection of Mary Beard's writings that instructively portrays her views. An important source for classroom and other lay introductions to Mary Beard's work and views. Part I is a good survey. Useful index.

Lerner, Gerda. *The Majority Finds Its Past: Placing Women in History.* New York:

Oxford University Press, 1979. Lerner's introduction is particularly instructive as are her references to Mary Beard throughout. Lerner credits Beard with originating the modern concept of women's history, among her other contributions. Lerner also agrees that Beard raised critical issues with which feminists were still grappling into the late 1970's. Notes, bibliography, index.

Smith, Bonnie. "Seeing Mary Beard," *Feminist Studies* 10 (Fall, 1984): 399-416. Especially useful for Smith's examination of Mary and Charles Beard's close collaboration and Mary's influence on her husband's shift in the 1930's toward explicit relativism.

Turoff, Barbara K. *Mary Beard as Force in History*. Dayton, Ohio: Wright State University, 1979. A study of the several ways in which and reasons why Mary Beard was, and continues to be, influential among those interested in gender issues. Focus is on Beard as a "student and writer" from the 1930's to 1950's. Many photos. Notes, short bibliography, useful index.

Zinsser, Judith P. *History and Feminism: A Glass Half Full*. New York: Twayne, 1993. A clear, cogent survey and comparative analysis of men's history, women's history, and the impact of feminism on each. Chapter 3 places Mary Beard in context as a pioneer in women's studies. Informative annotated notes and references, and annotated suggestions for further reading. Fine index of special value in this type of study. Wonderful introduction to its subject and sources.

Clifton K. Yearley

CECILIA BEAUX

Born: 1855; Philadelphia, Pennsylvania
Died: September 17, 1942; Gloucester, Massachusetts
Area of Achievement: Art
Contribution: As a portraitist of the intellectual and social elite of America in the
decades surrounding 1900, Beaux served as a model of success in the fine arts.

Early Life

Cecilia Beaux was born, probably in 1855, to Cecilia Leavitt, a woman of English
Puritan stock, and Jean Adolphe Beaux, an idealistic French Huguenot. Although—or
perhaps because—her mother died almost immediately after her birth and her father,
despondent over his wife's death, deserted his two young daughters, Cecilia felt
intensely connected to Europe, especially England and France, and the cultural
traditions of her mother and father. She was reared by her maternal grandmother in an
extended, mostly female family. Her uncle, the only male member of the household,
was a positive and supportive figure; but it was her grandmother and aunts who
assumed responsibility for her education.

Beaux's upbringing was genteel, even though the family was of quite limited
means. Her grandmother taught her the importance of self-reliance and discipline:
Any task assumed was a task to be completed. Observing her aunt Eliza, an accomplished musician and watercolorist, Cecilia learned that one could approach the arts
seriously. She also learned to prize self-sufficiency.

Beaux was educated at home. In addition to learning to read and write and learning
to speak French, she was introduced to history, literature, and music. Her aunt taught
her to draw a little by having her copy English lithographs. At fourteen, she went
briefly to an exclusive girls' school for "finishing." Drawing was part of a proper girl's
education, so Beaux was then sent to study with a female relative, Katharine Drinker.
Of independent mind and unusual upbringing, Drinker was at the time in her mid-
thirties and unmarried. She was a professional artist, not a dilettante, supporting her
family through her paintings and through her occasional income from teaching at the
Pennsylvania Academy of the Fine Arts. She proved to be a powerful role model
throughout Beaux's life. After a year, Beaux entered the art school of Adolf van der
Whelen, a Dutch artist living in Philadelphia.

In spite of this instruction, Beaux says in her autobiography, *Background with
Figures* (1930), that she had "not the slightest idea of being an artist." Even as she
began to teach at Miss Sanford's school for girls (assuming the post left vacant by
Drinker when she married) and to take on private students, Beaux did not see herself
as an artist. She drew fossils for publication in scientific journals and painted
children's portraits on porcelain plates, but these were commercial activities taken on
to achieve financial independence. She did not associate them with the elevated nature
of Art. Only when she joined a painting class critiqued by the New York artist William
Sartrain did she turn "a very sharp corner . . . into a new world."

Life's Work

Radical commitment demanded radical action: Cecilia Beaux renounced her commercial work and turned to oil paintings. Her first major piece, *Les Derniers Jours d'Enfance* (*The Last Days of Childhood*, 1883), received accolades when first exhibited in Philadelphia. Thanks to a friend, the painting was entered and accepted in the Paris Salon of 1887. Encouraged by this success, Beaux planned her next step. No American artist could pretend to professional status without an extended European experience. Therefore, Beaux convinced her family to permit her, at age thirty-two and properly chaperoned, to live in Paris from the winter of 1888 to the summer of 1889. In Paris, she attended the Académie Julien, refining her already strong drawing skills and copying Old Masters in the museum of the Louvre. On this, the first of many voyages to Europe, she also became acquainted with the work of Edouard Manet and John Singer Sargent, to whom she was frequently compared. This first experience also confirmed her belief that she was indeed heir to European artistic traditions and convinced her that her dedication to an artistic career required that she forego marriage.

Two considerations may have influenced Beaux's commitment to remaining single. First, late nineteenth century attitudes toward the fine arts likened a career as an artist to a divine calling: Just as a religious vocation required celibacy, an artistic one demanded sacrifice as well. Second, social realities mitigated against marriage for women professionals. The absence of birth control, combined with strong social expectations that a married woman, especially one of the middle or upper class, should not work for pay but should dedicate herself to the well-being of husband and children, created an environment in which marriage inevitably curtailed female ambition. Although Beaux, an intelligent and strikingly attractive woman, had suitors in her youth and, evidently, well into her middle years, she believed that marriage would demand unacceptable compromises in her ambitions. She was not alone among American women artists in making this decision.

She returned to Philadelphia and established a thriving portrait studio. Her work in this period shows a debt to the Americans Thomas Eakins and James McNeill Whistler as well as to the French Barbizon school. These tendencies are modified in her work through a study of the paint handling techniques of William Merritt Chase and Sargent, the design concerns of the Impressionists and, in the early twentieth century, artists such as Henri Matisse. Throughout her career, however, Beaux was careful never to give herself over to an enthusiasm for any single source. She tempered what she could learn from contemporary artists with her lessons from the Masters (especially Peter Paul Rubens, Titian, and Diego Velázquez); in this way, she maintained a stylistic and personal independence. She constructed her portraits with firm designs, using composition as well as accessories to reveal the character of her sitters. She was less likely to flatter than were many other portraitists. Nevertheless, her noncommissioned paintings, portraying close friends and family members, have been considered her strongest works.

By 1900, Beaux was recognized as one of America's premier painters. She opened a studio in New York, and received prestigious commissions from Washington, D.C., to Boston. She was appointed to full faculty membership at the Pennsylvania Academy, the first woman so honored, and taught there from 1895 to 1916. Throughout her life, Beaux strove to establish a disciplined pattern to her day and, in fact, to her year. Winter she spent in New York, but her "long, long summer" months (really April through December) were passed in Gloucester. Most productive in the morning and early afternoon, she would paint during these times, reserving the late afternoons for business arrangements and the evenings for family and her large circle of friends, a circle that included the social and intellectual leaders of the time.

Beaux left a body of works including more than three hundred finished portraits. Key works on which to base a study of her development include, in addition to *Les Derniers Jours d'Enfance*, her portrait of *Fanny Travis Cochran* (1887), *Sita and Sarita* (1893-1894), *Mother and Daughter* (1898), and *Dorothea Gilder* ("After the Meeting," 1914). There is also a series of "white paintings," in which the basic white is modeled with virtuoso passages of pinks, mauves and greens: *Fanny Travis Cochran*, the first, followed by *Ernesta with Nurse* (1894), *New England Woman* (1895), and *Henry Sturgis Drinker* (1898). To this series might be added one of Beaux's political commissions, *Mrs. Theodore Roosevelt and Daughter Ethel* (1901-1902).

Her honors and awards were numerous. Beaux had six works exhibited as a group in the 1896 Paris Salon. This showing received very positive critical notice; one of the paintings, *Sita and Sarita*, was purchased by the French government for the Luxembourg collection. In addition to receiving medals and prizes for individual paintings *(Mother and Daughter*, for example, received no fewer than four gold medals, including the gold medal of the Carnegie Institute), Beaux was elected a member of the National Academy of Arts and Letters in 1894, and an associate of the Société Nationale des Beaux-Arts in 1896. She received honorary degrees from both the University of Pennsylvania and Yale University. The honor that she allowed to crown her professional career in her autobiography, however, was her selection in 1919 as one of five artists to paint portraits of heroes from World War I for a series that was scheduled to tour the United States before being presented to the United States government. Her portraits of Cardinal Mercier of Belgium, President Georges Clemenceau of France, and Admiral Lord Beatty of Great Britain reside in the collections of the National Portrait Gallery in Washington, D.C.

After fracturing her hip during a transatlantic crossing in 1924, Beaux was able to walk only with the support of a crutch or cane. She continued to paint, but began to devote more attention to writing her autobiography. Fond of living a secluded life at her summer home in Massachusetts, Beaux died there of complications from heart disease in 1942.

Summary

Cecilia Beaux was part of a generation of artists who demonstrated that, although study in Europe was still required for complete professional training, one could excel as a professional artist without becoming an expatriate. She left a body of work that includes more than three hundred portraits depicting the cultural and social elite of America's gilded age, and she helped define American portraiture. Furthermore, through her twenty years as an instructor at the Philadelphia Academy of the Fine Arts, she trained innumerable young artists, not only in painting but also in the proper conduct of a career. In developing her style, Beaux remained an independent. She was not the protégé of a famous male artist, nor did she mimic anyone or respond to current fads. Critics of the time consistently evaluated her portraits as among the best produced, equal to those of John Singer Sargent. Her attachment to realism and to traditional forms of modeling led to a decline in her reputation after her death, as avant-garde and abstract styles gained critical favor. Still, through the example of her life, her works, and her teaching, she became a model of professionalism for women and men who aspired to be artists.

Bibliography

Beaux, Cecilia. *Background with Figures*. Boston: Houghton Mifflin, 1930. The autobiography of the artist, written in old age. It gives a full and interesting account of her family life and much information about her training and her attitudes toward art. Not forthcoming about her personal life, although it alludes to her close ties with her circle of friends.

Burns, Sarah. "The 'Earnest, Untiring Worker' and the Magician of the Brush: Gender Politics in the Criticism of Cecilia Beaux and John Singer Sargent." *The Oxford Art Journal* 15, no. 1 (1992): 36-53. This essay examines the language used by nineteenth century critics to evaluate the works of Beaux and Sargent and the ways in which gender distinctions were thus constructed and maintained. Copious end-notes and illustrations.

Cecilia Beaux: Portrait of an Artist. Philadelphia: Pennsylvania Academy of the Fine Arts, 1974. This catalog accompanied the largest retrospective exhibition of Beaux's work to be held; and it includes essays on her life and place in American art. Richly illustrated and the best published source for representations of her work.

Harris, Ann Sutherland, and Linda Nochlin. *Women Artists: 1550-1950*. Los Angeles: Los Angeles County Museum of Art, 1976. The catalog for a traveling exhibit of works by women artists, this is a fundamental and scholarly treatment of the careers of women artists, analyzing the production of each and the social conditions affecting her work. Included are illustrations of Beaux's works and a bibliography.

Rubinstein, Charlotte Streifer. *American Women Artists: From Early Indian Times to the Present*. Boston: G. K. Hall, 1982. A comprehensive study of women in the fine arts in America. In addition to presenting biographical sketches, Rubinstein pays attention to influential teachers and the relationships between artists. Many black and white illustrations; endnotes and selected bibliography, arranged by artist; several useful appendices noting the women participating in key cultural events.

Stein, Judith. "Profile of Cecilia Beaux." *The Feminist Art Journal* 4 (Winter, 1975-1976): 25-33. Biographical essay exploring the psychological make up of the artist and her decision to remain unmarried. Some illustrations.

Tappert, Tara L. "Cecilia Beaux: A Career as a Portraitist." *Women's Studies* 14, no. 4 (1988): 389-411. A biographical essay stressing the importance of female role models to Beaux's success and discussing the artist's ambivalence toward the category of "woman artist" into which she was habitually put. Illustrated; includes endnotes.

Jean Owens Schaefer

CATHARINE BEECHER

Born: September 6, 1800; East Hampton, Long Island, New York
Died: May 12, 1878; Elmira, New York
Areas of Achievement: Education and women's rights
Contribution: In pursuit of higher status and influence for women in the domestic arena, Beecher promoted women's education, urging professionalization and appreciation of women's traditional roles.

Early Life

Catharine Esther Beecher was born on September 6, 1800, in East Hampton, Long Island, New York. The eldest of nine children, Catharine was influenced most deeply by her father, Lyman Beecher, a Presbyterian minister descended from a long line of Calvinist colonial ancestors. Her mother, Roxana Ward Beecher, also from a prominent family, was reared traditionally and passed many of her domestic skills to her children. Catharine resisted these domestic tasks initially, preferring intellectual and outdoor activities.

Lyman Beecher played a major role in the Second Great Awakening, an evangelical movement that spread throughout the United States during the early 1800's. He used revivals to seek conversion and social cohesion in his communities. As a child, Catharine was enveloped by her father's dominant personality and religious zeal, and all of her life she struggled with her faith, never completely embracing it or completely deserting it.

In 1809, the Beecher family moved to Litchfield, Connecticut, a conservative town and site of a renowned law school as well as a celebrated school for young ladies. Catharine entered Miss Pierce's school in 1810, keeping a journal which reveals not only the school's emphasis on the social graces but also on the development of a social consciousness. She flourished in those years, exercising leadership and other social skills.

After Roxana died in 1816, Catharine left school to take on domestic duties, supervising her younger siblings, cooking, and sewing. Her father remarried in late 1817, but Catharine lived at home for a while longer, the ties between father and daughter remaining very strong. At the age of eighteen, she left Litchfield to teach in New London, Connecticut.

In 1822, Catharine became engaged to Alexander Fisher, a Yale professor in natural philosophy. Her father approved of Fisher wholeheartedly, but Catharine was uncertain about his potential as a husband, finding him somewhat lacking in affection. In April of 1822, Fisher died at sea when his ship crashed into cliffs on the west coast of Ireland. Catharine remained single throughout her life, devoting herself to the education of women.

Life's Work

In 1823, Catharine Beecher opened a school in Hartford, Connecticut; it flourished, allowing her to exert social, religious, and intellectual leadership. The Hartford Female Seminary offered courses in rhetoric, logic, chemistry, history, philosophy, Latin, and algebra. As principal, Beecher's status rose, and she socialized with Hartford's most respected citizens of both genders. Her self-confidence grew along with her competence as an educator. She began expanding and expounding her ideas of good pedagogy.

Beecher placed great emphasis on molding the moral character of her students. In 1829, she published an essay entitled "Suggestions Respecting Improvements in Education." In it, she stated that the most important objective of education was "the foundation of the conscience, and the direction of the moral character and habits." To accomplish such training, Beecher tried to hire an associate principal to direct the religious teaching but she was unsuccessful. Suffering a nervous collapse, she took several months rest away from Hartford while her sister, Harriet Beecher, filled in for her at the school. Upon her return to Hartford, Catharine herself gave moral instruction.

During the 1830's, Beecher became focused on women's roles and the need for more professionalism. She clearly expected women to exercise power in the home as mothers and outside it as schoolteachers. The means for enhancing this power would be a better-crafted education. Beecher viewed teaching as a noble profession, enabling women to have influence, respectability, and independence while maintaining themselves within the accepted boundaries of femininity. The time was ripe for such thinking.

The 1830's and 1840's were decades of dramatic population growth in the United States. This growing population called for more teachers. Although men had dominated the profession, fewer males were available to teach, since many of them chose to go into industrial or commercial careers. Tax-supported schools, a leisured female middle class, and the emphasis on women's nurturing qualities all aided Beecher as she began to focus on teacher training.

Resigning her position in September of 1831, Beecher left Hartford to be with her father, who had accepted the presidency of Cincinnati's Lane Theological Seminary. They arrived in Cincinnati in the spring of 1832. Within a year, Catharine Beecher founded the Western Female Institute, dedicated to both the acquisition of knowledge and moral development.

Choosing not to be fully employed in the school, Beecher busied herself with social activities and some writing. She spoke to a group of women in New York in 1835 and her lecture, "An Essay on the Education of Female Teachers," was published in New York and Cincinnati. She presented a plan for women to educate the children of immigrants and working-class families in the West.

Beecher noted that one-third of Ohio's children were without schools and that thousands of teachers would be needed to staff new schools. She envisioned her Western Female Institute as the model seminary for a national system whereby women would be trained and, in turn, would train others to educate American children and youth. She began a fund-raising campaign, appealing to Cincinnati's wealthy citizens to endow the seminary and others like it. The Cincinnati elite did not contribute, however, in part because Catharine Beecher and her father were regarded as troublemakers. Some members of Cincinnati society were angered by what they believed was a certain cultural snobbery expressed by Catharine Beecher. Further antagonism was generated by the Beechers' strong support for abolition in a city much divided over the issue even before their arrival.

The Western Female Institute closed in 1837 because of low enrollment and Beecher's alienation of her constituency. Some of Cincinnati's aristocratic families saw her as an "intellectual and social upstart." That same year, Beecher began developing a new constituency as she urged a broader image of women's role in American society. Her "Essay on Slavery and Abolition with Reference to the Duty of American Females" attempted to shape a unified consciousness in American women.

Unlike social reformers such as Sarah and Angelina Grimké, Beecher believed that female influence could best be utilized within the traditional family hierarchy and that this influence was at the core of national morals. Women would exemplify domestic virtues and by their superior moral sensibility would be a stabilizing force in the nation. The foundation of her future work was laid in this essay and Beecher turned to what she hoped would be a lucrative literary career.

Beecher wrote copiously, but only one book, published in Boston in 1841, gave her the financial base she craved. By 1843, her *Treatise on Domestic Economy* was in its fourth printing and it gave her access to a national audience. Her book intended to give women a sense of purpose, of mission: the formation of the moral and intellectual character of the young. Beecher saw that women needed specialized training for this mission. She stressed that, because of their service to others, women needed more education that would be specially tailored to prepare them for this responsibility.

Glorifying domesticity, Beecher assured women that they were engaged in "the greatest work that was ever committed to human responsibility." Women's subordinate status, Beecher stated, was not imposed by nature; rather, it was necessary to promote the general welfare. Domesticity knew no boundaries and therefore could be a focus for a new, unified national identity. Beecher intended to transcend divisions between women of different social classes by emphasizing the universality of domestic values as she built on traditional distinctions between the sex roles.

Women were uniquely able to be constructive agents of social change. The home, therefore, was not a place of isolation but rather a base from which to influence all of society. Beecher's reasoning was particularly comforting to a nation undergoing dramatic changes, as it did not require elimination of the traditional male prerogatives.

Beecher's treatise was published by Harper and Brothers after 1842, ensuring it national distribution. Reprinted almost every year from 1841 to 1856, it became Beecher's best-selling work. Previously, women had to read separate books on health, childcare, cooking, and general well-being. The treatise pulled together all the domestic arts, giving simple rules for resolving the contradictions and ambiguities of daily life.

With the continuing popularity of the treatise, Beecher's career entered a second phase in which she founded and directed the American Woman's Education Association which was to aid in the establishment of numerous women's schools. Traveling widely during the 1840's and 1850's, she helped define women's potential both within and outside the home, though primarily the former.

The last two decades of Beecher's life were given to extensive travel, fund-raising, promotion of her books, and publicizing women's education. A major focus was the founding of colleges in the West to train women for professions as teachers and homemakers. The American Women's Education Association (founded in New York in 1852) was a source of educational funding; although it helped raise respectable sums of money, the association did not meet all of Beecher's needs or expectations. For this she relied on private help, especially from well-to-do relatives and longtime friends. Beecher continued her efforts on behalf of women's education until her death in 1878.

Summary

Catharine Beecher's last years were active ones, attending teachers' conventions, keeping up a wide correspondence, and giving public lectures. Based in the East again, Beecher lived with her siblings' families on and off, becoming closest to Harriet Beecher Stowe. She continued to travel and write on behalf of women teachers, even after the disbanding of the American Woman's Educational Association in 1862.

With Harriet, Catharine coauthored *The American Woman's Home* in 1869, a sequel to the *Treatise on Domestic Economy*. It repeated much of that first book while emphasizing the family as a model of how society should function: in harmonious social interdependence. The post-Civil War years saw an urgent need for such a model since society was experiencing much change at a rapid pace. Catharine Beecher argued that an expanding democracy needed the stability provided by families supporting one another—parents and children sacrificing themselves for the good of all. In her schema, men were also tied into domesticity, although women were to be the chief ministers.

Above all, the *Treatise on Domestic Economy* assured Beecher's reputation and place in history. In it she asserted women's active role in society, according them a greater degree of dignity and respect than had been theirs. The keystone of her programs and policies was the promotion of a superior education for all females. She helped enlarge the world and role of women, offering strategies for autonomous growth. Catharine Beecher's vision of strong womanhood added much to the expansion of nineteenth century feminism.

Bibliography

Barker-Benfield, Graham J., and Catherine Clinton. *Portraits of American Women.* New York: St. Martin's Press, 1991. A history of gender roles and relations from the period of early settlement to the 1980's. Gives a broad scope of social history. One succinct chapter on Catharine Beecher.

Flexner, Eleanor. *Century of Struggle: The Woman's Rights Movement in the United States*. Rev. ed. Cambridge, Mass.: The Belknap Press of Harvard University Press, 1975. An excellent overview of the women's rights movement. Chapter 11, "Early Stages Toward Equal Education" very helpful. Extensive chapter notes and an index.

Kerber, Linda K., and Jane S. DeHart, eds. *Women's America*. 3d ed. New York: Oxford University Press, 1991. A collection of essays on women and their roles from 1600-1990. Selections in part 2 provide excellent background for Beecher's thinking and experiences. One essay on Beecher's educational efforts in the West. Chapter notes, bibliography, and an index.

Parker, Gail T., ed. *The Oven Birds: American Women on Womanhood, 1820-1920*. Garden City, N.Y.: Anchor Books, 1972. An anthology of women's writings. A lengthy excellent introduction, situating each woman in her era, relating themes and experiences. Two excerpts are included from Beecher's *Woman Suffrage* and *Woman's Profession*, published in 1871.

Sklar, Kathryn Kish. *Catharine Beecher: A Study in American Domesticity*. New York: W. W. Norton, 1976. An analytical study of Beecher and her times. Very thorough on her writings. Detailed chapter notes, a bibliography, and an index.

Tyler, Alice Felt. *Freedom's Ferment: Phases of American Social History to 1860*. Minneapolis: University of Minnesota Press, 1944. Reprint. New York: Books for Libraries Press, 1970. Traces the crusades, reforms, and reformers in U.S. society from colonial times to the Civil War. Especially helpful are chapter 2 on "Evangelical Religion," and chapter 10 on "Education and the American Faith." Bibliography, chapter notes, and index.

Woloch, Nancy. *Women and the American Experience*. New York: Alfred A. Knopf, 1984. Examines main themes of women's history in given eras by reference to particular lives. Connects public and private spheres and women's strategies, individual and collective, as agents of change. Chapter 6, "Promoting Women's Sphere, 1800-1860," is particularly useful. Contains suggested sources for each chapter and an index.

S. Carol Berg

RUTH BENEDICT

Born: June 5, 1887; New York, New York
Died: September 17, 1948; New York, New York
Area of Achievement: Anthropology
Contribution: Depicting culture as an integrated set of traits chosen from the vast range of behavioral possibilities, Benedict directed the focus of American anthropology in the 1930's and 1940's toward the search for describable cultural configurations.

Early Life

Two traumatic events, one physical and one psychological, profoundly affected Ruth Fulton as a child. In 1889, Ruth's father, Frederick Fulton, a gifted homeopathic surgeon, died at the age of thirty-one. His young widow Beatrice Shattuck Fulton publicly expressed her immense grief, insisting that twenty-one-month-old Ruth view her father in his coffin, an image which retained potency for Ruth throughout her life. Shortly after her father's death, she began exhibiting signs of emotional trauma, initially with violent tantrums in which members of her family feared for her safety and that of her sister Margery, and later as she became old enough to check her temper, through bouts of depression. Ruth was emotionally withdrawn as a child, preferring solitude and shunning physical contact. She idolized her dead father and disliked her mother, whose frequently recurring expressions of grief Ruth found appalling. Her traumatic response to her father's death was exacerbated by substantial hearing loss sustained as a complication from measles. The condition had occurred when Ruth was an infant, but was left undiagnosed until she was five years old. Her partial deafness contributed to her surliness and isolation from her family.

During Ruth's childhood, her mother uprooted her family several times in search of employment before finally settling in Buffalo, New York, where she became head librarian for the Buffalo Public Library. Beatrice Fulton's pay was relatively low, but the job provided security. Although the family settled in the prosperous upper-middle-class area of the then thriving city, the Fultons were poor in contrast to their neighbors. As scholarship students, Ruth and Margery attended the private St. Margaret's Academy where they were distressingly aware of their poverty relative to their socially privileged schoolmates.

After attending Vassar on a full scholarship, Ruth Fulton sought to balance the desire for public accomplishment with personal satisfaction. She returned to Buffalo after graduation, and for two years she was employed as a social worker. She then moved with her family to California where she taught school in a private girls' academy. Both occupations left her unfulfilled and bored. Her marriage in 1914 to Stanley Benedict, a talented young biochemist, and their subsequent move to the New York City suburb of Bedford Hills, left her similarly unsatisfied. Although she wrote poetry, which she published with moderate success under the pseudonym Anne Singleton, and feminist biographies which at the time remained unpublished, she found domestic life and suburban isolation abhorrent. Winter-induced depressions led her to seek external fulfillment and in 1919, at the age of thirty-one, Benedict enrolled in graduate work at the New School for Social Research in New York City. Later, through the influence of anthropologists Elsie Clews Parsons and Alexander Goldenweiser, she met and convinced Franz Boas of Columbia University to admit her to the doctoral program in anthropology.

Life's Work

Assisted by Boas' acceptance of her coursework from the New School of Social Research, Ruth Benedict earned her Ph.D. in three semesters. As Boas' graduate teaching assistant, personal friend, and aide, and later as a lecturer in anthropology, she assumed a progressively significant role at Columbia.

Her 1923 dissertation, "The Concept of the Guardian Spirit in North America," was the result of library research rather than fieldwork. While narrow in scope, her study contributed to the knowledge of American Indian religion and myth. Although she took several trips into the field, including excursions made between 1922 and 1926 to the Serrano, Pima, and Zuni, Benedict's partial deafness made the collection of oral myths and folk culture difficult. Because she used lip reading to enhance her limited hearing, it was impractical for her to immerse herself in a foreign linguistic tradition, depending instead on interpreters for interviewing informants. Benedict's forte was interpreting and organizing other anthropologists' data. Her expertise was most evident in her 1934 publication of the seminal *Patterns of Culture*, in which she combined her own fieldwork on the Zuni with Boas' among the Kwakuitl, and Reo Fortune's among the Melanesian Dobus. *Patterns of Culture* was the culmination of more than a decade's ruminations on the definition of culture, including the function of the individual within, and his or her effect on, culture. Furthermore she described the cultural foundations of abnormality.

Benedict's work reflected what was then a preeminent debate among social scientists about the nature of culture and its effect on the individual. In *Patterns of Culture*, she rejected biological determinism, which views immutable biological roles as determining human behavior. She also disdained the British-influenced functionalism of Bronislaw Malinowski and A. R. Radcliffe-Browne in which every aspect of culture had a particular function which needed only to be deciphered by anthropologists. Instead, Benedict adapted a configurationist approach in which individual cultures select attributes from a "great arc" of possible human behavioral traits. Cultures discard some characteristics while emphasizing others, thereby developing their own identifiable cultural configuration or pattern. The pattern is more than the sum of its parts; instead, it is an integrated whole or a gestalt which can be described by anthropologists. Culture was "personality writ large," a describable reflection of the psychological group mind. Unlike functionalism, which defined culture as static and ignored history and diffusion as agents of cultural change, Benedict's patterns were fluid and therefore could be influenced by individuals within cultures.

Within her configurationist approach Benedict also explained deviance, an issue about which she was preoccupied partially to explain her lack of fit in her own culture. While she had always felt herself to be an outsider, Benedict became increasingly aware of her differences as her marriage deteriorated and she attained emotional fulfillment in an intimate and ultimately lesbian relationship with Margaret Mead. In *Patterns of Culture* she emphasized the cultural specificity of abnormality; conduct which is defined as normal in one culture was often considered abnormal in another. Because of the malleability of human beings, the vast majority of members of any culture will conform to dictated behavior. A small percentage, however, will discover that their inborn temperaments or potentialities do not coincide with cultural patterns and will find culture uncongenial, thereby participating in what is culturally defined as abnormal behavior.

Stemming from her belief in the plasticity of human beings, her personal commitment to social reform, and her conviction that anthropologists could be agents of change, Benedict devoted considerable energies to social causes in the form of "applied anthropology." She became a principal spokesperson against racism with her 1940 publication of the popular *Race Science and Politics*. In addition she developed a resource unit on racism with high school teacher Mildred Ellis in 1942, collaborated with a Columbia University committee to write a public affairs pamphlet in 1943, and coauthored a children's book on racism with anthropologist Gene Weltfish in 1948.

During World War II, Benedict, along with many of her fellow social scientists, worked for government intelligence agencies. In 1943, she joined the Office of War Information (OWI), where she initiated her pioneering work on national character—the determination of cultural patterns in complex nations. Since fieldwork was infeasible during the war, she perfected techniques for determining "culture at a distance," including analysis of films, fiction, propaganda, and interviews with immigrants. Under the auspices of the OWI, she prepared reports on Thailand, Romania, Finland, Norway, Poland, and Italy. The publication of Benedict's *The Chrysanthemum and the Sword: Patterns of Japanese Culture* (1946) was the pinnacle of national character studies, profoundly influencing public opinion toward Japan by explaining the foreignness of Japanese culture to the American public.

Benedict's final contribution to anthropology involved her directorship of Columbia University's ambitious Research in Contemporary Cultures (RCC) project, an interdisciplinary program sponsored by the U.S. Navy and begun in 1947 to study national character. The program's potential was never realized since it ran counter to then-dominant trends in anthropology including movement from interdisciplinary work to specialization, emphasis on quantifiable data in the form of statistics, and distancing from "cultural relativity" which denied ethical absolutes, claiming cultures could only be judged on their own terms (a position many found untenable in the wake of Nazi Germany's concentration and death camps). Benedict, weakened by overwork and a postwar trip to Eastern Europe, died of a heart attack on September 17, 1948.

Summary

Ruth Benedict's work in the field of anthropology, while highly influential in the

1930's, lost prestige in the 1940's as it went against the grain of the then-dominant tradition among American social scientists. Her work was criticized as impressionistic and too similar to the humanities to be properly scientific. Nevertheless, her popular impact continued. By the early 1990's, *Patterns of Culture* continued to be a standard work in anthropology classrooms, popularizing anthropological concepts such as cultural relativity, and challenging notions of racial superiority and homophobia.

Benedict's quest for self-fulfillment was a monumental struggle during an era when women's roles were narrowly proscribed by Victorian social convention. Her battle for professional recognition was similarly a tribute to her persistence in the face of blatant academic discrimination. During the early years after she earned her Ph.D., Benedict, because of her age, was ineligible for grants and fellowships. To achieve professional recognition, she was forced to accept a series of yearly renewable appointments as an unpaid lecturer in anthropology at Columbia University. She earned a small salary teaching in the Columbia Extension and with what little money she could spare supported students' fieldwork. By the late 1920's, Benedict was increasingly influential in the anthropology department, but it was not until 1931 that Columbia finally granted her an untenured assistant professorship. Despite these slights and the subsequent decision to choose a less experienced male colleague as chair of the department when Boas retired, Benedict persevered to become one of the most notable women in the field of anthropology.

Bibliography
Caffrey, Margaret M. *Ruth Benedict: Stranger in This Land.* Austin: University of Texas Press, 1989. Caffrey examines Benedict's life from the perspective of her contribution to American intellectual history and as a "case history in cultural feminism." Illustrated, footnoted, with bibliography.
Mead, Margaret. *An Anthropologist at Work: Writings of Ruth Benedict.* Boston: Houghton Mifflin, 1959. A collection of Benedict's writings including journal entries, professional publications, and an autobiographical sketch interspersed with biographical essays written by Mead. Fully footnoted with chronology of achievements and bibliography.
———————. *Ruth Benedict.* New York: Columbia University Press, 1974. Again Mead used Benedict's own writing interspersed with her comments to provide a biographical sketch of Benedict. Included are several publications not found in *An Anthropologist at Work.*
Modell, Judith Schachter. *Ruth Benedict: Patterns of a Life.* Philadelphia: University of Pennsylvania Press, 1983. A detailed biography and analysis of Benedict's work by anthropologist Modell. Contains citations, full bibliography.
———————. "Ruth Fulton Benedict," *Women Anthropologists: A Biographical Dictionary*, edited by Ute Gacs et al. New York: Greenwood Press, 1988. A thorough biography and analysis of Benedict's major anthropological contributions. Includes select bibliography of primary and secondary sources.

Mary E. Virginia

PATTY BERG

Born: February 13, 1918; Minneapolis, Minnesota

Area of Achievement: Sports
Contribution: An original organizer of the Ladies Professional Golf Association (LPGA), Berg became the most decorated woman golfer in history and the foremost promoter of golf as the game of a lifetime for professionals and amateurs alike.

Early Life

The tomboy daughter of a Minneapolis, Minnesota, grain merchant, Patricia Jane Berg was born on February 13, 1918. As early as grammar school, she achieved notoriety as a natural athlete. Her first great love was football. She played blocking quarterback in the single-wing formation for the self-dubbed 50th Street Tigers, a local boys' football team. She masterminded the team's uncommonly successful attacks and was known as Dynamite by her teammates because of her determination and enthusiasm.

Her football days ended when her parents, Herman Berg, Sr., and Therese Kennedy Berg, despaired of their daughter's penchant for constantly shredding new clothes in pursuit of athletic glories. In her early teen years Patty Berg moved on to speed skating, winning numerous local events and placing third in the 1932 National Junior Class Speed Skating competition.

The woman who would go on to unmatchable achievements in women's golf took up the sport because her father bought her brother, Herman, Jr., a golf club membership. When Patty complained of unequal treatment, her father cut down four old clubs to her size and showed her the rudiments of the swing. Among Herman Berg's hobbies was the photographing of famous golfers so he could study their swings. He convinced his daughter that combining golf scholarship and practice was the way to success.

The young Patty Berg had always been impressed that golf great Bobby Jones had won the 1930 U.S. Open at the Interlachen Country Club in Minneapolis. In 1932, when she began to improve, her family joined Interlachen, at the time considered to be the most challenging golf course in Minnesota. Simply in the process of learning to play the game, Patty learned to adjust her technique to the variety of difficult situations a championship golf course affords.

Her father arranged for her to take lessons from Willie Kidd, Jr., and Lester Bolstad, two of Minnesota's most renowned teaching professionals. Almost immediately she gave notice that she would be a champion. She was Minneapolis city champion in 1934 and won her first of three Minnesota State Amateur Championships in 1935. Patty even enrolled at the University of Minnesota in 1938, while she was still competing as an amateur. By 1940, when she turned professional, she had captured twenty-eight titles, including the United States Amateur Championship in 1938.

Because Patty clearly possessed the potential to be the greatest woman golfer of all time, the Bergs began spending their winters in Florida so Patty could practice full time. Patty Berg benefited from her father's love of golf and his financial success, but she benefited most because Herman Berg was a man of stern character. She practiced religiously because she understood that the will to achieve depended upon dedication and hard work.

In tournaments, she was a strong competitor, but even as a young person Patty was developing a reputation as an ambassador for the game itself. Her sportsmanship and fellow feeling set her apart. Honest, sincere, and gracious, she was totally unassuming. Herman Berg insisted that his daughter capitalize on her celebrity for the benefit of the less fortunate. Any weekend she was not at a tournament, her father saw to it that she played an exhibition for charity. In 1939, she toured the western United States, giving exhibitions and clinics to raise money for a new student union building at the University of Minnesota.

Life's Work

Patty Berg turned professional in 1940 at the age of twenty-two. At the time there were three tournaments open to professionals: the Western Open, the Titleholders, and the Ashville Invitational. The total prize money was approximately five hundred dollars. Professionals in those days earned their livings through clinics and exhibitions and endorsements. Patty accepted an endorsement offer from Wilson Sporting Goods because she was already accomplished at clinics and exhibitions. She was thrilled to have found a way to earn a living at golf. Her contract with Wilson called for $7,500 plus commission from the sale of Patty Berg golf clubs. The Patty Berg model was the first line of golf clubs in America named for a woman.

In the next few years, new tournaments appeared here and there, but the prize money remained too small for an adequate living. Berg continued to give clinics and exhibitions as a goodwill ambassador for golf and Wilson Sporting Goods. In December of 1941, en route to an exhibition in Memphis, Tennessee, to raise money for British war relief, Patty sustained cuts and bruises to her face and a compound fracture to her knee in a car crash. After months in a cast, her knee would not bend properly. For six months, she bicycled and worked out in a gym to return to competitive shape. Eventually she could begin a regimen of hitting hundreds of golf balls a day. Her determination paid off when she won the Women's Western Open, a major tournament at that time, in her first outing after the accident.

Berg enlisted in the Marine Corp Reserve in the fall of 1943. She ultimately was stationed in Philadelphia, where she worked in public relations. She received an honorable discharge with the rank of first lieutenant in 1945.

Berg emerged from the Marine Corps when the short-lived Women's Professional Golf Association (WPGA) was forming. The WPGA added more tournaments, including the very first U.S. Women's Open, won by Patty Berg in 1946, her only U.S. Open title. Most of the players were local amateurs, however, and the WPGA just did not catch on with the public. Nevertheless, the WPGA was important in a number of significant respects. It established the notion of a women's tour, it published the first golf-specific magazine, *The Woman Golfer*, and it deleted "Caucasians only" from its bylaws years before its male counterpart, the Professional Golfers' Association (PGA).

In late 1949, Patty Berg, then president of the WPGA, and Babe Didrikson Zaharias were instrumental in forming the Ladies Professional Golf Association (LPGA) with financial backing from Wilson Sporting Goods. This support proved vital to the LPGA's credibility and financial stability, allowing it essentially to replace the faltering WPGA. Patty Berg served as president during the organization's first four years and immediately established herself as the number one spokesperson for women's competitive golf in general, and the LPGA in particular. In addition to keeping her own game at its highest competitive level, she would go anywhere at almost any time to give a clinic or a speech. She has continued this practice well into her eighth decade of life. Billing herself as "The Patty Berg Golf Show," she is renowned for her humor and collection of bizarre hats which complement her trick shot wizardry and sound instruction on the fundamentals of golf.

In the 1950's, Patty Berg was at her competitive best. During this period, she won thirty-eight of her fifty-seven professional victories. The first half of the decade, Berg and Babe Zaharias were the tour's major stars. Although Louise Suggs and Betsy Rawls established themselves as champions with equally impressive golf skills, Berg and Zaharias became the names synonymous with women's professional golf in the public's mind.

Those who know golf and the women's tour readily proclaim that Patty Berg possessed a sounder arsenal of golf skills and a greater knowledge of the game—and some would argue a more altruistic personality—than Babe Didrikson Zaharias, but it was Babe who captured the imaginations of the sportswriters and fans. Berg has never balked at having a spotlight slightly smaller than that of Zaharias. Her feeling is that at that time in history the women's tour needed a flamboyant personality in order to capture public attention. In their most publicized confrontation, the Weathervane Tournament series of 1951 and 1952 for the then unheard of prize of five thousand dollars, Berg and Zaharias were tied for the championship after the regulation 144 holes. They tied the first eighteen hole playoff with 71's and Patty Berg won the second playoff, 75 to 76. After 180 holes played in four sections of the United States, one stroke separated the pair. The truth is that the two women were close friends—competitive spirits with great respect for each other's golf games.

In 1956, Babe Zaharias died an untimely death, cut down at age forty-five by cancer. Patty Berg's last championship came in 1962 when she was forty-four. In the end, both captured more than eighty championships. Patty won fifteen majors, Zaharias won ten. As Patty Berg began to retire from tournament golf and spend more and more time on the lecture circuit, she never tired of regaling audiences with memories of how life on tour with Zaharias was never dull.

From the mid-1960's on, Patty's tour appearances became more and more sporadic, and she increased her clinic and exhibition schedule. In 1962, she toured Japan, the first woman professional to do so. In 1963, she toured Europe. The clinics became Patty Berg's way of giving something back to the game. In spite of cancer surgery in 1971, hip surgery in 1980, and back surgery in 1989, Berg has remained before the public, giving clinics, serving as honorary chairperson for a multitude of humanitarian causes, and receiving numerous awards for her dedication to golf and golfers.

Summary

Patty Berg was voted Woman Athlete of the Year in 1938, 1943, and 1955. She has been elected to a dozen halls of fame, including the World Golf, the LPGA, the PGA and the Minnesota PGA. She has been honored for her sportsmanship and dedication to golf by organizations, large and small, too numerous to mention. In 1978, the LPGA established the Patty Berg Award, given only when deemed suitable to individuals who have made outstanding contributions to women's golf.

Patty Berg won fifteen major championships, a record not soon to be matched. Yet, her record as a champion is second to her reputation as golf's foremost goodwill ambassador. Even at the height of her competitive career, Patty Berg gave as many as six clinics a week. Wilson Sporting Goods estimates that she has presented more than 25,000 clinics since 1940. Schooling her audiences in the sound fundamentals of golf is her primary objective, but she promotes just as intently sportsmanship, dedication to goals, and respect for other individuals. She remains one of the greatest golf legends of all time.

Bibliography

Barkow, Al. *Gettin' to the Dance Floor: An Oral History of American Golf.* New York: Atheneum, 1986. Reminiscences that chart the development of golf in America before it became a multimillion dollar industry. Especially useful for clarifying the differences in the profession for women and men, especially in matters of race.

Glenn, Rhonda. *The Illustrated History of Women's Golf.* Dallas, Tex.: Taylor Publishing, 1991. A richly detailed look at nearly one hundred years of women's competitive golf, carefully constructed from archives, print sources, and oral histories. Excellent photographs, solid bibliography.

Hahn, James, and Lynn Hahn. *Patty!: The Sports Career of Patricia Berg.* Edited by Howard Schroeder. Mankato, Minn.: Crestwood House, 1981. Written for a juvenile audience, this work provides a good introduction to Berg's career. Contains a number of photographs from Berg's career which are available nowhere else.

Nickerson, Elinor. *Golf: A Women's History.* Jefferson, N.C.: McFarland, 1987. The first book to concentrate on the role of women in golf's development. A tight rendering of the essential data without the richness of Rhonda Glenn's book.

Raque, Sally. "You've Come a Long Way, Ladies," *Women's Sports and Fitness,* 12 (May/June, 1990): 61-64, 66. A celebration of the first forty years of the LPGA. Includes a sidebar on Patty Berg, the oldest living member of the organization.

Dexter Westrum

MARY McLEOD BETHUNE

Born: July 10, 1875; Mayesville, South Carolina
Died: May 18, 1955; Daytona Beach, Florida
Areas of Achievement: Education and social reform
Contribution: A leading voice and activist for democratic ideals before World War I
and up to the early Civil Rights years, Bethune was instrumental in founding
organizations to advance the education and rights of blacks, inspiring others as she
was herself inspired.

Early Life
Mary Jane McLeod was born on July 10, 1875, in Mayesville, South Carolina, to
Sam and Patsy McLeod, who were former slaves. She was the seventeenth child to be
born to the couple and the first to be born free. Her father was a farmer and her mother,
Patsy, probably did laundry to supplement the family income in addition to her own
work on the family farm. Many of the older McLeod children were either married or
on their own, but the younger children assisted with the support of the family by
picking cotton. By her own report, Mary Jane McLeod, at nine years of age, could
pick 250 pounds of cotton a day.

One incident in particular is reputed to have inspired her determination to become
educated. While she was in a neighboring house being shown around by the white
family's young daughters, they happened into a room with books. Mary Jane picked
up one of the books and was examining it when one of the girls spoke sharply to her
about putting the book down, reportedly telling Mary Jane "You can't read, so you
shouldn't even handle a book!" Shocked at this response and perhaps vaguely aware
of the insult, Mary Jane McLeod became determined to read. As it happened, a young
black woman was in the neighborhood to start a school for black children. This teacher
approached the McLeods about having Mary Jane attend. The likelihood of one of the
children of this poor family being allowed to go to school seemed remote. Nevertheless, Mary Jane's desire to go was so strong and apparently so heartfelt that her mother
convinced her father to let her go. When she was able to read the Bible to her parents
as a result of this schooling, they all, parents and child, appreciated the benefits of
education.

She did well at the little country school. Her teacher recommended her for further
schooling, and her tuition was paid in part by Mary Chrissman, a white dressmaker
from Denver, Colorado. The new school, known as Scotia School, was located in
Concord, South Carolina. Mary Jane contributed to her education by doing odd jobs
at the school. Having done well in her studies at Scotia, she was again recommended
by her teachers for scholarships to continue her studies. She was accepted as a student
at the Moody Bible Institute in Chicago, Illinois, and received additional financial
support from Chrissman.

At the Moody Institute, Mary Jane McLeod became a member of the Gospel Choir
Team which went out to preach and sing throughout Illinois. She had hoped to become

a missionary in Africa upon completion of her studies, but because she was so young, she was not considered a suitable candidate. Therefore, she took a teaching assignment at Haines Normal and Industrial Institute in Augusta, Georgia, where she met a black woman who was to affect her life in important ways: Lucy Laney, the school's principal and founder and a trailblazer in the education of blacks. Sympathizing with McLeod's compassion for the uneducated black children of the neighborhood around the school, Laney allowed McLeod to teach them on Sunday afternoons. Soon, McLeod had the children singing familiar songs, and she encouraged them to listen to Bible stories later.

The sponsoring Presbyterian Board of Haines Institute sent Mary McLeod to other schools nearby. One of those schools was the Kendall Institute in Sumter, South Carolina. It was here that she met Albertus Bethune, also a teacher, whom she married in May of 1898. Their son, Albert McLeod Bethune, was born a year later. The family soon moved to Palatka, Florida, where Mary established a Presbyterian mission school. Her husband did not share her enthusiasm for missionary work, however, and the couple was eventually separated.

Life's Work

Having been born in the South during Reconstruction undoubtedly saddled Mary McLeod Bethune with many adversities. She was black, poor, and female, none of which made her more remarkable than other young women alive during the same period. What did distinguish her was her ability to conquer those misfortunes, to share her accomplishments with others, and to choose to devote her life to acts of service to others. From the time she read the Bible to her parents, she seemed to recognize and become inspired by the power of words and their effects on others.

Bethune's lifework began in Daytona Beach when she saw other young black women in need of all varieties of education. Her ambition to provide a place for their schooling took the form of grasping at any possibilities, becoming inventive as the needs arose: discarded, crumpled paper could be smoothed out to write lessons on; burned wooden twigs could become charcoal for pencils; cracked plates or broken chairs—anything that could be salvaged was recycled and returned to useful service. Her crowning achievement in these salvage operations was an area in the city which had been used as a garbage dump, but which she saw could be used for a school. Selflessness and determination proved to be the hallmarks of Bethune's character. She had a dollar and a half as her original budget, but she made do and found creative ways to recruit both students and community assistance for her projects.

The years following the founding of the school with five students on October 3, 1904, led to the rapid growth of her program of education for blacks. By 1906, Bethune had 250 students and employed a few teachers who worked for salaries of fifteen to twenty-five dollars a month. In order to lessen the drain on the meager finances and to become more independent, she stopped renting and began to buy land for her needs. By 1925, Bethune School merged with the Cookman School for boys to become Bethune-Cookman College. The merged institution included a grade school, high school, and college. Because southern policies of segregation at the time extended to the care of hospital patients, Bethune was led to erect a hospital near the college in 1911 to provide better treatment for the black community. It was named for her father and proved to be another example of her vision.

During the years of the Wilson Administration, Bethune became more active in social organizations devoted to protest and social reform. She served on the executive board of the Urban League as well as on committees resisting the discriminatory policies of the Young Women's Christian Association (YWCA). Since many of the positions taken by the YWCA were either condescending or blatantly biased, Bethune became one of several women opposing the racist stance of that association. She was also active in the formation of the National Association of Wage Earners, an organization dedicated to informing women of their rights as workers.

In 1921, Bethune was one of the executive leaders of the International Council of Women of the Darker Races of the World. The intention of this group was to raise the esteem and awareness of darker peoples about themselves and others from what has been called the "Third World."

She continued her activities on behalf of black children and women in order to combat the injustices and inequities they faced. Founding the National Association of Negro Women in 1935 and working with the Franklin D. Roosevelt Administration, Bethune directed the Negro branch of the National Youth Administration. She was also founder and president of the National Association of Colored Women's Clubs.

Although she served as president of Bethune-Cookman College from 1904 to 1942, and was one of its trustees until her death in 1955, her influence was not exclusively focused on education. She was a special assistant to the Secretary of War during World War II and served on the committee for National Defense under President Harry Truman. She also served as a consultant to the conference that drafted the United Nations charter. These activities and her many honorary degrees and medals never caused her to abandon her main concern: the education of every black child.

Bethune's imagination was not restricted to what she, or anyone, could see immediately. She was known to say "just because you can't see a thing, does not mean that it does not exist." During many of her talks, Bethune would frequently compare the peoples of the world to flowers. Some students would remark that there were no black flowers in the world's gardens. At first, she had only her visionary remark to offer, since there appeared to be no way to rebut the observation. On one of her trips to Europe, however, she was presented with a "black" tulip by one of her hosts in The Netherlands. She later planted the tulips on her campus as proof of her maxim.

Bethune's ability to maintain her lofty vision allowed her to endure in the face of great challenges. The black community was hard hit by the era's wars, economic depressions, riots, and lynchings. For the most part, there was little government intervention on behalf of black victims. Protests by black organizations went unheard, were ignored, or were suppressed. The activities of organizations such as the Ku Klux Klan were accepted, permitted, or even encouraged while blacks were denied their civil rights despite their achievements as responsible citizens. Poverty and ignorance, combined with racism, did much to inhibit black people. None of these conditions could quench Bethune's spirit. Working with Eleanor Roosevelt and some of the nation's top businessmen, Bethune enhanced her effectiveness as a representative of the black community and as an individual educator. She died of a heart attack in 1955 and was buried on the campus of her beloved college.

Summary

During times when being an African American often meant being invisible, being disheartened, and being denied chances to achieve intellectually, especially if female, Mary McLeod Bethune became a person whose entire life disproved such stereotypes. By white American standards, she possessed little physical beauty, but by any standards her spirit, her energy, and her compassion were evidence of great inner beauty. Bethune's drive to give women access to worlds that had been closed to them, to give all blacks intellectual choices that had been denied them, and to give children an example to follow in providing service to others made her one of the most notable African American leaders of her time. Before her death, she had lived to see Bethune-Cookman become one of the finest of the historically black colleges in the country. She had left her mark on the administrations of two American presidents. Using her keen understanding of human behavior and harnessing her ability to negotiate change in the face of great opposition, Bethune became one of the most influential voices in the struggle for racial equality.

Bibliography

Carruth, Ella Kaiser. *She Wanted to Read: The Story of Mary McLeod Bethune*. New York: Abingdon Press, 1966. A biography written for juveniles that presents a portrait of Bethune's early years. Also includes some coverage of her involvement as a presidential adviser as well as her activities as an organizer and founder of groups concerned with women's rights and labor relations.

Lerner, Gerda, ed. *Black Women in White America: A Documentary History*. New York: Pantheon Books, 1972. Contains excerpts of works and speeches by notable black women including Bethune. Extremely useful for accurate firsthand accounts of her life and her activities in entries such as "A College from a Garbage Dump," "Another Begging Letter," and "A Century of Progress of Negro Women."

McKissack, Patricia, and Fredrick McKissack. *Mary McLeod Bethune: A Great Teacher*. Hillside, N.J.: Enslow, 1991. Another biography directed at juvenile readers that provides an excellent introduction, broadly describing Bethune's life and achievements in fighting bigotry and racial injustice. Focuses much of its attention on Bethune's courage in overcoming adversity. Illustrated.

Salem, Dorothy. *To Better Our World: Black Women in Organized Reform, 1890-1920*. New York: Carlson, 1990. Salem's work is the fourteenth volume in Carlson's *Black Women in United States History* series. Provides a chronological narrative of the efforts made by black women's organizations to improve the lives of African Americans in the United States. A well-researched historical account that provides insights into the backgrounds of black women reformers, highlighting their resiliency of character in the face of failures as well as successes.

Smith, Elaine M. "Mary McLeod Bethune and the National Youth Association." In *Clio Was a Woman: Studies in the History of American Women*, edited by Mabel E. Deutrich and Virginia C. Purdy. Washington, D.C.: Howard University Press, 1980. An excellent assessment of Bethune's work in supervising the activities of the National Youth Administration with respect to African Americans. Although aimed at a scholarly audience, this essay is accessible to general readers and helps place Bethune's accomplishments within the context of her own time as well as the larger field of women's studies.

Maude M. Jennings

ELIZABETH BISHOP

Born: February 8, 1911; Worcester, Massachusetts
Died: October 6, 1979; Boston, Massachusetts
Area of Achievement: Literature
Contribution: Elizabeth Bishop wrote some of the most elegantly structured and moving poems in twentieth century American literature.

Early Life

Elizabeth Bishop was born on February 8, 1911, in Worcester, Massachusetts. Her father, Thomas Bishop, was a member of a wealthy family that owned a successful contracting company, so Elizabeth's family was financially well off. The shock of her father's death from Bright's disease when Elizabeth was only eight months old precipitated mental problems in Elizabeth's mother, May Gertrude Bulmer Bishop, and she was committed to a mental institution soon after. Elizabeth only saw her mother a few times after her commitment; May Bishop was in and out of mental institutions in the United States and Canada until her death in 1934. After her father's death and her mother's madness, Elizabeth lived with her maternal grandparents in Great Village, Nova Scotia. Despite the trauma of her parents' troubles, she found life with her grandparents in Canada to be very pleasant. It was an organic environment in which Elizabeth could see nature every day, and she had a home with people who cared deeply for her.

Despite this affectionate upbringing, Elizabeth's paternal grandparents, the Bishops, were distressed to see their granddaughter grow up in provincial Nova Scotia; they brought her to their mansion in Worcester, Massachusetts. Life was financially better for Elizabeth, but her grandparents were cold and had little sense of a child's needs. She had servants to wait on her, but she had no understanding or affection.

Elizabeth attended country day school in Swampscott before enrolling at Walnut Hill School, a boarding school in Natick, Massachusetts. She had a number of close friends at Walnut Hill and did very well academically. She later entered Vassar College, where she majored in English literature. She wrote poems and stories at Vassar that appeared in student publications, and she received an honorable mention in a literary contest sponsored by the prestigious magazine, *Hound and Horn.*

After graduating from Vassar in 1934, Bishop moved to New York. Later that year, she met Marianne Moore, the noted American poet who was to become her poetic mentor and supporter. Bishop worked briefly at a few unimportant jobs, and she spent most of her time traveling. She toured Europe with some friends from Vassar in 1934 and later went to Morocco and temporarily settled in Key West, Florida. She had a small income from her father's estate, and her friends from Vassar were often wealthy and helped her with travel arrangements. Bishop's compulsive traveling suggests that she was looking for the home and security she lost when her father died and her mother went mad.

Although she did not have a steady job in this early period, Bishop was busy writing poems and stories that gradually would win for her a national reputation as a writer. She published poems and stories in such important magazines as *The New Yorker*, *Partisan Review*, and the *New Republic*. In 1940, she signed a contract with Houghton Mifflin for a book of poems. Bishop felt that more poems were necessary for the collection, however, and she did not publish that first book, *North & South*, until 1946.

Life's Work

Elizabeth Bishop published four books of poetry and a number of short stories and reviews during her life. After her death, the poems were brought together into *The Complete Poems, 1927-1979* (1983), and her stories and reviews were published as *The Collected Prose* (1984). Her body of work is truly distinguished and marked by a careful and precise phrasing. The poems are closely structured and deal with a number of subjects and themes. The stories are fewer and less interesting on the whole, but many of them reveal facets of Bishop's life and mind, especially the dislocating experiences of her youth.

Her first book, *North & South*, was very different from the usual first book by a poet. Each of the poems was tightly structured with an imaginative choice of words and images. It was a mature and polished book and its critical reception was quite favorable. Randall Jarrell stated: "Her work is unusually personal and honest in its wit, perception, and sensitivity." Another important poet of the period, Robert Lowell, praised Bishop's first book highly; he was to become a lifelong friend and supporter of Bishop. The main themes in *North & South* are geography, nature, and love. In the poems using geography, Bishop consistently contrasts the land with the sea. Such a contrast is found in "The Map," a poem in which she also contrasts the imaginative world that a map can create to the factual certainty and fixity of the "historian." "The Fish," which became one of Bishop's most popular poems, also appears in this book. It tells of catching a fish, describing the fish as an old warrior who has "medals" and "ribbons." The poem ends with the speaker claiming a victory, only to say, "And I let the fish go." Bishop acknowledges the power and beauty of the fish and refuses to take him out of his natural element.

Bishop's second book of poems, *Poems: North & South—A Cold Spring*, was published in 1955. It, too, was met with critical acclaim, and some critics noticed a development in Bishop's poetry. Richard Eberhart detected a new "confessional" element in her poetry, while Howard Nemerov commented on the change "away from thought and towards vision." Bishop was awarded the Pulitzer Prize for this second volume of poems. Many of the poems have the same themes as her first book, but there is a playfulness in some of the poems that was not apparent in the first book. "Invitation to Miss Marianne Moore" is a delightful fantasy in which Bishop invites Marianne Moore to "please come flying" over the Brooklyn Bridge to Manhattan where Bishop is living. She asks Moore to "come like a daylight comet with a long unnebulous train of words." The poem conveys Bishop's affection for Moore and her work in a fantasy style that fits the subject and occasion perfectly. Another important poem in this collection is "At the Fishhouses," in which Bishop describes the land in images of jewels and "silver"; these beautiful colors, however, have been created by the dead fish. In contrast, the sea "is like what we imagine knowledge to be: dark, salt, clear, moving, utterly free." The contrasting images suggest both the gain and the bitterness that comes with any true knowledge.

The next book of poetry by Bishop, *Questions of Travel*, was published in 1965. Bishop was living in Brazil when the book was published, and many of the poems use Brazil as a subject. Perhaps the most interesting poem in the book is "Sestina." Bishop uses the very elaborate rhyme and stanzaic patterns to portray her experience with her grandmother in Nova Scotia when she was very young. The girl in the poem is portrayed as drawing an "inscrutable house," an image that suggests her loss of parents and home. This sense of unspoken loss is reinforced by the references to tears and to "planting" tears. The grandmother with her wonderful "Marvel stove" may try to provide a normal life, but the girl's tears remain.

Another poem in the book worth noting is "Visit to St. Elizabeth's." The poem uses the form and style of a nursery rhyme, "The House that Jack Built" to portray Ezra Pound in the madhouse. The form expands from stanza to stanza and each stanza uses a different adjective to reveal the many sides of the controversial Pound. The poem is brilliant in its haunting style and rounded character portrait of Pound.

The Complete Poems was published in 1969, gathering together Bishop's scattered work into a single volume. Among the work's glowing reviews was one written by Robert Lowell, in which he noted: "Once her poems, each shining, were too few. Now they are many. When we read her, we enter the classical serenity of a new country." The book later received the National Book Award.

Bishop's next book of poems, *Geography III*, appeared in 1976. Helen Vendler praised one poem from the collection, "Crusoe in England." She said "A poet who has written this poem really needs to write nothing else." The poem does bring together many of the themes of Bishop. It deals with geography and travel, and, above all, with displacement. Crusoe, who was shipwrecked on an island, has returned to England, but he now longs for the home he has left behind and mourns the loss of his companion Friday. In Bishop's poems, home is the place you have lost; it can never be recovered.

Another fine poem in this book is "One Art," which uses the difficult form of the villanelle. Bishop manages to use and vary the form for her own purposes. She alters some of the fixed lines to show a progression in the poem's theme of loss. The losses move from the trivial to larger elements. For example, Bishop moves from losing "house keys" to "Houses," and, finally, a "continent." The last stanza speaks of losing a beloved person, and Bishop varies the last line of the villanelle to read, "though it may look like (*Write* it!) like disaster." The line not only alters the rhyming lines but also allows Bishop to express the emotion that the poem has been burying in the form.

Elizabeth Bishop died in 1979, three years after the publication of *Geography III*.

Summary

With the publication of *The Complete Poems, 1927-1979* in 1983 and *The Collected Prose* in 1984, the achievement of Elizabeth Bishop was evident to all readers and critics. She did not follow literary trends, but created instead a world of her own in which her imagination could flourish. Bishop managed to avoid simple classification as a poet. In addition, Bishop both used and altered traditional forms. She breathed new life into such fixed forms as the sestina and the villanelle. Many critics have praised her "famous eye" and her ability to describe memorably places and things. Her achievement goes beyond description, beautiful as it may be in so many poems. There is a moral dimension in her poems and stories. She transformed her own loss and dislocation into poems and stories that portray human suffering and the pain of childhood in precise and sympathetic detail. In addition, her poems about the poor people in Brazil expose the social system, especially colonialism, that creates such conditions. She was not a feminist, but a number of feminist critics have praised her poetry and seen in it elements that support the feminist view. Adrienne Rich praises her honesty and courage in her portrayal of family, class, and race. Other critics have seen in her indirect poetic method a key principle in literature written by women. She was, as Richard Wilbur said, "an incomparable poet," and one of the major voices in twentieth century American literature.

Bibliography
Costello, Bonnie. *Elizabeth Bishop: Questions of Mastery.* Cambridge, Mass.: Harvard University Press, 1991. Costello reveals some of the most important literary techniques that Bishop used to structure her poems.
Kalstone, David. *Becoming a Poet.* New York: Farrar, Straus, & Giroux, 1989. Kalstone discusses the influence of Marianne Moore and Robert Lowell upon Bishop's life and art.
MacMahon, Candace. *Elizabeth Bishop: A Bibliography, 1927-1979.* Charlottesville: University Press of Virginia, 1980. A useful bibliography of Bishop's works and the criticism of her poems and stories.
Millier, Brett C. *Elizabeth Bishop: Life and the Memory of It.* Berkeley: University of California Press, 1993. A critical biography of the poet that discusses her life and works. Millier creates a readable narrative of Bishop's life and provides excellent analysis of Bishop's poems.
Rich, Adrienne. "The Eye of the Outsider: The Poetry of Elizabeth Bishop." *Boston Review* 8 (April, 1983): 15-17. Rich discovers some feminist elements in the austere poems of Elizabeth Bishop.
Schwartz, Lloyd, and Sybil P. Estess, eds. *Elizabeth Bishop and Her Art.* Ann Arbor: University of Michigan Press, 1983. An excellent collection of critical essays on Bishop's poetry and fiction. Reviews of the poetry are included along with Bishop's own prose writings.
Stevenson, Anne. *Elizabeth Bishop.* New York: Twayne, 1966. A life and works discussion of Bishop that provides some insight into Bishop's themes and poetic structures. Written thirteen years before Bishop's death, it lacks critical assessment of Bishop's final works.

James Sullivan

SHIRLEY TEMPLE BLACK

Born: April 23, 1928; Santa Monica, California

Areas of Achievement: Film and diplomacy
Contribution: A juvenile film star of international renown, Shirley Temple Black devoted her adult years to diplomacy, working for the U.S. Department of State and serving as an ambassador to Ghana and Czechoslovakia.

Early Life

Shirley Temple was born in Santa Monica, California, the daughter of George Francis Temple, a bank teller, and his wife Gertrude. Shirley's early life was not merely a waiting period in which she prepared for an adult career; she was a child actor with starring roles in more than forty motion pictures and fifty television productions. It is significant, however, that in her adult résumé of three pages, Shirley Temple Black's childhood achievements are listed in a mere three lines.

From the very start, Shirley was a tough little girl with a surprisingly logical mind. At the age of five, she courageously endured having her lip sewn up without anaesthetic; her father fainted. When placed into the infamous black box on a film set as punishment for delaying the shooting, she quickly deduced that time was a valuable commodity and should not be wasted. An intelligent child, Shirley was full of questions. When challenged by the query, "Why do you ask?," her logical reply was, "Because I do not know."

Her road to stardom was initiated and fully supported by her loving and ambitious mother Gertrude, who took her to dancing school at the age of three for lessons that cost the family fifty cents per week. Her mother was constantly at her side, serving as chauffeur, as chaperone, as seamstress of Shirley's costumes, and as hairdresser of her legendary curls (which were rolled on fifty-four curlers each day).

Shirley was soon discovered and hired at a salary of $50 per week to appear in short films. Among others, she acted in a series of eight Baby Burlesk pictures, which parodied films featuring adult actors. From the waist up, Shirley was dressed as a Parisian seductress, with an off-shoulder blouse and a rose behind her ear, while below, she and the rest of the juvenile cast were in diapers. The series was extremely popular, in spite—or perhaps because—of silly titles such as *Polly Tix in Washington* and *Morelegs Sweettrick*, a take-off on Marlene Dietrich.

After the eight Baby Burlesks, five comedy shorts, and various walk-on roles, Shirley Temple was signed to a contract by Fox Studios, later to become Twentieth Century-Fox. She started with a salary of $150 per week, with $25 for Gertrude. Shirley's first full-length picture for Fox was *Stand Up and Cheer* (1934). Several additional films were released by Fox that same year, the most memorable of which were *Little Miss Marker* and *Bright Eyes*. The latter film contained her famous rendition of "On the Good Ship Lollipop," which became a trademark song for Temple and a classic of its genre. The year 1935 marked the release of *The Little*

Colonel, the first of three films in which Shirley danced with Bill "Bojangles" Robinson, the legendary black tap dancer. Known for its memorable scene of the pair dancing on a staircase, *The Little Colonel* marked the appearance of the first interracial dance team in American motion picture history.

For five consecutive years, from 1934 to 1938, Shirley Temple was named as the most popular film star in the United States; she received star billing at the top of the cast lists for all of her pictures, and thousands of fan letters addressed to her poured into Fox Studios. In 1935, she received a special Academy Award for her "outstanding contribution to screen entertainment during the year 1934"—an impressive testament to her unprecedented box office appeal. She was the darling of Depression-era filmgoers—a cute, curly-haired moppet who could make them forget their problems simply by her ability to sing, dance, and cry on cue. The lead role in the 1937 film adaptation of Rudyard Kipling's *Wee Willie Winkie* was conveniently transformed into a female role for Shirley. Adaptations of children's classics provided other starring vehicles for Temple in the films *Heidi* (1937) and *Rebecca of Sunnybrook Farm* (1938). Her next-to-last film at Twentieth Century-Fox was a 1939 adaptation of Maurice Maeterlinck's masterpiece, *The Blue Bird*, but it did not fare as well as the rest in its Hollywood transfiguration.

As Shirley Temple progressed into adolescence, her star status declined. She left the studios at Twentieth Century-Fox for those at Metro-Goldwyn-Mayer, but was dropped after appearing in one production. Temple made additional films at other studios during the 1940's, but none matched the success of her earlier productions. While continuing her acting career, she entered the private Westlake School for Girls in Holmby Hills, California, in 1940 and was graduated in 1945. At the age of seventeen, she married John Agar, a marine sergeant who launched his own acting career and appeared with Temple in John Ford's *Fort Apache* (1948), and in *Adventure in Baltimore* (1949). Another costar in Temple's later films was the young Ronald Reagan in *That Hagen Girl* (1947).

Temple decided to give up her film career in 1949 and eventually obtained a divorce from Agar, who suffered from alcoholism. On December 16, 1950, Shirley Temple married Charles Alden Black, a naval commander from a prominent California family who went on to establish himself as a successful business executive. After her second marriage, Temple chose to remain in retirement in order to devote attention to rearing her children. Although Temple attempted a comeback, appearing in the NBC television series *The Shirley Temple Storybook* in 1958 and again on *The Shirley Temple Show* in 1960, she was discouraged by the shows' poor reception. Undaunted, she turned her attention to politics.

Life's Work

While living in Washington, D.C., with her second husband, Shirley Temple Black got her first taste of national and international politics. By 1960, she had begun to participate actively in Republican politics, serving as a successful speaker at various fund-raisers for party candidates, including Richard M. Nixon. As governor of

California, her longtime friend Ronald Reagan appointed Black to serve as a member of his finance committee and to serve on the California Advisory Hospital Council. She made her own foray into the political arena when she ran for the congressional district seat representing her home county of San Mateo, California. The seat became vacant in 1967 as a result of the death from leukemia of Republican incumbent J. A. Younger. Facing an all-male field of seven Democrats and four Republicans, Black was unprepared for the rough political campaign that followed. With her child star image satirized in an Off-Broadway play and on television and her political aspirations written off as the misguided ambitions of a rich society matron, Black lost the election to fellow Republican Peter McCloskey.

Determined to devote her life to public service, Black was gratified when President Richard M. Nixon appointed her to serve as a U.S. representative to the United Nations' Twenty-fourth General Assembly from 1969 to 1970. Black became a member of the U.S. delegation to the United Nations Conference on Human Environment held in Stockholm, Sweden in 1972, and a member of the U.S. Commission for UNESCO. She also served on the U.S.S.R.-U.S.A. Joint Commission for the Cooperative Treaty on the Environment held in Moscow between 1972 and 1973.

Personal tragedy threatened to curtail Black's political career. She was diagnosed with breast cancer and had a mastectomy on November 3, 1972. In a news release issued after the operation was deemed successful, Black expressed her hope that other women would be encouraged by her example and would not allow fear to prevent them from undergoing this life-saving surgery. The response to her plea was gratifying: The American Cancer Society reported a 30 percent increase in women seeking information on the detection of breast cancer. Three weeks after her operation, Black wrote a well-informed article on breast cancer for publication in *McCall's* magazine.

Although the Watergate scandal and subsequent upheaval within the Republican Party also threatened to prevent Black from further advancement, President Gerald R. Ford eventually rewarded her for her faithful support of the party by naming her to the post of U.S. Ambassador to the Republic of Ghana in western Africa. Black had demonstrated a long-standing interest in African affairs and had established friendships with many of the African representatives at the United Nations. Quickly dispelling rumors about having attained the appointment in return for reputedly large campaign contributions to the Republican Party, Black focused her attention on learning more about Ghana by attending numerous State Department briefings and studying the history and native languages of the country. Arriving in the capital city of Accra in December of 1974, Black and her family were greeted warmly. Benefiting from the country's respect for matriarchal leadership and its admiration of her as a film celebrity, Black conducted herself well under trying circumstances and made strides in improving relations between Ghana and the United States. Despite her success, she was recalled from her post in 1976 as a result of a diplomatic snafu over Ghana's last minute cancellation of a visit from U.S. Secretary of State Henry Kissinger.

Upon her return to the United States, Black was appointed to serve as chief of protocol under President Ford. The first woman to hold this post, Black was responsible for making proper presentation of foreign diplomats to the president and for overseeing all ceremonial matters connected to the executive branch. Black's finely honed social skills and ease in making public appearances allowed her to complete her duties with distinction. Her final assignment as chief of protocol was to prepare for the presidential inauguration of Jimmy Carter in 1977.

When Ronald Reagan succeeded Carter as president in 1981, Black was invited to share her expertise as a foreign affairs officer by cochairing State Department seminars that prepared appointees for their future duties as ambassadors and diplomatic envoys. For her extraordinary services, Secretary of State George Shultz named Shirley Temple Black a Career Foreign Service Officer in 1988, the only person to receive such an honor. In the spring of 1989, Black accepted an appointment as U.S. ambassador to Czechoslovakia extended to her by President George Bush. During her tenure in Prague, Black witnessed Czechoslovakia's "Velvet Revolution," which marked the country's peaceful transition to a democratic government, and she worked closely with the new republic's president, Václav Havel, before leaving her post as ambassador in 1992.

Summary
Shirley Temple Black's legendary popularity as a juvenile film celebrity opened the door for her later success as a government appointee, but it also served as something of an obstacle. Undaunted by allegations that she was not fully qualified to serve as an international diplomat, Black employed her no-nonsense flair for public relations and demonstrated her determination to master the skills necessary to work as a foreign affairs officer. Always eager to help others, she used the occasion of her own battle with breast cancer in 1972 to help educate women about the importance of early detection. Proud of her accomplishments as an actor, Black was recognized by the Academy of Motion Picture Arts and Sciences with a second special Oscar in 1980. Most of all, drawing upon the international goodwill created by her well-loved film image, Black managed to establish impressive credentials as an American diplomat and helped train other foreign service officers who followed. Few individuals, male or female, have negotiated such a successful transition between such diverse careers.

Bibliography
Black, Shirley Temple. *Child Star: An Autobiography.* New York: McGraw-Hill, 1988. By far the most reliable source on the author's life as a child star who was exceptionally intelligent and unspoiled by fame. Black leaves her narrative unfinished, saving room for a projected sequel. A perceptive and competent work, filled with humor and honesty that reflect Black's adult personality. Contains forty-eight pages of black-and-white illustrations, a filmography, and an index.
Edwards, Anne. *Shirley Temple: American Princess.* New York: William Morrow, 1988. A substantial work by an experienced author of celebrity biographies. Covers Black's life up through the mid-1980's. Illustrated with thirty-two pages of black-

and-white photographs in addition to a detailed filmography, copious notes, and an index.

Fiori, Carlo. *The Story of Shirley Temple Black: Hollywood's Youngest Star.* New York: Dell, 1990. Intended for younger readers, this juvenile biography provides a concise summary of Black's life. Contains a list of film titles and twelve pages of illustrations.

Greene, Graham. *Graham Greene on Film: Collected Film Criticism, 1935-1940.* Edited by John R. Taylor. New York: Simon & Schuster, 1972. Among other pieces, this work includes Greene's biting review of *Wee Willie Winkie* written for London's *Night and Day* magazine, in which he called Shirley Temple "a complete totsy" whose "dimpled depravity" emerged from beneath a "mask of childhood." Furor over the article resulted in a lawsuit that Greene and the magazine lost.

Haskins, James. *Shirley Temple Black: Actress to Ambassador.* New York: Viking Kestrel, 1988. A short work written by a leading author of juvenile biographies. Lacks notes or a filmography, but is charmingly illustrated with twelve drawings by Donna Ruff.

Minott, Rodney G. *The Sinking of the Lollipop: Shirley Temple vs. Pete McCloskey.* San Francisco: Diablo Press, 1968. This small press book chronicles Black's unsuccessful 1967 campaign for California's Eleventh Congressional District seat and analyzes the factors leading to her defeat by fellow Republican Pete McCloskey.

Vera Laska

ELIZABETH BLACKWELL

Born: February 3, 1821; Counterslip, England
Died: May 31, 1910; Hastings, England
Area of Achievement: Medicine
Contribution: The first woman ever to receive a degree from an American medical
school, Elizabeth Blackwell became a leading figure in the drive to open the field
of medicine to women.

Early Life

Elizabeth Blackwell was born on February 3, 1821, in a small town near Bristol,
England. The third of nine surviving children of Samuel and Hannah Blackwell,
Elizabeth joined a family heavily influenced by the progressive and reformist values
held by her father. In addition to being a successful sugar refiner, Samuel Blackwell
was an outspoken member of his community, having wedded the practice of his
Puritan faith with the support of various liberal causes, such as women's rights,
temperance, and the abolition of slavery.

The destruction of his refinery by fire in 1832 led Samuel Blackwell to move his
family to America. After a few years spent in New York and New Jersey, the
Blackwells came to settle in Cincinnati, Ohio, in May, 1838. Pursued to the end by his
monetary troubles, Samuel Blackwell died in August of that year, leaving Hannah, her
two eldest daughters, and Elizabeth responsible for providing for the family. They
were able to do so by opening what would become a successful boarding school,
where Elizabeth spent the first four of her seven years as a teacher.

It was during these seven years, which also included one year in Kentucky and two
more in North and South Carolina, that Elizabeth Blackwell began to grow frustrated
at the limits of the teaching profession, both in its poor remuneration and its low social
status. She also became aware of her growing aversion to the idea of marriage, an
institution which, at the time, imposed even greater restrictions than did teaching on
the women who entered into it. These realizations became important factors in
Elizabeth Blackwell's decision to pursue a career in the highly respected field of
medicine, a field so utterly dominated by men that no woman had ever before received
a diploma from an American medical school.

Life's Work

It was during her final two years teaching in the Carolinas that Elizabeth Blackwell,
within the personal libraries of the distinguished physicians John and Samuel Dickson, began her study of medicine. These years of self-education served to prepare
Blackwell for her move, in May of 1847, to Philadelphia, the home of several
well-respected medical schools to which she would subsequently apply. This application process forced Blackwell to confront the institutional prejudices of the day.
Although they were often supported by sympathetic faculty members, her applications were rejected by every medical school in Philadelphia and New York as well as

by several rural colleges of much less stellar reputations. It was only when the administration of Geneva Medical College in upstate New York put her application up for review by the all-male student body that Elizabeth Blackwell's determination won her a chance for a legitimate education. Presented with a woman's name, the students had thought the submission was a joke and passed it unanimously.

Immediately upon beginning her studies, Elizabeth Blackwell experienced the scorn of both townspeople and fellow students alike. Even the women within the community were taken aback by what they perceived as brash and unfeminine behavior by Blackwell in her pursuit of medical training, and she was often made aware that the idea of a woman physician upset many of those who would one day benefit from the course of action she was endeavoring to take. Gradually, however, Blackwell's intelligence and doggedness won her great measures of respect from important faculty members and the other students with whom she worked. After completing an internship in 1848 at the Philadelphia Hospital and writing a thesis based on her experiences there, Blackwell emerged from her course work with a focus that would last throughout her professional career: the importance of preventative care in the form of improved personal hygiene. With this focus established and her studies complete, Elizabeth Blackwell received her medical degree from Geneva Medical College on January 23, 1849. She became the first woman in the United States to ever earn such an honor and was ranked first in her graduating class.

Before she was to begin her career in earnest in New York in August of 1851, Elizabeth Blackwell spent a year and a half abroad, in both England and France, with the intention of enhancing her education. Though received graciously by the medical community in England and invited by prominent staff members of several hospitals to tour their grounds, Elizabeth Blackwell found that in France the only kind of advanced training available to her was as a midwife. This period in Blackwell's life is most notable for the eye disease she contracted from a patient during her midwives' course at La Maternité in Paris, the resulting loss of sight in one eye dashed her hopes of ever becoming a surgeon. Through these trials, Blackwell's strength of character enabled her to overcome adversity. Toward the end of her stay in Europe, she returned to England and gained valuable clinical experience under the supervision of Dr. James Paget at St. Bartholomew's Hospital. In retrospect, the setbacks she experienced in this interlude abroad helped steel Blackwell for the resistance she encountered in her attempts to establish herself as a practicing physician in New York.

For a woman doctor during the 1850's, merely finding a place in which to practice proved a near impossibility. Blackwell's applications to city dispensaries for positions in the pediatric wards were flatly rejected, as were her requests to visit the female wards of a city hospital. These rejections were handed down despite her rather impressive array of degrees and recommendations. Even more indicative of this era's prejudice was Blackwell's inability even to rent a space of her own for private practice. No landlord would lease a space for such a disreputable practice, knowing that every other tenant who might be sharing a building with a "female physician" (the contemporary euphemism for "abortionist") would be forced to move or be shamed.

While overcoming these obstacles and patiently awaiting the growth of her practice, she succeeded in publishing a series of lectures on hygiene in 1852. Later, in 1853, Blackwell opened a dispensary for the poor, supported by funds she raised herself. Four years later, her dispensary became the New York Infirmary for Women and Children, the first hospital completely organized and operated by women. Outside her professional life, Blackwell in 1853 took on the responsibility of adopting a seven-year-old orphan named Katherine Barry who would remain her closest relation for the rest of her days.

In her battle to open the infirmary in 1857, Elizabeth Blackwell was joined by two other women doctors: her younger sister, Emily, who had followed Elizabeth into the profession, and Marie Zakrzewska, a Polish émigré who had been educated at Western Reserve College (later Case Western Reserve University) and who would become the resident physician at the infirmary until 1859. Once this hospital was established, Blackwell's next major goal was to create a medical college for women with a commitment to rigorous preparation and to the cause of good hygiene. Before this goal was to materialize, however, Blackwell departed in August of 1858 for a one-year stay in Great Britain, where she both practiced medicine and lectured, and also made the acquaintance of such admirers as Dr. Elizabeth Garrett and Florence Nightingale. Upon her return to the United States, Blackwell's plans were interrupted by the outbreak of the Civil War, during which she became involved in a committee concerned with the status of care for soldiers and also helped to select and train nurses going out into the field. Finally, in 1868, Elizabeth Blackwell brought her quest to fruition as she founded the Woman's Medical College of the New York Infirmary and served as the first chair of hygiene at the college. (The college eventually became part of Cornell's medical school in 1899, after the university decided to grant admission to women.)

In 1869, Elizabeth Blackwell left the United States to live and work in Great Britain. At first, she took up residence in London, where she practiced privately until she accepted a position at the New Hospital and London School of Medicine for Women in 1875. As a result of her ill health, Blackwell was forced to retire after just one year. Leaving London, she moved with Katherine Barry to Hastings, where Blackwell spent most of her last thirty years. Never one to remain idle for long, Elizabeth Blackwell spent these days writing books, essays and articles addressing a wide variety of topics, but especially focusing upon the issues of medicine and morality. She also visited the continent and traveled to the United States in 1906. In 1907, she suffered injuries as a result of falling down some stairs at her summer house in the Scottish highlands. Blackwell died at her seaside home in Hastings in 1910 and was buried in Scotland.

Summary

It would not be difficult to present Elizabeth Blackwell's achievements as a list of breakthroughs in the process of opening the field of medicine to women. As the first woman to ever receive a degree from an American medical school, the founder of the first hospital run solely by women, and the founder of one of the earliest medical colleges for women, Blackwell stands as a distinguished pioneer in the fight for a woman's right to become a practicing physician. To focus on her breakthroughs alone, however, would unfairly limit the scope of Blackwell's contribution. From the moment she decided to pursue her degree, Blackwell committed herself to more than mere medicine. Desiring a greater status than was afforded by traditional feminine pursuits and seeking a level of freedom that she could find nowhere else, Blackwell chose to challenge the various obstacles that hindered women from pursuing professional careers. Medicine was the avenue she selected in order to accomplish her ultimate goal of advancing the opportunities available to women. Immersed in her era's atmosphere of social activism, Blackwell dedicated her work and her writings to causes of morality and equality. The breadth of Elizabeth Blackwell's influence is amply illustrated by the names of those individuals—people as various as Herbert Spencer and Florence Nightingale, as Dante Gabriel Rossetti and George Eliot—who came to admire and respect Blackwell's ideas and accomplishments.

Bibliography

Abram, Ruth J., ed. *"Send Us a Lady Physician": Women Doctors in America, 1835-1920.* New York: W. W. Norton, 1986. Compiled to accompany a museum exhibit, this collection of essays celebrates the pioneering spirit of early women physicians and describes the experience of women in the health professions during the nineteenth and early twentieth centuries.

Blackwell, Elizabeth. *Pioneer Work in Opening the Medical Profession to Women.* Reprint. New York: Source Book Press, 1970. Originally published in 1895, this work consists of autobiographical sketches which delineate the enormous struggle Blackwell had to endure in order to enter and graduate from medical school. That she was fully conscious of her historical role is clear.

Brown, Jordan. *Elizabeth Blackwell.* New York: Chelsea House, 1989. This biography is part of the publisher's American Women of Achievement series. Although primarily intended for young adult readers, this work provides an excellent introduction to Blackwell's life and examines the various issues that confronted her in her quest for providing opportunities for women in the medical profession.

Buckmaster, Henrietta. *Women Who Shaped History.* New York: Collier Books, 1966. Six remarkable women of the nineteenth century are the subject of this group biography. Elizabeth Blackwell's life is included with those of Prudence Crandall, Dorothea Dix, Mary Baker Eddy, Elizabeth Cady Stanton, and Harriet Tubman.

Hume, Ruth Fox. *Great Women of Medicine.* New York: Random House, 1964. Hume devotes her first chapter to Blackwell and offers the reader a compact biography that emphasizes Blackwell's early life and career in the United States and ends with her retirement to England.

Morantz-Sanchez, Regina. "Feminist Theory and Historical Practice: Rereading Elizabeth Blackwell." *History and Theory* 31 (December, 1992): 51-69. A scholar analyzes Blackwell's writings in order to demonstrate how the discussion of scientific topics in these works reflected Blackwell's feminist concerns. Morantz-Sanchez also notes that the growing predominance of laboratory-based treatment of disease and the rigorous application of scientific methodology moved the practice of medicine away from many of the nurturing, feminine aspects of health care championed by Blackwell and her colleagues.

Ross, Ishbel. *Child of Destiny: The Life Story of the First Woman Doctor.* New York: Harper, 1949. Ross wrote a full-length biography of Blackwell with the aid of interviews with family members. Full of fascinating detail, the book chronicles Blackwell's work as well as her personal life and her many associations with major figures of the nineteenth century. It places her within the swell of reform characteristic of the era.

Wilson, Dorothy Clarke. *Lone Woman: The Story of Elizabeth Blackwell, the First Woman Doctor.* Boston: Little, Brown, 1970. Novelist, dramatist and biographer, Dorothy Clarke Wilson brings her dramatic skills to enliven the solid biography which is based on family reminiscences and papers as well as extensive research in primary sources.

Bonnie L. Ford

LINDA BLOODWORTH-THOMASON

Born: April 15, 1947; Conway, Arkansas

Area of Achievement: Television
Contribution: A powerful force in Hollywood, Bloodworth-Thomason uses her television shows in order to educate viewers.

Early Life
On April 15, 1947, Linda Joyce Bloodworth was born in Conway, Arkansas. Her grandfather, who was half Cherokee Indian, had received no formal education beyond the sixth grade. While continuing his self-education, he clerked for a judge, became a lawyer, was a civil rights activist, served as editor of a newspaper, and was selected as chair of the Republican Party in Arkansas. (Republicans were considered to be members of the reform-minded party of the day, particularly in the South.) Linda was often told the family story that he carried President Teddy Roosevelt's telephone number on a slip of paper in his back pocket and regularly called to report how the six Republicans of Arkansas were doing. Her mother, Claudia Bloodworth, was a homemaker who went to business college. Her father, Ralph Bloodworth, was an antiwar activist and an exceptional liberal litigator who never lost a murder case.

As a child, Linda and her family moved across the Arkansas border to Missouri, where she grew up in Poplar Bluff. Described as a prissy tomboy, she developed toughness in order to play in neighborhood games dominated by boys, including her older brother, Randy. As a youth, while the other girls watched from the shore, she water-skied, dodging tree stumps. She was friendly and outgoing: In high school, she was a cheerleader and was voted "Most Popular Girl."

Linda learned much about creating realistic characters from observing the divergent personalities of her mother and father and their strong romantic relationship. At a young age, she became the mediator between her hard-drinking father and her mother. She later spoke of them both in glowing terms and credited them for making her childhood a liberated one, instilling in her ideals, and molding her into the complex person she later became. She credits her gracious southern charms and her beliefs about women to her mother. Her father ingrained in her the idea that she could do or be anything she wanted to be.

In the 1970's, Linda Bloodworth graduated with a degree in English from the University of Missouri. She planned to obtain a law degree and then move to Washington, D.C., but on the spur of the moment, she decided to travel with some friends to Los Angeles. Upon her arrival, Bloodworth began to teach English at Jordan High School, located in riot-torn Watts. The conditions were difficult in her overcrowded and underfurnished classroom, but she was motivated by the desire to combat injustice in the world. While teaching, she met actress Mary Kay Place. Both displaced southerners, they became fast friends and began to write together. For money, Bloodworth worked selling advertisements by phone for *The Wall Street*

Journal and writing free-lance articles for a local law journal.

In 1974, after Bloodworth and Place had had only a few months of writing together, Larry Gelbart hired the two to write for his popular television show, *M*A*S*H*. Female writing teams were extremely unusual at the time, and Bloodworth and Place were the first women to write for the hit series. As a result of her work there, Linda Bloodworth received her first accolades and launched her career in the entertainment industry.

Life's Work

For their first episode, "Hot Lips and Empty Arms," Linda Bloodworth and Mary Kay Place were nominated for an Emmy Award and Bloodworth was presented with a Woman of the Year award on a live television broadcast from Lincoln Center. After their success with writing for *M*A*S*H*, Place went back to acting and Bloodworth wrote television pilots on a free-lance basis, including the one for *One Day at a Time* in 1975, but she yearned for her own show.

Linda Bloodworth met her future husband, Harry Thomason, on the Columbia Studios lot in 1980, and they were married in 1983. Together, they formed Mozark Productions, which they ran as partners. In addition to taking on some directing duties, Harry Thomason chose to handle most of the business side of the production work, while Linda Bloodworth-Thomason continued to write and develop new programs. The couple shared duties as executive producers for all of their series.

Bloodworth-Thomason's first hit series came after the cancellation of two failed series: *Filthy Rich*, which ran for twelve episodes in 1982-1983, and the Robert Wagner series *Lime Street*, which only ran briefly in 1985. Having worked with Delta Burke, Dixie Carter, Jean Smart, and Annie Potts on the previously named shows, Bloodworth-Thomason cast them in her next series, *Designing Women*. The show premiered in 1986 and became a hugely successful CBS series, airing first-run episodes in prime time until May 24, 1993.

Describing herself as a man-loving feminist, Bloodworth-Thomason created a show featuring four women like herself whose southern femininity served as the perfect foil for their strong, independent opinions. She later confessed that much of the show's topical and opinionated banter was based on conversations between her father and his buddies. The show centered around four women running an Atlanta interior decorating firm, assisted by an African American delivery man who was later promoted to full partner. These women were not primarily defined by their relationships with men; rather, the focus was placed squarely on their relationships with one another.

In addition to creating, writing, and producing *Designing Women*, she also created, wrote, and produced two other hit series: *Evening Shade*, which first aired in 1990, and *Hearts Afire*, which came out in October of 1992. *Evening Shade* featured Burt Reynolds as Wood Newton, a small-town high-school football coach married to a city prosecutor, played by Marilu Henner, and surrounded by an eccentric bunch of family members and friends played by a star-studded ensemble cast that included Hal

Holbrook, Ozzie Davis, and Charles Durning. *Hearts Afire*, a romantic political comedy, starred John Ritter as John Hartman, a Washington political aide, and Markie Post as Georgie Anne Lahti, an unemployed journalist. Desperate for work, Lahti begs for a press secretary position with Hartman's boss, a conservative U.S. senator, played by actor George Gaynes. Like all of Bloodworth-Thomason's shows, these series depict complete female characters who have strong identities and opinions, as well as important relationships with one another.

In addition to achieving distinction as a powerful woman in a male-dominated arena, Bloodworth-Thomason has chosen not to conform to convention in other ways. As head of her own production company, Bloodworth-Thomason decides which actors she wants to cast in her shows, and her husband goes directly to them to work out a deal. At Mozark Productions, there is a huge emphasis placed on working as an ensemble. In fact, Bloodworth-Thomason does not actually write the pilot for a show until the casting is finalized. She is notorious for completing scripts at the last minute, regularly staying up all night to finish them. She wrote thirty-five consecutive episodes of *Designing Women* during the show's first two seasons, writing by hand on yellow legal pads at a furious pace, reportedly finishing some scripts in the amazingly short time of six hours. Regardless of deadlines, she displays grace under pressure and appears imperturbable and serene—nothing seems capable of disturbing her even keel.

As a politically active woman, Bloodworth-Thomason reveals her strong personal political beliefs in her work and life activities. She does more than make donations and attend fund raisers. For example, when former Vice President Dan Quayle attacked the television show *Murphy Brown* for undermining "family values" by depicting a single mother, Bloodworth-Thomason responded by debating Quayle's press secretary on public radio. In 1992, she and Harry played a major role in the Clinton campaign. Bloodworth-Thomason first met Hillary and Bill Clinton in the early 1980's through her husband Harry, and the two families are close friends. When Bill Clinton was running for President, Bloodworth-Thomason and her husband were enormously helpful and supportive. They used their professional skills to produce campaign advertisements for the New Hampshire primary, to arrange Bill Clinton's appearance on *The Arsenio Hall Show* on television, and to oversee the campaign's finances. In addition, although she was busy with her own shows and had no documentary experience, Bloodworth-Thomason made a video on Bill Clinton for the Democratic National Convention called "The Man from Hope." She collected ten hours of film and compiled a 1,000-page manuscript. Extremely moving and skillfully created, the finished version of this fourteen-minute video contained remarkable footage, including an adolescent Clinton shaking hands with President John F. Kennedy, and helped to emphasize Clinton's new image as a man of the people. The video was later credited with boosting Clinton's poll results. Bloodworth-Thomason continued to work with the Clintons after the election, providing them with her expertise.

Bloodworth-Thomason has used her shows as platforms to discuss topical issues such as acquired immune deficiency syndrome (AIDS), breast cancer, pornography, women clergy, racism, domestic violence, menopause, political conservatism, incest, and sexual politics. Her characters have also discussed current political events, including the 1991 Senate hearings involving law professor Anita Hill's allegations of sexual misconduct and harassment against Supreme Court nominee Clarence Thomas.

In addition, Bloodworth-Thomason spends $1 million each year to finance her own charitable foundation, which is based in Missouri. Named after her mother, the Claudia Company funds women's scholarships, literacy programs, and anti-domestic-violence programs.

The unrelenting personal tragedies that plagued Bloodworth-Thomason between the ages of thirty-five and forty not only exemplify her amazing optimism but also show that her personal experiences and beliefs are reflected in the content of her work. Her father died a difficult and painful death from cancer. One year later, her mother contracted AIDS from a contaminated blood transfusion during open heart surgery. Claudia Bloodworth suffered from the disease for three years before dying in 1986. Cancer also was responsible for the deaths of several uncles, Bloodworth-Thomason's mother-in-law, and her sister-in-law. Bloodworth-Thomason has helped rear the three children of her widowed brother, Randy, a successful Poplar Bluff lawyer.

A self-confessed workaholic, Bloodworth-Thomason regularly puts in eighteen-hour days, doing whatever she feels necessary, whether it is dancing off-camera to inspire an actor or sitting in an editing room to fine tune or shift the tone of a scene. She never rests on her laurels, but is constantly reworking and rethinking her shows, striving to make them all that she envisions. This hard work has paid off handsomely. In the early 1990's, she and her husband signed a $50 million deal with CBS television for five new series within an eight-year period—the largest contract in the network's history.

Summary

At the suggestion that people who work in television entertainment should refrain from involvement in politics, Linda Bloodworth-Thomason has responded, "I have 30 million viewers every week. Pick out the Top 5 White House correspondents, and they don't have that many readers." It was actually this realization that her work could have an impact on a mass audience that initially hooked Bloodworth-Thomason on television. "I am a Populist by nature," she has said, "and this is a way to combine whatever artistry I have with my populism." Convinced that art is more interesting if it is political in content, Bloodworth-Thomason has labored to make her political voice less threatening by delivering it with humor and charm, so that viewers who might otherwise feel uncomfortable with the content may absorb what she has to say.

Linda Bloodworth-Thomason's huge successes have not been greeted with total support in Hollywood. Striving to maintain artistic control, she writes as many of the episodes as she can, and she is prolific. During the first season of *Designing Women*, she was reprimanded by the Writers Guild for not hiring more writers. Since her first success writing for *M*A*S*H*, she has practically been ignored by the Emmys.

As of 1993, *Evening Shade* had received seven nominations (although none had her name attached) and went on to win two: one for actor Burt Reynolds and one for actor Michael Jeter. *Designing Women* received eighteen nominations, three for Bloodworth-Thomason as producer of an outstanding comedy series, but only received one Emmy Award—for outstanding achievement in hairstyling.

Nevertheless, Linda Bloodworth-Thomason remains a powerful force on television. A top writer/producer, she is one of a handful of powerful women in the male-dominated world of Hollywood to have a successful independent production company. Although she has experienced little in the way of overt discrimination in her work with CBS, she has acknowledged the limitations created by the expectation that rich and powerful women are jealous, loud, and obnoxious. Recognizing that her prominent role affects other women's lives, Bloodworth-Thomason feels a great responsibility to women and molds her life accordingly. Through her creative endeavors and direct efforts to improve women's lives, Linda Bloodworth-Thomason is not just paving the road for other women, she is building it.

Bibliography
Alexander, Shana. "Linda Bloodworth-Thomason." *Interview* 23 (August, 1993): 98-106. An interview with Linda Bloodworth-Thomason that covers her personal history, her current projects, her role as woman in Hollywood, and her relationship with the Clintons.
Carson, Tom. "Funny Ladies." *Harper's Bazaar* 125 (October, 1992): 68. This brief article discusses women producers of CBS sitcoms.
DeVries, Hilary. "Southern Exposure." *Vogue* 182 (October, 1992): 190-194. Interview with Linda Bloodworth-Thomason that focuses on her creative roots in the South and her vivid female characters.
Griffith-Roberts, Carolanne. "Their Work Stars the South." *Southern Living* 25 (June, 1990): 106-115. A comparative profile of the regional influences found in the work of Bloodworth-Thomason and of Jon Jory, a playwright/director with Actors Theatre in Louisville, Kentucky. Includes a valuable perspective on Bloodworth-Thomason's southern heritage.
Proffitt, Steve. "Linda Bloodworth-Thomason: Pursuing That Arkansas Connection." *Los Angeles Times*, November 22, 1992, p. M3. Covers Bloodworth-Thomason's biographical background, political involvement, "The Man from Hope," and role as a woman in the entertainment industry.
Rochlin, Margy. "The Prime Time of Linda Bloodworth-Thomason." *Los Angeles Times Magazine*, September 27, 1992, pp. 20-22, 42-47. In-depth and extremely informative interview covering all aspects of Bloodworth-Thomason's life, both her personal and professional history.
Weisberg, Jacob. "Southern Exposure." *New Republic* 207 (November 2, 1992): 13-15. The author discusses the Thomasons' relationship with Bill Clinton and their work in producing the documentary "The Man from Hope."

Ursula Burton

AMELIA JENKS BLOOMER

Born: May 27, 1818; Homer, New York
Died: December 30, 1894; Council Bluffs, Iowa
Areas of Achievement: Journalism and women's rights
Contribution: Bloomer is best remembered for her support of dress reform for women. Her greatest contributions, however, were as publisher of the first women's rights newspaper and leader of the Iowa suffrage campaign.

Early Life

Amelia Jenks entered the world on May 27, 1818, in the small town of Homer, New York. Her parents, Ananias and Lucy (Webb) Jenks, were married in Rhode Island in 1806, and then moved to central New York. Amelia was the youngest daughter and possibly the youngest child (a brother may have followed) of the six surviving Jenks children. Ananias Jenks was a clothier whose family managed well enough on his modest earnings. Amelia's parents were Presbyterians, her mother being particularly devout.

Little is known about Amelia Jenks's education and early life. She received instruction from her mother at home in matters both religious and domestic before attending the local public school. During the course of several terms at school, she acquired basic skills in reading, writing "with a little grammar," and arithmetic. In the year 1835, at the age of seventeen, Amelia found herself employed as a teacher in one of the district schools in Clyde, New York. Her teaching career was short-lived, ending abruptly for reasons unknown after only one term.

Shortly thereafter Amelia Jenks took up residence with her married sister Elvira in Waterloo, New York in 1837. Once there, Amelia found employment for two to three years as a governess and tutor for the three youngest children of Oren Chamberlain. During her tenure as governess, Amelia established a circle of friends that included Dexter Chamberlain Bloomer, a young Quaker lawyer from Seneca Falls. In 1840, their friendship led to marriage. Their wedding ceremony reflected the essence of their spousal partnership in that "obey" was omitted from Amelia's vows—a harbinger of Amelia's future endeavors.

The Bloomers settled in Seneca Falls, New York, where in 1843 they joined the Episcopal Church, an affiliation they would actively maintain throughout their lives. Though they never had children of their own, the Bloomers loved children and their household was often increased by the extended visitations of relatives' children. After the Bloomers moved to Iowa in 1855, they adopted a boy, and then later his sister, whose Mormon mother had died en route to Utah.

Life's Work

The year 1840 was significant for Amelia Bloomer in both her professional and personal life. The same year that the Bloomers were married, Amelia helped to organize the first Temperance Society in Seneca Falls. She proved an active and energetic member whose burgeoning literary talents had not gone unnoticed by her new husband. Impressed by her well-versed letters composed during their courtship, Dexter Bloomer encouraged his new wife to further develop her natural talent for writing. He saw to it that many of her articles found their way into the *Seneca County Courier*, the local newspaper of which he was part owner. She wrote for other reform papers as well, such as the local temperance society's *Water Bucket* and the *Free Soil Union*. Because it was considered unseemly for a woman's name to appear in print, Amelia Bloomer used various pseudonyms, both male and female, to disguise her identity.

In 1848, after publishing an announcement for the first women's rights convention to be held in Seneca Falls, the Bloomers decided, out of curiosity, to attend the meeting together. Amelia was acquainted with Elizabeth Cady Stanton, the radical women's rights advocate and one of the convention organizers who also happened to be a resident of Seneca Falls. While initially not a woman suffrage supporter, Amelia Bloomer listened and was not unaffected by what she heard at the meeting. Women temperance advocates were dissatisfied with the limited, inactive role assigned to them, that of financial supporters of their more active male counterparts. Consequently, in 1849, Amelia Bloomer and the other temperance women created a female auxiliary group with its own corresponding newspaper, the *Lily*.

This paper—written, edited, and published by women—was the first of its kind in the country. Though it began as a temperance journal, the paper's motto was "Devoted to the interests of women." Almost from its inception, Bloomer printed articles pertaining to women's rights. Serving as editor and publisher from 1849 to 1855, she was one of the journal's most prolific contributors. It was Amelia Bloomer who introduced Susan B. Anthony to Elizabeth Cady Stanton in 1850 during a temperance meeting in Seneca Falls. Meanwhile, Dexter Bloomer, who had been appointed postmaster following the presidential election of 1848, convinced authorities to appoint his wife deputy in 1849. Amelia Bloomer was the first woman to serve as a post office clerk. One day while working in that capacity, she encountered her cousin, Elizabeth Smith Miller, and Elizabeth Cady Stanton wearing what would soon become known as the Bloomer costume.

The idea of dress reform was not new to Amelia Bloomer, but seeing women actually wearing the "Turkish trousers" in public encouraged her to follow suit. Impressed by the ease of movement and grace that the new costume allowed its boosters, Bloomer donned the new attire and then heartily endorsed it in the *Lily*. The response was immediate and nearly overwhelming. The costume's loose waist provided comfort, its shortened skirt cleanliness, and its matching pantaloons modesty. Women clamored for a more detailed description while subscriptions for the *Lily* rose from five hundred to four thousand. The Bloomer costume symbolized the women's rights movement and the appearance of a Bloomer woman on the streets was sure to warrant mentioning in the local press. The debate produced by the controversial garb eventually convinced most women's rights advocates to abandon it after a few short years. Amelia Bloomer continued to wear the outfit until 1859, five or six years after everyone else had given it up. Though she was not the first to don it, and repeatedly said so, the outfit would forever bear the name of its greatest promoter, Amelia Bloomer.

In 1853, the Bloomers moved to Mount Vernon, Ohio, where they each resumed their work in reform. Amelia continued editing and writing for the *Lily*, witnessing the paper's circulation increase to six thousand. Dexter Bloomer had purchased an interest in another reform newspaper, the *Western Home Visitor*. He appointed Amelia assistant editor and she wrote weekly for the *Visitor* while pursuing other reform activities. She proceeded with the lecture tour that she had begun in 1852 on behalf of temperance and women's rights. Prior to one speaking engagement, Amelia discovered that she would be lecturing on the same platform used by Horace Mann, crusader for public education, only a few days before. She had drawn as big a crowd and, consequently, asked for as big a fee. The lecture committee was astonished at the suggestion that a woman be granted the same fee as her male counterpart, but paid her anyway.

Another controversy erupted when Amelia Bloomer hired a female compositor to work for the *Lily*. In protest, the male typesetters went on strike and could not be persuaded of the wisdom of hiring women. The Bloomers proceeded to dismiss the stubborn male printers and hired four women typesetters and three enlightened men for other, more physical tasks. Two issues of the *Lily* were delayed, but soon after the reorganization of the print shop, the paper appeared with praiseworthy regularity.

The Bloomers relocated again in 1855, settling in Council Bluffs, Iowa, a town of three thousand people at the edge of the western frontier. Council Bluffs lacked printing facilities and good rail connections for distribution of the *Lily*, so the paper was sold to Mary E. Birdsall of Richmond, Indiana, who had been editor of the *Indiana Farmer* ladies' department. Without the vitality and devotion of Amelia Bloomer, the *Lily*'s spirit was lost and it ceased publication in late 1855. Not until 1868, with the publication of the *Revolution*, would the women's rights movement again have a newspaper of national scope.

Amelia Bloomer's reputation for oratory had preceded her in Iowa, and she quickly became one of the busiest suffrage campaigners in the West. Six months after arriving in Council Bluffs, she began a speaking tour for "Woman's Enfranchisement." Having been won over to the idea earlier, she was the only woman to support female suffrage publicly before the Civil War. Asked to speak before the Nebraska state legislature in 1856, her persuasive eloquence helped to induce the lower house to pass a woman suffrage bill, only to have it filibustered in the upper chamber. Following her well-publicized speech, she was in great demand throughout the West. In 1869, she represented Iowa at the American Equal Rights Association convention held in New York and served as a vice president for the same organization from 1867 until her death in 1894. At the state level, she became president of the Iowa Woman Suffrage Society in 1871, a year after it was initially organized. Because of Bloomer's ardent involvement in the state's crusade for female suffrage, Stanton and Anthony asked her to write the Iowa chapter for their *History of Woman Suffrage*. While urging her female friends in the East to move west and homestead, to own their own land, Bloomer was instrumental in securing the passage of an 1873 law protecting the property of married women in Iowa. Until the time of her death in Council Bluffs, Iowa, in 1894, Amelia Bloomer wielded considerable influence in the press, continuing to defend her views in national newspapers and journals.

Summary

While not an original thinker, Amelia Bloomer possessed literary talent and did much to advance the cause of women's rights in nineteenth century America. Initially, she gained notoriety when her name became synonymous with pantaloons. While she was insistent that the wearing of Turkish trousers was not her original idea, she parlayed the phenomenon into a symbol of women's rights, earning for herself the recognition necessary to becoming a spokeswoman for the movement.

Bloomer represents the earliest variety of American feminist, diligently working to reform political inequality while attempting to address the social underpinnings of women's status. In a lifelong writing campaign, she championed various forms of women's rights including: female suffrage, divorce for wives married to drunkards, women's education, married women's property rights, and dress reform. Most important, she established the movement's first newspaper, facilitating communication among the nation's early feminists as well as providing information to an interested public.

Bibliography

Bloomer, Dexter C. *Life and Writings of Amelia Bloomer.* New York: Schocken Books, 1975. Reprinted since the 1895 original edition, this early biography by the subject's husband chronicles Amelia Bloomer's reform work, especially for the Iowa suffrage campaign. Texts of editorials she wrote and speeches that she gave are included.

Gattey, Charles Neilson. *The Bloomer Girls.* New York: Coward-McCann, 1968. A narrative history of the "bloomers" and the women who wore them, with particular attention paid to Amelia Bloomer's role in it.

Gurko, Miriam. *The Ladies of Seneca Falls: The Birth of the Woman's Rights Movement.* New York: Macmillan, 1974. A collection of biographies of early women's rights advocates, including a chapter on Bloomer's contributions to the movement. Its narrative style provides a good general background of the nineteenth century woman's rights campaign.

Noun, Louise R. *Strong-Minded Women: The Emergence of the Woman-Suffrage Movement in Iowa.* Ames: Iowa State University Press, 1969. Bloomer is a central figure in this penetrating case study of the intricacies and personalities involved in the Iowa woman-suffrage campaign. Thorough analysis of the external antisuffrage forces as well as the internal strife of the movement permeate this work.

Steiner, Linda. "Finding Community in Nineteenth-Century Suffrage Periodicals," *American Journalism* 1 (Summer, 1983): 1-16. The importance of women's news-

papers such as the *Lily* in sustaining relationships between woman's rights supporters is highlighted.

Thorp, Margaret Farrand. *Female Persuasion: Six Strong-Minded Women.* New
Haven, Conn.: Yale University Press, 1949. One of the six chapters is devoted to
Amelia Bloomer, which includes a critique of her achievements and a detailed
account of the bloomer phenomenon.

Rosanne M. Barker

NELLIE BLY
Elizabeth Cochrane Seaman

Born: May 5, 1864; Cochran's Mills, Pennsylvania
Died: January 27, 1922; New York, New York
Areas of Achievement: Journalism and social reform
Contribution: Her newspaper writing allowed women to be accepted as journalists
and stimulated countless cases of needed reform in living conditions, politics, and
businesses in Pittsburgh, Pennsylvania, and New York City.

Early Life

The journalist known as Nellie Bly was born Elizabeth Cochran on May 5, 1864,
to Michael and Mary Jane (Kennedy) Cochran in Cochran Mills, Pennsylvania, the
youngest of three children from her father's second marriage. Michael Cochran rose
from a laborer to a mill owner to an associate judge. He eventually owned most of the
land in the area. Elizabeth's mother, who had been widowed before she married
Cochran, came from an old, well-to-do Pittsburgh family. Elizabeth, who was known
to her family as "Pink," also had seven half-siblings from her father's first marriage,
including five older brothers with whom she continually tried to keep pace. She
climbed trees and ran races against them, despite their teasing.

Elizabeth received her early education from her father. Part of that education
included helping him research law cases, a skill that would come in handy when she
became an investigative reporter. After her father died in 1870 and her mother endured
a miserable third marriage that ended in divorce, Elizabeth was sent to be educated at
a nearby normal school to be trained as a teacher. Although she was a lackluster
student, she excelled in writing. Her stories contained heroines who looked like her
and defeated dragons and supernatural beings. By the time she was sixteen, her
father's savings had been spent, and she and her mother moved to Pittsburgh to be
near family.

Life's Work

Elizabeth Cochrane (she added the "e" to her last name supposedly to give it more
class) did not want to be a burden on family members. She needed a job, but none of
the common occupations for single women of her era—working as a schoolteacher or
as an escort for a rich woman—appealed to her. She wanted to write.

In January of 1885, Cochrane read an editorial column in the *Pittsburgh Dispatch*
entitled "Woman's Sphere." The column argued that women belonged in the home,
not in politics or business. Cochrane was infuriated. She wrote an anonymous letter
to the *Dispatch* contending that women were capable of thinking and working, and
she signed her letter "Lonely Orphan Girl." Intrigued by the letter, *Dispatch* Editor
George A. Madden published an advertisement asking that the writer of the letter
contact him. Cochrane responded and set up a time to meet.

Madden, who had been impressed with the sincerity and spirit of her letter, was pleased to meet Cochrane. After some questioning, he asked Cochrane what she would write if given the chance. She told him she wanted to write stories about people's everyday lives. Instead of printing her letter, Madden asked her to submit an article on the plight of women, which she did.

After editing and publishing her first piece, Madden invited Cochrane to select her own topic for the second. She suggested a piece on divorce, but Madden was skeptical. Divorce was obviously an interesting topic, but not one a young unmarried woman would know much about. Nevertheless, he gave her a chance. Cochrane used her father's notes on the topic and interviewed some of the women who lived in the same building with her. Her piece impressed Madden, who agreed to publish it, but not under her name. The use of her "Orphan Girl" pseudonym was inappropriate for her new article, yet female writers customarily adopted pen names to conceal their true identities. One legend recounts that Madden and Cochrane decided on Nellie Bly after a copy boy strolled by singing Stephen Foster's popular song, "Nelly Bly." However it evolved, this pseudonym remained with Cochrane throughout her journalistic career.

Cochrane, or Bly as she was now known, was hired at $5 a week. She wrote human interest stories, often immersing herself in her assignments. She worked in a factory she described as a firetrap and wrote about the women who were paid poorly, worked long hours, and could not leave their posts without permission. She visited Pittsburgh's slums and wrote about children forced to work long hours so their families could eat.

Readers were outraged by these revelations. Unfortunately, so were the newspaper's advertisers, the people who owned the unsafe factories and slums. Reform began, but advertising pressure forced Bly's editors to give her softer, less controversial assignments. As a result, Bly reviewed theater and art, and wrote about weddings and lectures. Her stories were thoughtfully written and popular with readers, but Bly was not satisfied. She missed writing reform stories.

She decided to visit Mexico, where she believed her reform stories could be helpful. Once there, Bly found families in rags, sleeping in the streets, while the wealthy wore the latest designs from Paris. She wrote about the contrasts in Mexican life for nearly six months, mailing the stories to the *Dispatch* for publication.

She returned to Pittsburgh in 1886 and decided to move to New York City in 1887. there, she sold stories about Mexico and went from newspaper to newspaper looking for a job. No editor wanted to hire a woman who wanted to be a real reporter. After selling the story of her failed interviews to the *Dispatch*, she negotiated a meeting with Colonel John Cockerill, the managing editor of Joseph Pulitzer's *The New York World*. Cockerill and Pulitzer himself were impressed with her stories, but wanted something more creative and attention-getting.

Together, Bly and Cockerill hit upon the idea of Bly feigning insanity in order to be admitted to Blackwell's Island lunatic asylum. Meant as a refuge for poor, supposedly insane people, the institution was rumored to be filled with horrors. Pulitzer and Cockerill promised Bly a full-time job and agreed to obtain her release if she successfully managed to get herself admitted.

Dressed in a nice outfit, Bly put 73 cents in her purse. She expected that someone with no money who was acting insane would immediately be sent to the institution.

Bly went to the Temporary Home for Females, using the name Nellie Brown in order to gain admission. Her strategy was to convince the residents of the boarding-house that she had become insane. Her act began after dinner. She screamed and cried, insisting that the other women in the house were out to get her. She shrieked that she must have her pistol for protection and demanded to be taken home. The women tried to console her, but she curled up in a corner and wailed.

Police were called, and Bly was dragged to the station. She kept up her act, yelling and fighting to get free. She was taken before a judge, who allowed reporters to interview her in the hope that her story would attract the attention of her relatives or friends. After the meeting with the reporters, doctors examined Bly. They took her temperature and pulse, and looked into her eyes. None bothered to test her sanity, convinced that her delusions and strange behavior were evidence of hysteria.

Bly was condemned to Blackwell's Island on September 25, 1887. She quickly dropped the act, speaking rationally and logically. She explained that she was not insane. The doctors and nurses ignored her.

Bly found other sane women at the institution, one of whom was merely physically ill, another who was admitted when her husband caught her with another man. The patients were viciously teased and beaten by nurses, forced to bathe in the same ice cold water and to use the same towel and comb, even though some patients had oozing sores and lice. They were forced to sit on hard chairs all day without anything to do. Patients were given inedible food. Rancid butter was spread on spider infested bread. The doctors and nurses, however, were served good food.

The *World*'s lawyer freed Bly from the island after ten days. She wrote a two-part series about the horrors she experienced, winning a job and forcing improvements at the institution. Money was given to get better food, and better wages were offered to attract better personnel. Her exploits also made news around the nation and her career as a stunt journalist was launched.

Bly's efforts to effect reform did not end there. She faked a theft and discovered the city prison had no female officers to search female prisoners and no way to keep male officers from watching the women being searched. Among other exposés, Bly investigated an employment agency that was cheating immigrants by charging finder's fees for nonexistent jobs, a New York state lobbyist who bought off politicians to pass or kill bills, and a health clinic for the poor that allowed inexperienced doctors to experiment on people.

Bly's time, however, was not completely consumed by crusading for reform. She interviewed various celebrities, including Buffalo Bill and the wives of Ulysses S. Grant, James Garfield, and James K. Polk. She also went on stage as a chorus girl.

Perhaps her most famous journalistic stunt was her race around the globe, inspired by Jules Verne's book *Around the World in Eighty Days* (1873). Bly decided to attempt a journey around the globe in seventy-five days. Initially, her proposed stunt met with opposition, because the journey was long and dangerous, and it was considered highly improper for a women to travel alone. Nevertheless, Cockerill and Pulitzer finally agreed to sponsor Bly's trip.

Using only commercial transportation, Bly left New Jersey on the ocean liner *Augusta Victoria* on November 14, 1889. She traveled from New Jersey to London to Paris; took a detour to Amiens, France, in order to meet Jules Verne; continued to Italy, the Suez, Ceylon, Singapore, Hong Kong, Yokohama, and San Francisco before returning to New Jersey. During the course of her journey, she got seasick, found out that American money was worth little in the East, received two marriage proposals, fought her way through storms and blizzards, wrote about the poor, and bought a monkey in Singapore.

Meanwhile, the *World* kept tabs on Bly's progress through cables. When she was unable to cable, they wrote stories speculating where she might be. They turned her into a celebrity, sponsoring a national contest as to when she would return. Clothes that imitated her traveling wardrobe, a game, and even a song entitled "Globe Trotting Nellie Bly" swept the country. On January 25, 1890, after seventy-two days, six hours, and eleven minutes, Bly returned, beating her own estimated time. The city welcomed her with canon blasts and a parade. After her adventure, Bly continued to write, taking on the cause of striking train workers and drought victims in the American Midwest.

On April 5, 1895, Bly married Robert Livingston Seaman, a millionaire industrialist who was nearly seventy years old. Although their first year of marriage was stormy and Bly went back to work as a reporter, she eventually retired from journalism to help him run his business. Seaman died in 1904, making Bly president of Iron Clad Manufacturing Company and American Steel Barrel Company. She proved to be a better champion of underdog causes than businesswoman. Bad judgment and dishonest employees forced Bly into bankruptcy by 1911. She returned to journalism, becoming the first woman to report from the Eastern Front during World War I. She later worked at the New York *Evening Journal* in 1919.

Bly died of pneumonia on January 27, 1922. Long detached from the spotlight, her death went nearly unnoticed by the New York newspapers. The *Evening Journal*, however, paid her a fitting tribute, describing her as "the best reporter in America."

Summary

Nellie Bly fought to be accepted in the male-dominated world of journalism, but acceptance was not what she really wanted. This acceptance was necessary for her to reach her true goals—expose injustices in order to accomplish reform and, at the same time, earn a living by writing.

Bly's investigative reporting brought about reform in factories, jails, politics, slums, and on Blackwell's Island. Convinced that instances of injustice should be made right and that individuals who preyed upon the unfortunate should be stopped, she challenged the mighty on behalf of the poor, battled the powerful, and demanded change. With her knack of seizing attention for herself as well as her subjects, she even made people laugh once in awhile.

Bly advanced journalism by taking newspaper audiences with her into situations and allowing them to experience those situations vicariously through her stories. In this way, she took her readers into worlds they might never have seen without her. Through her, they traveled to far-off places in a race against time. Through her, they also experienced the horrors of trying to convince those who would not listen that they were sane.

Bly advanced journalism as a career for women by refusing to adhere to societal concepts of a woman's role. Although she did not overtly fight for women's rights, her persistence opened the door for equal opportunities in journalism. Because she refused to be satisfied with writing fluff pieces about weddings and doilies, other women were undoubtedly taken more seriously when they too demanded to write about real stories. Most of all, Nellie Bly proved that women were capable of thinking and working, and that society would be better off because of their efforts.

Bibliography

Belford, Barbara. *Brilliant Bylines: A Biographical Anthology of Notable Newspaperwomen in America.* New York: Columbia University Press, 1986. A straightforward and concise biography complete with the second part of Bly's series on Blackwell's Island insane asylum. Wonderful for a quick but thorough look at Bly's life.

Davidson, Sue. *Getting the Real Story: Nellie Bly and Ida B. Wells.* Seattle: Seal Press, 1992. Another work aimed at juvenile readers, this biography presents an interesting comparative portrait of two women who broke down barriers in their chosen profession as journalists. Lightly fictionalized in places, this work contains useful chronologies of both women's lives and accomplishments.

Kroeger, Brooke. *Nellie Bly: Daredevil, Reporter, Feminist.* New York: Times Books, 1994. One of the most up-to-date assessments of Bly's career, this biography provides a useful corrective to conflicting and erroneous stories about Bly's life and exploits—many of which were circulated by Bly herself. Places Bly's achievements within the context of the sensationalistic journalism of her era and the struggle of women to carve out careers for themselves as independent, self-supporting individuals.

Noble, Iris. *Nellie Bly: First Woman Reporter (1867-1922).* New York: Julian Messner, 1956. A full-length biography written for young readers. Although told in story form, this work is more detailed and informative than the work by Rittenhouse below. Includes a list of sources.

Rittenhouse, Mignon. *The Amazing Nellie Bly.* New York: E. P. Dutton, 1956. A somewhat useful, though dated, biography of Bly. Written in a narrative story form, this work seems to take some liberties with the facts, making it less reliable than the biography by Kroeger.

Julie Foegen Frederick

LOUISE BOGAN

Born: August 11, 1897; Livermore Falls, Maine
Died: February 4, 1970; New York, New York
Area of Achievement: Literature
Contribution: A woman of rare and severe talent, Bogan left an enduring legacy of lyric poetry and fine criticism.

Early Life

Louise Marie Bogan was born on August 11, 1897, in Livermore Falls, Maine. Her father, Daniel Joseph Bogan, was the eldest son of an Irish sea captain who sailed out of Portland. Daniel Bogan did not follow his father down to the sea, however, and instead became a clerk at a local paper company. It was this respectable but hardly dashing job that he held when he met and married Mary Shields in Portland in 1882. A handsome and volatile woman, "May" Bogan dominated the household with both her presence and her occasional absences. The couple had two children besides Louise; one died in infancy, and the other, Charles, was killed in France in 1918.

Although Daniel Bogan had risen through the ranks to become superintendent of another successful paper company, New England at the turn of the century was beginning its bleak decline. Throughout Louise's early childhood, the family moved from one mill town to another, to New Hampshire and Massachusetts, finally settling in a Boston suburb in 1909. They were never quite poor, but neither were they prosperous enough to insulate themselves entirely from the deadening atmosphere of poverty, illness, and violence around them. There was also the taint—even for a white-collar family—of being Irish Catholics in a respectable Yankee Protestant world. Finally, there was the uneasy marriage of Daniel and Mary Bogan, marked by secrecy, explosive rages, and violent, bitter quarrels. Louise Bogan's famous reticence has kept the details obscure, but the upshot was a childhood without stability, alternating between love and dread. It was an alternation that would control much of her life and remain at the heart of her poetry.

She escaped into books, and once she had learned to read, she never stopped. Whatever else, the family valued education, and in Boston, Louise attended the Girls' Latin School, a public school with a rigorously classical curriculum. It was here, at age fourteen, that she began to write poetry.

Her gifts were obvious from the beginning, and on the strength of her first year at Boston University, she won a scholarship to Radcliffe. She did not accept it. Instead, just short of her nineteenth birthday, she married a military man named Curt Alexander and moved with him to New York. When the United States entered World War I in 1918, Alexander was transferred to Panama and Louise, four months pregnant, followed him. It was there that a daughter, Mathilde (Maidie), was born. Louise and her daughter soon returned to the United States. Brief reconciliations notwithstanding, the couple could not sustain their marriage and separated permanently in 1919. Leaving Maidie to live with her parents near Boston, Louise returned to New York to live and write alone. Curt Alexander died in 1920 before any divorce proceedings could begin. At age twenty-three, Louise Bogan had made her first attempt at achieving a conventional family life; judging the attempt to be a failure, she channeled her entire attention to her writing.

Life's Work

In New York during the 1920's, Louise Bogan found employment at bookstores and at various branches of the New York Public Library and set about establishing herself as a serious lyric poet. Driven by her gift as well as her ambition, she soon became part of the city's literary scene and developed friendships with other writers, including poets such as Allen Tate, Léonie Adams, and Hart Crane. Bogan also made the acquaintance of critic Edmund Wilson, who was first to be her mentor and later her friend for many years. Soon her work was published in the leading literary journals of the day: *The New Republic*, *Vanity Fair*, *Poetry*, and *The Literary Review of the New York Post*. Her literary successes, however, were accompanied by ever-growing depression and despair—the worsening of a chronic inner pain that had been part of her life since childhood. As she always did in the face of such inner crises, Bogan took action: She sailed for Europe for six months of concentrated reading, writing, and music lessons in Vienna, Austria. Though the sojourn in Vienna seemed unproductive while it lasted, she wrote a number of new poems soon after her return to the United States and by 1923 had published her first collection, *Body of This Death*.

The poems in this first collection focus on the nature of romantic love, the nature of passion, and on the disappointments that, in Bogan's world, are inevitable in relationships between men and women. The poems also deal with the dilemma of the artist in general and of the woman artist in particular. As personal as Bogan's lyrics may be, they are not simply autobiographical and confessional. Bogan is direct heir to the English metaphysical tradition in poetry; she uses traditional forms and devices and employs symbols to focus and intensify emotion. The formal quality of the verse distances both writer and reader from the raw feeling, but does not diminish its power.

Body of This Death was for the most part well received, but other developments marked Bogan's life in the mid-1920's. She married writer Raymond Holden in the summer of 1925 and her daughter Maidie soon came to live with them. For the first time in her unsettled private life, Bogan enjoyed some kind of domestic peace and stability. Then, at Edmund Wilson's insistence, Bogan began writing critical reviews. These reviews served two purposes: They allowed her to keep writing without wrestling with the self and subconscious that underlay all of her lyrics and they developed and refined an incisive, critical prose style. These reviews eventually led to Bogan's thirty-eight-year stint as chief poetry critic for *The New Yorker*.

A measure of Bogan's growing reputation was an invitation to be part of the first group in residence at Yaddo, the artists' and writers' colony founded by Elizabeth Ames in 1926 in Saratoga Springs, New York. Several years later, Bogan and Holden bought an old farmhouse in Hillsdale, New York, and set about making it livable. Bogan's work at the time reflects that relative peace: a truce, at least, with her restless self and a growing sense of living within seasonal cycles and natural rhythms. In her poems, she moves away from the paradoxes and conflicts of sex and love and approaches the natural world with a keener, more perceptive eye. The mood is somber, but at least tempered by joy. These poems were to be collected in her second volume, *Dark Summer* (1929).

The Hillsdale farmhouse burned, taking with it not only furniture and other material possessions but also Bogan's notebooks and journals. Although she and her family were able to return to relative comfort in New York City, Bogan's emotional and psychological reserves were dwindling. In 1931, she checked herself in for treatment at the city's Neurological Institute. Confident of her doctors' ability to repair her damaged psyche, Bogan returned home within a few months. Despite her optimism, Bogan's mental state and her marriage were still precarious. Although she claimed at the time that the process of recalling her "disastrous childhood" would be insufficient to put her stark memories to rest and that the past was best forgotten, Bogan undertook to write an autobiography in 1932.

Finding it increasingly difficult to work on the autobiography and continue her day-to-day work as a reviewer, Bogan welcomed the offer of a Guggenheim Fellowship in 1933 that allowed her a year away from these pressures. Again hospitalized upon her return home, Bogan made the decision to leave Raymond Holden; their divorce became final in 1937.

After beginning to write short stories in the 1920's, Bogan published thirteen stories in *The New Yorker* between 1931 and 1935. Severe, economical, yet witty, these stories describe contemporary life with ironic detachment. Nevertheless, Bogan remained rather skeptical of prose, or else of her own suitability for writing it. In 1937, she published what some consider her richest, most complex collection of poetry, *The Sleeping Fury*. Conflict in love, the follies of youth, and destructive emotion all figure in these poems, but for once Bogan ends on a note of serenity and acceptance. The inner violence of her early work subsides and she allows the Fury—the avenging creature of Greek mythology—to sleep.

Throughout the 1930's and into the 1940's, Bogan found herself estranged from both political and literary fashion. Many of her fellow writers espoused or at least flirted with Marxism. Perhaps by nature or by virtue of her Catholic upbringing, Bogan was chary of universal systems and ideologies, particularly those that relied on insult and invective as argument. By the 1940's, formal poetry had fallen out of favor with younger poets. Literary fashion opined that formal confines—rhyme, meter, traditional stanza structure, and so forth—presumed a lack of talent and absence of free-ranging imagination in the writer. Discouraged by the general atmosphere and finding herself at an impasse in her own creative life, Bogan wrote no new poetry between 1941 and 1948.

Her growing reputation as a critic did not allay her gloom about either the cultural situation or her own inability to write, yet it did stimulate the kind of public recognition that she had once both openly disdained and secretly craved. In 1944, Bogan was appointed a fellow in American letters at the Library of Congress, and she held a one-year appointment as chair of poetry there from 1945 to 1946. In addition to her appointments to lectureships at various universities, Bogan received various awards. With Léonie Adams, Bogan received the Bollingen Prize for selected criticism (poetry and prose) in 1955. She also received honors from the Academy of American Poets in 1959 and from the National Endowment for the Arts in 1967.

Throughout the 1950's and 1960's, Bogan worked as a translator, compiled anthologies, and wrote criticism in which she made an effort to be fair-minded and generous in her assessment of new poets temperamentally alien to her, including the Beat Poets, Robert Lowell, and Anne Sexton. Bogan worked sporadically on her memoirs, which were published posthumously as *Journey Around My Room* (1980). Her final poetry collection, *The Blue Estuaries: Poems 1923-1968* (1968), won great acclaim for her, but she was nevertheless convinced that the book had passed unnoticed. Outwardly busy and productive, she again struggled inwardly with poisonous depression and anxiety. After resigning from *The New Yorker* in 1969, she seemed ever more withdrawn, and her health deteriorated. On February 4, 1970, she was found in her New York apartment, dead of a coronary occlusion.

Summary

Louise Bogan was never a widely recognized poet, but she was an important one. Her power and skill were evident to many of her fellow poets, who read her work, praised her talent, and sought out her advice and criticism. Bogan oversaw the poetic apprenticeships of Theodore Roethke and May Sarton and directly influenced many other novice poets, including Sylvia Plath. Professional, elegant, and acute, Bogan's critical work has survived several generations of schools and trends.

Bogan had to fight on several fronts. She fought against inner demons, the source of her poetry and her debilitating despair, and she battled an outer world of American culture that placed little value on her lyric poetry and almost automatically classed all writing by women as minor. Bogan herself, while citing women's contributions to the writing tradition, seemed to believe, or fear, that this belittling assessment might be accurate. Nevertheless, her compact, paradoxical, and highly charged poetry has established Louise Bogan among the finest American poets of the twentieth century.

Bibliography

Bogan, Louise. *What the Woman Lived: Selected Letters of Louise Bogan, 1920-1970.* Edited by Ruth Limmer. New York: Harcourt Brace Jovanovich, 1973. Bogan's letters to the famous and near-famous are a part of American cultural history; they are also witness to Bogan's wit.

_____ , and Ruth Limmer. *Journey Around My Room.* New York: Viking Press, 1980. Ruth Limmer, Bogan's literary executor, gathered both published and unpublished sketches, letters, poetry, and criticism to flesh out Bogan's memoir. As an autobiography, it is enigmatic and incomplete, but it is beautiful and unsettling reading.

Bowles, Gloria. *Louise Bogan's Aesthetic of Limitation.* Bloomington: Indiana University Press, 1987. Bowles approaches Bogan from a feminist standpoint, arguing that Bogan so internalized what male literary tradition expected of the "poetess" that cultural limits and her own self-imposed limits were identical.

Collins, Martha, ed. *Critical Essays on Louise Bogan.* Boston: G. K. Hall, 1984. A collection of reviews of Bogan and her work over the years. Includes poet W. H. Auden's keen estimation of her work, one of the best available.

Frank, Elizabeth. *Louise Bogan.* New York: Alfred A. Knopf, 1985. A major work on Bogan, this is a readable and thoroughly researched biography that intertwines Bogan's life with her work.

Ridgeway, Jaqueline. *Louise Bogan.* Boston: Twayne, 1984. Ridgeway discusses the formal aspects of Bogan's poetry as a result of intellect and temperament rather than technique.

Jane Ann Miller

LOUISE BOURGEOIS

Born: December 25, 1911; Paris, France

Area of Achievement: Art
Contribution: An internationally recognized sculptor, Bourgeois has created works that are characterized by a singular fusion of the intellectual purity of formal abstraction and the unconscious affect of her personal psyche.

Early Life

Louise Bourgeois was born in Paris in the Left Bank district of Saint-Germain-des-Près, on December 25, 1911, to Josephine Fauriaux and Louis Bourgeois. She was the middle child in her family, her sister Henriette being six years older and her brother Pierre fifteen months younger. Louise was undoubtedly named in part after her father, who was hoping for a son, but also after the French Socialist Louise Michel, a feminist, whom her mother admired. She grew up in Aubusson, where the family lived with relatives during the war years while her father was engaged in military duty, and then, after 1919, in Antony outside Paris on the banks of the Bièvre River, where her parents established a workshop for restoring antique tapestries. At the age of ten, Louise began to assist in the family enterprise, her first exercise being to draw a foot that had been worn away at the bottom of an eighteenth century tapestry. As a teenager, Louise continued to assist with the drawing for the tapestry restorations, and attended the Lycée Fénelon in Paris, where her family maintained an apartment and a gallery in which the restored antique tapestries were sold.

Louise's mother, who ran the workshop establishment, insisted on using natural dyes—cochineal shells for red, indigo for blue—when the Gobelin factories had begun using chemical colors. Later, Louise would incorporate similar muted natural colors into her own paintings and graphics. Josephine, with a staff of many other women under her, could be imposing and forceful at work, but at home with the children she was warm and nurturing.

Louise's father handled the external business, the buying and selling of the antique tapestries. Handsome, charming, and also promiscuous, he became involved with a number of other women, including Sadie, the English tutor who lived with the family. Josephine, who did love her husband, looked the other way and continued to forgive Monsieur Bourgeois. Louise, who of the three children looked most like her father, later recalled deeply resenting his promiscuity and the resulting tension from the hypocrisy at home. The stormy emotions she felt as a child would continue to surface later in such sculptures as *The Blind Leading the Blind* (1947-1949), *Angry Woman* (1969), and *The Destruction of the Father* (1974).

In 1932, when she was twenty, Louise received her baccalaureate from the Lycée Fénelon. That same year her mother, the one parent with whom she had had a close relationship, died. Her memories of the deep maternal love she experienced from her mother would be reflected in such later works as the nestlike "lair" series of the early

1960's and the vulnerable, yet protective, figures of pregnant women at various points in her oeuvre.

That same year, Louise enrolled at the Sorbonne, where she studied mathematics. In the universal laws of mathematics, especially geometry, she found a kind of peace and stability which she did not trust the vicissitudes of human relationships to provide. For Louise, the realm of mathematics became a haven from emotional pain and the alienation of human existence: In mathematics, she said, relations are constant and eternal. The grid designs of some of her early paintings such as *Reparation* (c. 1938-1940), *Natural History* (c. 1944), and *Connecticutiana* (c. 1944-1945) seem to reflect, at least in part, the peace and calm she found in her studies of geometry, in addition to evoking the patterns of tapestries. About these grid designs, Bourgeois has said, "The grid is a very peaceful thing because nothing can go wrong . . . everything is complete. There is no room for anxiety . . . everything has a place . . . everything is welcome." For her, geometric designs seem to suggest the desire for and possibility of a harmonious collective gestalt. The minimalist formal abstraction of many of her sculptures and their purity of proportion would also evoke a kind of still serenity.

After graduating from the Sorbonne, Louise decided to study art. Between 1936 and 1938, she studied drawing and color theory at the École du Louvre and the École des Beaux-Arts, and also at a number of the ateliers of well-known artists. She credits the post-Cubist Fernan Léger with influencing her in the direction of sculpture: One day as she listened to Léger lecture about creating the illusion of the sculptural on a flat surface, she found herself wondering if it might not make more sense to make the actual sculpture.

During this time, she met the American art historian Robert Goldwater, who was in France completing a book on primitivism in modern painting. They married in 1938 and moved to New York. Their marriage, resulting in three children, was to be a happy one, and Louise's satisfying personal life would serve as a psychological ballast, permitting her to explore a wide range of memories and emotions from the depths of her psyche as she pursued her artistic career.

Life's Work

Shortly after Louise Bourgeois and Robert Goldwater moved to New York, other Parisian émigrés arrived as well, including such Surrealist artists as André Breton, Max Ernst, and Marcel Duchamp. Bourgeois was undoubtedly influenced by the philosophical views of Surrealism, which sees the exploration of the deep emotions of the unconscious as the primary function of art. Some of her early paintings, displayed in her first solo show in 1945, reflect her feelings of anxiety at the separation from her family in Europe, and her *Woman House* paintings (1947-1948) suggest feelings of entrapment and loss of personal identity in a woman's identification with domesticity. Thirty years later, art critic Lucy Lippard and artist Judy Chicago would acclaim Bourgeois' *Woman House* paintings as protofeminist works. Interestingly, Bourgeois herself did not consciously identify with the feminist movement when she painted her *Woman House* series and would not do so until the early 1970's.

The intense feelings of the primal unconscious—anxiety, fear, abandonment, aggression, anger, sexuality—that Bourgeois has expressed artistically, both in her early work and throughout her career, are mainly based, she believes, in her childhood family experiences, as well as in the human condition. She has said that, for her, the artistic process involves the "recall" and "articulation" of the memories of feelings and experiences through an artistic medium. Thus, in the process of creating a work of art, she is able to exorcise these feelings; they are sublimated in the work of art. For Bourgeois, the artistic process is cathartic and redemptive so that, while she is profoundly connected with these feelings in the studio while she is working, by evening she has released them and is free to enjoy her relationships with friends and family. The vitality of these deep feelings remains dynamically imminent in her works, animating them, so that through identification and projection the viewer experiences their haunting power, the indwelling energy of their sublimated forms.

Her first gallery exhibitions of sculpture—*Standing Figures* at the Peridot Gallery in October of 1949, and again in October of 1950—already demonstrated this evocative power: A variety of stark, white, vertical abstract forms configured in a room, each tenuously balanced at its base, evoked such paradoxically conflicting feelings as existential alienation, precariousness, and the desire for escape and a longing for connection, stability, and community. Bourgeois has said, "we're made of completely contrary elements, opposed elements; and this produces formidable tensions." The tensions arising from the ambivalent and conflicting emotions and states of being of the human condition—such as love and hate, joy and sorrow/mourning, vulnerability and violence/anger, masculinity and femininity, paralysis and adventure, the desire for security and protection and the desire for freedom, panic and peace—would be explored by Bourgeois throughout her career.

Despite the strength of her oeuvre, in the thirty years between 1949 and 1978, Bourgeois had only five solo shows as a sculptor. Numerous reasons may be advanced to explain this lack of attention: her innate shyness and scrupulousness about not wanting to take advantage of her husband's connections to further her career; her inner sense of needing to create but not necessarily to show her work; the discrimination against women in the art world; and the uniqueness of her creativity, which defies definition according to styles and movements. With the advancement of feminism in the 1970's and the concurrent beginning of a more pluralistic atmosphere in the art world, Bourgeois' work became increasingly acclaimed and shown, with seven solo shows (including five in New York) between 1978 and 1981 alone, a major retrospective at the Museum of Modern Art in 1982, and a European retrospective in 1989.

Summary

It is difficult to examine Louise Bourgeois' work in terms of a progressive development by stages; rather, her sculptural work is best understood as an organic whole, with various shapes and themes appearing and reappearing in a wide variety of versions and media—painted wood, plaster, bronze, clay, latex rubber, plastic, wax, cement, steel, marble, and alabaster, as well as environmental and performance art.

While Bourgeois identified, in part, with prevailing contemporary movements such as Surrealism and postwar Abstract Expressionism, her work has always remained singular and unique. Neither mainstream nor revolutionary, she defines herself as "eccentric." "Eccentric," she says, "means away from the center." Thus, while her work may be viewed in a contextual relationship with other artists or artistic movements, she remains independent and original in her artistic expression.

Bourgeois' reputation as a renowned national and international sculptor earned her the Honorary Doctor of Fine Arts degree from Yale University in 1977, the citation for which reads in part:

> You have reminded us through your sculpture that art speaks to the human condition. You have offered us powerful symbols of our experience and of the relations between men and women. You have not been afraid to disturb our complacency. The precision of your craftsmanship, the range of your imagination, and your fearless independence have been exemplary.

Other honors and awards have followed, in recognition of Louise Bourgeois' remarkable creativity as a sculptor.

Bibliography
Gardner, Paul. "The Discreet Charm of Louise Bourgeois." *ARTnews* 79 (February, 1980): 80-86. This article provides an overview of Bourgeois' career from her early beginnings in the mid-1940's as an important modernist sculptor to her emerging international stature in the early eighties.
Heller, Nancy G. *Women Artists: An Illustrated History*. New York: Abbeville Press, 1987. A well-documented and richly illustrated study (with two Bourgeois illustrations) of significant women painters and sculptors in the Western world from the Renaissance to the present, with attention to the range of their styles, subjects, and techniques. Describes, in brief, Bourgeois' contextual relationship to Barbara Hepworth's abstract organic sculpture, the emotional subtext in Germaine Richier's work, and Louise Nevelson's environmental sculpture.
Lippard, Lucy R. "Louise Bourgeois: From the Inside Out." In *From the Center: Feminist Essays on Women's Art*. New York: E. P. Dutton, 1976. Reprinted from *Artforum*, March, 1975. This essay notes Bourgeois' formal affinities with such artists as Joan Miró, Jean Arp, Barbara Hepworth, and Alberto Giacometti, but emphasizes the unique creativity of her fusion of the primal affect of her personal psyche with the formalism of abstract art. Examines the complexity of polarized tensions in Bourgeois' work.
Miller, Lynn F., and Sally S. Swenson. "Louise Bourgeois." In *Lives and Works: Talks with Women Artists*. Metuchen, N.J.: Scarecrow Press, 1981. This biographical interview contains Bourgeois' reasons for becoming an artist and considers several important themes in her work.
Munro, Eleanor. "Louise Bourgeois." In *Originals: American Women Artists*. New York: Simon & Schuster, 1979. A biographical overview, this essay highlights the

continuous importance of Bourgeois' personalized view of geometry, and also the emergence of feminist perspectives, in her life and work.

Pels, Marsha. "Louise Bourgeois: A Search for Gravity." *Art International* 23 (October, 1979): 46-54. In this in-depth interview, Bourgeois discusses her inner necessity to create art and describes the psychological stages of her creative process.

Wye, Deborah. *Louise Bourgeois.* New York: The Museum of Modern Art, 1982. Based on the Museum of Modern Art's 1982 retrospective of Bourgeois' work, this book includes a comprehensive essay on Bourgeois' stylistic progression, numerous illustrations (black-and-white and color), and a complete biographical chronology and list of exhibitions.

Jean T. Strandness

MARGARET BOURKE-WHITE

Born: June 14, 1904; New York, New York
Died: August 27, 1971; Stamford, Connecticut
Area of Achievement: Photography
Contribution: Margaret Bourke-White was a pioneering news photographer who helped develop and define the field of photojournalism.

Early Life

Margaret Bourke-White was born June 14, 1904, in the New York borough of the Bronx, the second in a family of three children. Bourke-White's father, Joseph White, was an engineer and inventor, and her mother, Minnie (née Bourke), was trained as a stenographer. The White children were reared in a strict but loving household. Joseph and Minnie White encouraged their children's curiosity about the natural world and strove to instill in them the values of determination and hard work. Margaret later remembered that her mother taught her to "never take the easy path."

When Margaret was a small child, her family moved to Bound Brook, New Jersey, where she attended public schools. She later attended Plainfield High School, where she served as yearbook editor and, as a sophomore, won a school literary competition—activities that highlighted her talent for writing. Upon graduation from high school in 1921, she attended Columbia University for one semester, during which she took a photography course. She left school after her father died in 1922, but returned to college the next year after winning a scholarship to study at the University of Michigan at Ann Arbor.

At the University of Michigan, Margaret met Everett Chapman, a doctoral candidate in engineering. They were married in the spring of 1924, and she accompanied her husband when he obtained a teaching position at Purdue University, where she also attended classes. When her marriage to Chapman failed in 1926, she moved to Cleveland, Ohio, to study natural sciences at Western Reserve University. She completed a bachelor's degree in biology at Cornell University in Ithaca, New York, in 1927. While at Cornell, she was unable to find suitable employment to support herself, and instead earned money by selling prints of her dramatic, artistic photographs of campus buildings. Her photographs were very popular with students and alumni and sold briskly. After the failure of her marriage, she was determined to make something of herself, and although she had never before considered photography as a profession, her success at Cornell convinced her to pursue a career in photography.

Life's Work

Soon after her graduation from college, Margaret Bourke-White returned to Cleveland, where she opened the Bourke-White Studio in 1927. (She began using her mother's maiden name together with her own maiden name after her marriage to Chapman ended.) She continued to pursue architectural photography, but was especially fascinated by machines and industry. She saw endless artistic possibilities in photographing the skyscrapers, smokestacks, derricks, and titanic machinery of industrial Cleveland. She made a name for herself after producing a stunning series of photographs of the steelmaking process for Otis Steel Mills. On the strength of those photographs, she received numerous other industrial commissions.

Her work caught the attention of Henry Luce, the publisher of *Time* magazine. Luce was also interested in telling the story of American industry in immediate, visual terms, and in 1930 launched *Fortune* magazine to do just that. An associate showed Luce some of the remarkable steelmaking photographs taken by a "girl photographer" in Cleveland, and Luce was so impressed that he brought Bourke-White to New York and offered her a position as *Fortune*'s first staff photographer.

Bourke-White was happy to accept. She moved her studio to the newly opened Chrysler Building in Manhattan and split her time between assignments for *Fortune* and more traditional commercial and advertising photography. She traveled around the country for *Fortune*, producing a visual record of American industry—from steel and aluminum plants, to coal mines and quarries, to the slaughterhouses and meat-packing plants of the Midwest. Her eye for composition and her sense of drama made the dirt and smoke of heavy industry appear strangely beautiful in her photographs. Throughout this early period in her career, her work emphasized the gigantic scale of the machinery, construction, and output of American business. *Fortune* also sent her to photograph the rapid industrialization of the new Soviet Union under Stalin's 1928 Five-Year Plan. Bourke-White's were the first photographs to emerge from that country since the Bolshevik Revolution of 1917. She returned to the Soviet Union twice in the 1930's, and produced a book, *Eyes on Russia* (1930), and a series of articles for *The New York Times* about her experiences there.

Yet the focus of Bourke-White's work started to shift away from machines and industry as a more compelling subject presented itself—the Great Depression. In 1934, she photographed the tragedy of the Dust Bowl in the midwestern United States, concentrating on the human aspect of that disaster. Around this time, she met Pulitzer Prize-winning author Erskine Caldwell and agreed to collaborate with him on a project documenting the effects of the Depression in the South. The two embarked on an automobile tour of the region, interviewing and photographing the rural poor, who were among those hardest hit by the devastating effects of the economic crash. Their interviews and photographs were published in the book *You Have Seen Their Faces* (1937).

In 1936, Luce made Bourke-White one of the first four staff photographers for his *Life* magazine. By 1937, she had given up her studio work to photograph full time for *Life*. Her assignments took her across the United States, and her photograph of Montana's Fort Peck Dam appeared on the cover of the magazine's first issue.

Always adventurous and willing to take considerable risks to get a shot, she was eager to travel to Europe to cover the growing political crises that would eventually lead to World War II. She traveled to Czechoslovakia and Hungary with Caldwell to cover the conflict in the Sudetenland. In addition to producing photo-essays for *Life*, Bourke-White and Caldwell collaborated on *North of the Danube* (1939). Bourke-

White and Caldwell were married in 1939, and in 1940 published an account of their travels around the United States entitled *Say, Is This the U.S.A.?* (1940). Although their creative partnership was successful, the couple's personal relationship was stormy, and they were divorced after two years of marriage.

Bourke-White continued to travel to the world's hot spots for *Life*. She photographed London as it prepared for war and was the only American photographer in the Soviet Union in 1941, when the Nazis violated their nonaggression pact and bombarded Moscow. She immediately set down those experiences in her next book, *Shooting the Russian War* (1942). In 1942, she also became the first female war correspondent to be accredited to fly combat missions with the U.S. Army Air Force. She shipped out for Europe, arriving in England. En route to an assignment, her convoy was torpedoed off North Africa; the several days she spent afloat waiting to be rescued are said to have inspired Alfred Hitchcock's wartime film, *Lifeboat* (1944).

In 1943, Bourke-White was assigned to Italy, where she covered the war near Naples. While there, she shared the lot of the U.S. infantry and photographed and reported on one of the most intensive bombing campaigns of World War II at Monte Cassino. While her journalistic reports and photographs went to *Life* magazine, her personal experiences of the Italian campaign were recorded in *They Called It Purple Heart Valley* (1944). Bourke-White accompanied General George S. Patton's Third Army as it rolled across Germany in the spring of 1945. She and *Time* correspondent Bill Walton reached the Erla concentration camp near Leipzig even before the American troops, and her photographs of newly liberated inmates at the Buchenwald death camp are among the most enduring images of the war and the Holocaust.

After the war, *Life* sent Bourke-White to India in 1946 to cover that country's growing struggle for independence from the British Empire. Although careful to present a balanced view of the complex conflict, she was sympathetic to Mahatma Gandhi and the Congress Party. She befriended the great Indian leader, frequently traveling with him. In 1948, she was the last journalist to interview Gandhi, completing her work only hours before he was assassinated. Other assignments for *Life* in the 1950's took Bourke-White to South Africa, where she covered the inequities of apartheid and the exploitation of black diamond miners and laborers. She also covered guerrilla warfare during the Korean conflict.

Bourke-White first began to notice severe pain in her legs in 1953 after returning from Korea. The problem was diagnosed as Parkinson's disease, and its onset forced her to retire to her home in Darien, Connecticut, where she fought the ailment. For several years, she worked on her autobiography, *Portrait of Myself*, which appeared in 1963. Her last photographic contribution to *Life* magazine appeared in 1957, but she continued to write for the magazine. Although she had two brain surgeries and underwent extensive therapy, Bourke-White eventually lost her battle with Parkinson's disease on August 27, 1971.

Summary

Margaret Bourke-White was a pioneer industrial photographer, who differed from others in the field in her ability to see the genre's artistic possibilities. She was among the first women to work as a photojournalist, and her pioneering pieces for *Fortune* and *Life* magazines helped to develop and define the photo-essay. A witness to some of the most significant events of the twentieth century, Bourke-White captured memorable photographs of the Depression, World War II, and the struggle for Indian independence.

A superbly talented photographer and a skilled writer, Bourke-White competed on equal terms with her male colleagues. Although she was one of the very few women working in her field, she subjected herself to the same hazardous conditions and dangerous assignments as her male counterparts. She was willing to take great personal risks to get a photograph and was known for her adventurous spirit and fearlessness.

Bibliography
Bourke-White, Margaret. *The Photographs of Margaret Bourke-White*. Edited by Sean Callahan. Greenwich, Conn.: New York Graphic Society, 1972. This large format collection of Bourke-White's work spans the photographer's career, from her earliest architectural and industrial work to her later photos of India, Korea, and South Africa. It includes a lengthy biographical introduction by Theodore M. Baron and a foreword by Bourke-White's friend and colleague, the noted photojournalist Carl Mydans.

——————. *Portrait of Myself*. Simon & Schuster, 1963. Margaret Bourke-White's autobiography, which appeared eight years before her death, focuses on her adventurous career and includes a discussion of the author's battle with Parkinson's disease. The lively text is illustrated with a large selection of photographs, enabling the reader to appreciate Bourke-White's talents as both photographer and writer.

——————. *A Taste of War*. Edited and introduced by Jonathan Silverman. London: Century Publishing, 1985. This volume brings together selections from Bourke-White's writings about World War II: *Shooting the Russian War* (1942), *They Called It Purple Heart Valley* (1944), and *Dear Fatherland, Rest Quietly* (1946). More than simply reporting on the war, the selections are also vivid personal accounts of her experiences in wartime Russia, Italy and Germany.

Brown, Theodore M. *Margaret Bourke-White: Photojournalist*. Ithaca, N.Y.: Andrew Dickson White Museum of Art, Cornell University, 1972. This catalog of a Bourke-White retrospective exhibit includes a short biography and lengthy critical comment that places Bourke-White's photography in context of the technological, historical, and social developments of the times in which she lived and worked.

Goldberg, Vicki. *Bourke-White*. Hartford, Conn.: United Technologies Corporation, 1988. This collection of Bourke-White photography includes an informative critical/biographical essay by Bourke-White biographer Vicki Goldberg. The selection of photographs is notable for its inclusion of several rarely seen examples of Bourke-White's work in color photography.

——————. *Margaret Bourke-White: A Biography*. New York: Harper & Row,

1986. Perhaps the definitive narrative biography of Bourke-White, Goldberg's volume is thoroughly researched, documented, and expertly written. In preparing this biography, Goldberg had access to the photographer's journals and diaries—resources that allowed her to provide readers special insight into Bourke-White's work and personality.

Silverman, Jonathan. *For the World to See: The Life of Margaret Bourke-White.* New York: Viking Press, 1983. Silverman compiled and edited a large selection of Bourke-White's photographs for this visually oriented biography. He also added a comprehensive biographical narrative that draws liberally from Bourke-White's writings.

Catherine Udall Turley

ANNE BRADSTREET

Born: 1612 (?); Northampton, Northamptonshire, England
Died: September 16, 1672; Andover, Massachusetts Bay Colony
Area of Achievement: Literature
Contribution: Not only the first American woman poet, Anne Bradstreet ranks as the first true American poet of either sex.

Early Life

Although no record of Anne Bradstreet's birth survives, she was the daughter of Thomas and Dorothy Dudley of Northampton, England, and according to a reference in one of her poems she must have been born in 1612. Her father, though not highly educated, was a substantial man who valued books and learning. Dorothy, apparently also literate, probably taught her daughter religion, and the Dudley children grew up with books. The Dudleys claimed kinship to a much more prominent branch of the family: Robert Dudley, Earl of Leicester, was a favorite of Queen Elizabeth I, while John Dudley, Duke of Northumberland, was the grandfather of Sir Philip Sidney, famed courtier and important English poet. Several other members of the Sidney family had literary talent, including Philip's sister Mary, later Countess of Pembroke, and his niece Mary, later Lady Mary Wroth. It is clear that early in life Anne Dudley became acquainted with the poetry of Sidney. Another favorite was the Protestant French poet Guillaume Du Bartas.

In a letter to her own children years later, Bradstreet explained that she was an obedient child who took comfort in reading the Bible but confessed that at the age of fourteen or fifteen was beset by "carnal" desires. Meanwhile, the family had moved to the coastal town of Boston in Lincolnshire, where Thomas Dudley served as a steward to the earl of Lincoln. At the age of sixteen Anne suffered from a common but deadly disease, smallpox; her face may well have been scarred for life as a result. Also at sixteen she was married to Simon Bradstreet, a Lincolnshire man and Cambridge graduate.

The Dudleys were Puritans, oppressed by religious authority and eager to make a new livelihood abroad, and Thomas Dudley became one of the founders of the Massachusetts Bay Company. Still much under the influence of her father, the eighteen-year-old Anne Bradstreet and her husband sailed from the Old World Boston in 1630 to settle a new Boston across the Atlantic.

Life's Work

It is well to remember that the work of Anne Bradstreet existed on two fronts. When she arrived as part of the earliest wave of Massachusetts Bay settlers, she was a young wife who, in the years that followed, became the mother of eight children. The duties implicit in such a life in a newly planted colony represented all the work that even a healthy woman might reasonably be expected to perform, and Anne Bradstreet suffered frequent illnesses. This work would not of itself have made her famous, but the work for which the world knows her is intimately connected with her status as colonial wife and mother.

Her earliest poems cannot be dated precisely, but by 1647, when she was thirty-five, someone, generally conceded to be the Reverend John Woodbridge, her brother-in-law, returned to England with a stack of her poems in manuscript. Three years later the first book of original poetry by an American, *The Tenth Muse Lately Sprung up in America*, appeared in London. Most of the poems now considered Bradstreet's best had presumably not yet been written, but the book has become justly famous.

The poems therein represent an apprenticeship rendered long by circumstances. Even the bookish Dudleys and Bradstreets could not have carried any great library to Massachusetts. For a number of reasons, poets thrive on fruitful contacts with other poets, and, the possibility of a few amateurish versifying friends aside, Anne Bradstreet had no such contacts. The time and energy she could devote to the lonely task of composing poetry must have been severely limited. Few poets can have learned their craft under more trying conditions.

Her book, which in a later poem she claimed to have been "snatched" from her in an "unfit" state by friends "less wise than true," consists mainly of long poems, primarily quaternions, or four-part poems. There are four of these interrelated quaternions, on the four elements, the four humors, the four ages of man, and the four seasons, respectively. The subject matter is traditional, the "elements" being the classification of the physical universe into fire, air, earth, and water which goes back at least as far as Plato. The four humors represented four different mixtures of the elements in humans which determined their physiological and temperamental types. Modern English vocabulary still retains the adjectives—choleric, sanguine, melancholy, and phlegmatic—used to describe the four basic types. The poems, varying in length from 264 to 610 lines, are all written in rhymed pentameter couplets. These poems hardly show Bradstreet at her best, nor does her unfinished *The Four Monarchies* in 3,572 lines, many of which paraphrase Sir Walter Raleigh's *History of the World* (1614).

The Tenth Muse contains a few other poems. "A Dialogue between Old England and New" indicates that Bradstreet maintained a strong interest in contemporary events in the early 1640's, when the policies of King Charles I that had sent people such as the Dudleys and Bradstreets to Massachusetts were leading toward civil war in England. Yet the most interesting poem in the collection for most people is the first one, appropriately called "The Prologue." In the poem, Bradstreet writes in a personal vein about her vocation as poet.

"The Prologue" is essentially a plea to accept the work of a woman invading a man's province. Most critics have taken its humility at face value, and it is true that Bradstreet is often humble and even apologetic about her poetry, but it is also true that talented people usually recognize that they *have* talent, and it is possible to read some passages as ironical needling of the "superior" men. Her wit cannot be disputed. Instead of the "bays" (i.e., laurels) that men poets receive, she asks for "thyme or parsley wreath." She surely knew (as doubtless many men did not) that laurel is indeed a botanical cousin to the housewife's kitchen spice, the bay leaf. Whether ironical or not, Bradstreet displays in "The Prologue" a sincere desire for "some small acknowledgement" of women's artistic capacity and a discernible indignation that such recognition has been so long forthcoming.

Because *The Tenth Muse* was presumably published without her consent, in "The Author to Her Book," written for a possible second edition, she compared her book to an "ill-formed" child, an embarrassment to its mother. Of her literal children, however, Bradstreet was proud. In a poem of 1659, they become "eight birds hatched in one nest, of whom five have flown, while three remain in the nest." In most of her later poems—some included in a posthumous 1678 edition of her book, some unpublished until 1867—the long, earnest, and fairly dull poems on set subjects have given way to highly personal domestic poems.

Several take the form of letters to her husband, who, as a figure of some consequence in the colony, made frequent business trips. Although her marriage most likely was an arranged one, these poems attest that a deep love had developed between them. She depicts Simon as her "mine of gold" or her "Sun" whose absence is her "winter." She writes also of her illnesses, of her children, and, as time goes on, of the deaths of grandchildren, several of whom proved less hardy than their parents; also, in 1666, of a fire that destroyed their home.

Some of her poems refer to events that are dated or datable; one of her most admired, "Contemplations," does not. She may well have begun it relatively early in her career, but it was not published until after her death. It is a mature poem in thirty-three stanzas, all but the last containing seven lines. Various critics have described it as a religious meditation, as an example of the seventeenth century emblem poem, even—because of its interest in landscape and vegetation—as an anticipation of romantic nature poetry. It blends elements of the "public" quaternions and of the more personal family poems. She also composed for her son Simon a series of *Meditations Divine and Moral* in prose urging that his appreciation of "mortal things" ultimately yield, like hers, to a Puritan faith in eternal ones.

Anne Bradstreet died on September 16, 1672 at the age of sixty.

Summary

Anne Bradstreet was both a meditative and a lyric poet. The scope of her work was circumscribed by religious and domestic boundaries beyond which modern women poets have plunged successfully. Yet as an artist, she was not only unique in her time and place but also progressed far beyond the level reached by the numerous religious and domestic female writers who flourished a full two centuries later. In culturally limited Massachusetts of the middle decades of the seventeenth century, she was able to apply the techniques she had learned from English and French Renaissance poets to the raw material of her own life. In her time for a woman to be an original meditative and lyric poet was a bold step, "obnoxious," as she put it, to men in general and probably more intensely so to the men who were fashioning the New England Puritan commonwealth.

So in her way Bradstreet was a torchbearer for women. She apparently took no initiative in publishing her work, but she persisted in writing original poems, her last datable one, "As Weary Pilgrim," coming in 1669, only three years before her death. Virtually all English women writers before her had concentrated their efforts on translations of works by men. The next woman to challenge men's poetic hegemony pointedly, Anne Finch, Countess of Winchilsea, was born the year before Bradstreet died.

In 1953, an important twentieth century poet, John Berryman, composed a major poem called *Homage to Mistress Bradstreet*. Although male critics had come to credit her achievement over the intervening centuries, Berryman's poem, an imagined dialogue, even an imaginative identification, with this woman who had lived three centuries earlier, symbolizes the full, ungrudging recognition of her as a sensitive victor in the dual struggle with environment and language—in other words, as a poet.

Bibliography

Bradstreet, Anne. *The Works of Anne Bradstreet*. Edited by Jeannine Hensley. Cambridge, Mass.: The Belknap Press of Harvard University Press, 1967. The best modern edition of Bradstreet's poems, Hensley's boasts several attractive features: a foreword by Adrienne Rich, an informative introduction by the editor, and an index of proper names in Bradstreet's poems. Hensley orders the poems chronologically insofar as this order is known or can be inferred.

Cowell, Pattie, and Ann Stanford, eds. *Critical Essays on Anne Bradstreet*. Boston: G. K. Hall, 1983. A selection of colonial and nineteenth century essays followed by twenty-one modern ones from a variety of critical perspectives with emphasis on the feminist. An unusual and useful feature in an anthology of this type is its thorough index.

Martin, Wendy. *An American Triptych: Anne Bradstreet, Emily Dickinson, Adrienne Rich*. Chapel Hill: University of North Carolina Press, 1984. Martin regards Bradstreet as the initial figure in a "female counter-poetic" linked to traditional Puritan values. For the most part the three essays are separate entities, the one on Bradstreet emphasizing her struggles with religious faith and with her numerous illnesses.

Rosenmeier, Rosamond. *Anne Bradstreet Revisited*. Boston: Twayne Publishers, 1991. Intended to supersede Josephine K. Piercy's study for the same publisher, this work's format is unusual in a Twayne book. Its approach is suggested by the titles of the three main chapters: "Daughter-Child: Actualities and Poetic Personas," "Sister-Wife: Conflict and Redefinitions," and "Mother Artist: A Typology of the Creative."

Stanford, Ann. *Anne Bradstreet: The Worldly Puritan*. New York: Burt Franklin, 1975. A biography with criticism by a leading Bradstreet scholar. The subtitle alludes to the conflict between the "invisible world" of Bradstreet's Puritan heritage and the "visible world" of her poetic vision. Stanford also casts light on Bradstreet's reading and her interest in American landscape.

White, Elizabeth W. *Anne Bradstreet*. New York: Oxford University Press, 1971. The most thorough Bradstreet biography. White includes useful discussions of the religious and political influences on Bradstreet's family, of the difficulties faced by the first wave of Massachusetts immigrants, and of the way Bradstreet transmuted these difficulties and numerous family griefs into impressive poems.

Robert P. Ellis

FANNY BRICE

Born: October 29, 1891; New York, New York
Died: May 29, 1951; Los Angeles, California
Areas of Achievement: Music and theater
Contribution: A celebrated singer and comedian whose extensive career extended from vaudeville to radio, Brice defied commonly accepted standards of beauty and created an individual niche in comedy for her own specialized talents.

Early Life

Fanny Borach was the third child born to immigrants Rose (Stern) and Charles Borach on the lower East Side of Manhattan on October 29, 1891. Fanny's earliest years were spent in the often romanticized Jewish neighborhood of the lower East Side. She carefully observed the people she met there, studied their lives, and practiced the Yiddish/Eastern European dialects that would later become the basis for much of her original humor material. Despite her frequent interviews to the contrary, Fanny moved after a few years to the newly developed area of Newark, New Jersey, where her bartender father had purchased a saloon. Unfortunately, her father's gambling tendencies forced much of the actual running of the saloon onto her mother. Both saloon and family prospered until an exhausted Rose decided to sell the business, leave her husband, and move with the children to Brooklyn, New York, late in 1903. There is no further record of Fanny's father in either public documents or interview material.

Fanny's earliest interest was performing in the neighborhood. She missed no opportunity to produce plays or perform heartrending ballads for the local residents. In fact, Fanny spent so many days truant from her Brooklyn schools harmonizing with newsboys on street corners that she was able to persuade her mother to allow her to drop out of school when she was fourteen. By 1906, Fanny began performing on the local amateur talent circuit and had won prizes producing an income of approximately $70 a week.

Fanny's skilled amateur performances, although prize-winning, did not provide her with the necessary skills for immediate employment in the entertainment venues of the 1900's. New York at this time was an exciting hub of theatrical activity with vaudeville, burlesque troupes, and numerous touring companies hiring artists from its performing population. The existing musical theater demanded sophisticated dance and vocal skills as well as a standard feminine beauty for chorus employment. Vaudeville circuits were composed of tightly developed and highly skilled single or group acts that were honed to perfection and presented on a national tour of privately owned theaters. On the other hand, burlesque had lenient standards regarding appearance and dance skill, and offered the only potential employment to the talented but untrained singer. She perceived her thin, lanky body and ethnic appearance as a handicap, but she characteristically found an opening which capitalized on exactly those attributes.

Life's Work

Fanny Brice's first professional job after leaving the amateur circuit was singing newly published sheet music to induce sales in a local store. It was here that she met then unknown composer, Irving Berlin, who was to become instrumental in her later career. As a strong emotional singer, she was hired as a chorus member for *Talk of New York*, a musical produced by Broadway great George M. Cohan in 1907, but she was later fired when her employers discovered that she could not dance. A job with a production of *A Royal Slave* (1907) put her in the position to bribe stagehands and dancers into teaching her the steps of the day. By the time the show had gone bankrupt, Fanny could work her way through numerous routines and was thankful to leave her bit parts as an alligator and moving water behind her.

After this aborted tour, she joined a burlesque wheel, or circuit, where she performed for three years as a singer and comedian. Between 1907 and 1910, Brice performed with three shows of increasing quality: *Transatlantic Burlesques* (1907-1908), *The Girls from Happyland* (1908-1909), and *College Girls* (1909-1910). Unlike current burlesque, the shows of this period were wholesome general entertainment featuring a chorus line of average-looking dancers, songs, and comedy sketches. The addition of striptease artists came much later, and Brice often tried to downplay her involvement in burlesque as it became detrimental to her image in the industry.

This touring proved invaluable in the development of Brice's improvisational skills and aided her adaptation to various audiences. A little-known burlesque comic named Willie Weston provided Fanny with her earliest instruction in spontaneous comedy work. Eventually, an emergency in *College Girls* led Irving Berlin to give Fanny the song "Sadie Salome" and make the suggestion that she use a heavy Yiddish accent during her performance. The enthusiastic reception to this song led to her discovery by successful impresario, Florenz Ziegfeld, Jr., and her introduction to Broadway performance in 1910.

Florenz Ziegfeld, Jr., was the creator and producer of the glamorous *Ziegfeld Follies*. This revue contained bright comedy acts interspersed with large chorus numbers. Ziegfeld believed that his showgirls were the most classically beautiful women anywhere, and Brice's brand of physical comedy appeared to be a natural contrast to Ziegfeld's elegant showgirls. Once again, Brice did not meet the required beauty prototype, but her thick auburn hair, brown eyes, and strong ethnic features caused her to stand out among the showgirls and helped create a niche for her.

After appearing in the Follies of 1910 and 1911, Brice left Ziegfeld for four years to work in a variety of vaudeville and musical comedy shows. Her career foundered during this period and she seemed limited as a performer to broad, visual clowning which was not always appropriate for all productions.

Upon returning to Ziegfeld's *Follies* in 1916, Brice adopted a style that would aid her work for years to come—creating parodies of famous people. In the shows of this era, racial stereotypes that would be considered offensive during the late twentieth century were presented commonly in ethnic songs and acts, and she was compelled to develop her Jewish characters based on these existing attitudes. An important development was the formation of the Anti-Defamation League of B'nai B'rith to protest humiliating stage characterizations of Jews. While Brice continued to use Yiddish accents and Jewish characterizations throughout her career, she was scrupulous that her performances were satirical and never demeaning.

It was during this phase of her career that she developed a desire to be taken seriously as a dramatic actress, and hoped to move away from ethnic comedy and concentrate on dramatic work. Unfortunately, her play *Why Worry* (1918) was a dismal failure and was followed by the equally unsuccessful *Fanny* (1926). During the period between her two plays, the twenty-nine-year-old actress became associated with three songs: "Second Hand Rose," "Rose of Washington Square" and "My Man." "My Man" became an audience favorite because it detailed Brice's well-publicized marital woes with her second husband, gambler Nick Arnstein. (She was later married to impresario Billy Rose in 1930.) Soon Brice went back to vaudeville even though it was facing some serious competition from the new silent pictures and recordings. In an effort to keep her career vital, she recorded "Second Hand Rose" and "My Man" for the Victor Talking Machine Company in 1922.

Brice herself was not immune to the lure of motion pictures and soon released *My Man* (1928), a film based around her song, to dismal reviews. *Be Yourself* (1929) fared no better, and it became obvious that Brice had several things working against her as Hollywood performer. Her exotic appearance was not standard enough to be considered pretty by filmmakers, and yet she was too attractive to be used as a strictly character actress. Also, her Jewish characters with their strong Yiddish accents did not play well in most areas outside New York City. In fact, both her humor and style were deemed to be too regional for national appeal. Worst of all, Brice was unable to establish herself as a believable dramatic actress. In addition, vaudeville was officially dead by 1933, and even the famed Palace Theater discontinued live shows and ran films all day. As a result, Brice concentrated on adapting her purely visual style to one that would translate to the vocal world of radio.

In 1934 and 1936, Brice appeared in two *Ziegfeld Follies* produced after the impresario's death in 1933. She was the undisputed star and was able to bring her career around full circle from a nineteen-year-old beginner to an experienced professional in her forties. It was at this time, after a brief successful appearance in the film *The Great Ziegfeld* (1935) that she came to terms with her great strengths as a comic performer and decided to forgo her dreams of dramatic stardom.

Finally, in 1938 she perfected the character that was to carry her through the final thirteen years of her career: Baby Snooks. Snooks, a mischievous and rowdy four-year-old girl, was one of Brice's most endearing creations and was based on a baby-talking character she created to amuse friends at a party. Brice's radio show made it possible for a middle-aged woman to be loved as the endearing Baby Snooks until her death of cerebral hemorrhage on May 29, 1951.

Summary

Perhaps Fanny Brice's greatest impact was her use of broad, physical comedy in an era when female comics were generally used passively as "straight men" to bolster the male comic's punchline. Brice also was determined to be a successful stage performer at a time when the standard for feminine beauty was strictly Anglo-Saxon. Despite prevailing standards, she used her unusual features as part of her humor in order to be both noticed and appreciated. She was more than willing to appear ridiculous and self-deprecating in front of her audiences and won their loyalty in return.

Brice's life story became a popular film vehicle, both before and after her death. In 1939, Twentieth Century-Fox released a film entitled *The Rose of Washington Square* that included characters loosely based on Brice and Nick Arnstein. After her death, Brice's life was the subject of two film musicals starring Barbra Streisand. Streisand made her film debut and earned an Academy Award for her portrayal of Brice in *Funny Girl* (1968), which chronicled Brice's early career in the Ziegfeld Follies and her marriage to Arnstein. The film's sequel, *Funny Lady* (1975), portrayed Brice at the height of her career with husband Billy Rose.

In an age when racial songs and routines were commonplace, Brice made use of her Jewish heritage to good advantage and with respect. She claimed in interviews that her characters were researched on the Lower East Side and were often based on a combination of her observations of real people. Required to play to the prejudices of her times in order to find employment, Brice refused to use her humor in order mock Jewish life or values. Her adaptation of heavy Yiddish dialect typed her briefly as an ethnic comic, but she was soon able to rise out of that somewhat limiting category. Brice's characters captured the audience's interest and acceptance by combining cultural authenticity, universal emotion, and an ability to poke fun at the most pretentious characters of the day.

Bibliography

Ewen, David. *New Complete Book of the American Musical Theater.* New York: Holt, Rinehart, & Winston, 1970. The history of the American musical theater from the earliest formal stage musical, *The Black Crook* (1866), to *Zorba* (1968). Provides main cast lists and synopses of all major American musicals produced on Broadway during this period. The text also includes biographical information on major producers, librettists, lyricists, and composers. Provides context for understanding Brice's work in musical comedy and theater.

Goldman, Herbert G. *Fanny Brice: The Original Funny Girl.* New York: Oxford University Press, 1992. An overview of Brice's life and career, this biography focuses particular attention on her relationships with men, especially her second husband, Nick Arnstein. Contains extensive additional resources including a filmography, radiography, discography, bibliography, and stage credits. In addition to providing Brice's complete vaudeville touring schedule, the film and stage credits give detailed cast and production data for works Brice performed in, including song titles and composers.

Grossman, Barbara W. *Funny Woman: The Life and Times of Fanny Brice.* Bloomington: Indiana University Press, 1991. A detailed biography devoted to Brice that stresses performance details, career development, societal pressures, and a modern interpretation of her significance to theatrical history. The author focuses primarily on career details and gives less attention to Brice's personal relationships.

Stein, Charles W., ed. *American Vaudeville As Seen by Its Contemporaries*. New York: Alfred A. Knopf, 1984. Personal memories and career highlights of vaudeville performers working from the earliest days to its demise in the 1930's. Famous and unknown performers alike describe in detail the background atmosphere, development of acts, problems, and joys of American vaudeville.

Unterbrink, Mary. *Funny Women: American Comediennes, 1860-1985*. Jefferson, N.C.: McFarland, 1987. Fanny Brice is one of several women comedians profiled in chapter 2, "Vaudeville Legends." Although the biographical sketch on Brice is somewhat brief, it does provide a good introduction to her career and includes details about her personal life.

Susan Chainey

ANTONIA BRICO

Born: June 26, 1902; Rotterdam, The Netherlands
Died: August 3, 1989; Denver, Colorado
Area of Achievement: Music
Contribution: Antonia Brico was an internationally recognized conductor who had two careers in her lifetime: the first in the 1930's and 1940's, and the second toward the end of her life in the 1970's and 1980's, after the release of the documentary film *Antonia: A Portrait of the Woman* in 1974. This film was instrumental in showing the severe discrimination suffered by Brico in penetrating the formerly all-male field of conducting.

Early Life

Antonia Brico was born in Rotterdam, South Holland, The Netherlands, on June 26, 1902. In 1906, her foster parents brought her to the United States, where she attended high school in Oakland, California. She began piano studies early with the intention of becoming a concert pianist, but after hearing a concert conducted by Paul Steindorff, the director of the San Francisco Opera, she decided to study conducting instead.

Brico studied with the famous physician, missionary, and musician Albert Schweitzer, and she would later conduct a benefit concert on behalf of the Albert Schweitzer Foundation. She persuaded her high school to admit her to music appreciation classes, in which, according to some sources, she demonstrated theoretical and stylistic points on the keyboard and accompanied the school orchestra. Believing that a musician needed a well-rounded education, she matriculated at the University of California at Berkeley in 1919 and was graduated with honors in 1923.

During her years at Berkeley, she worked as an assistant to Paul Steindorff, who also directed the music program on the Berkeley campus. In order to support her education, she began performing recitals in her freshman year.

A story that expresses the practicality and resourcefulness of the determined musician involves a concert given by Ignacy Paderewski in 1923. The only ticket available to Brico was too far to the side for optimal acoustics, so she moved a camp stool into the center aisle for the duration of the concert. The story was eventually related to another pianist, Sigismund Stojowski, by one of Brico's university professors. Apparently, the story eventually influenced him to accept the aggressive student as a pupil when she later studied in New York.

In 1927, Brico received a graduate scholarship from the University of California to enter a master class in conducting at the Berlin State Academy of Music, where she became the first American graduate. While in Berlin, she took a letter of introduction to the head of the Hamburg Philharmonic, Karl Muck. Despite the fact that he had never taken on a pupil before, Brico convinced him to become her mentor. In her five years of study with Muck, she acquired a mature comprehension of orchestral literature and a superb conducting technique.

Life's Work

Antonia Brico's professional career began in 1930 when she served as a guest conductor for the Berlin Philharmonic. The reviewers the next day were quick to point out the superiority of her conducting to that of many of the male conductors then working in Berlin. She returned to the United States later in the year to conduct in Los Angeles and San Francisco, and during the next few years she conducted major symphony orchestras in the principal cities of Germany and Poland. During the early 1930's, she worked constantly, to great acclaim, throughout Europe.

She made her New York debut during the height of the Depression conducting the Musicians' Symphony Orchestra at the Metropolitan Opera House in 1933. This orchestra was composed of unemployed union musicians who were led regularly by guest conductors. A reviewer stated that after only three rehearsals she made the orchestra play as it had never played before. This concert began her conducting career in the United States, and over the next few years she was engaged regularly in most major American cities.

Life as a visiting conductor involves constant travel and learning to produce music from an unfamiliar orchestra within severe time constraints. It requires that the conductor arrive not only with the music fully prepared but also with the ability to instruct and lead a new orchestra quickly. During these years, Brico was the only woman conductor working, and her skill and musicality were heralded as novel and almost abnormal. Although the orchestras of that era were composed only of male musicians, Brico never felt discriminated against by the men who served under her baton; professional musicians gave her the respect that her skill and talent deserved.

On February 18, 1935, an invitation arrived that would allow Brico to make a point about women's suitability to handle non-traditional musical roles and instruments. A group of fifteen female musicians approached Brico and asked her to lead them. This became the foundation of the Women's Symphony Orchestra, which would attract the attention of First Lady Eleanor Roosevelt and eventually would include as many as eighty-six musicians. Within a few months, Brico had molded the group of musicians into a professional-level symphony. It remained an all-woman organization until 1939, when it allowed male musicians to audition. By that time, however, the point had been made. Women were indeed able to play all symphony instruments with a professional level of skill; not only the flute, violin, and piano, as previously had been thought. During the years that the Orchestra performed, the reviews were generally impressive. World War II and the decline of Brico's "marketability," however, finally ended the symphony.

Brico's brilliant career had begun to dissolve as early as 1937, when the "novelty" of a female conductor had begun to wear off. In fact, Mrs. Charles S. Guggenheimer, a strong contributor to the New York Philharmonic Orchestra at that time, believed that it was a "disgrace" for a woman to conduct the orchestra. Brico was allowed a guest spot only because a petition of four thousand had demanded it. Unfortunately, these attitudes were not unusual, and although Brico had the support of major male conductors, orchestra managers, and soloists, she was not able to withstand the tyranny and the necessity of adequate financial backing.

Antonia Brico spent the war years conducting and organizing choral groups around the East Coast, and conducting municipal and federal orchestras. As her early fame began to diminish, she moved to Denver in 1942, where she founded the Denver Community Symphony in 1948. Conducting this orchestra became her primary occupation, and she spent the next forty years of her life in relative creative obscurity. Although Brico was a noted lecturer throughout the United States and a director of concert tours, she was still longing for an opportunity to work with major symphony orchestras.

It was not until one of Brico's former piano students, folk singer Judy Collins, coproduced the 1974 award-winning film *Antonia: A Portrait of the Woman* that a new career began for Brico. The film depicted Brico's life and aborted career, and after its release the fame that Antonia Brico had sought for forty years was finally attained. At the age of seventy-three, she began her career again in the public eye.

Antonia Brico spent the last sixteen years of her life back in the limelight of the classical world. She served as a mentor for thousands of female musicians whose paths were made easier through her struggles. Despite progress, however, she found that the struggle was still far from over. In 1975, Brico was one of three judges in the International Bach Competition, in which the competition was held with the players behind screens, as is common in most symphony auditions. The purpose of this procedure is simple: Musical talent should be the only criterion judged in any competition or audition. When the first- and second-place winners turned out to be women, one of the male judges was unable to believe that he had voted for a "girl." Brico was disgusted.

Brico's final years were spent actively conducting prestigious symphony orchestras, receiving more honors and tributes, and offering the world the music that societal attitudes had almost destroyed. Antonia Brico died on August 3, 1989, at the age of eighty-seven.

Summary

As the first woman orchestra conductor in the United States, Antonia Brico was a true pioneer. For years, she was lost in the shadow of discrimination and the financial domination of the professional musical industry. She spent those years with a small local symphony in Denver, Colorado, and in a private studio where she taught two generations of young future instrumentalists, singers, conductors, and audience members the majesty of beautifully produced and intelligently interpreted music.

Antonia Brico helped to break the male domination in the major symphony orchestras of the 1930's by bringing the New York Women's Symphony into being. This was the first orchestra to allow women instrumentalists to participate in making classical music. Despite the difficulties caused by the lack of salaries until after expenses had been covered and missed rehearsals because of second jobs, the women succeeded until the orchestra disbanded at the beginning of World War II. By this time, however, men were able to audition for membership, since Brico opposed segregation of any kind and sought to make musicianship the sole criterion for employment. Antonia Brico's primary contribution is simply that she made good, intelligently interpreted music. It is of little importance whether her story in *Antonia: A Portrait of the Woman* brought new fans because of outrage, anger, or mere curiosity. During the renaissance of her career, the concert halls were finally packed for Antonia Brico, and the people in them once again received a gift of interpretive and conducting talent that remained as bright and vibrant in her seventies as it had been in her thirties.

Bibliography

Cocks, Jay. "A Woman's Place." *Time* 104 (October 21, 1974): 4-9. This brief review of the cinematic release of *Antonia: A Portrait of the Woman* provides a fine assessment of her career as a musician at the same time that it conveys the content of the documentary itself. Cocks praises the film as being a fine example of what he calls "a new feminist consciousness" in motion pictures, showing how Brico was "scarred but not humbled by the problem of being both a woman and an artist in America."

Dizikes, John. *Opera in America: A Cultural History*. New Haven, Conn.: Yale University Press, 1993. Although his survey of opera history contains little direct information on Brico's field of expertise—conducting—Dizikes does provide a summary of Brico's significance as the first notable American woman conductor and mentions her work as an opera coach. Provides a context for understanding Brico's neglect within the prestigious field of conducting and the arduous struggle of many other American women to achieve recognition on the operatic stage.

LePage, Jane Weiner. *Women Composers, Conductors, and Music of the Twentieth Century: Selected Biographies*. 3 vols. Metuchen, N.J.: Scarecrow Press, 1980-1988. A well-written and concise work that serves as a truly excellent source of information on female musicians who rarely have been written about in such detail. The work takes a feminist approach to the lives and careers of important musicians and provides an analysis of their difficulties, if any, in achieving a career in the field. Includes a useful sketch on Brico. The only drawback of this series is that only a few women can be covered in such detail.

Saal, Hubert, with Abigail Kuflik. "Music, Maestra." *Newsweek* 86 (August 18, 1975): 52-53. A brief overview of Brico's career written during her comeback period. In addition to providing information about her early career, the interview provides a glimpse of the impact that the 1974 release of the documentary on Brico's life had in resuscitating her career as a conductor.

Slonimsky, Nicolas. "Antonia Brico." In *Baker's Biographical Dictionary of Musicians*. 7th ed. New York: Schirmer Books, 1984. A dictionary of brief but useful entries giving personal and performance/composition data on the careers of significant musicians, conductors, composers, instrumentalists, and vocalists, including Antonia Brico.

Laurie Dawson

GWENDOLYN BROOKS

Born: June 7, 1917; Topeka, Kansas

Area of Achievement: Literature
Contribution: The winner of the Pulitzer Prize for Poetry in 1950, Brooks elevated the image of African Americans from a plain, invisible people to a humble people with a rich and complex culture.

Early Life
Gwendolyn Brooks was born on June 7, 1917, in Topeka, Kansas, to poor but proud black parents. Her father, David Anderson Brooks, hoped to become a doctor, but the need to feed his family during the Great Depression eventually forced him to abandon his dream. He had already begun and discontinued his medical training at Fisk University by the time he met the woman who would become Gwendolyn's mother. Keziah Corine Wims, a fifth-grade teacher, married David Brooks in Chicago in 1916, where David found work as a mechanic and a custodian.

Keziah Brooks had high hopes for her daughter, who demonstrated an exceptional literary ability at an early age. As a preschooler, Gwendolyn was reciting poetry, and before she was a teenager, she was writing plays for performance by other teens (including her brother Raymond, who was sixteen months her junior). Keziah encouraged Gwendolyn's talent as well as her pride in her racial heritage, telling her daughter, "You are going to become the *lady* Paul Laurence Dunbar." A conscientious mother, Keziah also arranged for the young Gwendolyn to meet such famous black poets as James Weldon Johnson and Langston Hughes, whose poetry had a lasting influence on Gwendolyn.

Gwendolyn attended an all-white high school and an all-black one before settling in at the Englewood High School. Englewood's racially diverse student body was better suited for a shy, dark-skinned girl. Although her self-esteem was well cultivated by her loving parents and brother, as well as by the readers of her weekly poetry contributions to the *Chicago Defender* newspaper, Gwendolyn was nevertheless a socially awkward girl. She would later attribute her shyness primarily to the invisibility and other forms of racism that she believes all dark-skinned African Americans suffer from whites and lighter skinned blacks.

Gwendolyn became more active between 1934 and 1936 as a student at Wilson Junior College. She participated in such church, social, and race-related organizations as the Young Women's Christian Association (YWCA) and the National Association for the Advancement of Colored People (NAACP). As a member of the Chicago NAACP, Gwendolyn befriended Henry Lowington Blakely II, another aspiring poet, whom she married in 1939. Their son Henry, Jr., was born in the following year.

When her son was two years old, Gwendolyn Brooks's life was dramatically transformed: She and her husband began studying poetry at the South Side Community Art Center with Inez Cunningham Stark, a wealthy white member of Chicago's elite literary circle. Although her associates at internationally acclaimed *Poetry* magazine did not believe she would find any talented black writers in Chicago's ghetto, Stark discovered several gifted students who later acquired national renown, including John Carlos and Margaret Burroughs. Nurtured by Stark's classes, Gwendolyn's work developed rapidly. In 1943, she won the Midwestern Writers' Conference poetry award. With that achievement, the young writer began her professional career.

Life's Work

Gwendolyn Brooks's life became forever altered when she was honored with the Midwestern Writers' Conference prize. Immediately thereafter, Alfred A. Knopf, a prestigious publishing company, solicited her poems for publication. Her correspondence with Knopf gave her the confidence to submit poems to other publishers, and in 1945, Harper and Brothers issued *A Street in Bronzeville*, Brooks's first volume of poems.

Dedicated to her parents, *A Street in Bronzeville* contains some of Brooks's best-known works. The poems describe the daily lives of humble blacks in "Bronzeville," a poor Chicago neighborhood named for the skin color of such residents as "Hattie Scott" and "Satin-Legs Smith."

Like the poems of Langston Hughes and Paul Laurence Dunbar, Brooks's poems detail both the African American pursuit of the American Dream and the disappointment of black men and women when they find themselves unable to achieve that dream because of racism and oppression. Some of the poems describe ways that black people are oppressed not only by whites but also by one another. Poems such as "the ballad of chocolate Mabbie" and "Ballad of Pearl Mae Lee" condemn light-skinned blacks who discriminate against darker skinned blacks, creating a rupture within the race.

The poems of *A Street in Bronzeville* have also been compared to the early poems of T. S. Eliot, Ezra Pound, and other Modernist poets. Like them, Brooks uses European rhyme patterns and verse forms. In addition, Brooks creates Modernist characters who are too flawed or too human to be considered heroic or admirable.

Despite her use of Modernist characters, Brooks creates some poems with black characters who are truly heroic and noble. For example, "Negro Hero" is based on the life of Dorie Miller, an African American mess steward who was awarded the Navy Cross for saving white American troops during the Japanese attack on Pearl Harbor in 1941. Brooks identifies Miller's moral dilemma, noting that it was unlawful for blacks to handle weaponry during World War II. She expresses the Negro Hero's bitterness when she begins, "I had to kick their law into their teeth in order to save them."

In recognition of the genius of *A Street in Bronzeville*, Brooks earned numerous honors. In 1945, she was named Woman of the Year by *Mademoiselle* and was granted that magazine's Merit Award. The next year she received the American Academy of Letters Award, and in both 1946 and 1947, she was awarded the distinguished

Guggenheim Award. Also, she joined prominent literary society by contributing reviews of other writers' works to such notable publications as the *Chicago Tribune*, *The New York Times*, and *Negro Digest*.

In 1949, Harper and Row published *Annie Allen*, for which Brooks was awarded the highly acclaimed Pulitzer Prize in poetry the following year. Brooks was only thirty-two years old when she became the first African American to receive any Pulitzer Prize.

Annie Allen was considered worthy of the Pulitzer Prize because, even more brilliantly than *A Street in Bronzeville*, it illustrated the social, psychological, and economic factors that prevented the progress of African Americans. Whereas Brooks's first collection had emphasized the negative effects of the Depression on urban black people, *Annie Allen* describes the difficult adjustments black men and women had to make to life in America after two world wars.

After her daughter Nora was born in September, 1951, Brooks wrote her only novel. *Maud Martha* (1953) is based loosely on the author's own life. Although not as successful as her volumes of poetry, the novel explores some of the same themes. *Maud Martha* chronicles the life of a young woman who lives in a black ghetto. Because Maud has dark skin, she is not cherished and not considered attractive. In this novel, as in her poetry, Brooks forces the reader to reconsider what is meant by words such as "ordinary" and "beautiful," and how these descriptions apply to African Americans.

Brooks did not publish again until after her father's death in 1959. In 1960, she released *The Bean Eaters*, a collection of poems that mourn the racism of her father's lifetime. These poems explore ignorance, violence, and black manhood. One poem, for example, analyzes the psychology of the white murderers of Emmett Till, a fourteen-year-old Chicago boy slain in Mississippi in 1955.

In 1963, the publication of Brooks's fifth book, *Selected Poems*, coincided with the first of her many teaching jobs—a position at Columbia College in Chicago. The following year, Columbia College became the first of many institutions to grant the poet an honorary doctorate degree.

Brooks underwent an important change in her life when she attended the Black Writers' Conference at Fisk University in Nashville in 1967. She has described this experience as the "awakening" of her race consciousness. Also attending the conference were many younger artists and writers of the Black Arts movement, such as Don L. Lee and LeRoi Jones, later known as Haki Madhubuti and Amiri Baraka, respectively. The passionate black-centered politics of these young artists deeply affected Brooks and inspired her to adopt a more African style. Her poems assumed a new poetic sensibility, using jazz rhythms and black solidarity themes.

Brooks's next volume of poetry, *In the Mecca* (1968), forms a call to all black people, but especially black elders who, like the poet herself before the Fisk conference, perhaps did not fully understand or accept the ideas of the Black Arts movement. This work expresses the belief that blacks need to work together for racial progress.

Also in 1968, Brooks was named Poet Laureate of Illinois. In this position she developed the arts in communities across the state, mainly by sponsoring writing contests in all levels of educational institutions. Over the years, Brooks has continued to collect, edit, and publish poems by young writers.

In 1969, Brooks chose to have her own work published by Broadside Press, a black-owned company in Detroit that specialized in books by African American authors. This decision marked the end of her twenty-five-year relationship with Harper and Row, the white-owned firm that had published all of her books up to that point. Her Broadside books include three volumes of poetry—*Riot* (1969), *Family Pictures* (1970), and *Beckonings* (1975)—and her autobiography, *Report from Part One* (1972). Later books, including *To Disembark* (1981) and *The Near-Johannesburg Boy and Other Poems* (1986), were published by Haki Madhubuti's Third World Press in Chicago.

Summary

Gwendolyn Brooks's lifelong commitment to writing poems that proudly depict black life as complex—sometimes virtuous and worthy and other times ignoble and commonplace—enabled later African American poets to create a wide variety of black personality types. Her skillful use of poetic devices from both the European and the African traditions resulted in extraordinary poems that deeply moved readers and enhanced understanding among the races in the early Civil Rights movement. Her greatest contribution lies both in her own sensitivity and insights into human nature and ability to share them through her poetry and in her vision and generosity in the development of talented youth.

Bibliography
Brooks, Gwendolyn. *Report from Part One*. Detroit, Mich.: Broadside Press, 1962. Brooks's experimental autobiography. Provides poet's own retrospective look at her life, times, artistic development, and accomplishments; especially insightful are the comments on her coming to race consciousness in the 1960's. Includes photographs of the poet, her family, and her contemporaries.
Evans, Mari, ed. *Black Women Writers (1950-1980): A Critical Evaluation*. Garden City, N.Y.: Anchor Press/Doubleday, 1984. Contains several selections on Brooks, including a short essay by the poet herself and an appreciation by Chicago poet Haki Madhubuti.
Miller, R. Baxter, ed. *Black American Poets Between Worlds, 1940-1960*. Knoxville: University of Tennessee Press, 1986. Includes two exceptional essays on Brooks. In " 'Define . . . the Whirlwind': Gwendolyn Brooks' Epic Sign for a Generation," Miller shows how Brooks's 1968 epic *In the Mecca* uses Judeo-Christian theology, folklore, and history to portray Chicago as an urban "mecca." Harry B. Shaw's "Perceptions of Men in the Early Works of Gwendolyn Brooks" examines Brooks's pre-1960 treatment of black men as patriots, victims, youth, fathers, and lovers and reads these diverse portraits as details in Brooks's total picture of African American life.

Mootry, Maria K., and Gary Smith, eds. *A Life Distilled: Gwendolyn Brooks, Her Poetry and Fiction*. Urbana: University of Illinois Press, 1987. Best chronological appraisal of Brooks's lifetime achievement. The eighteen essayists include some of the scholars most familiar with Brooks's complete works, as well as leading critics of African American literature. Several essays examine Brooks's use of European poetic forms versus African American poetic forms; some essays offer insightful feminist commentary on *Maud Martha*.

Shaw, Harry B. *Gwendolyn Brooks*. Boston: Twayne, 1980. Provides thorough critical overview of Brooks's personal and professional lives. Draws on wide variety of autobiographical, biographical, literary, and sociological sources to place the poet in an early Modernist context.

Tate, Claudia, ed. *Black Women Writers at Work*. New York: Continuum, 1983. Acclaimed collection of interviews with some of the most celebrated African American women writing in the 1970's and 1980's. Includes an interview with Brooks about her personal and artistic development. By situating Brooks among younger poets such as Sonia Sanchez and Ntozake Shange, Tate demonstrates how Brooks's early fame opened doors for later black women writers.

Joycelyn K. Moody

ROMAINE BROOKS

Born: May 1, 1874; Rome, Italy
Died: December 7, 1970; Nice, France
Area of Achievement: Art
Contribution: Romaine Brooks's lifestyle, paintings, and drawings exemplify female strength, ingenuity, and power of expression. Her portraits of females provide some of the earliest images of modern and independent women.

Early Life

Beatrice Romaine Goddard was born on May 1, 1874, in Rome, Italy, to upper-class American parents. Romaine was her parents' third child, after Henry St. Mar (then age seven) and Mary Aimée (then age five). Romaine's father, Major Harry Goddard, was a mysterious figure who abandoned his family soon after Romaine's birth. Romaine's mother, Ella Waterman Goddard, was an heiress to a fortune made in a Pennsylvania coal-mining industry. Ella Goddard spent most of her adult life traveling in Europe with her three children.

Romaine's early life was one of terror and anguish. Ella Goddard was unpredictable, mentally unbalanced, and involved in the occult. She was devoted to St. Mar, who began going insane at the age of seven. Ella Goddard was resentful of Romaine because she was attractive, bright, and talented while St. Mar was not. Ella tended to ignore Romaine or treated her cruelly. She gave Romaine the job of caretaker of St. Mar, who often behaved in a bizarre or violent manner.

Ella Goddard unexplainably sent Romaine to live with her laundress in a New York tenement in 1880. It was at this time that Romaine began to draw, an activity she had become interested in at the age of five or six, but in which her mother had forbidden her to engage.

In 1882, Romaine's Waterman relatives sent her to an Episcopalian church school in New Jersey, where she remained until 1886. She then rejoined her mother and St. Mar in Europe and attended a convent school in northern Italy from 1887 to 1890. Later, she was sent to Mademoiselle Bertin's Private Finishing School in Geneva, Switzerland, to be instructed in the manners and behavior which would be expected of an upper-class woman of the late nineteenth century.

Although in this period it was deemed inappropriate for an upper-class woman to seriously pursue a profession or an art career, Romaine was becoming interested in art and music. In 1895, she was sent to Neuilly, France, to study voice. She made a dramatic change in her life the following year when she was twenty-two. She escaped from Neuilly, went to Paris, and proclaimed independence from her mother, while retaining a monthly allowance of three-hundred francs. For a time, Romaine continued to study voice and sang in operettas.

Romaine decided to turn her attentions to painting in 1898. She moved to Rome, Italy, and studied art at La Scuola Nazionale and the Circolo Artistico, where she was the only woman in her classes. She spent the summer of 1899 painting on the island of Capri. It was here that she began to paint the subject matter for which she was to become known: portraiture. With the money Romaine had made from the sale of a painting on Capri, she returned to Paris to continue her studies at the Académie Colarossi.

Life's Work

After her brother, St. Mar, died in 1901 and her mother died in 1902, Romaine Goddard became an enormously wealthy heiress. In 1902, she married a British pianist and writer, John Ellington Brooks, whom she had met on Capri. The marriage was unhappy and short (lasting about one year), but Romaine retained the last name Brooks.

From 1902 to 1904, Romaine Brooks lived in London and spent time on the Cornish coast of England, where she developed the color-scheme which was essential to her painting style: subtle tones of grays, blacks, and whites. This color-scheme may have been inspired by the paintings of American expatriate artist, James McNeill Whistler. Brooks painted several portraits at this time.

In 1905, Brooks returned to Paris and concentrated on painting. By this time, her artistic identity was beginning to be recognized. She associated with the intellectual, artistic, and homosexual elite of Paris and she was sought after for her unusual, eerie, gray-toned portraits. She was given her first solo exhibition in 1910, at the important Parisian art gallery, Durand-Ruel.

Romaine Brooks painted the portraits of many intellectuals, writers, and aristocrats of her day. She worked in oil on canvas, and she became known for her stark, severe style of painting and for her unusual use of color. She was celebrated for her ability to capture the psychology, spirit, and essence of her sitters. For this reason, she was called the "Thief of Souls," a name originally coined by the French writer, Robert de Montesquiou in an issue of *Le Figaro* in May of 1910.

Brooks's portraits often include environments or objects which relate to the life, personality or work of the sitter. In 1914, Brooks painted the full-length portrait of the French artist, Jean Cocteau, standing in front of the Eiffel Tower in Paris. His long, slender form echoes that of the Tower. In 1909 in Paris, Brooks met the famous Italian poet and aerial commander, Gabriele d'Annunzio, with whom she was to have a long involvement. In 1916, Brooks painted d'Annunzio in military uniform with an airplane in the background. In both paintings, Brooks's interest in modern technology and design is revealed.

Above all, Romaine Brooks's portraits reflect her own spirit, her own overriding melancholic mood, influenced by her life with St. Mar and Ella Goddard. Brooks's subjects are isolated, single figures that seem to be frozen eternally in a gray and eerie world. Brooks was an independent woman, she was alone, sometimes afraid, often obsessed with her past and haunted by the memory of St. Mar and her mother.

Brooks's portraits also reveal her courage, her daring, and her modernism. At a time when many modern artists were painting with intensely bright colors—Henri Matisse and the Fauves—or experimenting with geometric abstractions—Pablo Picasso, and the Cubists—Brooks remained dedicated to the subject matter, style, and color-scheme that best suited her own personality. At a time when women were being depicted in art primarily as decorative objects designed for the pleasure of men, Brooks was painting women who were solitary, independent, thoughtful, spiritual, and modern.

Romaine Brooks was one of the first artists, if not the first, to paint women who were modern, who were independent or unconventional, or who were known lesbians. She was one of the first to depict women wearing simple modern, or masculine attire. In 1920, Brooks painted a portrait of the pianist, Renata Borgatti, sitting at the piano, wearing masculine clothes and short-cropped hair. She later painted *Una, Lady Troubridge* (1924), whose subject was a lesbian, wearing a mannish suit and a monocle. In Brooks's *Self-Portrait* of 1923, she presents herself in a top hat, white shirt, and severe black jacket, which was the type of apparel she ordinarily wore.

It is not only the face of Brooks's subjects that confronts viewers of her portraits; the upper body or the entire figure is often included. Brooks's paintings of the female form, especially the nudes, are important because they reveal her preference for androgynous figures not normally depicted by male artists who were her contemporaries. Brooks painted female bodies that were long, thin, and elegant. Her ideal female form was that of the famous Russian ballerina, Ida Rubenstein. In paintings such as *Azalées Blanches* (white azaleas) of 1910 and *Le Trajet* (the crossing), believed to have been painted in 1911, Brooks displays Rubenstein's elongated, nearly emaciated, pale figure in haunting, mysterious settings. It is a body which is not exceedingly female or male. It is the type of body which was praised by the American expatriate writer, Natalie Clifford Barney.

Romaine Brooks met Natalie Barney in 1915. Barney lived an openly unconventional, lesbian lifestyle in Paris. Barney was to become the major love of Brooks's life and her companion for forty years. In *The Amazon* (1920) Brooks depicted Barney as a solitary, serious, meditative figure.

By the time of her 1910 exhibition in Paris, Brooks was generally regarded as an exceptional artistic talent. In 1920, she was awarded the Cross of the Legion of Honor. In 1925, her work appeared in three major exhibitions: at the Galerie Jean Charpentier in Paris, at The Alpine Club Library in London, and at the Wildenstein Galleries in New York. This last was her first major showing in America and it was reviewed positively in *Art News* on November 21, 1925. These exhibitions were to mark the high point of Brooks's career.

In 1931, the Galerie Théodore Briant in Paris exhibited 101 of Brooks's drawings; in 1935, fifty of her drawings were shown at the Arts Club of Chicago. It is in Brooks's delicate and expressive line drawings that one can see her spirit and subconscious world reflected even more clearly than in her portraits. With a singular, precisely flowing line Brooks was able to depict poetic, fantasy-like figures which she gave revealing titles such as *We Weep and We Weep Alone* (1930) and *It Makes the Dead Sing* (c. 1930).

Brooks traveled to the United States for the Chicago drawing exhibition and for a time rented a studio space in New York's Carnegie Hall in 1936. She painted the portraits of two Americans at this time: the writer, Carl Van Vechten, and the writer and lecturer, Muriel Draper.

After 1936, Romaine Brooks stopped painting. She returned to France and concentrated on drawing and writing her memoirs. From 1940 on, she spent more of her time with Natalie Barney, living in villas she purchased in Florence and Fiesole, Italy. In 1961, Brooks painted her last portrait, of the Italian duke, Uberto Strozzi.

Brooks moved to her apartment in Nice, France, in 1967. There, she began to live the life of a recluse, isolating herself from her friends, including Natalie Barney. She died in Nice on December 7, 1970.

Summary

By the time of her death, Romaine Brooks and her art had been virtually forgotten. In the 1960's, however, Brooks had given twenty-three of her paintings and thirty-seven of her drawings to the National Museum of American Art in Washington, D.C. In 1971, that museum put on a major exhibition of Brooks's art which traveled to the Whitney Museum of Art in New York. This exhibition marked the beginning of her rediscovery as an artist. After 1971, Brooks's art was shown in over eighteen exhibitions in America and Europe, and in 1974, Meryle Secrest's landmark biography of Brooks, *Between Me and Life*, was published.

Although it was perhaps little recognized during her lifetime, Brooks was a strong woman who pursued a life and career that directly challenged the strictures placed on women of her era. At a time when upper-class women were living lives prescribed for them according to strict social mores, Romaine Brooks was living a life she daringly and courageously designed for herself. In an epoch when upper-class women were viewed primarily as decorative ornaments, Romaine Brooks was living a life of independence and serious dedication to the pursuit of an artistic career. In an age when women were barred from most art schools and training programs because it was seen as inappropriate for them to dedicate themselves to the serious study of any art form, Romaine Brooks was taking her place as the only woman attending classes at La Scuola Nazionale and the Circolo Artistico in Rome.

Brooks's art was revolutionary in that it revealed a strongly individualistic artistic personality. Her portraits present modern personalities in modern settings in a style that is powerfully expressive. Her depictions of women were undeniably new and modern in their own time and they continue to emanate a sense of female strength and individualism. Brooks's spontaneous, emotionally charged drawings are abstract fantasies which daringly explore an inner consciousness in an unprecedented manner. For these reasons, Romaine Brooks has an unquestionable position among modern American painters in general and also among such prominent American expatriate painters as James McNeill Whistler, John Singer Sargent, and Mary Cassatt.

Bibliography

Breeskin, Adelyn D. *Romaine Brooks*. 2d ed. Washington, D.C.: Smithsonian Institution Press, 1986. An important catalog of Brooks's art which includes a discussion of her life and work as well as black-and-white and color reproductions of her paintings and drawings at the National Gallery of American Art. The reproductions are accompanied by thorough documentary and bibliographic information.

Chadwick, Whitney. *Women, Art, and Society*. New York: Thames and Hudson, 1990. A scholarly examination of the history of women artists and their position in society, which presents Brooks as an example of a modern woman of the 1920's in a chapter which includes a discussion of Coco Chanel and Sonia Delaunay. Excellent general bibliography. Two black-and-white reproductions.

Romaine Brooks: Portraits-Tableaux-Dessins. Paris: Braun & Cie, 1952. This book contains brief, general introductions to the life of the artist in English and French. It is useful for its black-and-white reproductions of thirty-two paintings and ten drawings, several of which are not included in the other publications.

Rubinstein, Charlotte Streifer. *American Women Artists: From Early Indian Times to the Present*. Boston: G. K. Hall, 1982. An extensive overview of women artists of America which includes a discussion of Brooks's life and work and identifies her as an "independent" modern artist. Good general bibliography. One black-and-white and one color reproduction.

Secrest, Meryle. *Between Me and Life: A Biography of Romaine Brooks*. Garden City, N.Y.: Doubleday, 1974. This well-written biography provides a thorough and complete treatment of Brooks's life and work and is informed by Brooks's unpublished memoirs, including *No Pleasant Memories*. Illustrated with many color and black-and-white reproductions of paintings and drawings as well as photographs of Brooks and family and friends. Includes a bibliography and an appendix with letters of Ella Goddard, a short story by Brooks, and poetry by Gabriel d'Annunzio and Natalie Barney.

Nannette Fabré Kelly

JOYCE BROTHERS

Born: October 20, 1929; New York, New York

Area of Achievement: Psychology
Contribution: Joyce Brothers has filled a void in television programming by offering mass therapy to the dejected, lonely, and troubled with gentleness and sincerity on such matters as sex and child-rearing.

Early Life

Joyce Diane Bauer was born one of two daughters of Morris K. Bauer and Estelle Rapoport Bauer. Joyce grew up in Far Rockaway, in the borough of Queens, a suburb of New York City. She was instilled by her lawyer parents with a high regard for hard work and academic achievement. She demonstrated great powers of concentration whenever she tried to learn everything. At Far Rockaway High School, Joyce demonstrated the kind of intelligence, charm, and poise that made her popular with her contemporaries.

While attending Cornell University as an undergraduate, Joyce majored in psychology and graduated with a B.S. degree with honors. She then enrolled at Columbia University for advanced work in behavior and personality. From 1948 to 1953, she served as an assistant in psychology at Columbia and an instructor at Hunter College in New York City. Several weeks after Joyce received her M.A. degree from Columbia University in 1949, she married a medical student, Milton Brothers. After her marriage, she continued her teaching and research. Following a year (1949-1950) as a research fellow on a United Nations leadership project, Joyce Brothers pursued postgraduate work at Columbia University and received her Ph.D. degree in 1953.

Although she was a woman with advanced degrees, Joyce Brothers thought it important after the birth of her first child to remain at home to rear her newborn daughter. She left her teaching posts at Columbia and Hunter, and the family scraped by trying to live on Milton Brothers' medical student salary of fifty dollars a month. To help them out of their financial straits, Joyce Brothers tried for and qualified for an appearance on a popular television quiz show called *The $64,000 Question.* Contestants had to choose unusual categories in which to compete, and Joyce's category was boxing. To prepare herself for the show, she memorized twenty volumes of a boxing encyclopedia. She said she had good motivation because she and her husband were hungry.

Brothers first appeared on the show in late autumn of 1955, and she was an immediate success. Each week she reached a new plateau, and her winnings went up from week to week until she won the $64,000 question in December. Her studying paid off handsomely since she knew such extraneous bits of information as the full name of the Marquis of Queensberry and the number of rounds fought in the 1923 Dempsey-Firpo contest. Joyce Brothers was the second person and the only woman ever to win the top prize of $64,000.

Life's Work

Unlike other quiz show contestants, Joyce Brothers remained on television. In 1956, she was hired to work as a cohost of *Sports Showcase*, commenting on sports events and interviewing prominent sports figures. She often appeared on television talk shows, and her intelligence, charm, and dignity reinforced her favorable image. In September of 1958, the National Broadcasting Company (NBC) offered Brothers an opportunity to try out an afternoon show based on counseling and giving advice on love, marriage, sex, and child rearing. Planned by the producers to be a publicity stunt for a limited run in the New York City area, the show with Brothers was an immediate success: Almost immediately Brothers began to receive more than one thousand letters a week from her listeners, and the show was telecast nationally. Within a year, Brothers added a late-night program to her schedule, expanding her discussions to canvass topics, previously taboo on the air, such as frigidity, impotence, sexual satisfaction, and menopause.

By 1962, Brothers' shows were receiving mixed reviews. Some critics said that they were too intimate while others credited her for exploring private concerns in a public forum without being offensive. A sizable and dedicated audience had been listening to Brothers' opinions and had taken her very seriously. Much of her success came from her genuinely sympathetic manner and her ability to dispense sound advice in simple language unencumbered by professional jargon.

When the 1970's arrived, the original format of *The Dr. Joyce Brothers Show* had been revamped several times and reintroduced as *Consult Dr. Brothers* and *Ask Dr. Brothers*. She also was heard on radio stations of the ABC and NBC networks and in taped short talks that went out on "Emphasis and Monitor" news spots. Brothers also was featured on station WMCA in New York City, answering personal questions from on-the-air telephone callers. Taped in advance, the television programs were thoroughly prepared, and Brothers often devoted fourteen and sixteen hours of background work to every half hour of discussion. The live radio shows, on the other hand, were spontaneous, realistic, and sometimes punctuated with drama.

Once, Brothers intervened directly to arrange a meeting between army officials and a young soldier who had gone AWOL. Other incidents involved disturbed individuals who threatened suicide. During the course of a telephone conversation with an extremely distraught woman early in 1971, Brothers averted the woman's suicide attempt by convincing her not to take an overdose of sleeping pills. Brothers talked calmly to the woman for three hours and ninety minutes on the air while the police traced the telephone number and staged a rescue operation.

Consulting psychologists have held mixed opinions about Brothers' shows. Some critics held that Joyce Brothers gave advice without knowing her callers well enough. Brothers responded to this criticism by stating that she did not attempt to treat mental illness nor did she practice therapy on the air. Whenever necessary, she said, she advised callers to seek professional help. Brothers' supporters praised her ability to offer individuals a chance to look at their personal problem with some detachment. By assuring them that their problems were shared by others and not at all unique,

Brothers was able to offer these individuals some of the benefits derived from group therapy techniques. Brothers insisted, however, that she was merely a link between the viewer and professional literature.

In addition to fulfilling her television and radio commitments, Brothers wrote a syndicated column that appeared in some 350 daily newspapers throughout the nation. She furnished a monthly column for *Good Housekeeping* and was a special feature writer for the Hearst newspaper syndicate and United Press International. She also served as business consultant for such companies as Magee Carpet Company and Greyhound Bus Lines, advising them on feminine tastes.

While starting out as a media psychologist, Dr. Brothers ventured into writing books on a variety of subjects including love, marriage, sex, success, grief, and loneliness. Among her works are *Ten Days to a Successful Memory* (1959), *Woman* (1961), *The Brothers System for Liberated Love and Marriage* (1972), *Better than Ever* (1975), *How to Get Whatever You Want Out of Life* (1978), *What Every Woman Should Know About Men* (1981), and *What Every Woman Ought to Know About Love and Marriage* (1984). Her 1990 book, *Widowed*, dealt with her personal experiences with bereavement after the death of her husband from cancer in 1989.

Although she prescribed tranquillity for others, Brothers herself led a fast-paced existence. She rejected the view that she was a compulsive achiever. She attributed her ability to get things done to efficient organizing of time so that not a moment was wasted. In private life, Joyce Brothers was the wife of Milton Brothers, a Park Avenue internist, and the mother of a daughter, Lisa, who later became an ophthalmologist. In ranking her multiple roles, Joyce Brothers considers herself first a woman, then a mother, a wife, and a psychologist.

Summary

Without tremendous organizational ability, Joyce Brothers could scarcely have managed her varied professional activities. Without her keen interest in learning new things, her multifaceted life would have been less stimulating and her impact on American society less significant. On the professional front, Joyce Brothers pioneered the psychological phone-in show in the 1960's, and the idea proliferated to such an extent that by 1985 there was an Association of Media Psychologists to monitor for abuses. In the 1970's, Brothers spoke out against sexist bias, citing the need to change textbooks because children quickly pick up sexist attitudes from them. She noted that nonsexist cultures tend to be less warlike because the man does not have to prove that he is big and strong and needs to protect the weaker woman. She called for children to learn that it is fine to be either male or female, thereby developing more positive attitudes about themselves.

Bibliography

Anderson, Walter. "Dr. Joyce Brothers and Risk Taking." *Good Housekeeping* 207 (October, 1988): 46-51. An interview with Joyce Brothers, excerpted from the book, *The Greatest Risk of All*. Deals with what was perhaps the biggest risk in

Brothers' life: appearing on the television show *The $64,000 Question*.

Brothers, Joyce. *How to Get Whatever You Want*. New York: Simon & Schuster, 1978. Using anecdotes from her own life, from the lives of her patients, and from the lives of many celebrities, Brothers supplies the tools that she believes will allow anyone to achieve success in nearly any area of life.

——————. *The Successful Woman*. New York: Simon & Schuster, 1988. Brothers shares her personal secrets to success and the success stories of various women who managed to get what they wanted most out of life. Contains some autobiographical information, since in one chapter, Brothers focuses on her own route to success and analyzes the decisions she made in pursuit of success.

——————. *Widowed*. New York: Simon & Schuster, 1990. A personal account of how Brothers overcame the grief and loneliness of widowhood and how she managed to put her life back together after the death of her husband from cancer in 1989. One chapter is devoted to her early life with her husband, from the time she met Milton Brothers up through the beginnings of her successful career as a psychologist and media personality.

Moran, Joseph J. "Newspaper Psychology: Advice and Therapy." *Journal of Popular Culture* 22 (Spring, 1989): 119-127. In this scholarly analysis of newspaper advice columns as an influential form of popular psychology, the author provides formal content analysis of a variety of columns authored by Brothers and by Ann Landers that were published during a six-month period in 1986. Gives some insights into the perceived therapeutic value of Brothers' advice.

Rodgers, Joann Ellison. "Psychologists at Home: How They Live." *Psychology Today* 26 (July, 1993): 48-53. Brothers is one of three psychologists profiled in this article, which focuses on how professional psychologists and psychiatrists cope with their own personal crises and problems.

Bill Manikas

HELEN GURLEY BROWN

Born: February 18, 1922; Green Forest, Arkansas

Area of Achievement: Publishing
Contribution: Author of several books on the single life and editor of *Cosmopolitan* magazine, Brown legitimized and defined the single lifestyle for a generation.

Early Life

Helen Gurley was born in Green Forest, Arkansas, on February 18, 1922. She grew up in Little Rock, Arkansas, and Los Angeles, California. Her parents, Ira and Cleo Gurley, were both schoolteachers, and the family, including Helen and a sister, lived in modest circumstances. Early in life, Helen grew to despise the "hillbilly" life surrounding her and sought to distance herself psychologically from the perceived crudeness of her neighbors and relatives. Her father died accidentally when she was ten years old, and several years later her sister contracted polio, forcing the family into even more financially straitened circumstances.

Helen attended Texas State College for women from 1939 to 1941. In 1942, she took her first secretarial job in Los Angeles, working for an announcer at radio station KHJ while she attended secretarial school at Woodbury Business College. While she claims that both she and the job were "dreadful," Helen was able to survive and helped support her family on her salary of six dollars a week. Sixteen secretarial jobs followed, including positions with Music Corporation of America (MCA) and the William Morris Agency. She discovered that it was not necessarily rewarding to work for a glamorous agency; in one company, the secretaries were actually required to use a back stairway rather than the lavish entry, complete with chandelier, reserved for clients. Helen Gurley worked for the advertising agency Foote, Cone & Belding for five years before her entertaining letters to her boss when he was away on business led to an invitation from him to write copy for the agency. She had a talent for writing advertising copy and won two of her three Frances Holmes Advertising Copywriting awards before she left Foote, Cone & Belding in 1958. The following year, Helen married David Brown, a motion picture producer with Twentieth Century-Fox, but continued her career in advertising until 1962.

Life's Work

Happily married and involved in her career, Helen Gurley Brown still had not accomplished what she considered "the one big important thing." Her successes in the field of advertising were remarkable for any woman at that time, as few had gained the opportunity to excel in the corporate world. From her own experience, Brown knew that a career was important to women, rejecting the traditional belief that women found fulfillment only within marriage and family life. She had worked as a single woman, supporting herself and struggling with the problems of single life, as well as appreciating its benefits, until she was thirty-seven years old. Those years of experience, her husband convinced her, would constitute a useful and much-needed book.

Published in 1962, *Sex and the Single Girl* caused an immediate sensation. It was both praised for its honest treatment of the realities of single life, especially the sexual activities of young single women, and condemned for those same reasons. One reviewer, *Los Angeles Times* critic Robert Kirsch, called it "As tasteless a book as I have encountered." Nevertheless, *Sex and the Single Girl* remained on best-seller lists into the next year. It was obvious that there was, indeed, an audience of young single women who craved the information and guidance Brown offered.

The book opens with a whole-hearted affirmation for the unmarried, working woman. In a style that is chatty, informal, and personal, chapter 1 explains why the single woman is the most glamorous star of the social scene—she is accomplished, economically self-sufficient (her actual salary and circumstances notwithstanding), and available, at least to the men she decides are worth her time. Stating the dismal marriage outlook for women during the early 1960's and conceding that some women may have no choice but to remain single for life, Brown insists that the prospect is not one to cry over, but holds excitement and opportunity. Independence, she holds, is a character development that will benefit a woman regardless of her marital prospects.

In succeeding chapters, Brown detailed a plan for a woman to enjoy being single, whether she is still in her twenties or approaching fifty. Topics covered begin with men and end with men, from what males are available to tips on conducting the modern affair. In between, chapters on fashion, makeup, cooking, finances, decorating an apartment, and keeping in shape cover the inward and outward self.

The format worked because Brown's approach was so personal, and she was able to remind the reader that these strategies certainly worked for her. She threw in plenty of anecdotes and borrowed from the experience of friends to create an atmosphere that encouraged success for those who were willing to work at it. Some of her advice is shrewd, some a little silly, and some of it bound by the definitions of women and sexuality in the time period in which *Sex and the Single Girl* was written. Nevertheless, the book proved to be a valuable guidebook of sorts for many young women, and its popularity helped propel Brown to her own success.

Subsequent to the publication of *Sex and the Single Girl*, Brown began receiving numerous fan letters from women, asking her advice on matters of romance and other topics addressed in her book. Although Brown had a popular syndicated newspaper column in the early 1960's called *Woman Alone*, her husband thought that these letters indicated that a forum for addressing these issues more extensively was needed.

The Browns set to work developing a prospectus for a magazine that they tentatively named *Femme*. They drew up a format and a list of possible articles and submitted the package to several publishers. After their plan was rejected by many prospective backers, the Browns approached the Hearst Corporation, which already possessed a magazine that was failing. Hearst agreed to turn *Cosmopolitan* over to the Browns, who could impose their new format on the old magazine. In 1965, Helen Gurley Brown became editor of *Cosmopolitan* and entered a new stage of her career.

As editor-in-chief of *Cosmopolitan*, Brown increased circulation from 700,000 to 2,800,000. Almost all sales of the magazine are from newsstands, sparing the publisher (and the readers) the pangs of subscriptions and renewals. Advertising revenues also jumped as *Cosmopolitan* proved to be popular with the increasing numbers of career-oriented single women who sought a little advice to augment their own growing tastes and reinforce their independent lifestyles. The magazine offered up-to-date information on fashion and advice for succeeding in the workplace, along with articles on relationship woes and pitfalls, how to avoid them, or how to deal with them when they are detected. The magazine's trademark questionnaires, introduced by titles such as "Are You . . . " or "Is He . . . ," provided a sort of self-help barometer and encouraged an attitude of vigilant self-awareness among readers.

Brown claims that her husband, David, has written the cover blurbs and has approved which articles should go into each issue, although he has maintained his own career as a motion picture producer. Brown herself has continued to write a column featured in each issue, "Step Into My Parlor," using her trademark comfortable, sympathetic, and personal style that has made all of her publishing efforts a success.

In addition to her career as a magazine editor, Brown continued to write books: *Sex and the Office* (1965); *The Outrageous Opinions of Helen Gurley Brown* (1967); *Helen Gurley Brown's Single Girl's Cookbook* (1969); *Sex and the New Single Girl* (1970), in which she updated her original book; and, in 1982, *Having It All*, in which she defines her favorite self-designation of "mouseburger." According to Brown, a mouseburger is a woman who is not particularly pretty, or smart, and certainly does not come from a good family background, but has the determination and common sense to work hard and make the most of, or more than, what she has been given. *Having It All* seems to resemble yet another attempt by Brown to update *Sex and the Single Girl*. In 1993, she published *The Late Show*, a survival guide for women over the age of fifty who continue to want to "have it all."

In the early 1990's, Helen Gurley Brown continued to be happily married to her husband, David. Despite persistent rumors through the 1980's, she did not step down from her position as editor-in-chief of *Cosmopolitan*. An avowed workaholic, she continued to squeeze as much from life as she possibly could.

Summary

Helen Gurley Brown struggled through lean years at low-paying jobs at a time when women were expected to find a husband and make their careers in the home. When she finally broke through into an advertising career, she discovered that her hard work was a reward in itself. After she met and married David Brown, she chose not to retire from the working world. Ultimately she was persuaded to share her secrets for success with the growing numbers of single working women.

The times were indeed changing: *Sex and the Single Girl* was a breakthrough book that openly dealt with the sexual lives of unmarried women, a topic not only considered taboo but also denied by "polite" society. Based on the experience of herself and her close friends, Brown gave advice for women conducting affairs, both with single and married men, urging them to keep their wits about them and enjoy themselves with a clear understanding of what they were doing.

Another area in which Brown contributed was the elevation of work outside the home as a source of pride and accomplishment, both personal and financial. Although some feminists may despair at Brown's insistence that men are still an integral, indispensable part of a woman's life, she did contribute much to the liberation of women from the traditional notion that domestic life was their only respectable choice. Brown remained childless and often voiced her opinion that the joys of children are not worth the demands they make upon their mothers, a radical viewpoint when she first stated it. Her life has provided an example of the success a hardworking woman can achieve and the satisfaction that can be hers.

Bibliography

Brown, Helen Gurley. *Having It All*. New York: Simon & Schuster, 1982. Brown advises the working woman of the 1980's who wishes to have a fulfilling career, marriage or not, a healthy body and mind, and an elegant, sociable life and reveals the intricacies of her personal philosophy.

——————. "Having It All." *McCalls* 120 (March, 1993): 84. Helen Gurley Brown discusses aging and its effects on her. Despite her own advice on vitamins, daily exercise, and nutrition, she concedes that one can only preserve good health, not youth, and admonishes older women to accept the changes a long life brings.

——————. *Sex and the Single Girl*. New York: Random House, 1962. The book that started it all. Brown sets forth the philosophy that led to the founding of *Cosmopolitan* magazine and which legitimized the experience of many single women.

——————. "What the Women's Movement Means to Me." *Ms.* 14 (July, 1985): 118. In this brief article, Brown ingenuously discusses the women's movement and the assumptions that she lived with in her early career days.

Falkof, Lucille. *Helen Gurley Brown: The Queen of Cosmopolitan*. Ada, Okla.: Garrett Educational Corp., 1992. An entry in the publisher's Wizards of Business juvenile biography series, this work provides a good introduction to Brown's career and her childhood in the rural South. Focusing primarily on Brown's role as an entrepreneur, Falkof offers useful insights into Brown's philosophy of business and her ability to supervise others.

Kornbluth, Jesse. "The Queen of the Mouseburgers." *New York* 15 (September 27, 1982): 36-41. An admiring overview of Brown's accomplishments on the publication of *Having It All*. Provides some details of her early life and much on her personal life and philosophy.

Mason, Margaret. "Still the Cosmo Girl." *The Washington Post*, March 19, 1993, p. F5. Describes the way in which Brown has dealt with aging and the personal philosophy that has helped her to achieve peace with the inevitable aging process.

Rothenberg, Randall. "The Cosmo Girl at Twenty-five: She Still Wants It All." *The New York Times*, April 21, 1990, p. A31. Profiles Brown's twenty-five years as editor of *Cosmopolitan* and offers examples of how her personal philosophy has shaped the editorial content of her magazine.

Patricia Masserman

MARGARET WISE BROWN

Born: May 23, 1910; New York, New York
Died: November 13, 1952; Nice, France
Area of Achievement: Literature
Contribution: The author of one hundred books for children, as well as numerous other works, Brown brought a new vitality and art to the field of juvenile literature.

Early Life

Born in the Brooklyn area of New York City on May 23, 1910, Margaret Wise Brown was the second of three children. Her father, Robert Bruce Brown, was an executive of American Manufacturing Company, specializing in rope, cordage, and bagging. Her mother, Maude Margaret Johnson Brown, spent her days pursuing a variety of aesthetic interests, including painting china plates and reading poetry.

The three children—Benjamin Gratz, Jr., Margaret, and Roberta—lived a life of freedom, peopled with fairy tale companions and surrounded by a menagerie of pets, including rabbits, squirrels, and the more typical cats, dogs, and goldfish. The bucolic existence was possible because the family moved to a large new home in suburban Beechurst, Long Island, in 1915.

Childhood for Brown and her siblings was overshadowed by pressure from her father's family. Their remote father and overbearing aunts doted on Gratz as the male heir of their Brown name which proudly traced its lineage from B. Gratz Brown, the antislavery governor of Missouri (1871-1873) and a vice presidential candidate in 1872. Despite this bias, all three children were well educated, although the girls frequently bounced from local schools to boarding schools. In 1923, Robert Brown made an extended trip to India. The family closed up the Beechurst home and took the opportunity to travel the European continent. During this period, Margaret and Roberta spent two years at Chateau Brillantmont, a French boarding school near Lausanne.

Returning home in 1925, the Brown family awaited the completion of their new home in wealthy Great Neck, New York. Other changes included Maude Brown's growing interest in Theosophy, which sustained her as her marriage became increasingly unhappy. Margaret and Roberta entered Dana Hall, a private girls' school in Massachusetts in 1926. Dana Hall focused on classical studies and preparation for college. Margaret, however, was not a scholar. Roberta, almost two years younger, was in the same class and was generally much more successful in her studies. Although she lacked a solid scholastic background, Margaret decided to attend her mother's alma mater, Hollins College, in Roanoke, Virginia.

Margaret Wise Brown's years at Hollins served as a turning point for her life. She began to dedicate her attention to writing. Her first publication appeared in the campus literary magazine, *Cargoes*. The essay was written as an assignment for Marguerite Hearsey's class on Chaucer. As Brown's professor, Hearsey encouraged Brown to persevere as a writer. Throughout Brown's life, women served both as mentors and as the emotional center of her life. More often than not, these relationships were with older women. Brown, known as "Tim" to her friends, spent spring break of 1932 in Little Rock, Arkansas, where she met the parents of her fiancé, George Armistead. For reasons that never became clear, Brown returned to be graduated from Hollins with the engagement terminated.

Life's Work

With her diploma in hand, her college friends married, and no job prospects, Margaret Wise Brown returned to her parents' home. In pursuit of her writing career, Brown enrolled in a fiction workshop at Columbia University in the fall of 1934. Her inability to sustain a plot led her to question her talent and to fear she would never be a writer. Disturbed by the growing turmoil between her parents, Brown moved into her own apartment in Greenwich Village that same fall.

Employment as a nanny in the winter of 1934 did not prove satisfying to Brown. Her neighbor, Inez Camprubi, suggested she enter the Bureau of Educational Experiments (later, the Bank Street College of Education). At the school, students pursued three levels of education—developmental research, teacher training, and preschool education. All of these efforts were overseen by the school's director, Lucy Sprague Mitchell. An advocate of John Dewey and the educational theories laid out in his work, *Democracy and Education* (1916), Mitchell believed the classroom should be a democracy. She developed her "curriculum of experience" in which each child was allowed to explore, play, and grow at an individual rate. Projects included psychological testing, sex education, and linguistics, among others. From this Brown derived her ideas of children's creativity as reflected in their languaging. Mitchell's ideas formed the basis of her work, the *Here and Now Story Book* (1921), and they also served as the foundation of Brown's life's work and of her success.

Mitchell became Brown's new mentor, and Brown absorbed all the ideas of integrating children's own words, such as "toot-toot," and their simple linguistic cadence into her own works. Brown, like Mitchell, removed the fairy-tale quality from her juvenile works and instead described the world of everyday things that children experienced. One of Brown's first works clearly demonstrated these ideas. The first *Noisy Book* (1939) described the sounds of the city, the "clop, clop" of horses and the "bang, bang" of men hammering. The success of this work was followed by several additional books, including the *Country Noisy Book* (1940), *The Seashore Noisy Book* (1941), *Indoor Noisy Book* (1942), *The Noisy Bird Book* (1943), *The Winter Noisy Book* (1947), *The Quiet Noisy Book* (1950), and *The Summer Noisy Book* (1951).

Brown's first years at Mitchell's Bank Street school proved remarkably productive. Within two years she completed several books, including *When the Wind Blew* (1937), *Bumble Bugs and Elephants: A Big and Little Book* (1938), *The Fish with the Deep Sea Smile* (1938), *The Little Fireman* (1938), as well as several other collaborations and adaptations. With these works, "Brownie" (the nickname she adopted at Bank Street) established several precedents. She "tested" the books on the children in the school to see if the children responded, a habit she maintained even after she left the school in 1943. Throughout her life she wrote the primary texts of her works in about twenty minutes and then spent months honing them. In addition, she established herself not only as the author but also as the artistic director of her works.

She collaborated with more than forty artists, some of the best in the business. Artists such as Garth Williams, Leonard Weisgard, Clement Hurd, Esphyr Slobodkina, and Charles Shaw became her close friends and confidants in addition to providing the art for her works. At first, her relationship with her publishing houses was also a congenial and friendly one. Although both Harper and Brothers and E. P. Dutton published some of her early works, Brown became an editor with the William R. Scott publishing house. Since Brown produced more than seven books a year, no single publisher could handle her output, so gradually Harper, with her friend Ursula Nordstrum as editor, became her chief publisher. Brown's professional relationship with Scott actually deteriorated by the end of the 1940's when Brown abruptly withdrew the publishing rights to new *Noisy* books from Scott.

While Brown's professional career could only be termed a success, her personal life was much more tumultuous and unsatisfactory. By 1938, she established the habit of summering in Maine on the island of Vinalhaven. She bought a home she called "The Only House" there later in 1943. Although it was one of several residences on the island, the house itself was unique, featuring a stairway that went nowhere but to the sky and a dressing table outside, since there was no indoor plumbing. During her 1938 summer in Maine, she met William Gaston, a New York attorney, and began an affair with him. The affair proved unsatisfactory when he married someone else. In 1942, Brown had a brief affair with journalist Preston Schoyer in New York.

It was between these two liaisons that Brown met the woman who would be both her mentor and companion for the next several years. Blanche Oelrichs, the former wife of John Barrymore, was a socialite, actress, and poet who had adopted the name Michael Strange. She was several years older than Brown. In 1943, Brown gave up her apartment and essentially moved in with Strange. The emotional interruptions and lack of privacy at her new home made writing difficult, so Brown began to use a small run-down house, built c. 1810 and called Cobble Court, as her office. Brown and Strange had an uneven relationship, with Strange invariably controlling their contact and Brown feeling inadequate. The quality of their relationship even affected Brown's working relationships, since certain illustrator friends disliked Strange while others approved of her. Brown actually removed art assignments from Clement Hurd to give to Garth Williams because of this estrangement. Only after Strange's death in 1950 did Brown break free. In fact, in 1952, at the age of forty-two, Brown became engaged to twenty-six-year-old James Stillman Rockefeller, Jr., a wealthy scion of the Carnegie and Rockefeller families who was known as "Pebble."

Despite inward turmoil, an unhappy personal life, and the death of her mother in 1947, Brown produced some of her most renowned works during this period, many of which remain in print nearly a half century after her death. Standouts from this period include *Baby Animals* (1941); *The Runaway Bunny* (1942); an adaptation of a medieval Provençal love ballad; *Little Fur Family* (1946); *Goodnight Moon* (1947); *The Color Kittens* (1949); and *Big Red Barn*, published posthumously in 1956. Several different publishing houses produced some eighty works by Brown from this period, including Simon and Schuster, Doubleday, and Random House. Some books, usually collaborations, were written under her pseudonyms Timothy Hay, Golden MacDonald, and Juniper Sage. At the time of her death, her new works were focusing on lyrics for children's songs, using adaptations of her works and the talents of personalities such as Burl Ives.

Her plans for her imminent marriage as well as her career were abruptly ended in late 1952. A seasoned traveler, Brown was in France in October of 1952, when she was assailed by severe abdominal pain. Unable to be transferred quickly to Paris, she underwent surgery in Nice, France, on October 31. Preparing to leave the hospital on November 13 after recovering from the removal of an ovarian cyst and her appendix, Brown kicked her leg in the air to demonstrate her vitality. An embolism in the leg broke free and Brown was dead in seconds. Her ashes were flown back to "Pebble" Rockefeller, who took them to Vinalhaven as she had wanted.

Summary

Margaret Wise Brown's work literally turned an industry around. During the Depression, publishing houses had cut back on book production, and the first cuts were often made in the category of juvenile literature. Brown, however, made children's books a marketable commodity. Barbara Bader in her work *American Picturebooks* summed it up best when she said Brown was the first writer of children's books "to be recognized in her own right . . . [and] to make the writing of picturebooks an art."

Aside from her writing legacy, Brown left behind the memory of a woman both competent and complicated. Reflecting the best of the educated Progressive woman and the best of Pragmatic philosophy, Brown stood alone in her career—editing, choosing and endorsing artists, making her own financial decisions and her own personal choices. The woman who wrote about cuddly bunnies, carried one on a train in college, skinned one as a child, and chased them as a member of a hunt club, is best remembered for her legacy of the "runaway bunny," but should also be remembered for her courage to make innovative choices. Brown herself said that her contribution was as a "writer of songs and nonsense."

Bibliography

Bader, Barbara. *American Picturebooks from Noah's Ark to the Beast Within*. New York: Macmillan, 1976. Basically an evaluation of Brown's contributions to her field of children's picture books and her role in elevating her profession to the rank of art.

Bechtel, Louise Seaman. "Margaret Wise Brown: Laureate of the Nursery." *Horn Book* 34 (June, 1958): 172-186. Originally a book critic, Bechtel interviewed Brown and maintained a personal correspondence with her. This article is taken from Bechtel's speech at the dedication of the Margaret Wise Brown collection at the Memorial and Library Association of Westerly (Rhode Island).

Bliven, Bruce, Jr. "Child's Best Seller." *Life* 21 (December 2, 1946): 59-61. Written during Brown's lifetime, this interview contains interesting anecdotes and presents a piquant view of Brown with quotes. Bliven was coexecutor of Brown's estate. Photographs included.

Fleischman, John. "Shakespeare of the Sandbox Set." *Parent's Magazine* 63 (July, 1988): 92-96. Fleischman provides a brief biographical sketch of Brown, discussing the enduring popularity of her stories and placing her work within the larger context of children's literature.

Marcus, Leonard S. *Margaret Wise Brown: Awakened by the Moon.* Boston: Beacon Press, 1992. The only comprehensive biography of Brown, this work draws on her letters, interviews, and publications. Includes family background with additional biographical information on other people mentioned in the book. Marcus places Brown in historical perspective and then tries to present readers with insight into Brown's own creative process, hence the subtitle of the work. Photographs included.

Sutherland, Zena, and May Hill Arbuthnot. *Children and Books.* 7th ed. Glenview, Ill.: Scott, Foresman, 1986. An overview of children's literature, this work provides a short summary of Brown's career and the influence of Lucy Sprague Mitchell on Brown's work.

Michaela Crawford Reaves

RACHEL FULLER BROWN

Born: November 23, 1898; Springfield, Massachusetts
Died: January 14, 1980; Albany, New York
Areas of Achievement: Biochemistry and medicine
Contribution: With microbiologist Elizabeth Hazen, Brown discovered and purified the first antifungal antibiotic used to treat human disease. This discovery led to the two scientists' becoming the first women to receive the Chemical Pioneer Award from the American Institute of Chemists.

Early Life
Rachel Fuller Brown was born on November 23, 1898, in the industrial town of Springfield, Massachusetts, to George Hamilton Brown and Annie Fuller Brown. Eleven months later, her only brother, Sumner Jerome, was born.

In 1905, soon after Rachel started grammar school, her father's business ventures necessitated the family's move to Webster Groves, Missouri. It was there that Rachel's early brushes with science took place, although her interest in science in general was, at this time, lukewarm at best. During her elementary school years, she was befriended by a retired school principal who encouraged her fascination with insects, helping her to collect and mount specimens and allowing her the use of his microscope to examine them. Despite this, Rachel's main interests were in art and history. Throughout her precollege years, she made every effort to avoid science courses.

The family in which Rachel grew up was in some ways quite progressive for the day. Rachel and Sumner were both taught all the household chores, without regard to gender, and were expected to trade sets of jobs weekly. Life changed, however, when Rachel was twelve. George Hamilton Brown deserted his family, leaving his wife and children to support themselves. Annie Fuller Brown, suddenly financially responsible for them all, decided to move back to Springfield, Massachusetts, where they could be with Annie's own family.

Rachel finished elementary school and went to high school in Springfield, enrolling briefly at the vocational high school on the advice of relatives but soon transferring to the college preparatory program at Central High. During this time, Rachel's mother supported the family by working as a secretary, then as director of religious education at various Episcopal churches in western Massachusetts. It did not seem likely that Rachel would be financially able to attend college. Nevertheless, she was set on it, focusing her dreams on Mount Holyoke College, a well-known institution for women in nearby South Hadley, Massachusetts. A friend of Rachel's grandmother, Henrietta F. Dexter, evidently impressed by Rachel's determination, offered her the funding for four years at Mount Holyoke. Rachel accepted, entering the college as a history major. She was dismayed to learn that for a Bachelor of Arts degree in history, she was required to complete a course requirement in the physical sciences. She chose chemistry, deeming it the lesser of two evils, physics being her other option. To her surprise, she loved it from the start. She decided to take a double major in chemistry and history and received her B.A. degree in 1920. With the encouragement of Emma Perry Carr, one of her Mount Holyoke chemistry professors, and additional funds from her "Aunt Etta," Rachel decided to attend the University of Chicago for a graduate degree in chemistry. She received her M.S. degree in organic chemistry the following year and chose to go into teaching.

For the next three years, she taught chemistry and, ironically, physics at the Frances Shimer School, a girls' high school and junior college near Chicago. Convinced that teaching was not for her, Rachel returned to the University of Chicago for further study, this time paid for from her own savings and her salary as a laboratory assistant. Electing a minor of bacteriology as well as her major of organic chemistry, she completed the course work, research, and thesis for her doctorate in two years. The acceptance of her thesis and the administration of her oral examinations, however, rested on the whim of the faculty, and as she waited for this approval, her savings ran out. Unable to wait longer, Rachel accepted an appointment as research chemist at the Division of Laboratories and Research at Albany, a division of the New York State Department of Health.

Life's Work

In accepting her research post, Rachel Fuller Brown was fortunate to have found employment at a place where her gender did not hinder her professional advancement. The Division, as it was familiarly called, had a good research reputation and a practice—surprising even in the late twentieth century in scientific institutions, but amazing then—of recruiting women as its primary researchers. Augustus Wadsworth, the Division's director, assigned her briefly to syphilis antigen research, then moved her to a project more closely related to her doctoral research, extracting the polysaccharides associated with particular bacteria known to cause pneumonia. Since penicillin, sulfa drugs, and other antibiotics were not yet available, each pneumonia-causing bacterium had to be fought separately, and there were many. In the next fifteen years, Brown identified more than forty pneumococcins (pneumonia-causing bacteria) and purified the antigens to counteract almost all of them. During her brief work with the syphilis antigen, she also devised a test for syphilis which was much less time-consuming than any previously available, and which is still used.

During this time, Brown was called upon to present a paper in Chicago. With Wadsworth's influence, the University of Chicago chemistry department finally arranged for her oral examinations—in the area in which she was now considered to be an expert. In 1933, she finally received her Ph.D. degree in organic chemistry and bacteriology.

Then, in 1948, the new Division director, Gilbert Dalldorf, introduced Brown to microbiologist Elizabeth Hazen. Involved in working with fungi, Hazen was in need of a chemist able to help her isolate and purify the antifungal agents she hoped to find.

When penicillin began to be commonly used in the 1940's, it was seen that often, while the antibiotic was phenomenal at curing infection, there were often decidedly unpleasant side effects. Eventually it was realized that, while penicillin killed the pathogenic bacteria as was desired, it was indiscriminate about killing many benefi-cial fauna as well. These latter bacteria often acted to keep endemic fungi under control, and when they were removed, the fungi grew unchecked.

Elizabeth Hazen had been working for four years on the search for an antifungal substance when she met Brown. Hazen focused on soil organisms, since other researchers had found unusual antibiotic activity in soil, and spent much of her time in her New York City laboratory testing soil samples for antifungal activity. Those samples that stopped fungal growth were sent on to Brown for further testing. Brown then extracted the active agents from the sample, purified them, and tested their effectiveness and safety. Two primary antifungal agents were found, but only one was determined to be safe to use on humans. (The other is used to control plant fungi.) Brown and Hazen tested this agent on laboratory animals and, in 1950, announced that they had succeeded in finding a fungicide that stood up to laboratory testing. They named it nystatin, in honor of the state that had supported their research.

There was immediate interest in the discovery of nystatin. Presumably somewhat overwhelmed, or possibly merely uninterested in the marketing and production of nystatin, the two women gave control of their discovery to Research Corporation, a private foundation which oversaw the patenting and licensing of inventions. They made only one stipulation: Any profits made from royalties were to be reinvested immediately into research or education. Neither woman ever accepted any financial reward for her discovery.

Very soon, E. R. Squibb and Sons, a pharmaceutical company, took over the testing and large-scale manufacture of nystatin. In 1954, the Food and Drug Adminis-tration (FDA) granted approval for the marketing of the drug under the trade name Mycostatin.

The profits from the market of Mycostatin were, and are, considerable. Brown and Hazen were very firm in their conviction that they not use the money for themselves. The royalties that accrue from sales are still split evenly between Research Corpora-tion, which is dedicated to the advancement of science, and the Brown-Hazen Fund.

The fund has provided money for a wide variety of research. Not surprisingly, a large portion of the fund is devoted to advancing the field of medical mycology. Another substantial slice is given to training women in the sciences. Beyond this, funds are donated to research programs in virtually every biological specialty as well as other scientific fields, and to projects in almost every one of the United States, plus Puerto Rico, Canada, and several other nations.

Besides funding research, the Brown-Hazen Fund provides scholarship monies at Mount Holyoke College and at the Mississippi University for Women, which Eliza-beth Hazen attended. These institutions have also received funds for laboratory equipment and facilities, as has the College of Physicians and Surgeons of Columbia University, where Hazen worked for many years. A special designation also funds study and research at the Division at Albany as well.

Brown and Hazen received many awards for their work, including honorary doctorates from Mount Holyoke and Hobart and William Smith Colleges, the Rhonda

Benham Award of the Medical Mycology Society of the Americas, and the Squibb Award in Chemotherapy. The most prestigious of these, though, was the Chemical Pioneer Award of the American Institute of Chemists, presented to them in 1975. Brown and Hazen were the first women ever to receive this award. As Hazen was too ill to attend the ceremonies, Brown accepted for both of them. Soon after, Hazen died.

Brown continued to work for the Division until she retired in 1968. She maintained an active life outside her job, very involved in her church and spending much time and energy in the administration of the Brown-Hazen Fund. She and her longtime friend Dorothy Wakerley opened their house to a steadily increasing stream of visiting Chinese scientists and their families. Brown also remained close to her brother, an Episcopal priest in Massachusetts. She died at the age of eighty-one on January 14, 1980.

Summary

The results of their scientific research were far more varied than either Rachel Fuller Brown or Elizabeth Hazen ever dreamed of in the beginning. Aside from its continued use on many severe, sometimes fatal infections in humans and animals, nystatin has been used to keep bananas fresh, to stop grain from spoiling, to cure Dutch elm disease, to preserve wine, and to save priceless art objects damaged by floodwaters in Italy. Nystatin has become a very useful research tool, invaluable for its ability to eliminate fungal contamination in tissue cultures. It has also been used to distinguish between different strains of fungi, since it is generally known which strains are resistant to nystatin and which are not.

The impact of Brown and Hazen's research has reached beyond their specific discovery of nystatin. The Brown-Hazen Fund and Research Corporation have collected more than thirteen million dollars in royalties, money that has been cycled back in research grants and scholarships. The money that was donated for Brown's education has been repaid many times over to the benefit of others.

Brown had a special concern for the scientific education of women throughout her lifetime and spent much energy encouraging the pursuit of scientific careers by women. Her moral and financial support for this endeavor and the example she provided have served to inspire young women seeking to make a profession of scientific research. Her story is a tribute to dedication and the achievement of one's goals. Rachel Brown committed a half-century to the advancement of science and medicine and ensured through her work that many other people will be able to do the same.

Bibliography

Baldwin, Richard S. *The Fungus Fighters*. Ithaca, N.Y.: Cornell University Press, 1981. An excellent, thorough biography of both Hazen and Brown with a particularly comprehensive account of their research years.

Salisbury, David F. "A Chemist's Discovery Saved Priceless Murals." *The Christian Science Monitor*, October 1, 1975, p. 20. Written from an interview with Rachel

Brown, this article gives insight on the personality of the scientist not found elsewhere.

Vare, Ethlie Ann, and Greg Ptacek. *Mothers of Invention: From the Bra to the Bomb—Forgotten Women and Their Unforgettable Ideas.* New York: William Morrow, 1988. Vare and Ptacek explore the forgotten contributions of women in a variety of scientific fields. They provide examples of several women's roles, including Brown's, in the advancement of medicine.

Yost, Edna. *Women of Modern Science.* New York: Dodd, Mead, 1959. Reprint. Westport, Conn.: Greenwood Press, 1984. Contains biographical accounts of eleven women scientists, including a nontechnical, easy-to-read biography of Rachel Brown. A useful source of information on Brown's life as well as the significance of her scientific work.

Margaret Hawthorne

RITA MAE BROWN

Born: November 28, 1944; Hanover, Pennsylvania

Areas of Achievement: Literature and women's rights
Contribution: Through her novels, poems, essays, and political activity, Rita Mae Brown has brought lesbian existence "out of the closet" and into popular awareness.

Early Life

Rita Mae Brown was born in Hanover, a Pennsylvania town just north of the Maryland border. Soon after her birth, she was adopted by Ralph and Julia Ellen Brown, and lived in Hanover until the family moved to Fort Lauderdale, Florida, in 1955. A fine student and star athlete, Brown graduated from Fort Lauderdale High School and earned a scholarship to the University of Florida at Gainesville, where she became a civil rights activist. As a result of these activities, she was expelled from the university. She then hitchhiked north, arriving friendless and penniless in New York City. In New York, she worked as a waitress and encountered for the first time an established, yet diverse, lesbian community. A combination of menial jobs and a scholarship allowed Brown to attend New York University, from which she graduated with a B.A. in English and Classics in 1968.

Brown's years in New York also marked her entrance into the embryonic gay rights movement. She was cofounder of the Columbia University Student Homophile League and was one of the few gay activists willing to use her real name. Increasingly disillusioned with male sexism within gay rights organizations, Brown gradually transferred her energies to women's liberation. She joined the National Organization for Women (NOW) and soon became the editor of NOW's New York newsletter. But in the late 1960's NOW and the women's liberation movement in general began to repudiate their alliance with avowed lesbians, not wishing to alienate mainstream America. In 1969, NOW president Betty Friedan referred to growing lesbian visibility as a "lavender menace." As a result, Rita Mae Brown was relieved of her duties as newsletter editor.

Stung, Brown denounced NOW's homophobia and resigned from the organization, vowing to form a lesbian-feminist movement. She cofounded Lavender Menace, a radical group that pushed the lesbian agenda within women's liberation. Under the name Radicalesbians, the group published the influential position paper "The Woman-Identified Woman" in 1970. Later that year Radicalesbians disintegrated, and Brown moved to Washington, D.C., drawn both by the Institute for Policy Studies (IPS), a leftist think tank, and by the lure of a lesbian-feminist commune. Together with activist and IPS associate Charlotte Bunch, Brown started a lesbian "consciousness-raising group" in early 1971 which evolved into the Furies collective. The Furies were perhaps the most influential of the lesbian-feminist cells in the early 1970's, not because they succeeded in toppling heterosexism, but because their revolutionary fervor ignited the lesbian movement and garnered attention for the lesbian agenda as a means of achieving real change for women. The Furies disbanded after a single turbulent year; nevertheless, that year crystallized Brown's thinking about the role of class, and enabled her to produce "The Last Straw," a perceptive analysis of class dynamics within the feminist movement.

Brown maintained her link with the IPS, working as a research fellow there until 1973, and eventually earning her Ph.D. in political science. Despite this academic success, however, since 1973 Brown has poured her primary energy into writing: poetry, essays, screenplays, and especially novels.

Life's Work

Rita Mae Brown had always wanted to write fiction, and in 1973, at the urging of friends, she completed *Rubyfruit Jungle*, her first full-length novel. *Rubyfruit Jungle* was originally published by Daughters, Inc., a feminist press; it achieved considerable notoriety among alternative readers. In 1977, growing interest in the work prompted Bantam to reissue the book as a mass-market paperback. The response was immediate and overwhelming. *Rubyfruit Jungle* sold more than a million copies and catapulted its author into overnight fame, placing her in the unofficial position of spokeswoman for American lesbians.

Rubyfruit Jungle, like many other Brown novels, is semiautobiographical. It traces the childhood and young adulthood of the symbolically named Molly Bolt (a molly-bolt is a fastener which, when inserted through wood into empty space beyond, opens and anchors itself to the away side). Like her author, Molly is born out of wedlock, is adopted, and spends her early childhood in southern Pennsylvania. A sexual outlaw even as a young girl, she has her first lesbian experience (although the word "lesbian" is not in her adolescent vocabulary) before her family moves to Florida. The novel follows her through her high school years, her expulsion from college for lesbianism, her discovery of the New York lesbian scene, and her graduation from college with a degree in film.

Rubyfruit Jungle is a novel in the tradition of Henry Fielding; Molly Bolt is a kind of female Tom Jones, romping through a series of humorous sexual escapades. Hers is a *Bildungsroman* with a picaresque heroine. Never afflicted with self-doubt, Molly faces repeated rejections without a ripple in her sense of identity. Naturally, *Rubyfruit Jungle* and its heroine represented an astonishing validation of lesbian existence. For lesbian readers especially, Molly was a tonic. Her boundless self-confidence contrasted strikingly with miserable, guilt-ridden Stephen Gordon, heroine of Radclyffe Hall's *The Well of Loneliness* (1928), the only previous lesbian novel to gain a wide "mainstream" readership. Like *The Well of Loneliness*, *Rubyfruit Jungle* awakened the general public to the existence of lesbianism; but unlike *The Well of Loneliness*, *Rubyfruit Jungle* painted a portrait of a well-adjusted, empowered lesbian woman.

After the phenomenal success of *Rubyfruit Jungle*, Rita Mae Brown's second novel *In Her Day* (1976) was decidedly a failure. It takes up many compelling issues central to the radical feminism of the time, but the humorless preachy tone is not Brown's natural voice, and *In Her Day* is heavy going.

Two years later Brown rediscovered the buoyant breezy style that had been so successful in *Rubyfruit Jungle*. Her third novel, *Six of One* (1978), revisits the area in southern Pennsylvania where she spent her early childhood. In this novel, Brown creates the fictional towns of North and South Runnymeade, invents a history for them, and populates them with eccentric and amusing people. Some of these characters—particularly Julie Ellen (Juts) and her adopted daughter Nickel, who just happens to have been born on November 28, 1944, and who grows up lesbian—bear a striking resemblance to Rita Mae Brown and her family. *Six of One* rambles, and it lacks the kind of conflict that leads to a coherent plot, but Runnymeade and its citizens come to life.

By contrast, Brown's next novel, *Southern Discomfort* (1982), abounds in conflict. Set in Alabama, it explores the intersecting oppressions of racism, classism, and sexism. Even more powerfully than in *Rubyfruit Jungle, Southern Discomfort* takes up the question of being publicly true to oneself, even when one's life violates society's accepted code of conduct.

Sudden Death (1983), Rita Mae Brown's fifth novel, explores this same theme. Set in the high-rent, high-tension world of the women's professional tennis tour, the novel's plot revolves around whether the tennis star protagonist will admit her lesbianism. Much of the real interest of *Sudden Death* lies in its description of the behind-the-scenes workings of top-rank women's tennis, an environment familiar to Brown as a result of her widely publicized relationship with Martina Navratilova. More than anything else *Sudden Death* is an intriguing *roman à clef*; readers cannot help but try to identify the real people behind the fictional characters.

As an avid student of Civil War history, Brown incorporated her familiarity with the period into *High Hearts* (1986), the Civil War novel she always wanted to write. The book has an air of authenticity about it, largely due to Brown's painstaking preliminary research. On the surface, the plots and subplots are typical historical romance devices; the novel's depth rests in its questioning of the nature of gender. In *High Hearts*, Brown explores the interplay between gender role expectation, behavior, and happiness.

Starting from Scratch, a fiction writer's manual written in 1988, represented a new direction for Rita Mae Brown. The book opens with a personal statement of Brown's beliefs about writing ("It's an act of faith to be a writer in a postliterate world"); it then discusses strategies for writing, for navigating tricky publishing procedures, for self-promotion, for dealing with fame, for branching out, for recharging flagging creativity.

In that same year, Brown's seventh novel, *Bingo*, appeared. This book revisits Runnymeade and the cast of characters from *Six of One*. It reintroduces us to the aging Juts and her sister Louise, but the primary focus is Nickel. In *Bingo*, Nickel faces several midlife challenges: how to live as a lesbian in a small town, how to handle her attraction to a man, and how to deal with an unexpected pregnancy.

Brown's next books represent something of a departure from her other works. The novels, entitled *Wish You Were Here* (1990) and *Rest in Pieces* (1992), are both "coauthored" by her cat Sneaky Pie Brown. They signal her entry into the rapidly expanding area of mystery novels featuring women detectives.

Rita Mae Brown's novel *Venus Envy* (1993) takes up an intriguing idea. The central character, believing she is terminally ill, writes letters to her closest friends and relatives revealing her lesbianism; she then must deal with the repercussions when she recovers. Although *Venus Envy* begins as a "grown-up coming out story," it ultimately wanders off into fantasy; one reviewer has seen this thematic unsteadiness as a sign of a literary "identity crisis" for Brown.

Summary

Since the late 1960's, Rita Mae Brown has battled for women's rights, for lesbian visibility, and for literary acceptance. Her early essays and novels profoundly inspired a generation of women who sought validation for their identity as lesbians. Her later writing deemphasizes lesbian consciousness in favor of historical romance, mystery, and Southern regionalism. In fact, Brown stated, "Next time anyone calls me a lesbian writer I'm going to knock their teeth in. I'm a writer and I'm a woman and I'm from the South and I'm alive, and that is that." This irrepressible voice is vintage Brown— impudent, iconoclastic, individualistic, egotistical. Refusing labels, Rita Mae Brown insists on her right to set her own literary, political, and personal agenda. Over the years, her participation in social change organizations has followed a pattern; she quit the Civil Rights movement, the Gay Liberation Front, NOW, and many lesbian-feminist groups when their rigid positions conflicted with her ideological independence. It is this independence that informs every piece of her writing.

Bibliography

Boyle, Sharon D. "Rita Mae Brown." *Contemporary Lesbian Writers of the United States: A Bio-Bibliographical Critical Sourcebook.* Edited by Sandra Pollack and Denise D. Knight. Westport, Conn.: Greenwood Press, 1993. This detailed discussion of Brown's life and work includes an overview of the criticism.

Brown, Rita Mae. *Rubyfruit Jungle.* Plainfield, Vt.: Daughters, 1973. New York: Bantam, 1977. Brown's first novel took first alternative, then mainstream readers by storm. It introduced Molly Bolt, a lesbian character who was upbeat, humorous, and most importantly, psychologically healthy.

Bunch, Charlotte, and Nancy Myron, eds. *Class and Feminism: A Collection of Essays from The Furies.* Baltimore, Md.: Diana Press, 1974. This collection includes Rita Mae Brown's important article "The Last Straw." The seven essays in this small volume make up a penetrating critique of the pervasive middle-class bias of early second-wave feminism. Their penetrating analysis has never been surpassed.

Chew, Martha. "Rita Mae Brown: Feminist Theorist and Southern Novelist." *Southern Quarterly* 22 (1983): 61-80. Chew points out similarities between Brown's fictional characters and her own life, noting in particular how the decrease in Brown's political activism is reflected in the attitudes of her characters. Nevertheless, Chew notes that even the most mainstream of Brown's heroines refuse to be limited by society's definitions.

Echols, Alice. *Daring to be Bad: Radical Feminism in America—1967-1975.* Minneapolis: University of Minnesota Press, 1989. The basic source book on the second wave of feminism. Specifically chapter 5, entitled "The Eruption of Difference," provides excellent background reading concerning the early lesbian-feminist movement and Brown's involvement in it.

Faderman, Lillian. *Odd Girls and Twilight Lovers: A History of Lesbian Life in Twentieth-Century America.* New York: Columbia University Press, 1991. Both a reference book and a very readable history, this is a helpful work for those who seek to place contemporary lesbianism in an historical context. Rita Mae Brown is mentioned and quoted both in connection with her early political activities, and with her later views on sexual liberation during the "Lesbian Sex Wars" of the 1980's.

Deborah T. Meem

LOUISE BRYANT

Born: December 5, 1885; San Francisco, California
Died: January 6, 1936; Sèvres, France
Area of Achievement: Journalism
Contribution: An international correspondent who published extensively on the subject of radical politics, Louise Bryant both witnessed and reported on the Russian Revolution.

Early Life

Louise Bryant was born December 5, 1885, and christened Anna Louisa Mohan in the Roman Catholic church. She was the third child of Hugh J. Mohan, a newspaperman, and Anna Louisa Mohan, a former dressmaker. Louise's parents divorced when she was three, and on June 11, 1892, her mother married Sheridan Daniel Bryant, who worked as a brakeman and later as a freight train conductor on the Southern Pacific Railroad. Subsequently, Louise was sent to live with her step-grandfather on a combination cattle ranch and mine in the Nevada desert, where she was schooled by a tutor.

When Louise was fourteen, her mother summoned her to Reno, where Louise learned piano and attended Wadsworth High School. Later, she enrolled in the University of Nevada, Reno, where she took commercial courses and made up requirements by taking courses at the University High School. By 1904, Louise entered the Liberal Arts College, where she proved an active student. Bryant played on the basketball team and worked as a staffer on two campus publications: the *Student Record* and the *Chuckawalla*. Bryant wrote short stories for the campus literary magazine, and both *Chuckawalla* and a third campus publication, *Artemisia*, published her signed sketches.

In September of 1906, Bryant registered at the University of Oregon at Eugene. During her time there, Bryant prepared essays, reviews, and pen-and-ink sketches for the *Oregon Monthly*, publishing them under the byline of "A. Louise Bryant" or "A. L. Bryant." While in Eugene, Louise acted in campus plays and participated in demonstrations for woman suffrage.

After graduation, Louise Bryant spent a brief time working as a schoolteacher, then ventured to Portland, where she joined the staff of a local newspaper. On November 13, 1909, Bryant was married to Paul Trullinger, an Oregon dentist. Although married, Bryant kept her name and a downtown Portland studio. The city directory continued to list her as an editor and artist. She contributed sketches and articles to the *Spectator*, and became that publication's society editor in 1913. Bryant continued to publish sketches and political cartoons. Her lifelong career as a writer had begun.

Bryant's political interests emerged early, leading to involvement with liberal causes. She sold subscriptions for her favorite leftist publication, the *Masses*, and in 1915, Bryant's poetry and sketches appeared in the *Blast*, a San Francisco anarchist weekly. These early encounters with the press, stage, and politics would set the groundwork for later accomplishments.

Life's Work

Many find it hard to separate a discussion of Louise Bryant's career from that of journalist/activist John Reed. Although Bryant and Reed may have met as early as 1912, it is certain that the two spent time together in December of 1915, during a visit to Portland by Reed. They became close, letters followed, and on New Year's Eve 1915, Bryant left Trullinger to join Reed in New York City. She arrived on January 4, 1916, and took up residence with John Reed in a Washington Square apartment in Greenwich Village. New York afforded Bryant the opportunity to write, as well as to discuss poetry and politics with such figures as the editors of the *Masses*, Max Eastman and Floyd Dell.

Bryant and Reed's professional partnership did not confine itself to accomplishments in journalism. In the summer of 1916, Bryant and Reed took up residence in Provincetown, Massachusetts, where they became associated with the Provincetown Players. They spent the summer working with this theater company, including playwright Eugene O'Neill, with whom Bryant was briefly romantically involved. In addition to performing with the Provincetown Players, both Reed and Bryant wrote drama for the group. Later, Bryant published six poems in the October issue of the *Masses*.

On November 9, 1916, despite their reputations as bohemians likely to deign wedlock as at best irrelevant to intimacy, Bryant and Reed married. Bryant made plans to accompany Reed on a 1917 assignment to China, but as the United States entered World War I, even the pro-socialist *Metropolitan* withdrew support from antiwar Reed. The trip never happened. In May, Bryant received press credentials for her first trip to Europe. On June 9, Bryant left for Europe without Reed. After spending time in Paris as a war correspondent, she returned to the United States in August of 1917.

On August 17, 1917, Bryant and Reed sailed for Russia, a trip that would prove to be a formative experience in both their lives and careers. She traveled with press credentials from the Bell Syndicate, *Metropolitan*, *Seven Arts*, and *Every Week*, along with passage sponsorship from the *Masses*. After an arduous journey, Reed and Bryant arrived in Petrograd (previously known as St. Petersburg). They attended meetings at the Smolny Institute, where Bryant met, and in some cases befriended, various leaders of the Russian Revolution. Bryant made the acquaintance of social revolutionaries Maria Spiridonova and Aleksandra Kollontai, figures widely known among leftist feminists. Bryant's work covering the Russian Revolution launched and helped sustain her fame as a writer.

In January of 1918, Bryant returned to New York, and set about recording her impressions of the figures she had met and events she had seen. Bryant worked on articles concerning Russia's October Revolution. In addition, on October 19, 1918, Bryant's book, *Six Red Months in Russia—An Observer's Account of Russia Before and During the Proletarian Dictatorship* was released. In February of the following

year, Bryant spoke in Washington, D.C., offering "The Truth About Russia."
Bryant and Reed's political activities abroad did not go unremarked at home. On October 3, 1918, Bryant was called to testify in the second trial of editors for the *Masses*. Bryant was also questioned at length as an unfriendly witness before Senator Lee S. Overman's Subcommittee of the Senate Judiciary Committee on February 20, 1919. The conveners of these hearings were charged with investigating Bolshevik propaganda, and Bryant published articles for *Pearson's* and the *Liberator* regarding her appearance before the subcommittee. Early in 1920, when Reed was indicted by a special grand jury for conspiracy to overthrow the government by force, Bryant resolved to go to Russia and see to it that Reed, already away on assignment, did not return. While she finalized her travel plans, Bryant continued to write, including a piece entitled "Russian Memories" for the *Dial*.

In July, she began her journey to Russia to reunite with Reed. While there, she planned to write articles for the International News Service. It was at this point that Reed's generally poor state of physical health worsened. In October, 1920, while still in Russia, Reed fell victim to a typhus epidemic, died, and was buried in the Kremlin. Bryant's poetic tributes to Reed appeared in *Current Opinion* and *Liberator* in 1921.

Following Reed's death, Bryant persevered with her journalism. She sought and was granted an interview with Russian leader Vladimir Ilich Lenin. From him, she secured permission to travel in the Middle East, where Bryant studied the effects of Soviet treaties with these nations. Upon her return to Russia, Bryant interviewed Russian leader Leon Trotsky. She subsequently went to Rome, where in 1922 she also interviewed Italian Premier Benito Mussolini. Hers was the first interview he gave to an American citizen. *Mirrors of Moscow*, Bryant's second book concerning Russia, appeared in February of 1923.

Acquaintances and colleagues alike were surprised when, on December 10, 1923, Bryant married a diplomat, William Christian Bullitt. Bullitt's semiautobiographical novel, *It's Not Done* (1926), dedicated to Louise Bryant, allegedly echoes their relationship in some measure. Bullitt and Bryant had a daughter, Anne Moen, in 1924. Throughout the pregnancy, Bryant worked on a book concerning Turkish revolutionary Kemal Pasha. It was during this time, however, that Bryant became ill with Dercum's Disease, a rare and incurable illness. By 1929, Bullitt sued Bryant for divorce, charging her with alcoholism and an extramarital lesbian relationship. He eventually won custody of their daughter. Bryant then settled in Paris with the long-cherished goal of publishing a biography of John Reed. At this point, though, her illness and depression in the wake of the custody battle left her significantly impaired. Along with suffering the effects of her disease, Bryant was rumored to be abusing alcohol and drugs. With only a partial memoir of Reed's life completed, she died of a cerebral hemorrhage on January 6, 1936.

Summary

Louise Bryant's career as an international correspondent was unprecedented in both its scope and concerns. Her on-the-scene global journalism made it possible for

Bryant not only to see events firsthand but also, through her activism, to participate in the political history those events represented. Bryant was one of only a few Americans, male or female, to work as a correspondent during the Russian Revolution. She was granted and conducted rare interviews with some of the most powerful leaders of her time, including Lenin, Trotsky, and Mussolini. In addition to her journalistic pieces and political cartoons, Bryant wrote poetry, short stories, plays, articles, reviews, essays, and books. Her writings appeared in a wide range of political papers and journals. Her books, *Six Red Months in Russia* and *Mirrors of Moscow*, provide her own impressions of the transformations in Russia. Louise Bryant's life is recalled in the motion picture *Reds* (1981), directed by Warren Beatty. This romantic and, at times, historically flawed treatment nevertheless conveys the passion of her life with Reed. As with many representations of Bryant, she appears in the film chiefly as Reed's satellite. Nevertheless, Louise Bryant demonstrated independence of thought and action that has sounded a keynote for many women who, regardless of their political affiliation, have benefited from Bryant's commitment to political dissent. Her advocacy of woman suffrage, of sexual and reproductive freedom, and of women's pursuit of professional careers foreshadowed many of the key issues in the struggle for women's empowerment during the 1970's and beyond.

Bibliography

Duke, David C. *Distant Obligations: Modern American Writers and Foreign Causes.* New York: Oxford University Press, 1983. References to Bryant appear in Duke's chapter on John Reed. This work is helpful in its efforts to situate Bryant and Reed in a larger context of writer activists, such as Waldo Frank and John Dos Passos.

——————. *John Reed.* Twayne, 1987. This biocritical monograph on Reed's work sheds light on some aspects of Bryant's career. It is especially attentive to her time with the Provincetown Players and her visits to Russia.

Gardner, Virginia. *"Friend and Lover": The Life of Louise Bryant.* New York: Horizon Press, 1982. A reasonably thorough biography, Gardner's book strives to keep Reed's life story from eclipsing Bryant's. Of particular interest is an extended treatment of the years following Reed's death of typhus, including Bryant's close friendship late in life with African American writer Claude McKay.

Gelb, Barbara. *So Short a Time: A Biography of John Reed and Louise Bryant.* New York: W. W. Norton, 1973. A significant portion of the information gathered here came from interviews with the pair's friends and associates. Unfortunately, the text concludes with Reed's death in 1920, relegating to an epilogue the final sixteen years of Bryant's life.

Gitlow, Benjamin. *The Whole of Their Lives: Communism in America—A Personal History and Intimate Portrayals of Its Leaders.* Reprint. Freeport, N.Y. Books for Libraries Press, 1971. Gitlow's approach to this era is something of a memoir, as he attempts to reconstruct conversations with Bryant. His central reference to Bryant attends to her discussion of the political implications of John Reed's physical decline.

Heller, Adele, and Lois Rudnick, eds. *1915, The Cultural Moment: The New Politics, the New Woman, the New Psychology, the New Art and the New Theatre in America*. New Brunswick, N.J.: Rutgers University Press, 1991. This interdisciplinary treatment concentrates on the cultural intersections of such diverse fields as theater, psychology, and visual art. Bryant's activities in the Provincetown Players and with Eugene O'Neill are detailed.

Lasch, Christopher. *The American Liberals and the Russian Revolution*. New York: Columbia University Press, 1962. Although his work refers only to Bryant's views on women's rights and her appearance before the Overman committee, Lasch does provide the historical context for Americans involved in this era's radical politics.

Rosenstone, Robert. *Romantic Revolutionary: A Biography of John Reed*. New York: Alfred A. Knopf, 1975. While this volume concerns itself chiefly with John Reed as a visionary, it also makes frequent reference to the intersections between the lives of Reed and Bryant. Bryant's relationships with painter Andrew Dasburg and playwright Eugene O'Neill receive mention.

Linda S. Watts

PEARL S. BUCK

Born: June 26, 1892; Hillsboro, West Virginia
Died: March 6, 1973; Danby, Vermont
Area of Achievement: Literature
Contribution: A novelist and Nobel laureate, Buck campaigned tirelessly for freedom and equal rights for all peoples of the world, both East and West.

Early Life

Born to missionary parents and taken to China at the age of three months, Pearl Sydenstricker always displayed her understanding and love for the Chinese people. Her scholarly father, Absalom Sydenstricker, was a student of comparative religion, spoke four languages, and translated the Bible from Greek to Chinese. Her mother, Caroline, was well versed in languages, art, and literature and taught her children at home. Instead of living in a missionary compound, Pearl's parents insisted upon the family living among the Chinese people. In addition to a Chinese nurse, Pearl had a Chinese tutor, a Confucian scholar who taught her Chinese writing, reading, and history as well as the principles of Confucianism.

Despite their peaceful ties with their Chinese neighbors, the Sydenstricker family was forced to flee temporarily during the Boxer Rebellion in 1900. Pearl left China at age seventeen to attend college at Randolph-Macon Woman's College in Lynchburg, Virginia, from which she graduated in 1914. That same year she returned to China to care for her sick mother and work in a nearby mission school. In 1917, she married John Lossing Buck, an American agricultural specialist, and they moved to Northern China. In 1921, her daughter Caroline, was born. As time passed, it became obvious that Caroline was mentally impaired. The next year the Buck family moved to Nanking, where Pearl frequently taught English literature over the next ten years. Motivated by her daughter's increasingly desperate condition, Buck accompanied her husband to America to seek medical advice. Unfortunately, she learned that Caroline's mental impairment was severe. During her stay in the United States, Pearl attended Cornell and received a master of arts degree before the family returned to Nanking in 1926.

Buck and her family again resumed their work in Nanking. China was beginning to show signs of political unrest as various factions lobbied for the elimination of foreign imperialism. Buck now felt herself the target of racial prejudice. On March 27, 1927, during the Nanking Incident, Buck and her family almost lost their lives when their home was attacked by an angry Chinese mob. Huddled in the hut of a poor neighbor woman, Buck and her family watched as their home was looted and burned. They were rescued by American gunboats and taken to Shanghai. The family returned to Nanking as soon as possible. Buck and her husband resumed their former life, yet their peaceful work within their adopted culture was gone. By the time Buck and her husband returned to the United States in 1932, Chiang Kai-shek's government had all but disintegrated and civil unrest had erupted. Although Buck returned to Nanking in

1933, the level of hostility toward foreigners was such that she was forced to leave China permanently in 1934.

Life's Work

By the time Pearl S. Buck left China in 1934, she had already published *East Wind: West Wind* (1930), *The Good Earth* (1931), *Sons* (1932), *The First Wife and Other Stories* and *All Men Are Brothers* (both in 1933). She had won the Pulitzer Prize for *The Good Earth* in 1932, and became the spokesperson for the Chinese people in America. In 1935, her trilogy, *House of Earth* which contains *The Good Earth, Sons* and *A House Divided* was published. This year, too, she divorced John Buck and married Richard Walsh, head of the John Day Company and publisher of all of her early books. The following year her biographies of her parents, *The Exile* and *Fighting Angel* (1936), were published. These two biographies and *The Good Earth* were cited by the Nobel Foundation when it awarded Buck the Nobel Prize in Literature in 1938. Her selection as the first American woman to win the Nobel Prize aroused a furor among critics. William Faulkner, Ernest Hemingway, Sinclair Lewis, and Theodore Drieser were alive and writing at the time, and all had published considerably more work and had achieved more critical acclaim for their literary achievements than Buck. Nevertheless, the Nobel committee cited Buck not only for her literary achievements but also for her compassionate and rich portrayals of rural Chinese life, the first to appear in American literature.

Although Buck's literary output in the wake of the Nobel Prize was considerable, it never achieved the level of excellence of *The Good Earth* and her two biographies. Instead, Buck used her influence as a literary figure to work for the causes she championed, such as rights of women. From the cultural vantage point of her life in China, she viewed American women from a new perspective. In *This Proud Heart* (1938), Buck portrays her heroine as a female genius torn between her career as a sculptor and her duties as a wife and mother. While the book does not match *The Good Earth* in literary excellence, it is one of the few works of its time to explain and study female genius.

Two of Buck's essays, "America's Medieval Women" (1938) and "America's Gunpowder Women" (1939), examine the difficulties and characteristics of American women. In the first essay, she describes American women as medieval because, even though they might be well rounded and well educated, they are prevented from fulfilling their potential. Buck viewed the possibilities open to American women of her time as limited to roles as subservient wives or as career women without families. In the second essay, Buck identifies women frustrated by these limited roles as "Gunpowder Women" who, if given the chance, would enter professions and politics and make a difference in American society and in the world. The ideas contained in these essays came to fuller expression in her book *Of Men and Women* (1941). As a friend of Margaret Sanger, founder of the birth control movement, Buck advocated birth control and supported the right of unmarried women to have children. Throughout her life, Buck's writings, speeches, radio broadcasts, and public appearances supported the self-realization of women through participation in national and world affairs.

Viewing women as natural advocates for peace, Buck herself became active in promoting international goodwill during the World War II years. In 1941, she founded the East and West Association to promote understanding between the cultures through bringing Asians into American communities. The association lasted eight years before coming under attack during the anti-Communist years of the 1950's. As early as 1947, Buck began work on the United Nations General Assembly's manifesto condemning the crime of genocide. Buck believed condemnation was not enough and continued to work until all the members of the United Nations declared genocide an international crime.

After World War II, Buck became concerned about the discrimination and poverty faced by children born of mixed American and Asian parentage. In 1949, she established Welcome House, an adoption agency for Amerasian children born in the United States. Hearing from Asian friends about the plight of children fathered in Asia by American servicemen during the war, she expanded Welcome House to include overseas children in its program. Buck lobbied intensely to get the restrictive immigration quotas lifted in Congress through the passage of a Refugee Act. She and Richard Walsh themselves adopted seven children of mixed parentage. Her concern for victims of the war motivated her to arrange medical treatment for young Japanese girls badly burned and disfigured by the atomic bomb. She was also instrumental in halting the detainment and deportation of Asian Americans brought to Ellis Island and questioned about communist activities.

In 1929, Buck had come to the decision to place her daughter Caroline in the Vineland Training School, a private boarding school for the mentally impaired. In 1950, she wrote a moving account of her experiences as a parent of a mentally impaired child, *The Child Who Never Grew* (1950). The response of the public was overwhelming. She received letters and personal visits from parents seeking help and expressing gratitude. Throughout her life, she continued her involvement by writing three nonfiction works describing advances in the field and supporting local and national organizations.

During the Cold War years, she wrote four novels condemning both Communist China and anti-Communist America, including *Imperial Woman* (1956), a history of the Empress Dowager Tsu Hsui. Although they sold well, they lacked the literary quality of her prewar Chinese novels. From 1945 to 1953, Buck published five novels under the pseudonym "John Sedges." Only one of these, *The Townsman* (1945) received critical attention, although they all sold well. In 1959, Buck resumed her name with *Command the Morning* (1959), a well-researched account of the development of the atomic bomb. The following year, 1960, her husband Richard Walsh died after a long illness. She recounted these difficult years in *A Bridge for Passing* (1962). The public response was again astounding; women throughout the United States wrote to express gratitude for her understanding and compassion.

In 1962, Buck tried to establish the Pearl S. Buck Memorial Fund to assist homeless

Korean American children living in Korea. She wanted the Fund to be a branch of Welcome House but was unable to gain support from Welcome House, in part because of her close relationship with her dancing instructor, Theodore Harris, whom she wanted appointed Director. She appealed to the John Day Company once headed by her husband, but the Company refused to lend its support. This brought about the final break with John Day. Buck established the Memorial Fund on her own in 1964, with Harris as director. In 1969, a *Philadelphia Magazine* article accused Harris of misappropriation of funds and the State of Pennsylvania withdrew its nonprofit status. Buck loyally supported Harris throughout the scandal and together they moved to Danby, Vermont. There Harris established Creativity, Inc., which managed most of Buck's later projects. During the last decade of her life, she continued to publish two to five books a year, many of them collections of previously published works. She published other books of a general nature, children's books, and fiction written earlier. In 1973, at the age of eighty-one, Pearl Buck died in Danby, Vermont.

Summary

To evaluate Pearl S. Buck's achievements on the basis of her fiction alone would be to ignore important aspects of her life's work. She viewed fiction as popular entertainment and was extraordinarily popular. In contrast to her contemporaries, her optimism and belief in the innate goodness of men must have come as a welcome relief to everyday modern readers, for her immense popularity extended world wide.

She is best remembered for her activism in the cause of freedom and understanding. In her liberal views of marriage and family, her advocacy of women and children, her support of China, her understanding of the dichotomy between America's idealism in world affairs and its disgraceful oppression at home she shows her amazing foresight and awareness of events that came to pass in her lifetime. Her books describing her own sorrow as a mother and widow display her willingness to offer compassion and understanding, especially to women. Perhaps this willingness to share her time and thoughts makes her such an appealing figure. Never aligned with a single cause, Buck supported any cause that advanced freedom and equality. The literary quality of *The Good Earth*, *The Exile*, and *Fighting Angel* will no doubt endure, but this is only a portion of Pearl Buck's accomplishments: She was a humanitarian, a liberal patriot, an advocate for peace and freedom.

Bibliography

Buck, Pearl S. *My Several Worlds*. New York: John Day, 1954. Buck's autobiography describes vividly her years in China and the impact these experiences had upon her life and work. Not strictly chronological, the book offers memories and scenes from her past. She discusses marriage, family, divorce, and child rearing and shows clearly her advanced ideas on these subjects.

Doyle, Paul A. *Pearl S. Buck*. Rev. ed. New York: Twayne, 1980. In this revised edition of the first book-length study of Buck's work since the 1930's, Doyle justly examines the most significant of Buck's writing.

Harris, Theodore F. *Pearl S. Buck: A Biography.* New York: John Day, 1969. An uncritical biography that consists primarily of Buck's selected letters and speeches edited and commented upon by Harris. Most evident in the work is Buck's activism and her sympathy and compassion for all those who sought her advice. Harris' comments are slanted by his adulation for Buck.

Mitchell, Barbara. *Between Two Worlds: A Story About Pearl Buck.* Minneapolis, Minn.: Carolrhoda Books, 1988. Although the text of this juvenile biography concludes with Buck's acceptance of the Nobel Prize in Literature in 1938, its coverage of Buck's early life and her struggle to care for her daughter is excellent and the afterword draws attention to Buck's humanitarian efforts on behalf of needy children and in support of improved cultural understanding between East and West. Contains useful bibliography of Buck's works for juvenile readers.

Stirling, Nora B. *Pearl Buck: A Woman in Conflict.* Piscataway, N.J.: New Century, 1983. Stirling's book is the only one written after Buck's death in 1973 and has the advantage of time and distance from Buck as a public figure. Hers is the only detailed objective account of Buck's final years and assessment of Buck's contribution to various causes.

Thompson, Dody Weston. "Pearl Buck." In *American Winners of the Nobel Literary Prize*, edited by Warren G. French and Walter E. Kidd. Norman: University of Oklahoma Press, 1968. An adulatory essay that discusses Buck's popularity as a writer and argues that her works have merit precisely because of their popular appeal and lack of high-brow literary attributes.

Jean McConnell

CAROL BURNETT

Born: April 26, 1936; San Antonio, Texas

Areas of Achievement: Theater and television
Contribution: Overcoming a childhood of poverty and abandonment, Carol Burnett launched a career on television, stage, and screen that eventually made her one of the most popular entertainers in the United States.

Early Life

Carol Burnett was born to Ina Louise Creighton and Joseph Thomas Burnett on April 26, 1936. Her father was an alcoholic who supported himself selling photo store coupons and her mother was a publicity writer and receptionist. When Burnett was two years old, her parents moved to Santa Monica, California, and left Carol with her maternal grandmother, Mabel Eudora White (known to Carol as Nanny). Carol never lived with her parents again. They were divorced when Burnett was six years old.

Nanny often wrote to Carol's parents asking for financial and emotional support, but Ina and Joseph were unable to offer anything more than regrets and promises. In 1940, when Carol was seven years old, Nanny, tired of excuses, packed both their bags and moved to Hollywood, where Carol's mother had settled. Ina Burnett was not happy that her mother had "rushed" the move, but promptly found them a one-room apartment in the same building in which she resided. This was Carol's home for the next twelve years.

Carol's life with Nanny, while somewhat stable, was far from secure. Nanny had brief spells of illness during which she was sure she was dying. Afraid of losing her lifeline, Carol would panic if she could not find Nanny, guessing that Nanny had finally succumbed to death. Although Nanny lived a long life, Carol's childhood experiences convinced her that there was only one person on which she could really depend—herself.

Despite these challenges, Carol later remembered her childhood as being a happy one, crediting this to her tremendous imagination. She would often act out film scenes with her friends or stage her own radio show from the window of her apartment. This rich fantasy life and her ability to forget the troubles of her own life helped Burnett in her later career as an entertainer.

After graduating from Hollywood High, Burnett received a scholarship to attend the University of California, Los Angeles (UCLA), in 1951. Majoring in English, she quickly became absorbed in the activities of the theater arts department. Her first attempt at dramatic acting, which ended in disaster, led her to discover her talent for comedy. Carol became completely hooked on performing and basked in the audience's laughter and acclamation.

After being chosen in 1952 as the year's most outstanding newcomer, Burnett spent the next two summers working with UCLA's Stumptown Players. Early in 1954, after performing with friends at a private party in a San Diego suburb, Carol was approached by a couple. They offered her a loan of $1,000 to help her start her career if she promised to never mention their name and to pay the money back in five years. Already planning to move to New York City, Carol gratefully accepted the money.

Life's Work

By August of 1954, Carol Burnett was a resident of the Rehearsal Club, a hotel for female entertainers in New York City. Taking the advice of an agent who was reluctant to represent her, Burnett gathered together friends and residents of her hotel and put together a show in March of 1955. Although it ran for only two nights, the show drew standing room only audiences. As a result, Burnett was offered a contract with the prestigious William Morris agency. Her reputation grew; in December of 1955, she was offered a thirteen-week contract with *The Winchell-Mahoney Show*, a television children's show.

In 1956, Burnett was a guest on CBS television's *The Garry Moore Show*. Garry Moore gave her an open invitation to return any time she had new material. Burnett put together an act which featured a tune called "I Made a Fool of Myself Over John Foster Dulles," a parody of a popular song of the era. In the original version, a girl is infatuated with a rock star, but Burnett drew howls of laughter for her version, in which the girl was in love with John Foster Dulles, the prim U.S. secretary of state of the time. She was asked to perform the song for Jack Paar's *Tonight Show*, Ed Sullivan's *Toast of the Town,* and *The Garry Moore Show*. From 1959 until *The Garry Moore Show* ended, Burnett was a regular performer; in 1962, she earned an Emmy for her work. The following year, Burnett won another Emmy for her performance with Julie Andrews in *Julie and Carol at Carnegie Hall* in June of 1962.

While appearing on *The Garry Moore Show*, Carol opened off Broadway in May of 1959 in George Abbott's production of *Once Upon a Mattress*, a parody of the fairy tale *The Princess and the Pea*. Burnett remembers learning the most about comedy from Abbott, who told her to play her characters "real" in order to heighten the humor. These sentiments were later echoed by Lucille Ball, whom Burnett met on the second night of *Once Upon a Mattress*. The two women remained friends until Ball's death.

Under contract to CBS from 1962 through 1967, Burnett made several television specials while the network developed a show for her. *The Carol Burnett Show* premiered in September of 1967, and ran until March of 1978. Based on the vaude-villian tradition of short skits, the show's skits spoofed famous films, commercials, and people. Her cast of regulars and special guests would join Burnett in several skits before she ended each episode with her theme song, "I'm So Glad We Had This Time Together," and a tug at her ear as a special hello to her grandmother. It was the longest running variety show in the history of television. Critics credit the show's success to Burnett's unlimited comedic range. The show did not venture into the biting social commentary found in situation comedies such as those produced by Norman Lear, but kept the comedy moderate, developing familiar recurring characters such as Mrs. Tuttle, Eunice, and the charwoman. *The Carol Burnett Show* eventually earned twenty-two Emmys.

Even though Burnett worked around a heavy production schedule with *The Carol Burnett Show*, she managed to perform in Los Angeles stage productions of Neil Simon's *Plaza Suite* (1971), *I Do! I Do!* (1973), and *Same Time Next Year* (1977). Burnett performed two plays adapted for television, Bob Randall's *6 RMS RIV VU* and George Furth's *Twigs*. In addition, Carol was cast as a lead opposite Walter Matthau in *Pete 'n' Tillie* (1972) and in a cameo role with Matthau and Jack Lemmon in *The Front Page* (1974). In addition, she won critical acclaim for her performance in Robert Altman's star-studded yet uneven film, *A Wedding* (1978).

By 1978, it became apparent to everyone involved with *The Carol Burnett Show* that it was time to make radical changes or end its eleven-year run. Burnett decided to end production. She wanted to leave the show before it hit rock bottom and she became stale, as she told her audience when taping the final episode.

The years following *The Carol Burnett Show* were busy with film and television appearances. In 1979, Burnett starred in two made-for-television films. It was her performance in *Friendly Fire*, a film about a mother who battles the government into admitting her son was killed in Vietnam by U.S. military bombings, that was a critical success. In 1982, Burnett played an orphanage matron in the little-noticed film adaptation of the hit Broadway musical *Annie* (1982). Her over-the-top performance as the drunken and oversexed matron was deemed the only notable performance in the film. By 1986, Burnett was back on network television with *Fresno*, a CBS comedy miniseries that parodied such prime-time soap operas about rich and oversexed people as *Dallas*, *Falcon Crest*, and *Dynasty*. The miniseries delighted Burnett's fans and received high ratings. Also in 1986, she published her autobiography, *One More Time*. The book, written to her three daughters, Carrie, Jody, and Erin, immediately hit the best-seller list.

In March of 1990, *Carol and Company* premiered on NBC television. The show, produced by Burnett's Koala Productions in conjunction with Disney's Buena Vista Television, presented a new type of comedy program. Each week, Burnett played one character in an anthology of situation comedies. *Carol and Company* was the top-rated show for the season, but could not hold the ratings when slotted against another hit show. In November of 1991, Burnett launched another variety show with the same name as her original, *The Carol Burnett Show*. The program was canceled by CBS executives after only four episodes, with critics claiming that the old variety show format could not compete with new wilder comedy shows.

Following the demise of her show, Burnett turned to other acting venues. She was awarded a starring role in the film adaptation of Michael Frayn's *Noises Off*, released in March of 1992. A comedy about life behind the scenes of a British sex farce, the film received mixed reviews. Critics praised the actors' performances, including Burnett's, but criticized the script. Never one to be idle, Burnett starred in a two-week run of the musical comedy *From the Top* in April of 1993.

Carol Burnett has been honored many times for her talent and contributions to the entertainment field. She has received four Emmys, three People's Choice Awards, two Photoplay Gold Medals for most popular television star, and eight Golden Globe

Awards for outstanding comedian of the year. Burnett was awarded the First Annual National Television Critics Award in 1977 and was named in a Gallup Poll as one of America's most admired women. In November of 1993, Carol Burnett was the first woman comedian to be inducted into the brand new Comedy Hall of Fame. Typical of her respect for her peers, Burnett suggested that this honor more properly belonged to Lucille Ball, who opened the door for all women comedians and provided them with an outstanding model for success.

Summary
Carol Burnett is an extraordinarily versatile performer whose talent, determination, and rejection of limitations has helped establish wider opportunities for women in television, film, and stage comedy. Although she started out as a bit player, Burnett achieved a level of success that allowed her to establish her own production company and take a more active role in selecting properties to showcase her talent. Burnett believes that women should be equal partners with men in the entertainment industry and in life in general. Her accomplishments, combined with those of colleagues such as Lucille Ball and Julie Andrews, have inspired other women entertainers to persevere and always stretch their talent. As a powerful advocate for education in the arts, Burnett has spoken out against the tendency of schools to not offer acting or art when budgets get tight because she believes that those classes in her own life allowed her to overcome the poverty and abandonment of her childhood. She advises young people to nurture their creative sides and be proud of their talents, rather than be afraid of problems or challenges.

Bibliography
Burnett, Carol. *One More Time: A Memoir.* New York: Random House, 1986. An autobiography of her early life, Burnett writes to her children in journal style about her family, her struggles, and her success.
Marc, David. "Carol Burnett: The Last of the Big-Time Comedy Stars." *Quarterly Review of Film and Video* 14 (July, 1992): 149-156. A quarterly journal of film studies which includes critical analysis of entertainment history, motion pictures, plays, video recordings, and television subject articles.
Martin, Linda, and Kerry Segrave. *Women in Comedy.* Secaucus, N.J.: Citadel Press, 1986. Biographies of various women comedians and comedic actresses in the United States.
Sochen, June, ed. *Women's Comic Visions.* Detroit, Mich.: Wayne State University Press, 1991. A historical and critical perspective of American women's wit and humor and women comedians in the United States.
Unterbrink, Mary. *Funny Women: American Comediennes, 1860-1985.* Jefferson, N.C.: McFarland, 1987. A history and criticism of women comedians in the United States between 1860 and 1985.

Sheryl Perry-Yannaccone

JANE BYRNE

Born: May 24, 1934; Chicago, Illinois

Area of Achievement: Government and politics
Contribution: Active in Democratic politics since 1960 and in Chicago city administration since 1964, Jane Byrne was the first woman to be elected mayor of Chicago.

Early Life

Jane Byrne was born Jane Margaret Burke on May 24, 1934, when her family resided at 6503 N. Claremont in Chicago. Her parents, William and Katharine (Nolan) Burke, had married in 1929; despite the Depression, their modest circumstances soon improved, and they moved their "lace curtain Irish" household to Sauganash, a fashionable neighborhood on Chicago's Northwest side. The warm, bright, ambitious son of a blacksmith, Bill Burke worked his way up from clerk to vice president of Inland Steel. In 1940, he formed Gordon-Burke Steel and later became the Steel Warehousemen Association's national president. Burke was a successful member of the "North Side Irish" elite.

"Janie" was the second of six children. Their mother, Katharine Nolan Burke, was strong-willed and well-read; she reared them by strict principles, within an insular Roman Catholic family structure. Janie attended Queen of All Saints Parish grammar school and all-girl St. Scholastica high school, graduating in 1951; she was an exemplary, serious student, though shy. At St. Mary-of-the-Woods College in Terre Haute, Indiana, she majored in biology and premedical studies, but grew homesick.

Transferring to all-female Barat College of the Sacred Heart, in wealthy north suburban Lake Forest, Jane Burke fit in well. She had impressive Catholic social credentials: Jane's uncle, the Right Reverend Monsignor Edward M. Burke, was the Chancellor of Chicago's Archdiocese; uncle Joseph Burke was also a priest. Jane had traveled with her uncle Ed to Rome in 1950, enjoying an audience with Pope Pius XII. She debuted at Samuel Cardinal Stritch's Presentation Ball of 1955.

Notably studious, shy, and ambitious, Jane made weekend treks to Notre Dame, where "Barat girls" hunted upwardly mobile Catholic husbands. During her junior year, Jane fell in love with William P. Byrne, a Naval ROTC student. They were graduated in 1955; Byrne was commissioned a Marine Corps officer, and from 1955 to 1956, Jane taught fourth grade at St. Juliana Grade School in Chicago. Rejecting a medical career, Jane Burke married Bill Byrne on New Year's Eve, 1956, satisfying 1950's social expectations.

The Byrnes were posted to Florida, Texas, and North Carolina. Jane delivered their daughter, Katharine Crane Byrne, in Chicago on December 31, 1957. Shortly before his scheduled discharge, Bill Byrne was killed on the foggy night of May 30, 1959, when his plane crashed at Glenview Naval Air Station. Jane Byrne was a widow at age twenty-five, with a seventeen-month-old daughter. This tragedy rerouted the course of Margaret Jane Burke Byrne's life: she would not follow her beloved mother's domestic footsteps.

Life's Work

Jane Burke Byrne assuaged her grief by joining her sister Carol on John F. Kennedy's 1960 presidential campaign. As a secretary for Margaret Zuehlke, executive director of Illinois Citizens for Kennedy, Byrne made important contacts with local and national Democratic Party supporters. After Kennedy was elected by a historically close margin—put over the top by Daley's Chicago machine—Jane Byrne attended education classes, received her master's degree from the University of Illinois at Chicago, and again taught grade school. A 1964 encounter with Chicago Mayor Richard J. Daley nudged Byrne back into politics.

Daley told Byrne to do political work in Sauganash, the city's Thirty-ninth Ward. As a reward for paying these political dues, Daley promised to secure a patronage position for Byrne. In the summer of 1964, Jane Byrne was hired at Head Start, controlled by the Chicago Commission on Urban Opportunity (CCUO), an agency created by Lyndon Johnson's Economic Opportunity Act. Byrne soon left Head Start for a personnel slot in the CCUO itself. She also continued her work on behalf of the city's Democratic machine, in part, organizing socials.

In March of 1968, Daley appointed Byrne to serve as commissioner of the small Chicago Department of Consumer Sales, Weights, and Measures. Some commentators believed her to be unqualified; she seemed Daley's "token woman." Commissioner Byrne controlled city inspection and regulation of consumer affairs, such as retail unit pricing, retail advertising, and toy safety. Byrne immediately leveled gender-based pay differentials among inspectors and began eliminating department corruption. She enforced fair inspection of retailers in poor neighborhoods, where grocery price gouging ran rampant; she pushed through a landmark ordinance banning phosphates in detergents. In 1973, her department prompted the Federal Trade Commission to undertake an antitrust investigation of Checker and Yellow Cabs, divisions of one company which controlled 80 percent of Chicago taxis. Consumer rights activist Ralph Nader applauded Byrne's efforts.

Byrne rode the consumerism wave of the 1970's to public visibility. As a relatively "clean" commissioner within the corrupt machine, her political clout rose. After the 1972 national convention, Mayor Daley made Byrne the new Illinois member of the Democratic National Committee, where she chaired the powerful Resolutions Committee. Daley appointed Byrne cochair of the Cook County Democratic Central Committee in January of 1975, clearly signalling Byrne's ascendance of the machine hierarchy.

Richard J. Daley died in December, 1976. Despite her status as a Daley protégé, Jane Byrne was maneuvered aside by male members of Chicago's Democratic political machine. Michael Bilandic became interim mayor; George Dunne replaced Byrne as cochair of the County Committee. Byrne, however, was still head of a second-class cog, the Democratic Women of Cook County and Chicago, and she remained in office as commissioner of the Department of Consumer Sales, Weights, and Measures. Oversight of the city's public vehicle licenses had been transferred to Byrne's department under Daley; when Bilandic sponsored a questionable cab fare increase in November of 1977, Byrne blew the whistle. The post-Daley machine cut Byrne off: her dismissal exploded into a media spectacle.

The public appreciated "Fighting Jane" Byrne's gutsy demeanor, and her speaking engagements established grass-roots support for a mayoral run. On St. Patrick's Day in 1978, Byrne married Chicago journalist Jay McMullen. Shortly thereafter, Byrne announced her candidacy for the office of mayor. Byrne's shoestring campaign used constant personal contact with the voters to advantage. Byrne preached "change" and reform, criticized "business as usual" in City Hall, and forged a multicultural voter coalition. Luck helped, since the frigid winter of 1979 burdened Chicago with catastrophic, record snowfalls. Bilandic's administration failed miserably at snow removal, and Byrne lambasted Bilandic and his machine for incompetency. Byrne won the February primary after a record turnout; she won the general election on April 3, 1979, with a startling 82 percent of the vote.

Jane Byrne was sworn in as mayor of the city of Chicago on April 15, 1979, the first female mayor of any major American city. Mayor Byrne faced grave problems. She had promised to improve Chicago's neighborhoods and aging infrastructure; she learned "the city that works" was verging on bankruptcy as 1970's inflation peaked in 1980. A transit strike loomed; Byrne had promised all city workers union contracts. The Democratic machine remained in place and was only semicooperative; State's Attorney Richard M. Daley (son of the late mayor) soon targeted Byrne's administration with investigations. Byrne's aggressive public persona both aided and hindered her progress.

Chicago Transit Authority workers went on strike in December of 1979, exposing Byrne's lack of a contingency plan, but shortly returned to work after succumbing to pressure from business interests. Chicago's end-of-year deficit of $102 million denied Byrne an easy solution to a $101 million shortfall in the public school system budget. The State of Illinois split bailout costs with the city, but in January of 1980, the teachers went out on strike. Byrne played a major role in the final settlement of the education crisis, but the city faced greater difficulties when it confronted what one historian has called a "strike-a-month schedule." Politically conservative firefighters struck in February of 1980, endangering the public safety during midwinter, and public opinion helped Byrne propel the firefighters back to work without a contract. The media often criticized Byrne for indecision and an acidic style during these three major strikes in her first mayoral year, yet she settled them by displaying a remarkable "sense of fiscal responsibility," according to Holli.

Byrne balanced the city budget every full year of her term (1980-1982); an unanticipated $15 million deficit occurred in 1983, when she left office at midyear. The balanced budgets were accomplished by adopting unpopular austerity measures, such as initiating city worker lay-offs, and some tax increases. To her credit, Byrne had not juggled the books or raided earmarked funds as previous administrations had.

The city's bond ratings dropped, then improved. Byrne even launched some major development initiatives, such as 1981 revitalization plans for the city's North Loop district, a transit extension to and major renovation plan for O'Hare International Airport, an extension of the Chicago Transit Authority's rail service on the city's southwest side, and basic infrastructure improvements. She continued to support ChicagoFest, begun by Michael Bilandic, while initiating Taste of Chicago and various neighborhood festivals.

Byrne believed in public drama and spectacle, gaining popular approval. Her battles with the Chicago media were legendary. Byrne's political postures could flip-flop dizzyingly: She apparently offered Jimmy Carter her support at a 1980 election fund-raiser, but announced support of Edward Kennedy two weeks later. Political drama sometimes backfired. In 1981, Byrne's two-week tenancy in Cabrini-Green, a Chicago housing project suffering protracted gang violence, was widely praised for boldness and widely ridiculed as "grandstanding." She increased police, maintenance, and education provisions in public housing, with only short-term consequence. She also increased, then cut minority hiring. One study noted that 47 percent of employees hired between 1980 and 1981 were black in a city with a black population at 40 percent; 28 percent of new hires in 1982 were black. Byrne seemed racist defending her white Chicago Housing Authority (CHA) head against a 1982 federal agency power grab, realigning the CHA board's racial balance with controversial white appointees.

Poor ethnic relations hindered Byrne's reelection bid. The 1983 Democratic primary pitted Byrne against African American Congressman Harold Washington and white State's Attorney Richard M. Daley; the contest was racially polarized. Incumbent Byrne was a woman, with a mixed record, with limited (white) machine support and flagging minority support. Harold Washington won the Democratic primary with 36 percent of the vote; Byrne received 34 percent, and Daley netted 30 percent. Byrne withdrew her brief write-in candidacy; Washington won the bitterly fought general election.

Twice more, Jane Byrne ran unsuccessfully for mayor. She and Washington squared off in the March, 1987, Democratic primary, in which Washington polled a scant majority of the record turnout. After his election, Washington attempted to slate Byrne for clerk of the circuit court, but the machine refused. Byrne challenged Richard M. Daley in the February, 1991, Democratic primary, but came in a distant third. Since that time, Jane Byrne has served as a political commentator; in 1992, she published her autobiography, *My Chicago*.

Summary

Jane Byrne's political career was startling in its contradictions. A privileged child, she became a civil servant. A machine functionary, she ran a "clean" city Department. A 1979 mayoral long shot, she became the first woman to hold that office, yet she failed to support the Equal Rights Amendment. A coalition-builder, she became a divisive figure in City Hall despite her various administrative achievements. In the final analysis, although her credentials as an Irish-Catholic Democrat were impeccable, she could not maintain the power for which Richard J. Daley groomed her. Because Jane Byrne was a woman, she faced constant opposition from male Democrats and the press. Her inability to present a stable, competent public image—regardless of actual performance quality—led to her rapid political downfall. One survey rating six recent Chicago mayors ranked Byrne fifth overall, but third for "accomplishments." Her most visible legacies are the Chicago Transit Authority and infrastructure projects as well as the summer festivals; her handling of "hard" issues—major strikes, budgeting, race relations—may acquire future cachet, but her later "perennial candidacy" seriously tarnished her reputation.

Bibliography

Byrne, Jane. *My Chicago*. New York: W. W. Norton, 1992. A sometimes self-serving, but readable, anecdotal autobiography that encompasses the history of Chicago, Byrne's genealogy, and her entire political career, especially her association with Richard J. Daley and her own term as mayor. Its Chicago-centered bibliography is wide-ranging.

FitzGerald, Kathleen Whalen. *Brass: Jane Byrne and the Pursuit of Power*. Chicago: Contemporary Books, 1981. Relying heavily on personal interviews of Byrne's friends and family, this extremely sympathetic biography is notable mainly for its germane explication of Byrne's Catholic, "lace curtain" Irish background and worldview.

Gove, Samuel K., and Louis H. Masotti, eds. *After Daley: Chicago Politics in Transition*. Urbana: University of Illinois Press, 1982. Essays by Samuel Gove and Milton Rakove in this academic collection address Jane Byrne's mayoralty, complementing other essays addressing Chicago concerns. Rakove's explicit analysis is interesting, though undocumented.

Granger, Bill, and Lori Granger. *Fighting Jane: Mayor Jane Byrne and the Chicago Machine*. New York: Dial Press, 1980. This critical, occasionally hostile, biased account coauthored by a well-known, reactionary Chicago newspaper columnist details the Byrne mayoralty through 1980, incorporating Byrne's biography.

Green, Paul M., and Melvin G. Holli, eds. *The Mayors: The Chicago Political Tradition*. Carbondale: Southern Illinois University Press, 1987. Holli's essay analyzing Byrne's mayoral administration offers an astute, concise account of major events and objectively assesses its positive and negative outcomes; his expert survey rating recent mayors provides perspective.

Rivlin, Gary. *Fire on the Prairie: Chicago's Harold Washington and the Politics of Race*. New York: Henry Holt, 1992. In explaining how Harold Washington, Chicago's first black mayor, succeeded Byrne, Rivlin lends significant perspective on Byrne's tenure and on her unsuccessful campaigns after 1983, particularly emphasizing minority communities and racial problems.

Penelope J. Engelbrecht

FRANCES XAVIER CABRINI

Born: July 15, 1850; Sant' Angelo Lodigiano, Lombardy, Italy
Died: December 22, 1917; Chicago, Illinois
Areas of Achievement: Religion and social reform
Contribution: Founder of a religious community dedicated to helping the poor, Mother Cabrini contributed to missions among Italian immigrants to America, eventually establishing convents, schools, and charitable orphanages all over the world.

Early Life

Frances Xavier Cabrini was the last of thirteen children born of Augustino and Stella (Oldini) Cabrini. She was baptized Maria Francesca, at which time miraculous evidence of her piety was said to have appeared in the form of white doves which flitted about the house on that day. Her family was well-known for its dedication to the Roman Catholic church, and one of her uncles, Luigi Oldini, was a priest and foreign missionary. Luigi taught her games associated with missionary work which helped to mold young Frances into a surprisingly serious and pious young girl.

By the time Frances was twelve, she began taking an annual oath of virginity, which she declared permanent at the age of eighteen. She attended a private normal school under the direction of the Daughters of the Sacred Heart of Arluno, where her sister Rosa was preceptress. Frances graduated in 1870. In September of that same year, the united Kingdom of Italy was established after the Papal States capitulated and acknowledged the sovereignty of Savoyard forces. The birth of a united Italy resulted in a severe curb on the traditional authority of the Roman Catholic church over schools, hospitals, and charitable enterprises.

In 1872, Frances fell victim to a smallpox epidemic while caring for the sick. While she was still recovering, she began teaching at the school of Vidardo, where she found her ability to teach Christian doctrine firmly repressed by secularizing laws. Unsatisfied with her limited opportunities to serve the Catholic church in this role, she petitioned in 1874 to become one of the Daughters of the Sacred Heart. Her petition was denied on the basis of her fragile health, but her zeal was noted by Father Antonio Serrati, who appointed her to supervise an orphanage in Codogno.

Three years later, in 1877, Frances founded a new convent, called the Institute of the Missionary Sisters of the Sacred Heart. Her foundation grew rapidly; in 1888, her society received an official decree of commendation. Mother Frances Xavier, as she then became known, led the sisters in founding orphanages and schools all over Italy. Pope Leo XIII commended her work and called her "a woman of marvelous intuition and of great sanctity."

Life's Work

Mother Frances Cabrini also expressed a strong desire to begin a foreign mission, preferably in China. Pope Leo XIII instead decided to send her to the United States, an area which was becoming a great concern among Vatican leaders. More than one million Italian immigrants were flooding into the United States between 1880 and 1902. These new arrivals crowded into makeshift tenements located in teeming neighborhoods in large American cities. They worked long and grueling hours for pitiful wages under the control of Italian *padrones*, agents who organized labor gangs to work in exchange for paying for their passage across the Atlantic, and American sweatshop owners. Practically all of these Italian émigrés considered themselves to be Roman Catholics, but their religious practices, if they engaged in any at all, consisted of an informal jumbling of local traditions from back home and family superstitions that bore little resemblance to official Catholic teachings.

By the 1880's, the Vatican was beginning to take an intense interest in the plight of Italian Americans. With the support of Pope Leo XIII, Giovanni Battista Scalabrini began a concentrated endeavor to minister to the spiritual and physical needs of these uprooted people. A Scalabrinian mission was sent to New York. As part of this ministerial program, the Catholic church would encourage female religious orders to assist Italian American Communities by providing staff for local orphanages and schools.

Cabrini was sent to New York to fulfill plans for an Italian orphanage for girls proposed by Countess Mary Reid DiCesnola. The countess' proposal to fund a Catholic charity was common in a day when the intellectual and social elite were expected to engage in at least a token attempt to alleviate the suffering of the illiterate and unwashed masses. Consequently, the countess designed an orphanage to provide young girls with basic schooling as well as training in fine needlework and fine laundrywork, all skills which would be useful to the countess' society friends, where the girls were expected to practice their crafts.

When Scalabrini and the pope suggested that Mother Cabrini go to New York, Cabrini was given the impression that her charitable work would be performed under the supervision of Archbishop Michael Corrigan of New York, and that preparations had already been made for the arrival of the sisters. Cabrini arrived in New York on March 31, 1889, only to find that her superiors in Italy had been gravely misinformed. No accommodations for the sisters had been secured; in fact, Corrigan had written to Cabrini shortly before her departure from Italy suggesting that she delay her journey, but the letter had arrived too late.

Corrigan greeted Cabrini coolly and suggested that the sisters return to Italy immediately. Cabrini stoutly refused. Corrigan finally agreed to allow the nuns to stay if they would establish an Italian school on the lower East Side of the city. He quickly came to loggerheads with the countess over this issue. The countess wanted the sisters to serve as inexpensive labor for her orphanage and suggested that they support themselves by seeking outside employment. In the end, the countess was forced to yield to the archbishop and turn control of the orphanage, along with all money previously collected, over to Mother Cabrini. The orphanage opened on April 21, 1889.

Growing tension between the countess and the archbishop convinced Mother

Cabrini of the necessity of acquiring another site for the orphanage. By June, 1890, she had raised sufficient funds to purchase a Jesuit novitiate which became the new site of Sacred Heart Orphan Asylum and a novitiate for the Missionary Sisters of the Sacred Heart. Cabrini also became more closely involved in the projects begun by the Scalabrinian missionaries in New York, including a proposal to build an Italian hospital, for which Cabrini and her sisters solicited the funds. Columbus Hospital was incorporated on May 18, 1891.

Not content to rest on her laurels, the dynamic Mother Cabrini left her New York projects in he hands of other sisters and traveled to Nicaragua in September, 1891, where she founded a house and school. From there she opened a school for Italian children in New Orleans, where she remained until recalled to New York to settle a dispute between the Scalabrinian priests and her nuns.

She returned to New York in April of 1892, where she found the Columbus Hospital in dire financial straits. The leader of the Scalabrinian mission, the Reverend Felice Morelli, had pushed the mission deeply into debt by borrowing money at exorbitant interest to purchase buildings and land. Morelli was unable to pay the debt on the hospital, which was threatened with public auction to satisfy his creditors. In Mother Cabrini's absence, Morelli had attempted to shift the debt onto the shoulders of the sisters. Cabrini decided to disassociate her order from the original hospital and, with a grant of $550 from Archbishop Corrigan and some wealthy Italians, she opened a new Columbus Hospital in two rented apartments. The new hospital was expanded in 1894.

The work of the Missionary Sisters of the Sacred Heart continued to grow after Corrigan's death in 1902 to include more schools and orphanages. The sisters also visited hospitals and almshouses, tombs and prisons. Quietly but persistently, the small and frail Frances Cabrini cultivated the support of bishop after bishop throughout the United States and around the world. She founded orphanages and schools in Denver, Los Angeles, Chicago, Seattle, and Philadelphia, as well as in such far-off locations as Buenos Aires, Paris, Madrid, London, and Brazil. She also founded several modern charitable hospitals in New York, Chicago, and Seattle.

Following a brief illness, Mother Cabrini died on December 22, 1917, at Columbus Hospital in Chicago. At her death, she was mother-general to some four thousand nuns and had founded seventy charitable institutions the world over. Her funeral was officiated by Archbishop (later Cardinal) Mundelein and her remains were laid to rest in New York. Soon after her death, her associates, led by Cardinal Mundelein, promoted her cause before the pope and the archdioceses of New York and Chicago. She was beatified by the Roman Catholic church on November 13, 1938, after the rule which required fifty years to elapse before the beatification process could be initiated was waived for her case. She became the first American to achieve this honor.

Summary

Frances Xavier Cabrini brought increased unity to the Italian community in New York through her charitable efforts. Her highest goal in her mission work was to strengthen the ties between the Italian immigrants and the Roman Catholic church. Although she was often frustrated in her failure to wipe out "the worldly spirit" that she felt all around her, she contributed greatly to the growth of popular faith in the Italian community in New York City and in cities throughout the United States. Her worldwide missions also established charitable organizations to help those living in less affluent parts of the world.

Mother Cabrini achieved a worldwide reputation for her religious zeal, her diplomatic skill, and her talents as a businesswoman. She fought valiantly to create a role for Catholic women in foreign missionary work. When reminded by a male colleague that missionaries historically had always been men, Cabrini is said to have replied, "If the mission of announcing the Lord's resurrection to his apostles had been entrusted to Mary Magdalene, it would seem a very good thing to confide to other women an evangelizing mission." Contemporaries often referred to her as "a great man" or "a statesman" for want of a better term. Pope Pius XI considered her name "equal to a poem—a poem of activity, a poem of intelligence, a poem above all of wonderful charity." Through her zeal and her intrepid determination, Mother Cabrini helped to establish a vital role for Catholic women in the area of foreign missions and to increase their visibility within the Roman Catholic church.

Bibliography

Border, Lucille Papin. *Francesca Cabrini: Without Staff or Script*. New York: Macmillan, 1945. An older biography meant for popular audiences, this work is extremely sympathetic to Cabrini and focuses primarily on her role as head of the Missionary Sisters of the Sacred Heart.

Di Donato, Pietro. *Immigrant Saint: The Life of Mother Cabrini*. Reprint. New York: St. Martin's Press, 1991. Originally published in 1960, this modern, scholarly biography of Cabrini gives the best background information on the period in which she lived. It uses archives of the Vatican opened to the public in 1978, as well as materials from the Congregation of Propaganda Fide which have been opened recently by Pope John Paul II.

DiGiovanni, Stephen Michael. "Mother Cabrini: Early Years in New York." *Catholic Historical Review* 77, no. 1 (January 1, 1991): 56-77. This is the most comprehensive account of the circumstances that led to Mother Cabrini's dispatch to New York and of her early work with the Italian population there. DiGiovanni sets Cabrini's work in the context of the political developments within the Roman Catholic leadership both in Rome and in New York in the 1880's.

Martindale, Cyril C. *Life of Mother Francesca Saverio Cabrini*. New York: Burns, 1931. Based on biographical materials collected by the Institute of the Missionary Sisters of the Sacred Heart, this brief treatment of Mother Cabrini was compiled as part of the campaign by her colleagues and friends to convene a hearing for Cabrini's beatification.

Maynard, Theodore. *Too Small a World: The Life of Francesca Cabrini*. Milwaukee: Bruce Publishing, 1945. An uncritical and simple biography, this book concentrates on Mother Cabrini's role as a worldwide ambassador for the Roman Catholic church. It is the best source for study of Cabrini's work outside the United States.

Kimberly K. Estep

SARAH CALDWELL

Born: March 6, 1924; Maryville, Missouri

Area of Achievement: Music
Contribution: A major force in producing, staging, directing, and promoting opera, Sarah Caldwell has broken new ground for women in the arts and has served as a role model for those who followed.

Early Life
Sarah Caldwell's parents were divorced when she was an infant. Her mother, Margaret, was an aspiring pianist who studied at Northwestern University and the Juilliard School of Music. As a result of her mother's frequent absence from home, Sarah lived with relatives who surrounded her with photographs and other memorabilia of her mother. As a child, Sarah studied the violin; revealing prodigious talent, she performed chamber music with adults at the age of five. By the time she was six, she gave her own recitals, some as far away as Chicago. At the same time, her gifts in mathematics were recognized and, thus, there emerged the homegrown legend of Sarah Caldwell, child prodigy. There was yet another side to this *wunderkind*; she staged elaborate fireworks displays in her backyard via the Roman candles, cherry bombs, sparklers, and firecrackers she managed to acquire from local stores.

After her mother's second marriage to Henry Alexander, a teacher of political science at the University of Arkansas, Sarah moved to Fayetteville and began to enjoy a brief period of stabilization in her life. She recalls that her stepfather kept a dictionary at the dinner table, and that he encouraged her to study music, but not to make it her life's work. After graduating from high school at the age of fourteen, Sarah declared psychology as her major at the University of Arkansas, but about a year and a half later she followed her own dream and moved from Fayetteville to the central Arkansas town of Conway in order to study violin with David Robertson at Hendrix College. Shortly thereafter, she received a scholarship to the New England Conservatory of Music to study violin with Richard Burgin, concertmaster of the Boston Symphony Orchestra. Burgin was not overly impressed with her violinistic talents but Georges Flourel, a violist with the Boston Symphony, soon accepted Sarah in his studio. By 1946, she received a scholarship to play viola in the student orchestra at Tanglewood, the summer residence of the Boston Symphony. There she had ample opportunity to observe the orchestra's famed conductor, Serge Koussevitzky.

During the regular academic year at the New England Conservatory, Sarah came under the influence of Boris Goldovsky, head of the opera department, and soon became his assistant. In the summer of 1947, Sarah conducted a performance of English composer Ralph Vaughan Williams' one-act opera, *Riders to the Sea* (1937) at Tanglewood. Koussevitzky expressed his admiration for her work, and, by the following summer, she was invited to join the faculty. As the only woman in her conducting class, she was a phenomenon. Strong-willed and independent, her work with Goldovsky came to an end in part because of a clash of personalities and in part because their views on opera production did not mesh. Thus, when Boston University invited her to head their fledgling opera workshop in 1952, Sarah Caldwell seized the moment to strike out on her own.

Life's Work

From 1952 until 1960, Sarah Caldwell taught, directed, and molded a small student enterprise into a sizable opera department, one which, like its founder, became identified with the exploration of new territory. A representative example of Caldwell's derring-do at the Boston University opera workshop was her direction of the American premiere of Paul Hindemith's *Mathis der Maler* (1934), an opera based on philosophical issues surrounding the Catholic church and the Renaissance painter, Mathis Grunewald. This 1957 production, so well-suited to a university environment, concerns the creative artist's conflict in being true to his art while dealing with the pragmatic issues of religious, political, and economic pressures of daily life. By the end of her tenure at Boston University, this fireball of energy had established a reputation for fearlessness in trying new things with old operas as well as introducing new operas to her growing audiences.

Known for dabbling in a variety of ventures at the same time and for creating a state of confusion in her wake, Caldwell began her own opera company, the Opera Group of Boston, in 1957. The group's inaugural performance in 1958 was an outdoor rendering of Jacques Offenbach's *The Voyage to the Moon*. When the Back Bay Theater, in which most of the group's early productions were given, was torn down to provide space for an apartment complex, Caldwell managed to secure a variety of locales as sites for her public offerings, ranging from the gym at Tufts University, to the indoor track at Boston College, to high school auditoria, to motion picture theaters. A more permanent home has been the Orpheum, a 2000-seat theater with no pit; thus, the orchestra is required to sit on the main floor. Caldwell, whose eccentricities include entering the hall through a side door wearing slippers and seating herself in a canvas director's chair from which she conducts, has, nevertheless, managed to stage, under these conditions, the American premieres of Hector Berlioz's *Les Troyens* (1855-1858), Jean-Philippe Rameau's *Hippolyte et Aricie* (1733), and Arnold Schoenberg's *Moses und Aron* (1930-1932). As a director who believes in bringing in stars to work with the local artists, she has engaged such celebrated divas as Joan Sutherland to appear in the first American staging of Vicenzo Bellini's *I puritani* (1835) and the first since 1906 of Gioacchino Rossini's *Semiramide* (1823).

Having demonstrated what could be achieved on a low budget in Boston, Caldwell envisioned a traveling troupe to bring opera to people throughout the land. In 1967, her American National Opera Company, aided by a $350,000 grant from the National Council on the Arts, the federal government's first major involvement in underwriting opera, began an eventful road trip in Indianapolis. The tour offered three works, Giuseppe Verdi's *Falstaff* (1893), an English-language performance of Alban Berg's *Lulu* (1937), and Giacomo Puccini's *Tosca* (1900).

Notorious for demanding long rehearsals, Caldwell is remembered by those in the opera world for her nine-hour final run-through for a 1973 production of Verdi's *Don Carlos* (1867). Also in the Caldwell lore are accounts of her researches, musical and otherwise, in order to bring a sense of reality to her recreations. Much time was expended in going to Mexico to look into the conquests of Hernando Cortés and the pyramids of Teotihuacán, all of which ultimately resulted in her 1976 performances of Roger Sessions' spectacular *Montezuma* (1941-1963). Beverly Sills has sung in many of Caldwell's presentations, including a spectacularly successful staging of Rossini's *Barber of Seville* in 1974, a year in which Caldwell also gave her audiences Sergey Prokofiev's monumental *War and Peace* (based on the novel by Leo Tolstoy), Puccini's *Madama Butterfly* (1904), and Juks Massenet's *Don Quichotte* (1910). On a seemingly never-ending treadmill, the grande dame of opera was called upon to conduct the venerable New York Philharmonic in November of 1975, only the second woman to be so honored (the first was theorist and teacher Nadia Boulanger in 1939 and 1962). Her program was sponsored by the Philharmonic and *Ms.* magazine. Billed as "a celebration of women composers," it featured works by Lili Boulanger (younger sister of Nadia), Ruth Crawford Seeger, Thea Musgrave, Barbara Kolb, and Lucia Dlugoszewski.

On January 13, 1976, the bicentennial year, Sarah Caldwell achieved another first when she was invited to conduct at the Metropolitan Opera in New York, another startling breakthrough for women in music. Her well-received direction of Verdi's *La traviata* (1853) with Beverly Sills dispelled any lingering doubts about Caldwell's skills to lead singers or to conduct that well-entrenched male bastion, the Metropolitan Opera Orchestra. As the years rolled on, Caldwell could claim to have directed opera companies such as the Dallas Civic, Houston Grand, and New York City Opera, as well as major symphony orchestras of Indianapolis, Pittsburgh, and Milwaukee in addition to the New York Philharmonic.

Further groundbreaking activity occurred in 1982 when Caldwell, by now the doyenne among women opera conductors, conducted Verdi's *La traviata* in Chinese in the Central Opera Company's performance of this masterwork in Beijing's Tian Qiao Theater. In that same year, she and her Opera Company of Boston forged a collaborative effort with the Philippines to develop opera in that nation. In 1983, she was named artistic director of the New Opera Company of Israel. Other international efforts include taking a leading role in developing a joint Soviet-American music-making venture. The result was a three-week event in Boston featuring 285 Soviet performers joining with American singers and instrumentalists to perform such Soviet compositions as Rodion Schedrin's opera, *Dead Souls* (based on the novel by Nikolai Gogol). While this first phase of the partnership took place in 1988, the Soviet reciprocation was delayed until January, 1991. Beginning in Moscow and continuing through the spring, concerts, recitals, symposia, and such operatic performances as that given Robert Domenico's *The Balcony* were offered to the Soviet citizenry as a way to promote American culture. As usual, Caldwell was a dominant personality in all aspects of this historic cultural pact.

Summary

Unlike so many women of valor, whose light shone for a brief moment on the stage of history and then dimmed or died out entirely, Sarah Caldwell has been a beacon of light, hope, and courage to all those who face adversity in their personal and professional aspirations. She has grown steadily as a force with which to be reckoned in the world of music, a world which has, for centuries, been a male-dominated enclave at all levels. Caldwell's list of "firsts" have shown what is possible when extraordinary talent is complemented by perseverance, independence, determination, and will. Caldwell's achievements have made it possible for women to aspire to the highest echelons of the music profession, most particularly in the realm of conducting and in the field of opera direction, staging, and production.

Apart from serving as a living example of how one can overcome professional obstacles, Sarah Caldwell has also shown that conformity to common standards of female beauty is not essential for the achievement of success; indeed, most writing about her refers to her obesity, and frequently it is accompanied by unflattering pictures of this extraordinary personality. For those with challenges of any kind, she serves to prove that there are no barriers to greatness.

Bibliography

Appleton, Jane Scovell. "Sarah Caldwell: The Flamboyant of the Opera." *Ms.* 3 (May, 1975): 26-31. A compelling account of Caldwell's triumphs over adversity, particularly with regard to mounting operas in theaters ill-suited for the purpose. Treats her philosophical and artistic approach to operatic production.

Ardoin, John. "Making Contact." *Opera News* 46 (March 6, 1982): 28-29. Reveals succinctly how Caldwell has dealt with foreign artists and politicians, specifically with regard to her historic production of Verdi's *La traviata* in the Tiam Qiao Theater with the Central Opera Company of Beijing.

Bender, William. "Music's Wonder Woman." *Time* 106 (November 10, 1975): 52-54, 59, 65. A comprehensive cover story on Caldwell. Illustrated with many excellent photographs, including one of Caldwell at age four. Provides background on Caldwell's childhood years, on her personal and professional idiosyncracies, and on her innovative approaches to opera production.

Dizikes, John. *Opera in America: A Cultural History.* New Haven, Conn.: Yale University Press, 1993. In this wide-ranging cultural overview, Dizikes includes a brief chapter entitled "Sarah Caldwell Presents" that touches on Caldwell's contributions to American opera by expanding the horizons of a small opera company and reviving interest in operas generally neglected by major companies.

Eaton, Quaintance. "Renaissance Woman." *Opera News* 28 (April 18, 1964): 26-29. Treats the multiple talents of Caldwell with special attention to personality and personal appearance vis-à-vis priorities in her life.

Kufrin, Joan. *Uncommon Women: Gwendolyn Brooks, Sarah Caldwell, Julie Harris, Mary McCarthy, Alice Neel, Roberta Peters, Maria Tallchief, Mary Lou Williams, Eugenia Zukerman.* Piscataway, N.J.: New Century, 1981. The author places

Caldwell's achievements in the context of an eclectic gathering of other women who have made important contributions in various cultural arts. Illustrated with photographs by George Kufrin.

LePage, Jane Weiner. "Sarah Caldwell." In *Women Composers, Conductors, and Musicians of the Twentieth Century.* 3 vols. Metuchen, N.J.: Scarecrow Press, 1980-1988. A fulsome account of Caldwell's career that includes reviews of many of her most important performances. Notes all of her groundbreaking efforts in the world of opera with specific dates, places, and personalities involved.

David Z. Kushner

KIM CAMPBELL

Born: March 10, 1947; Port Alberni, British Columbia, Canada

Area of Achievement: Government and politics
Contribution: As Canada's first woman prime minister, Kim Campbell advanced the quest of North American women for high political office.

Early Life

Avril Phaedra "Kim" Campbell was born on March 10, 1947, in Port Alberni, British Columbia. Her father George was a Canadian soldier in World War II who later became a lawyer. George Campbell married Lissa Cook in 1944. Their first child, Alix, was born in 1945, followed by Avril Phaedra two years later.

After struggling to establish himself professionally for several years, George became a successful lawyer and moved his family into the suburbs. A liberal, enlightened father, he encouraged his younger daughter to excel at her studies and explore her interests in the arts. By the time she entered high school, she was recognized as the most talented and intelligent student in her class. Yet behind the veil of serene success, there was trouble at home. The Campbells were divorcing, and in the aftermath of the split Lissa did not see her daughters for ten years. It was during this period that Avril Phaedra assumed the nickname "Kim."

Kim was valedictorian of her high school class in 1964. Despite her obvious promise, her life remained tentative and provisional during her early adulthood. Kim earned an Honors degree in political science from the University of British Columbia in Vancouver. Even though the late 1960's were the height of radical agitation in North America over involvement in the Vietnam War, Kim's politics had already taken on a moderate-conservative coloring.

In 1967, Kim began to date Nathan Divinsky, a mathematics professor twenty-two years her senior. Divinsky, a brilliant but erratic intellectual, introduced Kim to a wider world of thought and discourse. The couple began living together as Kim pursued her master's degree in international relations at the University of British Columbia. With Divinsky's aid, Kim won a scholarship to study at the London School of Economics. Here, her conservative political views were cemented. In 1972, she married Divinsky, and they returned to Canada shortly thereafter. Kim tried to look for teaching jobs, but since she had not completed any advanced degree she could only get the most lowly and temporary positions.

Life's Work

Kim Campbell decided to abandon a teaching career in academia and, like her father, earn a law degree. Once again, Campbell excelled as a student, and her achievement began to awaken thoughts of a political career. In 1980, Campbell won a seat on the Vancouver school board.

By 1983, Campbell was chairman of the school board. Her increasing public prominence strained her marriage to Divinsky, and in that year the couple divorced. As school board chairman, Campbell earned notoriety for her vociferous attacks on trade unions. At the same time that Campbell was accepted as an associate at a prestigious Vancouver law firm, she tried to move up in politics, running for the provincial parliament. Even though she lost, Campbell had found her true vocation.

Campbell abandoned her career as a private attorney when she was hired to work in the office of William Bennett, the premier of British Columbia. When Bennett resigned, Campbell entered the race to replace him. As a total unknown, she lagged far behind the leaders, but her effort nevertheless garnered her a seat in the provincial legislature in October, 1986.

Campbell generated controversy and earned acclaim as an advocate of women's rights when she opposed the anti-abortion views of the new premier. As a consequence, she alienated the right-wing leaders of the Social Credit party, known for its advocacy of conservative political views in British Columbia. Realizing that her climb up the political ladder would be severely restricted if she remained in provincial politics, Campbell began to cast her eye toward the federal arena.

Meeting with important local leaders of the ruling national Progressive Conservative (Tory) Party, Campbell impressed them with her drive and ambition. When a parliamentary seat opened up some months later, Campbell decided to run. Although she was unsure whether she would be happy in Ottawa, cherishing her pleasant British Columbia lifestyle, Campbell soon thrived in the political atmosphere. Strenuously championing Prime Minister Brian Mulroney's free trade agreement with the United States, Campbell won election by a narrow margin.

Campbell moved to Ottawa, where she began drawing attention. Campbell was soon named to Brian Mulroney's cabinet, as minister of State for northern affairs and political development. In the Canadian parliamentary system, unlike American politics, legislators must also be administrators. Campbell's smooth mastery of both challenges brought her much praise from senior Tories.

Campbell broke through to the leadership ranks of the federal party in 1990, when Mulroney appointed her to serve as Canada's first female attorney general. Campbell's agenda was primarily focused on one issue: gun control. Drafting a proposed bill that would fortify existing gun control laws, she devoted many months to shepherding her bill through a sullen and fractious Parliament. Her vigorous efforts were vindicated when the bill was successfully passed in September, 1991. Although staunch in her support of conservative law and order issues, Campbell emerged as an unconventional and unpredictable politician. Despite her conservative background, she argued that much of Canadian law was biased in favor of white males, and she overtly campaigned for women's rights.

The Mulroney government, like the administration of Ronald Reagan in the United States, had reaped political profit from the economic boom years of the 1980's. In the wake of the worldwide recession that began in 1990, Mulroney's popularity, which had been sufficient to ensure his reelection two years before, plummeted. By 1993, the Tories had been in power for nine years and were increasingly regarded as stale, outmoded, and likely to lose in the election that had to be called by autumn of 1993. As one of the few fresh faces in the party, Campbell saw her popularity and political eligibility soar. Her political strength was acknowledged when Mulroney asked Campbell to serve as defense minister in January of 1993. Once again, Campbell had broken a barrier, receiving an appointment to a post not traditionally occupied by women. No sooner, though, had she attained this post than Campbell began to be spoken of as a possible candidate to succeed Mulroney as prime minister.

After desperate attempts to secure, successively, the jobs of the Secretary-General of the United Nations and the commissioner of the National Hockey League for himself, the dismally unpopular Mulroney resigned in March of 1993, and Campbell immediately entered the race to be his successor as Tory party leader. Since in Canada's parliamentary system the leader of the ruling party automatically becomes prime minister, if Campbell won the Tory race she would be prime minister as well. Campbell took an early lead in the polls, spurred by the novelty of a woman prime minister and by her relative lack of association with the hated Mulroney regime. She was soon challenged, however, by an ambitious, articulate young politician from Quebec named Jean Charest. At the party convention, Campbell turned back Charest's unexpectedly strong challenge and became Canada's first woman prime minster.

Things did not look rosy in the polls for the Tory party in 1993. The perceived failure of Mulroney's economic politics, and his inability to resolve the constitutional crisis precipitated by the wish of many in the French-speaking province of Quebec to withdraw from the Canadian confederation, had shriveled the party's formerly wide-spread support. Not only were the party's traditional rivals, the moderate-left Liberals and the socialist New Democrats, looking to gain seats, but there were two new entrants in Canadian electoral politics. One was the Reform Party, which was based in the traditionally conservative western provinces and called for free enterprise, assaults on government waste, and an end to the so-called special pleading of the French Canadians for a distinct role in the country's society. The other was the Bloc Québécois, a Quebec nationalist party that siphoned off the support of many Tories in that province who had helped elect Mulroney.

Despite this severe erosion in the Tories' base of support, Campbell's first weeks in office were dynamic and impressive. She soon became the most personally popular of all the party leaders, and rallied the Tories from far behind to a respectable place in the polls. Campbell's casual, colloquial, apparently unrehearsed style was refreshing and appealing to many voters. Many women saw Campbell's prominence as a ratification of the gains of women in the workplace and in society over the past generation. Campbell generally made a good impression on Canadians and on the world during this period. Traveling to the G-7 economic summit in Tokyo to meet with the leaders of the six other major Western democracies, Campbell was compared with recently inaugurated U.S. President Bill Clinton as a member of the "baby-boom" generation who was bringing fresh ideas and energy into politics.

Campbell sought to capitalize on this exposure when the election was formally called in 1993. Her opponents did not think that her experience would be sufficient, intimating that Campbell's brief tenure as prime minister was only "a summer job." Campbell went on the offensive, reviling her principal opponent, Liberal Party leader Jean Chrétien, as "yesterday's man." Campbell was appealing to many Canadians not only as a woman but also because she was from British Columbia, an English-speaking province, and thus represented a change from the long hegemony of Quebec politicians as exemplified by Mulroney and Pierre Elliott Trudeau.

Campbell's dynamism, however, was not enough. Campbell's performance in the televised debates between the party leaders had to be superb in order for her to make any dent in the polls; but it was only workmanlike. Mulroney's legacy had saddled the Tories with an indelible stain of failure, and by the time election day came the question was not whether Campbell would lose but by how much. As fate would have it, the margin was wide. In probably the most humiliating defeat for a major party in the history of modern democratic government, the Tories lost all but two seats of the more than one hundred and fifty they had previously held. The heavy loss of support from traditional Tory voters, who had fled to either Reform or the Bloc Québécois, meant that the liberal Chrétien would be the next prime minister. There was not even any personal consolation for Campbell, as she lost her own seat in Vancouver as well. Campbell, though, was still only forty-six as she left office, a mere youth as far as political careers go, and many were predicting that this was not the last time her voice would be heard in Canadian politics.

Summary

Kim Campbell's brief tenure as Canadian prime minister was truncated by the unpopularity of her predecessor, which she was powerless to change. Nevertheless, Campbell for a short time illuminated the often drab face of Canadian politics with her individuality and irreverence. Overcoming personal disappointments and family unhappiness, Campbell's swift rise to political power demonstrated that high office in Western democracies had become as open to women as to men. Campbell's career serves as a hopeful sign of a day when Western societies will be fully democratic and everyone can be seen as having potential for leadership, whatever their background. After Campbell's stint as leader of the second largest nation in the world, it is assured that the door will never be closed again to women seeking positions of political leadership and responsibility.

Bibliography
Davey, Frank. *Reading "Kim" Right*. Vancouver: Talonbooks, 1993. This unusual book, by a respected Canadian poet and professor at the University of Western Ontario, examines Campbell, especially as a media image and political symbol, from the perspective of contemporary literary and cultural theory.

Dobbin, Murray, with Ellen Gould. *Kim Campbell: From School Trustee to Prime Minister*. Toronto: James Lorimer, 1993. The fullest book-length biography of Campbell, this work focuses attention on her early political career in the British Columbia of the 1980's.

Fife, Robert. *Kim Campbell: The Making of a Politician.* Toronto: HarperCollins, 1993. This book, written from the perspective of the political insider, examines Campbell in the context of the machinations of the federal government in Ottawa, especially with an eye toward evaluating her potential as a vote-getter.

Fulton, E. Kaye, and Mary Janigan. "The Real Kim Campbell." *Maclean's* 106 (May 17, 1993): 16-23. A long, detailed article that served as the primary source during the campaign for many Canadians' impression of Campbell's biography. Significant not only for what it says about Campbell but also for the image of her it presented to the voters.

Gray, Charlotte. "Singing in the Rain." *Saturday Night* 106 (October, 1991): 28-31. This early profile of Campbell on the national scene emphasizes her work as justice minister, and is the best contemporary account of those years.

Swan, Susan. "The Verge." *Mirabella* 5 (August, 1993): 71-75. Written by a Toronto novelist, this profile of Campbell provides American readers with an overview of her career and explains her phenomenal success from a variety of perspectives. Mentions Campbell's provocative pose that appeared in Barbara Woodley's photographic collection, *Portraits: Canadian Women in Focus.*

Nicholas Birns

ANNIE JUMP CANNON

Born: December 11, 1863; Dover, Delaware
Died: April 13, 1941; Cambridge, Massachusetts
Area of Achievement: Astronomy
Contribution: In her work at the Harvard College Observatory, Cannon cataloged stars according to their spectral class into the Draper Catalogue and discovered several new variable stars and novas.

Early Life

Annie Jump Cannon was born in Dover, Delaware, the only daughter and eldest of three children born to Wilson Lee Cannon and Mary Elizabeth Jump Cannon. The Cannon family also included a half-brother and three half-sisters, children of her father's first marriage. He was a wealthy merchant and shipbuilder of Scottish descent and was a state senator. Annie's mother was descended from seventeenth century Maryland settlers.

Annie's family home was prosperous and cultured. She was educated in the Dover public school and in a private academy. Her mother had become interested in stars as a schoolgirl herself and shared her knowledge and interest with Annie, arranging a makeshift observatory in the attic of the family home. During those years, Annie learned to recognize constellations and kept a record of her observations. She also was fond of observing the colored spectra produced by prisms on an ornate chandelier in the family home.

After Annie's graduation from the Wilmington Conference Academy at the age of sixteen, her father sent her to Wellesley College in Massachusetts. One of a group of colleges exclusively for women, Wellesley had opened just five years earlier in 1874. There, under the tutelage of Sarah Frances Whiting, professor of physics and astronomy, Miss Cannon (as Wellesley students were thus addressed at that time and as she was known throughout her life) furthered her studies in astronomy and spectroscopy, the study of the spectrum of colors produced when white light passes through a prism.

After her graduation from Wellesley College in 1884, Annie returned home to Dover and was a popular participant in the social life of that city. She traveled to Spain and made fine photographs on her journey, at a time when photography was not at all a common activity of tourists. She was a gifted pianist, but had early shown signs of deafness which increased as she aged.

In 1893, Annie's mother died. They had always been very close, and Annie decided to seek a change in her life. She returned to Wellesley College for a year of further study and to serve as an assistant to Professor Whiting. The following year she enrolled as a special student of astronomy at Radcliffe College, the women's college in Cambridge, Massachusetts. Instruction at Radcliffe paralleled that offered at Harvard College, then an exclusively male institution. As a Radcliffe student, Annie was allowed access to the Harvard College Observatory, where she began daytime study of photographic plates and evening observation of variable stars.

Life's Work

In 1896, Annie Jump Cannon became an assistant at the Harvard College Observatory. The observatory's director, Edward C. Pickering, was well acquainted with Professor Whiting at Wellesley College. Whiting had studied physics with Pickering at the Massachusetts Institute of Technology, where he had served as professor of physics before assuming the directorship of the Harvard College Observatory in 1877. Pickering had advised and assisted Whiting in setting up the Wellesley physics program and made special efforts to encourage the work of Whiting's students.

At the time Cannon joined the observatory staff, the principal work in progress was the cataloging of stars according to their spectral classification through funding from an endowment established in honor of Henry Draper. Draper, a New York physician, was an amateur astronomer particularly interested in stellar spectroscopy. He made the first photograph of the spectrum of a star in 1872, and was assisted in his work by his wife, Mary Anna Draper. After his death in 1882, his widow gave a large sum of money to Harvard to ensure the continuation of this activity.

The introduction of photography and spectroscopy into astronomy in the late nineteenth century made possible a whole new kind of investigation, one that eventually led to the development of astrophysics, the study of the physical conditions and processes prevailing among the stars. By inserting a prism into the light path and replacing the human eye behind the telescope with a camera film, the light from individual stars could be recorded and their spectra analyzed. From photographic observations, astronomers were able to obtain information about stellar temperatures and chemical composition, which varied markedly among the stars.

Pickering was eager to carry on this kind of work. Harvard had the required facilities to do so, not only in Cambridge but also in Peru, where the stars of the southern hemisphere could be photographed, analyzed, and cataloged.

This was the kind of work that Cannon was hired to do and at which she excelled. She joined a group of women working under the immediate supervision of Williamina Fleming. These women were called "computers," since some computation was involved in the analysis of the photographic plates. They worked seven hours a day, six days a week for an average wage of twenty-five cents per hour and were given a month of paid vacation each year. An income of more than $500 per year, while not generous, was sufficient to provide a modest livelihood for a single woman in those days. Cannon also had family money available. During her years at the observatory, her salary increased to $1,200 per year.

Cannon, a keen and careful analyzer, soon realized that the spectra provided new information about variable stars—stars whose brightness varied with time. In 1900, she established a card catalog of all the literature pertaining to variable stars. She also improved upon the spectral classification scheme that had been developed by Pickering and Fleming before Cannon joined the staff. In 1911, following Fleming's death, Cannon was named curator of astronomical photographs at the Harvard College Observatory, a post she held until her own death in 1941. Under her care, the photographic collection grew from 200,000 to 500,000 plates.

By 1918, Cannon began to supervise the publication of the Henry Draper Catalogue, which continued until 1924. Spectral classes for some 350,000 stars were included. Still more were added in the Henry Draper Extension, begun in 1925 and continued by others after Cannon's death until 1949. These publications remain the definitive compilation of information on the spectral classes of stars throughout the entire sky.

The wealth of information contained in the Draper Catalogue provided astrophysicists with what they needed to reach an understanding of the evolution of stars and the history of the universe. Because all the information was gathered at one site, the Harvard College Observatory, by one group of analyzers, under the direct supervision of Annie Jump Cannon, the catalog was especially valuable and reliable. The Henry Draper Catalogue became a bible for astrophysicists.

Cannon's work received worldwide recognition and appreciation during her lifetime. Among the honors she received were honorary doctoral degrees from the University of Groningen in 1921 and the University of Oxford in 1925. She was elected to membership in the Royal Astronomical Society of Great Britain, the American Philosophical Society, and the American Academy of Arts and Sciences. In 1938, Harvard University gave her a formal appointment as the William Cranch Bond Astronomer (named in honor of the first director of the Harvard College Observatory, 1839-1859), a singular distinction for a woman at that time.

The male-dominated National Academy of Sciences in Washington, D.C., never elected Cannon to membership, but it did award her its Draper Medal in 1931. She had been given the Nova Medal by the American Association of Variable Star Observers in 1922 and also received the Ellen Richards Prize by the Society to Aid Scientific Research by Women. The latter was a monetary award that Cannon donated to the American Astronomical Society to establish the Annie Jump Cannon Prize. Her namesake prize was to be awarded every three years to a woman astronomer of any nationality who had made a distinguished contribution to astronomy. She stipulated that the award should be a brooch, or pin, that the recipient could wear, rather than a ceremonial medal to be stored in a box.

Cannon retired from the Harvard College Observatory in 1940 and died the following year of heart failure and arteriosclerosis. She was buried in Dover, Delaware.

Summary

Annie Jump Cannon was a product of her particular social class and period in American history. The work she did was made possible by technical developments that had changed the work of astronomers and opened the door to the development of astrophysics. The fact that she was able to accomplish so much for the world of astronomy was due to her own intelligence, dedication and, she said, "patience."

Born into a privileged family, she benefited from American educational opportunities unavailable to previous generations of women anywhere. She was well aware that women, in general, found limited opportunities for participation in society. A believer in the woman suffrage movement, she joined the National Women's Party and was disappointed by the lack of enthusiasm for voting among the general population of women in the United States and elsewhere.

Her lifelong activities centered in Cambridge and in the world of astronomy. She traveled extensively, attending meetings of the International Astronomical Union and working at the Harvard College Observatory site in Peru from where the southern stars could be photographed.

Her visibility in the world of astronomy was an inspiration to other women and led to her being designated, in 1922, America's leading woman scientist by the League of Women Voters. Her establishment of the Annie Jump Cannon Prize provided encouragement to future generations of women astronomers. Yet there can be little doubt that her stellar classification scheme, incorporated into the Draper Catalogue, was her principal contribution to world knowledge. With only slight modification it has served several successive generations of astrophysicists. In particular, it was of great value to Henry Norris Russell and Ejnar Hertzsprung in devising their famous Hertzsprung-Russell diagram, which is considered one of the most important astronomical discoveries of the first half of the twentieth century. The scientific legacy of Annie Jump Cannon remains a permanent memorial to her dedication and industry.

Bibliography

Jones, Bessie Z., and Lyle Gifford Boyd. *The Harvard College Observatory: The First Four Directorships, 1839-1919*. Cambridge, Mass.: The Belknap Press of Harvard University Press, 1971. Chapter 11, "A Field for Women," contains a biographical sketch of Cannon and a photograph of her in her Oxford University robes. Other chapters provide extensive information on Edward C. Pickering, the Henry Draper Memorial, and on the work of women astronomers at the Harvard College Observatory in considerable technical detail.

Mack, Pamela E. "Straying from Their Orbits: Women in Astronomy in America." In *Women of Science: Righting the Record*, edited by G. Kass-Simon and Patricia Farnes. Bloomington: Indiana University Press, 1990. Has particular emphasis on the years up to 1920 and contains a section on Cannon's work at the Harvard College Observatory.

Mozans, H. J. *Woman in Science: With an Introductory Chapter on Woman's Struggle for Things of the Mind*. New York: D. Appleton, 1913. Reprint. Notre Dame, Ind.: University of Notre Dame Press, 1991. A historical sourcebook for women's contributions to science dating back to ancient Greece. Chapter 4, "Women in Astronomy," details the work of talented women astronomers, up to and including Cannon. Includes a bibliography of sources. H. J. Mozans is the pseudonym for John A. Zahm.

Ogilvie, Marilyn Bailey. *Women in Science: Antiquity Through the Nineteenth Century: A Biographical Dictionary with Annotated Bibliography*. Cambridge, Mass.: MIT Press, 1986. Contains an essay summarizing Cannon's career and achievements, followed by a list of sources including obituary notices.

Rossiter, Margaret W. *Women Scientists in America: Struggles and Strategies to 1940*.

Baltimore: The Johns Hopkins University Press, 1982. A scholarly survey of the opportunities and difficulties encountered by American women scientists and would-be scientists of the nineteenth and early twentieth centuries. Includes specific, referenced examples, pertaining to A. J. Cannon and her work.

Yost, Edna. *American Women of Science.* Rev. ed. Philadelphia: Lippincott, 1955. An informal biographical account of Cannon and her work, written as part of a series of sketches for high school girls seeking female role models in science.

Katherine R. Sopka

RACHEL CARSON

Born: May 27, 1907; Springdale, Pennsylvania
Died: April 14, 1964; Silver Spring, Maryland
Areas of Achievement: Biology and literature
Contribution: A marine biologist and gifted expositor, Rachel Carson wrote many articles as well as three lilting, lyrical books about the sea. She is most remembered, however, for her fourth book, *Silent Spring* (1962), an exhaustively researched exposé that sparked a national furor over the irresponsible use of pesticides in America.

Early Life

Rachel Louise Carson was born on May 27, 1907, in Springdale, Pennsylvania, approximately eighteen miles from Pittsburgh. Her father, Robert Warden Carson, had purchased at least sixty-five acres of land, intending to sell house lots, but the failure of this plan ensured that the young Rachel would be brought up in a fairly rural setting. Her mother, Maria McLean Carson, was the daughter of a Presbyterian minister and instilled her love of language, music, and nature in her three children. Rachel's long walks with her mother in the nearby orchards and woods awakened in her an awe for and joy in the natural world which lasted her entire life.

Rachel Carson soon conceived the goal of becoming a writer and proceeded toward that goal with alacrity: Her story "A Battle in the Clouds," which won a $10 prize, was published in *St. Nicholas*, a children's magazine, when she was only ten years old. Throughout her teenage years, she continued to write, and in 1925, at the age of eighteen she entered the Pennsylvania College for Women (later Chatham College) as an English major. During her first two years there, Rachel contributed many works to the literary supplement of the school newspaper.

Despite her success as a budding writer, Carson changed her major from English to biology midway through her college career. Years later, she was to say that biology gave her something to write about. One of Carson's mentors, a dynamic biology instructor named Mary Skinker who was returning to the doctoral program at The Johns Hopkins University, encouraged Carson to think about graduate school. Carson applied for admission to graduate school at The Johns Hopkins University for the fall of 1929 and was accepted. Following her graduation from Pennsylvania College for Women in the spring of 1929, Carson studied under a scholarship at the Marine Biological Laboratory at Woods Hole on Cape Cod. That summer, Carson saw the ocean for the first time. Henceforth, the sea remained an integral part of her life.

The following year saw many changes in Carson's life; her parents moved to Baltimore to live with her, and she received a teaching assistantship at The Johns Hopkins Summer School. Carson completed her master's degree in marine zoology in 1932, although she continued to teach until 1936.

In 1935, Carson's father died. Under pressure to support her family, she went to work part-time at the Bureau of Fisheries (which later became the U.S. Fish and

Wildlife Service), writing and editing radio scripts. While working there, she noticed an announcement of an opening for an assistant biologist at the bureau. She took the Civil Service examination (earning the highest score that year) and accepted the full-time appointment. Carson continued her work for the bureau for the next sixteen years, eventually rising in rank to become editor-in-chief of the publications department.

Life's Work

Oddly enough (considering the Department of Agriculture's subsequent vigorous opposition to her most famous book, *Silent Spring*), it was Rachel Carson's government work which led to her first article on the ocean. Carson had been asked, as she later said, to "produce something of a general sort about the sea. I set to work, but somehow the material rather took charge of the situation and turned into something that was, perhaps, unusual as a broadcast for the Commissioner of Fisheries." Her supervisor found the article unsuitable and suggested that she submit it to *The Atlantic Monthly* magazine. The article, "Undersea," was published in 1937.

As lyrical as it was informative, "Undersea" soon attracted the attention of an editor from the publishing house of Simon & Schuster, who encouraged Carson to write a book. After nearly four years of working in the evenings, during the weekends, and whenever her government job permitted, Carson published *Under the Sea-Wind* (1941). Although the book received excellent reviews, its publication was rather lost in the outrage over the bombing of Pearl Harbor and the entrance of the United States into World War II. Despite its dampening effect on the sales of her first book, the war effort not only provided Carson with a wealth of new information about the ocean but also provided the nation with many new pesticides that were developed as part of the research into chemical warfare.

As early as 1942, when she unsuccessfully proposed an article on the effects of the pesticide dichloro-diphenyl-trichloroethane (DDT) to *Reader's Digest* magazine, Carson was interested in the issues involving the use of untested pesticides. At this time in her life, however, she could not bring herself to believe that man's chemicals could fundamentally affect what she called the "stream of life" on the land, in the skies, or in the oceans. Thus, she returned to her first love—the sea—writing the lyrical and technically informative book, *The Sea Around Us*, published in 1951. One chapter, "The Birth of An Island," was published in 1950 in *The Yale Review* and won the George Westinghouse Science Writing Award. The book was enormously popular, winning the National Book Award in 1951 and the John Burroughs Medal in 1952 and remaining on the best-seller lists for more than a year. She was awarded a Guggenheim Fellowship, but returned the money after receiving substantial royalties from her best-selling book. Carson's resulting financial independence allowed her to resign from her government post and devote herself to her writing.

Just before the publication of *The Sea Around Us*, Carson had begun work on what originally was to be a field guide to the Atlantic shore, but later became *The Edge of the Sea* (1955), a careful, poetical portrayal of "the marginal world" between ocean and land. This book also became a best-seller and added to Carson's financial security as well as to her reputation as an author. These first three books contain themes that pervaded Carson's entire life: her belief that nothing in nature exists alone (for example, that all living things are interconnected by air and water) and her sense of what Albert Schweitzer called a "reverence for life," a phrase which she quoted often. These characteristics, together with her technical training and her expository gifts, made Carson the perfect person to write *Silent Spring*. Initially, Carson intended to write only an article on the effects of pesticides. The more studies she read, however, the more horrifying the picture became, finally driving her to relinquish her belief in the inviobility of the natural world. The widespread spraying of toxic chemicals (such as DDT) led to disastrous effects on wildlife and possible links with human diseases (such as cancer) which had not been thoroughly studied. These facts, together with the incomplete information from the chemical industry about its products and the ignorance of the American public about the effects of pesticides, convinced Carson that a book explaining these issues needed to be written.

In *Silent Spring*, Carson suggested that studies on long-term effects of pesticides needed to be conducted. She revealed documented evidence that showed a pattern of increasing concentrations of pesticides in higher animals. She conservatively combined the results of more than a thousand technical reports to form an unassailable foundation of documentation to support her alarming conclusions. At the same time, she beautifully encouraged love and respect for life in all of its forms. This feature of *Silent Spring*, together with her constructive suggestions for alleviating the damage already done, turned what could have been a doomsaying book into a hopeful guide to "the other road" (one of her chapter titles).

The publication of *Silent Spring* led to a national debate over the use of pesticides. Unable to discredit the scientific precision of the book, her opponents frequently misrepresented her positions, then attacked those misrepresentations as well as the author's scientific ability. Despite these attacks, the public outcry over *Silent Spring* led President John F. Kennedy to appoint a special commission charged with studying the pesticide controversy. This Science Advisory Committee eventually supported most of Carson's conclusions and duplicated many of her suggestions. Carson's work and her testimony before the United States Senate formed a large part of the impetus behind the formation of the Environmental Protection Agency (EPA) in 1970. Rachel Carson died of cancer and heart disease in 1964, approximately six years before the EPA opened its doors.

Summary

As the beloved author of three well-researched and beautifully written books about the sea, Rachel Carson was able to draw a large reading audience for her final book, *Silent Spring*; as a well-trained scientist who was able to consult with specialists in many fields, Carson was able to write with precision and confidence about the technical issues surrounding the use of pesticides; and as a gifted expositor, she was able to hold the audience's attention through understandable explanations and suggestions written in a graceful, impassioned style. Carson's well-documented book incited a national debate over the cavalier use of pesticides which led to the growth of the American environmental movement and the formation of the Environmental Protection Agency. Despite the passage of three decades, Carson's books were as readable in the 1990's as they were in the 1950's and 1960's because of her meticulous writing, which distinguished hypotheses and theories from demonstrated facts. The impact of Carson's *Silent Spring* on government, on industry, on everyday citizens, and, thus, on the natural world is unequalled in American history.

Bibliography
Brooks, Paul. *The House of Life: Rachel Carson at Work.* 2d ed. Boston: Houghton Mifflin, 1989. This biography of Rachel Carson and survey of her work was written by her editor. Based upon her private papers, Brooks's account is primarily made up of many wonderful samples of her writings, both public and private.
Gartner, Carol B. *Rachel Carson.* New York: Frederick Ungar, 1983. This readable discussion of Carson carefully blends her personal and public lives as well as providing a good bibliography for further reading.
Graham, Frank, Jr. *Since "Silent Spring."* Boston: Houghton Mifflin, 1970. This book provides an account of Carson's career and how she came to devote most of her energy during her final years to *Silent Spring.* The author also traces the progress of the pesticide controversy through the 1960's.
Hynes, H. Patricia. *The Recurring Silent Spring.* New York: Pergamon Press, 1989. This work focuses on *Silent Spring*, providing a brief but informative biography of Carson (elegantly refuting the "lonely spinster" stereotype) before discussing the impact and legacy of *Silent Spring* and the state of the American physical and social environment from Carson's time through the 1980's. A detailed bibliography is included.
McCay, Mary A. *Rachel Carson.* New York: Twayne, 1993. This excellent biography of Carson puts her major writings in the context of her personal development as a naturalist and analyzes her work as a part of the American naturalist tradition.
Marco, Gino J., Robert M. Hollingworth, and William Durham, eds. *Silent Spring Revisited.* Washington, D.C.: American Chemical Society, 1987. This collection of essays includes a summary of *Silent Spring*, as well as an essay about Carson's motives and the reaction to her book by a personal friend of Carson, in addition to eleven essays that explore the scientific, political, and environmental issues surrounding the use of pesticides.

Katherine Socha

MARY CASSATT

Born: May 22, 1844; Allegheny City, Pennsylvania
Died: June 14, 1926; Château de Beaufresne, France
Area of Achievement: Art
Contribution: As a painter and printmaker, Cassatt was a key member of the French Impressionist group.

Early Life

Born on May 22, 1844, Mary Stevenson Cassatt was the fourth of five surviving children of Robert Simpson and Katherine Kelso Cassatt. At the time of her birth, the family lived in Allegheny City (now a part of Pittsburgh), where her father served briefly as mayor. Robert Cassatt had achieved some financial success in real estate speculation and stock brokerage, but was too restless to remain long in any one business activity or location. In 1848, the family moved to Pittsburgh, leaving the following year for Philadelphia, and relocating in 1851 in Europe, where they settled first in Paris and later in Heidelberg and Darmstadt. During their four-year sojourn in Europe, the Cassatt children acquired a command of the French and German languages as well as a rather cosmopolitan culture. After the death of Mary's twelve-year-old brother, Robbie, in 1855, the family returned to Philadelphia, stopping in Paris to visit the Universal Exposition, which included a major exhibition of contemporary French art.

Upon reaching the minimum age of sixteen in 1861, Cassatt enrolled in the Pennsylvania Academy of the Fine Arts, where she attended classes for the next four years before deciding that her career goals required further study in Europe. Her father was at first dismayed by her determination to become a professional painter—she later recalled him saying "I would almost rather see you dead"—but after the initial shock, both parents offered her continuing support, moral as well as material.

At the beginning of 1866, Cassatt returned to Paris, where she studied with such fashionable French painters as Charles Chaplin, Jean-Leon Gérôme, and, later, Thomas Couture. She also copied old masters in the Louvre, and traveled the countryside, sketching scenery and searching for picturesque subjects. During the summer of 1870, she spent time studying in Rome. Her first submission to the Paris Salon in 1867 was rejected, but in 1868 and again in 1870 she had paintings accepted for this prestigious exhibition.

The outbreak of the Franco-Prussian War in 1870 sent Cassatt back to Pennsylvania, but not for long. She had difficulty selling her work in the United States and missed the inspiration of the great European museums. A commission from the Catholic bishop of Pittsburgh to copy two paintings by the sixteenth century Italian master, Correggio, for his new cathedral provided her a means to return to Europe. She spent eight months in Parma, Italy, in 1872, working on her copies and developing a profound admiration for Correggio before moving on to Spain. Her letters from Spain reflect her enthusiasm for the realism and brilliant execution of the Spanish painters, especially Velázquez. Cassatt's nomadic existence continued with extended stays in Antwerp and Rome, always involving study of the local artistic masterpieces, until she finally settled in Paris in 1874. By this time, Cassatt was receiving a degree of recognition in her adopted city: Her entries to the Paris Salon were accepted four years in a row, from 1873 to 1876. She was dissatisfied with the prevailing academic style, however, and was casting about for alternatives.

Life's Work

In 1875, upon her return from a summer visit to her family in Philadelphia, Mary Cassatt noticed some pastels by Edgar Degas, a leader of an emerging group labeled "Impressionists," in a dealer's window. Forty years later she recalled their impact: "I used to go and flatten my nose against that window and absorb all I could of his art. It changed my life."

Meanwhile, Degas had also become aware of Cassatt. On seeing her painting, *Ida*, on display at the 1874 Salon, he is said to have remarked, "Here is someone who feels as I do." In 1877, Degas invited Cassatt to exhibit with the Impressionists, or, to use the term they both preferred, the "Independents." Cassatt recalled that she accepted with joy and added: "I began to live."

The influence of her new associates could be seen in a painting of 1878, *Little Girl in a Blue Armchair*, which was more daring in its composition and viewpoint than any of her earlier works, too daring, in fact, for the jury of the American section of the Universal Exposition, which rejected it.

A portrait of her sister, Lydia, was one of eleven paintings and pastels shown by Cassatt in the fourth Impressionist exhibition in 1879, the first in which she partici- pated. Its light tonality and vibrant brush strokes demonstrate her affinity with the group.

In 1877, Cassatt's parents and Lydia had come to live with her in Paris, and her mother and sister, until the latter's death in 1882, were among her favorite models. Her two brothers and their growing families also visited regularly, and Cassatt's portraits of her nephews and nieces gave her practice in an area that was to become a specialty—the representation of children. Eager to promote the artistic efforts of her friends and colleagues, Cassatt tried to steer her brothers toward the purchase of contemporary French art. Particularly through her older brother, Alexander, a success- ful businessman who eventually became president of the Pennsylvania Railroad, she was able to introduce some Impressionist painting to American viewers. By far her most important contribution to American patronage, however, was through her long and close friendship with Louisine and Henry Havermeyer, whom she constantly guided and encouraged in their acquisition of an extraordinary collection of French and Spanish art, the bulk of which resides in the Metropolitan Museum in New York.

In the 1880's, Cassatt participated in three more exhibitions of the Impressionist group and in a show of Impressionist paintings in New York organized in 1886 by the dealer Durand-Ruel. She chose, however, to boycott the Seventh Impressionist Exhi- bition held in 1882, along with Degas. The close professional association of the two artists has inevitably given rise to speculation about the possibility of a romantic liaison, although most biographers regard this as unlikely. He did, however, produce some elegant studies of her in the Louvre and at the milliner's shop; they admired and bought each other's work; and, in the early 1880's, they collaborated on a projected print journal to be called *Le Jour et la nuit*. The journal never materialized, but the plan stimulated Cassatt's experimentation in this media.

A major influence on her printmaking was a show of Japanese woodblock prints in Paris in 1890. Cassatt was enthusiastic and responded with a set of ten color prints that reflect the simple linear patterns and decorative effects of her models. The following year these prints were the core of a highly successful solo exhibition, her first, where they were shown with pastels and paintings of mothers with babies. The mother-and-child theme was one that she had explored sporadically since 1880 and it was to play an increasingly important role in her later art.

Cassatt received an important public commission in 1892, an invitation to paint a mural on the subject of "modern woman" for the Woman's Building of the World's Columbian Exposition to be held in Chicago in 1893. The project reflected her own feminist sentiments and she undertook it with enthusiasm, but her experience had not prepared her to work on a monumental scale (the mural was fifty feet across) or in an allegorical mode. The painting was not well received and disappeared after the end of the Exposition.

Throughout the 1890's and the first years of the twentieth century, Cassatt was active and highly productive. She traveled extensively, including trips to Spain, Italy, and Egypt as well as two more visits to the United States. She was also increasingly honored. In 1904, she was named a Chevalier of the Legion of Honor by the French government, and in the same year one of her paintings, *The Caress*, won awards from her alma mater, the Pennsylvania Academy of the Fine Arts, and from the Chicago Art Institute. Characteristically, though, she turned down both prizes, explaining that she must be true to the principles of the Independents (Impressionists)—"no jury, no medals, no awards." Ten years later, however, she did accept a Gold Medal of Honor from the Pennsylvania Academy. Major museums in Europe and the United States began acquiring her work, and, in 1914, a monograph was published in French on her career.

These years of public recognition were also marked by private bereavement over the deaths of her parents in the 1890's and of her two brothers in the following decade. Her eyesight gradually began to fail as a result of cataracts; after 1915, she was no longer able to paint. She continued, however, to take an active interest in art and politics. In 1915, she was one of the organizers, along with Louisine Havermeyer, of an exhibition of her own art and that of Degas to benefit the cause of woman suffrage. Cassatt died, almost blind, at her French country home in 1926.

Summary

Mary Cassatt was the first American woman to gain international recognition in painting and printmaking. Her reputation, already well established in her lifetime, has continued to grow in recent years. Moreover, she was not only a woman painter but also a painter of women. Her works celebrate the daily lives of middle-class women, but often she presents them in somewhat unaccustomed roles. They read newspapers and go unaccompanied to the opera, where they return the gaze of male spectators; in one painting, a young lady drives a pony cart while a groom sits idly nearby.

Although she did not experience it herself, Cassatt viewed maternity as a woman's chief vocation, and the theme of mother and child plays an increasing role in her later career. She renders this motif with intimacy, honesty, and surprising variety: Her images range from casual, naturalistic scenes to compositions with symbolist overtones recalling the great art historical tradition of the Madonna and Child.

Cassatt also played a significant role in encouraging American patronage of art, both that of her Impressionist colleagues and of earlier, then undervalued masters such as El Greco and Gustave Courbet and thus she enriched American artistic culture.

Bibliography
Breeskin, Adelyn. *Mary Cassatt: A Catalogue Raisonné of the Graphic Work*. 2d rev. ed. Washington, D.C.: Smithsonian Institution Press, 1979. A complete catalog, with illustrations both black and white and color, of all Cassatt's work in various print media. Includes biographical introduction, a description of technical methods used by the artist, and chronology.

_____ . *Mary Cassatt: A Catalogue Raisonné of the Oils, Pastels, Watercolors and Drawings*. Washington, D.C.: Smithsonian Institution Press, 1970. A scholarly catalog of more than nine hundred of Cassatt's works with mostly black and white illustrations. Includes brief introduction, index and, chronology.

Getlein, Frank. *Mary Cassatt: Paintings and Prints*. New York: Abbeville Press, 1980. Color illustrations of a selection of Cassatt works with interesting commentaries.

Hale, Nancy. *Mary Cassatt*. Garden City, N.Y.: Doubleday, 1975. A popular biography with emphasis on human relations and psychological interpretation. Black-and-white illustrations and index.

Mathews, Nancy Mowll, ed. *Cassatt and Her Circle: Selected Letters*. New York: Abbeville Press, 1984. Contains more than two hundred letters from Cassatt herself, as well as her family and friends. Provides invaluable source material on her life and milieu. Letters are divided into periods, each with a brief biographical summary. Also includes black and white illustrations, chronology and index.

_____ . *Mary Cassatt: A Life*. New York: Villard, 1994. Mathews, an art historian, presents a compelling portrait of Cassatt as a brilliant, outspoken, and single-minded woman who devoted her life to the attainment of high artistic goals.

Pollock, Griselda. *Mary Cassatt*. New York: Harper & Row, 1980. A fairly brief discussion of Cassatt's career from an explicitly feminist perspective, followed by commentary on individual works. Illustrated in color and black and white. Includes chronology.

Sweet, Frederick A. *Miss Mary Cassatt, Impressionist from Pennsylvania*. Norman: University of Oklahoma Press, 1966. An early, somewhat uncritical, but thorough and reliable biography. Sweet was one of the first biographers to have wide access to letters belonging to Cassatt, her family, and her colleagues. Includes black-and-white illustrations and index.

Yeh, Susan Fillin. "Mary Cassatt's Images of Women." *Art Journal* 35 (Summer, 1976): 359-363. A discussion of Cassatt's innovative approach both to the representation of women and to the mother-and-child theme.

Jane Kristof

IRENE CASTLE

Born: April 7, 1893; New Rochelle, New York
Died: January 25, 1969; Eureka Springs, Arkansas
Area of Achievement: Dance
Contribution: A famous ballroom dancer known for her refined style and elegant fashions, Irene Castle popularized ballroom dancing in the second decade of the twentieth century. She also made several silent motion pictures and was an activist in protecting animals from abuse.

Early Life

Born April 7, 1893, Irene Foote was the second daughter of Annie Elroy Thomas and Hubert Townsend Foote. Irene grew up a privileged and pampered child playing amid the rural surroundings of her parents' thirty-five-acre estate in New Rochelle, New York. Hubert Foote was a wealthy medical doctor who specialized in herbal cures, and Annie Foote was an active, emancipated woman. Educated in Europe, Annie spoke fluent French and German and was an advocate of birth control and equal rights for women. She shot a rifle and rode and jumped her own horses with the same skill and flair that she planned and executed lavish entertainments for her family and friends. Irene admired her energetic mother tremendously. Annie Foote's bold action in having her hair cut short at a time when long hair was considered a woman's crowning glory particularly impressed the young Irene.

Irene was educated at St. Mary's Episcopal Convent School in Peekskill, New York, and later she attended the National Park Seminary, a finishing school for wealthy young girls near Washington, D.C. In addition to her regular studies, she was a member of the swim team. For convenience, and probably inspired by her mother's example, Irene cut her hair short. She created a commotion, however, when her classmates followed her example. As boarding school students, Irene and her older sister Elroy were able to continue their education while their parents spent winters in Mexico nursing Hubert Foote's tuberculosis. Irene reveled in the summers when the entire family was reunited in New Rochelle. The town had become a summer resort for New York's theater set. Irene enjoyed singing and dancing herself and appeared in many local theatrical productions. Her mother supported these efforts, even arranging an unproductive meeting with a relative in New York City who was connected with the theater.

During the summer of 1910, Irene met her future husband, Vernon Castle, a Broadway entertainer who was vacationing in New Rochelle. Irene was fascinated by the British-born Castle, who was six years her senior. As the months passed, the two spent considerable time together, and soon Vernon arranged an audition for Irene in New York. As a result she was given a dancing part in the road company of *The Midnight Sons*. Her parents did not allow the seventeen-year-old Irene to join the tour. When the Footes left for Mexico that winter, however, Irene and her sister were permitted to take an apartment in New York City.

Life's Work

Irene Foote spent her time in New York trying to get established in the theater and seeing a lot of Vernon Castle. He got her a part in the musical *The Summer Widowers* in 1910 and proposed to her that Christmas. They were married May 28, 1911, and honeymooned in England. Upon their return to New York, they were both cast in the musical comedy *The Henpecks* (1911), but Vernon's role was that of a slapstick comedian rather than a dancer.

When he was offered a job in Paris playing essentially the same part, Vernon took it even though both he and Irene preferred to dance. In *Enfin . . . une Revue* (1912), Vernon's comedy routine was a failure. Fortunately, the producers had included a dance number featuring Irene and Vernon Castle that was so successful it launched their dancing career. Soon the Castles were hired as dancers at an elegant supper club known as the Café de Paris.

As a performer, Irene was extremely fashion conscious. Aware that she was unable to compete with the extravagantly gowned and bejeweled guests, Irene decided to use that contrast to her advantage. She wore softly flowing gowns with simple elegant lines accompanied by a minimum of jewelry. On opening night, she chose to dance in her crepe de chine wedding dress and her only adornment was a single bar pin holding up the train of the dress for ease of movement.

Irene and Vernon's graceful and sophisticated performances were also different from the usual cabaret fare. The popularity of ragtime in the United States had spread to Europe, but the Castles modified that style's bouncing energetic animal dances such as the grizzly bear, turkey trot, bunny hug, and camel walk with their own swift yet smooth movements. Soon it was the Castle's dancing style that was being imitated. Another technique of the Castles that was later often copied was their strategy of beginning their performance by rising from a table at the supper club as if they were guests.

Becoming more and more popular, Irene and Vernon Castle were entertained by the rich and famous. Irene, however, decided to maintain her simple but elegant costumes. Her designs for her own dancing dresses were soon duplicated by the European fashion houses.

In 1912, Irene's father died and she and Vernon returned to New York City, where they started dancing at the Café de l'Opéra. They also entertained at wealthy clients' private parties. In addition they both appeared briefly in the Victor Herbert musical *The Lady of the Slipper* in Philadelphia and then performed in *The Sunshine Girl* on Broadway in 1913.

That same year Irene and Vernon Castle invented the Castle Walk, an innovative skipping dance step that became an immediate hit. By this time, the United States was fully involved in a dance craze, and a debate raged about the merits of dance itself. Supporters opened dance parlors across the country while detractors went so far as to say dancing was sinful. The tango was particularly targeted as being sensual and erotic and as encouraging lax morals. Irene and Vernon Castle were never embroiled in the debate. As a married couple known for their wholesome image and elegant style, the

Castles were considered above reproach and were acceptable to both sides of the dance debate. They enjoyed themselves when they danced and made others want to join in the fun. While they included innovative dips, twirls, bends, and lifts in their routines, their dancing always appeared elegant and refined. Irene and Vernon opened the Castle School of Dance to teach their techniques to others and soon expanded that successful endeavor into a posh dance palace called Castle House in New York City. In 1914, they wrote *Modern Dancing*, a book that included not only dance instructions but also their philosophy about dancing as well.

The Castles were extraordinarily successful and parlayed this success into operating a series of dance clubs and restaurants. The highest paid ballroom dancers in the United States, they opened their own restaurant with dance floor, the Sans Souci, in New York City. After it closed, they owned and operated Castles in the Air, another restaurant with dance floor on the roof of the Forty-fourth Street Theater in New York; the Castle Club, in the basement of the same building; and Castles by the Sea, a nightclub at Long Beach, on Long Island.

As a celebrity who introduced new fashion innovations by designing clothes to suit her way of life, Irene influenced countless others through her actions. When she appeared corsetless in loose flowing gowns of chiffon and silk, women found new freedom in similar styles. When she cut her hair short before going into the hospital for an appendectomy, her new style made the headlines. After she began wearing a band across her forehead to keep her fine hair in place, another new look was established as Castle Bands appeared everywhere. When she had her hair curled, Castle Bobs became popular.

In 1914, the Castles conducted a nationwide tour and dance contest that ended in a championship event in Madison Square Garden. They also danced in Irving Berlin's first complete Broadway musical, *Watch Your Step* (1914), in roles written specially for them.

Throughout their careers both Irene and Vernon Castle were concerned about the abuse of animals that occurred in theatrical and motion picture productions. Whenever possible they purchased the victimized animals, finding good homes for them later. After they had achieved star status, they had a clause put in their contracts stating that they would not appear in any production with animal acts.

In 1915, the Castles made the silent film *The Whirl of Life*, which was based loosely on their lives. Vernon enlisted as a pilot in the British Royal Flying Corps and fought in World War I. Meanwhile Irene was elected most popular motion picture actress in 1916 according to publicity that was in large part a promotion for her starring role in the silent serial *Patria* (1917). She also danced in Florenz Ziegfeld's Broadway revue *Miss 1917*.

Vernon Castle died in a plane crash in 1918 in Texas, where he was helping to train Canadian pilots. After his death, Irene worked feverishly making several silent pictures in rapid succession: *The Hillcrest Mystery*, *The Amateur Wife*, and *Convict 993* in 1918; *The Firing Line* and *The Invisible Bond* in 1919; *The Broadway Bride* (1921); *French Heels*, *No Trespassing*, and *Slim Shoulders* in 1922; and *Broadway*

After Dark (1924). She remarried three times: in 1919 to Robert Treman; in 1923 to Frederic McLaughlin, with whom she had three children (Barbara, born in 1925; Michael, who died at birth in 1926; and William, born in 1929); and in 1946 to George Enzinger.

Irene took a new dancing partner, Billy Reardon, toured, and even lectured occasionally, but her most important work later in life was the founding of Orphans of the Storm, an animal shelter in Chicago. She became active in exposing animal abuse of all kinds and often testified in court.

In 1939, Fred Astaire and Ginger Rogers starred in the film *The Story of Vernon and Irene Castle* based on two works by Irene, "My Friend" and "My Memories of Vernon Castle." Irene also served as the film's technical adviser. In ill health during her later years, Irene Castle died in 1969 at the age of seventy-five.

Summary

Irene Castle's work in silent films was not memorable, but her influence on modern social dance was extraordinary. With her dancing partner and husband Vernon Castle, she not only popularized ballroom dancing but also made it a respectable and enjoyable form of recreation. The Castles introduced new dance steps that were widely copied, changing the focus of dance from formal intricate routines to graceful, rhythmical movements. Irene also liberated American and European women from the confines of hobble skirts and corsets with her elegant flowing fashion designs. Her short hair created a new stylish female image. In addition Irene Castle was an animal activist who exposed animal abuse of all kinds and fought for strong laws for the humane treatment of animals.

Bibliography

Castle, Irene. *Castles in the Air*. Garden City, N.Y.: Doubleday, 1958. Reprint. New York: Da Capo Press, 1980. Written by Castle when she was sixty-five years old, this autobiography not only reveals her feelings about her family and career but also gives intimate details about many of the famous and powerful people with whom she interacted. Liberally illustrated, many of the photographs show Irene in her elegant fashions. An index is lacking, however.

——————————, and Vernon Castle. *Modern Dancing*. New York: Harper and Brothers, 1914. This book explains how to perform specific dances popularized by the Castles. It is, however, more than a dance instruction manual and includes philosophical essays revealing the Castles' attitudes toward the subject of dance.

Jasen, David A. *Tin Pan Alley: The Composers, the Songs, the Performers, and Their Times: The Golden Age of American Popular Music from 1886 to 1956*. New York: Donald I. Fine, 1988. An excellent background work that provides a musical perspective of the period when Irene Castle was most popular. A summary of her career, index, four-page bibliography, and many illustrations are included.

Kendall, Elizabeth. *Where She Danced*. New York: Alfred A. Knopf, 1979. An important overview of the history of dance in the United States with a thorough explanation of the tremendous influence of Irene Castle on both the worlds of dance and fashion and an analysis of their interrelationship. Includes an index, bibliography, and selected illustrations.

Shaw, Arnold. *Black Popular Music in America: From the Spirituals, Minstrels, and Ragtime to Soul, Disco, and Hip-Hop.* New York: Schirmer Books, 1986. A thorough analysis of the history of African American music with details about James Reese Europe, the Castles' famous black musical director and composer. Includes an index, a sixty-five-page bibliography, and a dance dictionary.

Virgilio, Carmela L. "Irene and Vernon Castle: Their Contribution to Social Dance in America." *The Journal of Physical Education and Recreation* 51 (September, 1980): 67. A well-documented article analyzing the Castles' dance innovations and their influence on particular dances such as the waltz and the tango.

Judith A. Oliver

WILLA CATHER

Born: December 7, 1873; Back Creek Valley, near Gore, Virginia
Died: April 24, 1947; New York, New York
Areas of Achievement: Literature and journalism
Contribution: A major American writer of the early twentieth century, Cather wrote
novels, short stories, poetry, and critical reviews.

Early Life
Willa Sibert Cather was born on December 7, 1873, in Back Creek Valley, Virginia,
to Charles Fectique Cather and Virginia Boak Cather. Willa, christened Wilella, was
the eldest of seven children. In 1874, the Cathers moved to Willow Shades, Virginia,
to Willa's grandfather's sheep farm, and in 1883, the family moved again to homestead in Webster County in Nebraska. A year later, the Cathers moved to Red Cloud,
Nebraska, where Charles Cather worked with farm loans and mortgages.

According to biographer James Woodress, Cather attended a rural grade school. In
contrast, Cather herself, in an autobiography written in third person and published by
Houghton Mifflin in 1915, claims she was educated at home until high school, that it
was her maternal grandmother, Rachel Boak, who taught Cather to read. Records
support Woodress' account. In fact, both Cather and her intimate friend Edith Lewis
often changed the facts of Cather's life, probably because of Cather's intense desire
for privacy. (For example, Cather insisted she was born in 1876, even though her birth
records indicate otherwise.) Accounts agree that Cather attended high school in Red
Cloud.

Critics focusing on gender issues in literature have emphasized a four-year span in
Cather's late teenage years when she cut her hair short, wore mannish clothing, and
referred to herself as William Cather. During those years, she was deeply interested
in science.

Throughout her life, Cather was an avid reader. As a youth, she read from the Bible,
Homer, Virgil, and *Pilgrim's Progress.* In high school, Cather read the fiction of
Rudyard Kipling and Robert Louis Stevenson. Later, Cather read from Leo Tolstoy
and French writers such as Honoré de Balzac, Gustave Flaubert, and Alphonse
Daudet. She had a particular passion for French literature, and was said to have hung
George Sand's portrait over her mantel. These authors, including Sand, provided little
in the way of models for women narrators for Cather's distinctly American fiction,
and even through Cather's university years, Cather was skeptical of women writers.

Intending to study science and become a doctor, Cather enrolled in the University
of Nebraska. Once there, however, she moved toward the study of journalism after her
essay on Thomas Carlyle was published.

Life's Work
Willa Cather's career as a writer began in March of 1891 at the University of
Nebraska, Lincoln, with the publication of her essay on Thomas Carlyle. With her

energy turned from science to journalism, Cather began writing and studying languages. In 1892, her first work of fiction, a short story entitled "Peter," was published. In 1893, Cather began writing a column for the _Nebraska State Journal_. By 1895, when she was graduated, Cather was a short story writer and a part-time journalist. From 1895 until 1906, Cather lived in Pittsburgh, Pennsylvania, where she worked as a journalist and as a teacher and a principal at two high schools. In 1903, Cather's first book of poems, _April Twilights_, was published, and, in 1905, Cather's first book of short stories, _The Troll Garden_, was published. In 1911, at the age of thirty-six, Cather completed her first novel, _Alexander's Bridge_ (1912).

Throughout the years of Cather's career, several significant friendships, all with women, profoundly influenced her. In 1908, Cather finally met the woman who was to serve as her literary mentor: Sarah Orne Jewett. It was a 1908 letter from Jewett to Cather that encouraged the young author to focus on her art, to be a solitary individual, and to maintain a wide outlook on the world. Jewett died in 1909 while Cather was on assignment in England for _McClure's Magazine_, and Cather paid tribute to Jewett's influence by editing a collection of her fiction in the 1920's. Other important influences were her friendships with Isabelle McClung and Edith Lewis.

Cather met McClung in 1899, when Cather was a member of the Pittsburgh _Leader_. They made several trips together, one to Europe in 1902. Cather lived in the McClung household at various times and did some of her writing there. When McClung became engaged, to Jan Hambourg, a violinist, Cather was devastated. Still, their friendship lasted until McClung-Hambourg's death in 1938.

Cather met Edith Lewis, a graduate of Smith College, in 1903. In 1906, when Cather began working for _McClure's_ in New York, she moved in with Lewis in Greenwich Village. In 1912, Cather and Lewis rented an apartment that they shared for the next fourteen years, and, in 1925, they built Whale Cove Cottage together. Lewis, who survived Cather, honored her wish for privacy. Even before Cather's death in 1947, Lewis helped Cather destroy her personal correspondence, and after Cather's death, Lewis, who was Cather's primary heir and executor, burned the bulk of her remaining correspondence. Lewis and Elizabeth Shepley Sergeant, another of Cather's close friends, each wrote a memoir of Cather. Although both memoirs are worth reading, the information they contain is not always accurate. Lewis, in particular, avoids the personal and focuses strictly on Cather's career. Lewis died in 1972 and was buried at the foot of Cather's grave.

In literary criticism of Cather's work, much as been made of the year 1922, a year Cather claimed was about the time that "the world broke in two." Perhaps her feelings stemmed from post-World War I politics and culture. Certainly war was on her mind. In fact, 1922 was the year that _One of Ours_, Cather's only war novel, was published. Cather was also experiencing a spiritual rebirth in 1922. That was the year that Cather joined the Episcopalian Church. Whatever the significance of 1922, the 1920's was Cather's most productive decade. She produced six novels and a book of short stories, and she edited and reissued a book of her poetry.

By the early 1920's, Cather's fiction was receiving literary acclaim. In 1923, she received the Pulitzer Prize for *One of Ours*, a war story that focuses both on civilian life, in the United States and in France, and on front-line action in France. While many critics were indignant that a woman would write a war story, critical support for the novel became increasingly stronger. In 1930, Cather won the Gold Medal award of the American Academy of Arts and Letters for her novel *Death Comes to the Archbishop*, an experimental "narrative" (as Cather called it) depicting the experiences of Father Latour, a French missionary. In 1933, Cather became the first recipient of the French Prix Femina Américaín award for her novel *Shadows on the Rock* (1931). This novel, set in Quebec, recounts the story of Jeanne Le Ber, a recluse nun, who never participates in the novel except as a narrative to sustain Cécile through the harsh winter. In 1944, the year of her last public appearance, Cather received a gold medal from the National Institute of Arts and Letters. In addition, Cather received honorary degrees, one from Yale and another from Princeton, where she was the first woman to receive the honor.

Cather's link to women's issues of the time, especially in her early years, was nebulous. According to Jamie Ambrose, in her biography *Willa Cather: Writing at the Frontier*, Cather had a low opinion of the suffragists. She also had a low opinion of writing by women. In 1895, in a discussion of Christina Rossetti and of women poets in general, Cather questioned "whether women have any place in poetry at all." She believed that most poetry by women was ineffectively emotional. In fiction, she said that she liked the Georges (Sand and Eliot) but that they were anything but women. Nevertheless, throughout Cather's fiction, the complexities of gender relations are repeatedly explored.

Susan J. Rosowski, in her essay "Willa Cather's Subverted Endings," contends that, despite the linear pattern of Cather's fiction, a pattern "emblematic of a traditional and often patriarchal social order," the endings of Cather's novels often posit "alternatives to tradition by creating a new and often female order." To illustrate her contention, Rosowski cites such novels as *Alexander's Bridge* (1912), *A Lost Lady* (1923), and *O Pioneers!* (1913). The first of these examples, *Alexander's Bridge*, focuses on the breakdown of Bartley Alexander, a world-renowned engineer drawn simultaneously to two women, who symbolize opposing feminine principles. One principle is that of civilization and order, represented by Winifred, Alexander's wife. The other principle is that of passion, represented by Hilda Burgoyne, Alexander's younger lover. Alexander is torn apart by the conflict. As Alexander drowns, it is, however, Winifred that he thinks of. After Alexander's death, Winifred remains in their home in Boston, while Hilda, with a sense of ending, stays on in London. In the second example, *A Lost Lady*, Marian Forrester refuses "to immolate herself on the funeral pyre," a clear break with feminine tradition. In the final example, *O Pioneers!*, Rosowski cites the nontraditional marriage between Alexandra and the youthful, sensitive Carl Linstrum, a marriage in which Alexandra belongs not to Carl but— more than ever—to the land. Cather's men, those unlike Carl Linstrum, are undone by linearity, undeveloped imaginations, and competitiveness.

Summary

Willa Cather has earned her place as a great twentieth century American writer. Her work includes at least twenty-four of her own books. In addition, Cather edited anthologies, including one of the writing of Sarah Orne Jewett, and wrote columns and short stories for various magazines. Though her novels (fourteen in all) have won her the most acclaim, she also leaves a body of short fiction, poetry, critical writing, and other essays. Such success is enough to hold her a place in American literature.

Yet Cather also has a position specifically in women's history. As one critic has pointed out, Cather establishes a new feminine order in her fictional conclusions. Cather's women have new roles, new options, that break with the options of women in fiction written by men. Cather, through her characters, explores gender issues, human passion, and human possibilities.

Cather looked with a critical eye at the writing of women, and sometimes she found their fiction and poetry wanting. For Cather's fictional women, however, she created better worlds, ones with complexity, with options, and with possibilities. Cather's vision of possibilities for women is probably her most significant contribution to the history of American women.

Bibliography

Ambrose, Jamie. *Willa Cather: Writing at the Frontier.* New York: St. Martin's Press, 1988. A biography written by a "single woman making [her] way in the world through writing," this book takes a close look at Cather's similar situation. Well documented, the work has notes, a bibliography, illustrations, a chronology, and an index.

Lee, Hermione. *Willa Cather: Double Lives.* New York: Pantheon, 1990. An analysis of Cather and her fiction, this book weaves together close readings of Cather's fiction and biographical material in order to illuminate the major themes and literary technique found in her works. Devotes significant attention to Cather's childhood and adolescence.

O'Brien, Sharon. *Willa Cather: The Emerging Voice.* New York: Oxford University Press, 1987. O'Brien combines biographical and literary analysis in her approach to Cather's work. She focuses particularly on Cather's relationships with women, both in Cather's life and in Cather's fiction. Contains illustrations and an index.

Rosowski, Susan J., ed. *Cather Studies: Volume 1.* Lincoln: University of Nebraska Press, 1990. This volume (189 pages with an index) contains twelve essays and covers such topics as literary influences on Cather's work, critical analyses of her work, and biographical discussion.

Woodress, James. *Willa Cather: A Literary Life.* Lincoln: University of Nebraska Press, 1987. Woodress' comprehensive biography (583 pages) covers Cather and her literary career. The book is illustrated and contains a prologue, epilogue, notes, and index. No chronology is included.

Carol Franks

CARRIE CHAPMAN CATT

Born: February 9, 1859; Ripon, Wisconsin
Died: March 9, 1947; New Rochelle, New York
Area of Achievement: Women's rights
Contribution: Recognized as one of the ablest leaders and organizers of the woman suffrage movement, Carrie Chapman Catt brought new life to a faltering National American Woman Suffrage Association (NAWSA) and designed the campaign which won the federal vote for women.

Early Life

Carrie Lane, the second of three children, was born on February 9, 1859, in Ripon, Wisconsin. Her parents, Maria Clinton and Lucius Lane, originally from the state of New York, had come west to live as farmers. In 1866, lured farther west by the Gold Rush, the family moved to Charles City, Iowa, where they remained throughout Carrie's adolescence.

Maria Lane had attended a woman's school, Oread Collegiate Institute, in Massachusetts. She encouraged her daughter to continue her studies beyond high school. Carrie entered Iowa State Agricultural College in March, 1877, and graduated in November, 1880, the only woman in her graduating class. During her college career, she supported herself by teaching, washing dishes, and working in the school library. After college, Carrie worked first as a law clerk and then as a schoolteacher in Mason City, Iowa. In 1883, she was appointed superintendent of schools, a post which she resigned in 1885, in order to marry Leo Chapman, editor of the *Mason City Republican.*

Like his new wife, Leo Chapman was highly interested in political reform and used his position at the paper to push for social change. When a local Republican candidate sued him for libel, Leo Chapman went to California to look for new employment opportunities. In 1886, Carrie was notified that Leo was ill with typhoid fever. She left Iowa to go to him, but while she was en route to California, she was notified that he had died.

Carrie Chapman decided to settle in San Francisco, where she earned a barely adequate living through freelance journalism. The following year, she encountered George Catt, a fellow student at Iowa State. He encouraged her to become a public lecturer. She returned home to Charles City in 1887, working as a professional lecturer and the temporary editor of the *Floyd County Advocate.*

Life's Work

Upon returning to Iowa, Carrie Chapman joined the Women's Christian Temperance Union (WCTU), the antialcohol, prosuffrage organization run by Frances Willard. The issue of woman suffrage increasingly interested Carrie; in 1889, she was elected secretary of the Iowa Woman Suffrage Association. In 1890, she spoke at the convention of the newly merged National-American Woman Suffrage Association

(NAWSA), held in Washington, D.C. In June of that year, she moved to Seattle, Washington, to marry George Catt.

A few months later, Carrie Chapman Catt went to South Dakota to work for a state referendum for woman suffrage, traveling throughout the eastern part of the state to speak. Although the campaign was unsuccessful, Catt gained valuable experience and began to be touted as a leading figure in the suffrage movement.

In 1892, Catt again attended the NAWSA convention in Washington, D.C., where Susan B. Anthony asked her to speak before Congress on the proposed suffrage amendment. After she and her husband moved to Bensonhurst, New York, Catt became more active and worked more closely with Anthony and other leaders of the suffrage movement. At the World Columbian Exposition in Chicago in 1893, Catt was approached about campaigning in support of a state suffrage amendment in Colorado. Initially reluctant, she agreed and was instrumental in making Colorado the second state to allow women to vote, on November 7, 1893.

Throughout the next decade, Carrie used her superlative organizational skills to establish political equality clubs, make speeches, and raise money for the suffrage movement. She headed the organizational committee within the NAWSA, which worked to coordinate suffrage campaigns throughout the United States and to educate women about suffrage.

When Anthony stepped down as president of the NAWSA in 1900, she chose Catt as her successor, citing her ingenuity and political sagacity. Catt served as president of the NAWSA for the next four years. During her tenure, she worked to raise money, increase enrollment, and establish links between the NAWSA and the International Council of Women, as well as the International Woman Suffrage Alliance. In 1904, she resigned her NAWSA presidency in order to care for her ailing husband. She became vice president at large under the organization's new president, Anna Howard Shaw.

On October 8, 1905, George Catt died of a perforated duodenal ulcer. The death of Susan B. Anthony in February, 1906, further shattered the grief-stricken Carrie. Concerned for her health, Carrie's friends and doctor urged her to travel, and she spent much of her time for the following nine years abroad, working with the International Woman Suffrage Alliance to promote woman suffrage around the globe.

Carrie Chapman Catt's international efforts helped make her even more well known at home, and she became recognized as a world leader in the suffrage movement. In 1914, she turned her attention to New York state, believing that if it passed a suffrage amendment, other states would soon follow suit. She toured the state, making numerous speeches and appearances. That same year, Mrs. Frank Leslie, a publisher's widow, died and left an estate worth more than $900,000 to Catt to use as she saw fit to promote woman suffrage. Because of legal difficulties arising from suits filed by Leslie's relatives, who hotly contested the will, Catt did not receive the legacy until 1917, when she used it to set up the Leslie Woman Suffrage Commission.

In 1915, Shaw announced her resignation as president of the NAWSA. The organization's members turned to Catt, asking her to resume the presidency. She resisted their request until she was promised a free hand in governing the organization. Then she accepted the presidency and proceeded to make the NAWSA the most powerful woman's organization in the history of the United States.

Following Anthony's example, Catt refused to allow the NAWSA to work on any cause other than suffrage, realizing that a single goal would unify the organization and allow it to use its energy and resources more effectively. Her "Winning Plan," put before the NAWSA in 1916, was to push for congressional passage of the suffrage amendment to the U.S. Constitution, rather than work on the slow process of getting the vote state by state. She proposed a campaign that would encompass every state, saying that each organization must run "a red-hot, never-ceasing campaign."

Catt's plan was hindered by divisions within the suffrage movement. Some of the movement's more radical members broke off to form the Congressional Union (later known as the National Woman's Party), headed by Alice Paul. Catt believed that the radical tactics adopted by such groups alienated the public and harmed the suffrage cause far more than they helped it. Another impediment to her goal was the inevitable involvement of the United States in World War I. Some suffragists, including Catt, were open advocates of peace, an unpopular premise in a country gearing itself for military action. Nevertheless, when diplomatic relations were broken with Germany in 1917, Catt and the NAWSA drafted a letter saying they would stand by the government in case of war. This act drew more criticism of Catt than anything else she had ever done. Despite her personal inclinations as a pacifist, Catt believed that getting women the vote must take precedence, and she would not let the peace activists stand in its way.

In designing her strategy, Catt took the Republican and Democratic parties as her model, knowing that the NAWSA could challenge these institutions only if it worked along the same principles. She wanted to establish a well-organized network that could affect public opinion in every state. Under her guidance, the NAWSA worked tirelessly to set up such a network and to educate the public about the importance of woman suffrage, distributing pamphlets, buttons, flyers, leaflets, posters, and even playing cards. The NAWSA purchased the popular suffrage newspaper *Woman's Journal*, renamed it *Woman Citizen*, and used it to spread even more information.

On January 10, 1918, the House of Representatives passed the suffrage amendment. Jubilant suffragists sang on their way out of the Capitol, and the Congressional Union threw down their picket signs. The Senate delayed their vote on the suffrage amendment for ten months, eventually voting it down on October 1. Catt and her supporters refused to give up hope, insisting that votes for women were just around the corner. Rallying her organization, Catt plunged into another year of intensive campaigning.

In 1919, both the House and the Senate passed the Nineteenth Amendment, paving the way for state ratification. Catt sent telegrams to the state governors, urging them to call immediate special sessions for ratification of the amendment. She also notified the women's organizations in each state to prepare themselves for the last desperate push. That fall, she went west on her "Wake up America" tour to drum up support for the amendment. On August 20, 1920, Secretary of State Bainbridge Colby signed the proclamation declaring the Nineteenth Amendment officially part of the United States Constitution.

After the ratification of the suffrage amendment, Catt stepped down from the presidency of the NAWSA, and was succeeded by Maud Wood Park. She continued to work with the International Woman Suffrage Alliance and founded the new League of Women Voters. Her main focus, however, was world peace; she stated "war is to me my greatest woe." Catt spoke across the country on behalf of the Versailles Treaty and the League of Nations, insisting that the United States must accept internationalism. In 1925, she founded the Committee on the Cause and Cure of War, whose purpose was to educate the public on peace issues and to pressure the U.S. government to work toward world peace. She was an influential political figure who worked for Prohibition and endorsed Herbert Hoover for the presidency in 1928, approving of his strong Prohibitionist views.

When the Nazis came to power in Germany in the 1930's, Catt worked to help Jewish victims of Nazism and was instrumental in the formation of the Protest Committee of Non-Jewish Women Against the Persecution of Jews in Germany in 1933. She helped organize the Women's Centennial Congress in 1940, and during World War II, she served as the honorary chair of the Women's Action Committee for Victory and Lasting Peace. Her last public appearance was in 1941, when she was presented with the Chi Omega Achievement Award, at a formal dinner at the White House. She retired to New Rochelle, New York, where she died on March 9, 1947, of heart failure following a gallstone operation.

Summary

A pragmatic, shrewd politician, Carrie Chapman Catt designed and implemented the plan of action which brought about the passage of the suffrage amendment at a time when its passage seemed doubtful. She worked tirelessly for the suffrage cause, giving literally thousands of speeches across the country and around the world. In her speeches, she stressed woman suffrage before suffrage for immigrants and American Indians, views which alienated some of her adherents. She would not have called herself a racist, however, since she saw herself as simply assessing realities. Her focus was always on voting rights for women; all other matters took second place.

Unlike some other suffragists, Catt did not believe the suffrage she worked so hard to establish would automatically change women's status, nor was she surprised that American politics were not transformed by the events of 1920. She believed that women's achievement of economic power, through their entrance into the workplace, would prove to be the key to improving women's lives, and she stressed the importance of women supporting other women in the workplace.

Bibliography
Campbell, Karlyn Kohrs, ed. *Women Public Speakers in the United States, 1800-1925: A Bio-Critical Sourcebook.* Westport, Conn.: Greenwood Press, 1993. This collection includes an article on Catt by David S. Birdsell focusing on her use of

rhetoric and her persuasive powers as a speaker. Contains a chronology of Catt's speeches.

Catt, Carrie Chapman, with Nettie Rogers Shuler. *Woman Suffrage and Politics: The Inner Story of the Suffrage Movement.* New York: Charles Scribner's Sons, 1923. Catt's book gives her own account of the events leading up to the passage of the suffrage amendment, and provides insight into her brilliant and reasoned political strategies.

Evans, Sara M. *Born for Liberty: A History of Women in America.* New York: Free Press, 1989. While not focusing specifically on Catt, Evans provides a thoughtful overview of the woman suffrage movement in the United States and the events leading up to women's achievement of the right to vote.

Fowler, Robert Booth. *Carrie Catt: Feminist Politician.* Boston: Northeastern University Press, 1986. Primarily interested in Catt's ability and vision as a leader, Fowler focuses for the most part on her political career, although he does provide a brief account of her early life.

Peck, Mary Gray. *Carrie Chapman Catt: A Biography.* New York: H. W. Wilson, 1944. Written by one of Catt's friends, who also worked in the suffrage movement, this first biography is the most detailed of the various accounts of Catt's life. Nevertheless, in her attempts to write an impersonal account of which Catt would approve, Peck ignores most of Catt's private life.

Van Voris, Jacqueline. *Carrie Chapman Catt: A Public Life.* New York: The Feminist Press at the City University of New York, 1987. A straightforward account of Catt's life, focusing on her suffrage activities.

Catherine Francis

LINDA CHAVEZ

Born: June 17, 1947; Albuquerque, New Mexico

Area of Achievement: Government and politics
Contribution: As a Hispanic conservative activist and public official, Chavez broadened the role of women and minorities in American politics.

Early Life

Linda Chavez was born in Albuquerque, New Mexico, on June 17, 1947, the daughter of Rudy and Velma Chavez. Rudy Chavez was the descendent of Spanish immigrants who had settled New Mexico in the early 1600's; his wife Velma was of Anglo-American heritage. The Chavezes were devout Roman Catholics and provided their daughter with a sturdy middle-class childhood. A veteran of World War II, Rudy Chavez possessed a sense of patriotism and a quiet pride in his Hispanic heritage—qualities that had a major influence on his daughter's later conservative political beliefs.

When Linda was nine years old, she moved with her family from New Mexico, where Hispanic Americans were comfortably established as a majority ethnic group, to Denver, Colorado, where racial prejudice against Hispanics and other minorities was more prevalent. During her teenage years, Linda reacted to this discrimination by developing a fierce determination to excel; she also marched against segregation and became involved in a range of social causes supporting civil rights for women and African Americans.

After she graduated from high school, Linda Chavez enrolled at the University of Colorado in 1965. As an undergraduate, Chavez became involved in teaching through tutoring Mexican American students in remedial studies. Although she was discouraged by patterns of discrimination she witnessed and the lack of motivation on the part of her tutorial students, Chavez remained committed to her ambition to become a teacher. Although the teaching profession was considered a conventional aspiration for women, Chavez believed the field of education presented women with a challenging opportunity to effect significant social change.

Near the middle of her undergraduate years, Chavez was married to fellow student Christopher Gersten in 1967 and chose to retain her maiden name after the ceremony. After graduating from the University of Colorado with a bachelor's degree in 1970, she pursued graduate studies in English literature at the University of California at Los Angeles (UCLA). As a graduate assistant, Chavez was persuaded to present a course on Chicano literature. Although she harbored serious reservations because of the lack of sufficient published material on which to base the course, Chavez bowed to academic pressure. She found that many of the students were unwilling to read the material she presented and were disrespectful during her lectures; some who were given failing marks retaliated by vandalizing Chavez's home. Discouraged by her experiences with teachers, colleagues, and students who made stereotypical assumptions about her because of her Hispanic heritage, Chavez left UCLA in 1972 and moved with her husband to Washington, D.C.

Life's Work

Despite her discouraging experience at UCLA, Linda Chavez did not abandon her interest in education. In Washington, D.C., Chavez became affiliated with the National Education Association (NEA), the largest union of schoolteachers in the United States, and worked for the Democratic National Committee in support of various liberal causes. She became increasingly discouraged by the way many organizations were courting her as an ethnic representative and lobbyist for Hispanic causes rather than respecting her opinions as an individual. After serving as an educational consultant for the Department of Health, Education, and Welfare, Chavez joined the staff of the American Federation of Teachers (AFT). As the second-largest national teachers' union, the AFT was known for its influence in policy making, and Chavez found an outlet for her own views while serving as editor of the union's quarterly journal, *American Educator*. Her series of articles in support of a return to traditional educational values and goals brought her to the attention of conservative politicians in Washington.

As the decade of the 1970's drew to a close, Chavez had reversed her previous liberal political stance after becoming alienated by liberal Democratic rhetoric that portrayed Hispanics as defenseless, victimized minorities who depended on the financial assistance of wealthy upper-class whites. Her own vision placed Hispanics in control of their own destiny—their success could be attained through hard work and personal dedication rather than the bureaucratic largesse represented by government handouts. Her opinions meshed with the growing national conservatism of the new decade that brought about the election of Ronald Reagan as president in 1980, and she began working as a consultant for the Reagan Administration in 1981.

Appreciative of her contributions, President Reagan appointed Chavez to serve as director of the U.S. Commission on Civil Rights in 1983. A nonpartisan agency, the commission was charged with the responsibility of monitoring the federal government's progress in enforcing civil rights legislation. Echoing the administration's position, Chavez began to denounce many traditional civil rights measures, including affirmative action programs and racial hiring quotas. Chavez also authorized a federal study to investigate the negative effects of affirmative action on members of minority group. Although she asserted that she was helping to direct the agency toward the stated goal of establishing a color-blind society in which minorities would advance based on merit rather than ethnic identity or gender, many civil rights activists criticized Chavez for transforming the agency into a partisan arm of the Reagan Administration. Chavez also found that the ideological differences between her and many Hispanic activists prevented her from persuading them to support her policy positions.

In 1985, Chavez was promoted to the position of director of the Office of the White House Public Liaison. As the highest-ranking woman on the White House staff,

Chavez found that her new post gave her more direct access to President Reagan. She switched her political affiliation to the Republican Party and lobbied hard to promote the administration's policies within Congress as well as among various public groups. After ten months, however, Chavez decided to leave the post to run for political office.

The Republican Party encouraged Chavez to become a candidate for the U.S. Senate seat in Maryland in 1986. Eager to retain their majority within the Senate, many prominent Republicans demonstrated their support for Chavez and helped her win the Republican primary race. Banking on her conservative credentials, her close ties to President Reagan, her solid middle-class background, and her potential appeal with women and Hispanic voters, the Republican Party launched a large-scale fund-raising effort and poured substantial funds into Chavez's election campaign.

Despite this demonstration of partisan support, Chavez found herself at a distinct disadvantage against Democratic challenger Barbara Mikulski. An ethnic, working-class populist who had represented her Baltimore district in the U.S. House of Representatives for many years, Mikulski had spent her life in the state, had close ties within the state's urban communities, and had deep support among the state's substantial majority of registered Democrats. All of these credentials negated Chavez's perceived strengths, and her ratings in the political polls trailed far behind Mikulski's as the fall election approached.

Placed in the unenviable position of having to counter criticism of her shifting political allegiance and her brief residence in the state of Maryland, Chavez adopted a campaign strategy of attacking Mikulski. The strategy backfired when Chavez, who was the mother of three children, called attention to the fact that Mikulski had never been married and accused her of being "anti-male." Indulging in further political mudslinging, Chavez's campaign staffers exacerbated the situation by attempting to link Mikulski with several lesbian groups in the greater Baltimore area. In a clear rejection of these accusations, Maryland voters endorsed Mikulski for the Senate seat by a substantial margin.

Shaking off her loss, Chavez realized that the electoral fray was unlikely to yield concrete rewards for her in the foreseeable future. Instead, she became president of U.S. English, a private nonprofit organization lobbying to establish English as the official national language. She soon resigned her post in late 1988, citing her distaste for the anti-Hispanic and anti-Catholic bias exemplified in sentiments expressed by the group's founder. Upon leaving the organization, Chavez became a fellow at a conservative Washington-based think tank known as the Manhattan Institute for Policy Research. She also became a freelance political commentator and wrote columns and editorials for various periodicals.

Capitalizing on her growing prominence as a policy expert, Chavez published a work entitled *Out of the Barrio: Toward a New Politics of Hispanic Assimilation* (1991). Arguing against the representation of the Hispanics as a part of a monolithic community, Chavez reiterated her belief that affirmative action programs and hiring quotas effectively segregated Hispanics. According to Chavez, the organized Hispanic movement's tendency to focus most of its attention on the plight of those who are impoverished and disadvantaged not only has prevented Hispanics from taking credit for the enormous gains made by those who have achieved middle-class status but also has reinforced a skewed perception of the Hispanic population by American society. The book was widely reviewed, and its success ensured Chavez a new level of visibility as a commentator during the early 1990's on shows such as *The McNeil/ Lehrer News Hour.*

Summary

Despite her failed bid for a seat in the U.S. Senate, Linda Chavez managed to establish impressive credentials during the course of her political career. A widely noticed and well-regarded commentator on American domestic affairs, Chavez has worked to break down the limitations imposed by stereotypical perceptions of Hispanic Americans. As differences within their community became more evident, Hispanic Americans began to be courted as an important political constituency by both the Democratic and Republican parties. Riding the crest of this attention, Chavez received prominent political appointments, and her success within the Republican Party helped inspire other Hispanics, such as Richard Pombo of California and Ileana Ros-Lehtinen and Lincoln Diaz-Balart of Florida, to campaign as Republicans and succeed in winning election to the U.S. House of Representatives. Although the election of Democratic candidate Bill Clinton to the presidency in 1992 shifted control of the executive branch of government out of the hands of the Republican Party, many Hispanic Americans continued to pursue elective office as Republicans.

As the 1990's ushered in new debates about multiculturalism and political correctness in the United States, Chavez continued to express her opinions regarding the advancement of Hispanic Americans. Affirming the long-cherished American ideal of respecting the political beliefs of those whose views run contrary to those of the political majority, Chavez has argued passionately for a new vision of Hispanic Americans. Chavez's greatest importance for women and for Hispanic Americans has been her willingness to challenge predictable stereotypes, regardless of the popularity of her beliefs.

Bibliography

Arias, Anna Maria. "Making People Mad." *Hispanic* (August, 1992): 11-16. This article, written by a Latina journalist, captures both Chavez's polemical fervor and the underlying seriousness of her conservative political convictions.
Brimelow, Peter. "The Fracturing of America." *Forbes* 149 (March 30, 1992): 74-75. An influential and sympathetic analysis of Chavez's opinions on a variety of political topics, including her views on Hispanic Americans and minority status.
Chavez, Linda. *Out of the Barrio: Toward a New Politics of Hispanic Assimilation.* New York: Basic Books, 1991. Chavez's own exposition of her views serves as an excellent introduction to her political thought and a vital primer on her influence on the shifting American cultural scene of the 1980's and 1990's.
Grenier, Jeannin. "The Woman Versus Woman Race." *Ms.* 15 (November, 1986): 27.

Grenier's piece centers on Chavez's contest with Mikulski, although it also includes some treatment of Chavez's earlier career and background. The author particularly highlights the issues of race, gender, and homophobia in the rhetoric of the two candidates and how their political views affected their campaign strategies.

Noonan, Peggy. *What I Saw at the Revolution.* New York: Random House, 1990. Although it contains no direct information about Chavez, this memoir, written by a female speechwriter for Reagan, provides insights into Chavez's encounter with Reagan-style conservatism. Noonan echoes some of Chavez's views, suggesting that, contrary to the settled conviction of most American liberals, Reagan's brand of political conservatism was an empowering, democratic force rather than a product of racist, reactionary tendencies.

Telgen, Diane, and Jim Kamp, eds. *Notable Hispanic American Women.* Detroit, Mich.: Gale Research, 1993. Filling a gap in the coverage of minority women in available reference works, this collection profiles more than 200 women of Hispanic descent. The entry on Chavez provides a thorough overview of her career through the early 1990's and is accompanied by a useful list of periodical sources.

Nicholas Birns

CHER

Born: May 20, 1946; El Centro, California

Areas of Achievement: Music and film
Contribution: Cher began her career in the mid-1960's as a pop singer, but gained wider acclaim after turning to acting and starring in a number of successful films.

Early Life

Cher was born Cherilyn Sarkisian on May 20, 1946, in El Centro, California. Her mother, Jackie Jean Crouch, later known as Georgia Holt, was part French and Cherokee Indian and worked as an actress and model. Cher's father, John Sarkisian, a gambler and drug addict, was of Armenian descent. Cher's parents were divorced soon after her birth, and she did not know her father until later when her parents were remarried for a brief period when she was eleven years old. Cher considers her sister Georgeanne's father, John Southall, to be her real father, but one of her mother's other husbands, Gilbert LaPiere, formally adopted Cher and Georgeanne.

Cher was an exotic-looking child in a family of blondes. With her black hair and prominent features, she considered herself to be unattractive. School frustrated her as she did well in some subjects and failed others. (When she was thirty years old, she was diagnosed with the learning disability dyslexia.) By her junior year in high school, Cher was disenchanted with academics and dropped out of school.

She left home when she was about sixteen years old to move in with a friend in Los Angeles. Living next door was Salvatore "Sonny" Bono, an aspiring songwriter and record producer. At the time, Bono was working as a songwriter and backup vocalist for Phil Spector, the record producer responsible for producing such groups as the Ronettes and the Righteous Brothers. Cher moved in with Bono and began singing. She spent time at Phil Spector's studio using her throaty voice to sing backup on the Ronette's hit "Be My Baby." She also recorded her own single "Ringo, I Love You" under the name Bobbie Joe Mason. Cher and Sonny wrote songs and began to perform in nightclubs under the name Caesar and Cleo before changing the name of their act to Sonny and Cher. The couple was married on October 27, 1964.

Life's Work

In 1965, Sonny and Cher's single "I Got You Babe" sold more than three million records and eventually reached the top of the pop charts that year. The couple, with their colorful, hip outfits (including fringed vests, patterned pants, and boots) became pop icons. They released a number of hit singles including "Bang, Bang (My Baby Shot Me Down)" (1966) and "The Beat Goes On" (1967). They starred together in a feature film called *Good Times* (1967).

By 1968, however, public taste was shifting. Rock bands such as the Rolling Stones and Cream were popularizing a harder-edged, blues-flavored sound. Sonny and Cher's brand of effervescent rock was no longer in vogue with the young people who were their record-buying public. In 1969, Sonny and Cher made a second film, *Chastity*. That same year, the couple's daughter, also called Chastity, was born. Out of favor with the counterculture, Sonny and Cher began performing in nightclubs in glittering evening wear rather than the outrageous hippie garb that had charmed America's youth.

In 1971, the head producer of programming at CBS television signed Sonny and Cher for a series of six hour-long comedy-variety shows that were telecast during the summer rerun season. Cher's deadpan barbs at Sonny's short stature and his lack of talent won over the show's audience, as did her daring, navel-baring outfits designed by Bob Mackie. In the wake of her newfound popularity as a glamorous television star, Cher recorded solo hit records including "Gypsies, Tramps, and Thieves" (1971), "Half-Breed" (1973), and "Dark Lady" (1974).

The Sonny and Cher Comedy Hour ran for three seasons until 1974 when the couple's marriage deteriorated, and they were divorced. CBS developed a solo comedy show for Cher, but it only ran for one season from 1975 to 1976. The network's attempt to revive the pair's old program as *The Sonny and Cher Show* from 1976 to 1977 also failed. Sonny Bono's show business career never recovered after his divorce from Cher. (Eventually, he went on to become a successful restaurateur and was later elected mayor of Palm Springs, California, in 1988.)

On June 30, 1975, three days after her divorce from Sonny Bono was final, Cher married rock musician Gregg Allman. Nine days later, she filed for divorce from the alcoholic, drug-addicted Allman. The couple attempted several reconciliations, but none were successful. Cher and Gregg Allman had one child, a son, Elijah Blue Allman, born in 1976.

In the late 1970's, Cher performed her solo act in Las Vegas. Although she was well paid, Cher was still dissatisfied with her accomplishments. She began looking for acting jobs in Hollywood and initially had no luck getting work. In 1981, she moved to New York, hoping to find stage work since the film industry had turned her down. Film director Robert Altman cast her in his stage adaptation of Ed Graczyk's *Come Back to the Five and Dime Jimmy Dean, Jimmy Dean*, set to run at the Martin Beck Theater on Broadway. Critically, the play was dissected, but Cher's performance received kind reviews. Altman's film version of the play was well received upon its premiere in 1982, as was Cher's performance in the role of Sissy.

Impressed by Cher's acting on Broadway, Mike Nichols offered her a part in his upcoming film *Silkwood*, about the life and mysterious death of a nuclear factory worker named Karen Silkwood. Released in 1983, *Silkwood* starred Meryl Streep, Kurt Russell, and Cher as Karen Silkwood's wisecracking, lesbian coworker and housemate Dolly Pelliker. For her performance as Dolly, Cher received an Academy Award nomination for best supporting actress in 1984.

While Cher fielded a variety of film offers and waited for the perfect part to showcase her talents, her money dwindled. To help her income, she appeared in a series of television ads for the Health and Tennis Corporation to promote the company's chain of Jack La Lanne Health Clubs. Cher's next film role was in *Mask*

(1985), in which she played Rusty Dennis, the unconventional biker mother of a son afflicted with craniodiaphyseal dysplasia, a disease which causes facial deformity and enlargement of the head. The part, based on the true story of Rusty Dennis and the early death of her son Rocky, earned Cher a best actress award at the 1985 Cannes Film Festival. Cher was disappointed that her performance failed to receive an Oscar nomination.

While pursuing success in films, Cher continued as a recording artist. In 1987 she released the hit album *I Found Someone* and made music videos for three of the album's songs. The year 1987 saw the release of three of Cher's films: *The Witches of Eastwick, Suspect,* and *Moonstruck.* In the first film, Cher played sculptor Alexandra Medford in a colorful script loosely based on John Updike's novel of the same name. The film allowed Cher to work with Michelle Pfeiffer, Susan Sarandon, and the devilish Jack Nicholson. *The Witches of Eastwick* earned mixed reviews but was a box-office success. In *Suspect*, Cher played Kathleen Riley, a workaholic public defender in Washington, D.C., who defends a homeless deaf-mute (Liam Neeson) accused of murder and is romanced by a juror played by Dennis Quaid. *Suspect* was directed by Peter Yates, noted for his work on the surprise hit *Breaking Away* (1979), but the film received poor reviews and quickly disappeared from theaters.

Both critics and filmgoers alike adored Norman Jewison's romantic comedy *Moonstruck.* Appearing with Nicolas Cage, Vincent Gardenia, Danny Aiello, and Olympia Dukakis, Cher was cast as Loretta Castorini, the lovestruck, frumpy widow who finds excitement and passion in the arms of her fiancé's brother. In 1988, Cher's performance in *Moonstruck* won her the best actress Oscar she coveted. In 1989 she also won the People's Choice Award for favorite female entertainer.

Mermaids, Cher's next film, opened in 1990. In it, Cher was cast as the libidinous and vibrant Rachel Flax, single mother to two young daughters played by Winona Ryder and Christina Ricci. Cher released another hit album, *Heart of Stone*, in 1989. The same year, in collaboration with nutritionist Robert Haas, she published *Forever Fit*, her diet and exercise book. Always a health fanatic, Cher revealed the details of her regular, arduous fitness program. Despite tabloid reports of compulsive plastic surgery, Cher insisted that her elegant, trim looks were the result of her rigorous health regime, and that she had undergone only three minor cosmetic surgeries. CBS/Fox released her exercise video *Cher Fitness* in 1991. Later that year, Cher released another album, *Love Hurts*, and 1992 saw the release of her second fitness video, *Cher Fitness: Body Confidence.*

In addition to her work in the music, film, and fitness industries, Cher became involved in many different environmental and charitable causes. After learning of the organization during her work in *Mask*, Cher became active in the International Craniofacial Foundation. She arranged for facially deformed children and their parents to attend her concerts as guests, and she contributed significant amounts of money to the foundation and to individual patients who needed expensive surgeries. In April of 1993, Cher traveled to her troubled ancestral homeland Armenia under the auspices of the United Armenian Fund, a nonprofit relief organization. She delivered medical supplies, toys, books, printing equipment, and candy to Armenia, which had been devastated by earthquake, economic ruin, and a relentless war with neighboring Azerbaijan. Cher toured the country, visited its people, and arranged for a paralyzed Armenian child to be transported to the United States for treatment. In 1994, Cher completed location work in New York City filming the Picture *Faithful*, directed by Paul Mazursky and featuring costars such as Ryan O'Neal and Chazz Palminteri.

Summary

Although Cher's musical talents were clearly evident during her early days with Sonny Bono, it was not until her later years that she emerged as a successful star in her own right. Her exotic appearance and her deadpan humor captivated many viewers who watched the *Sonny and Cher Show* and her subsequent self-titled show. After the breakup of her marriage and the cancellation of her musical variety show, Cher continued to fascinate the media and her fans with her outspoken interviews, her flamboyant outfits, and her well-publicized romances with various men, including many who were significantly younger than herself. In the course of dealing with broken marriages, single parenthood, and other challenges, Cher reached her forties and began to establish her credentials as a serious actor. Despite the limited nature of her formal dramatic training, Cher managed to draw upon her own experiences in order to create a range of memorable and believable characters, culminating in her Academy Award-winning performance as Loretta Castorini in *Moonstruck*. Establishing a name for herself in the fields of music, film, and physical fitness, Cher also found time to support a variety of charitable causes that provided much needed support for others who were much less fortunate than herself.

Bibliography

Bono, Sonny. *And the Beat Goes On*. New York: Pocket Books, 1991. Although this account certainly reflects Sonny Bono's personal biases, it is helpful for obtaining information about the early years of Cher's career as part of the Sonny and Cher team.

Cher, and Robert Haas. *Forever Fit: The Lifetime Plan for Health, Fitness, and Beauty*. New York: Bantam Books, 1991. While this book mainly discusses Cher's fitness plan, the work also devotes considerable space to Cher's discussion of her life, particularly her health and recent involvement in films, music, and music videos.

Petrucelli, Rita. *Cher: Singer and Actress*. Vero Beach, Fla.: Rourke Enterprises, 1989. This volume is a children's book that presents Cher's life story as the biography of a woman overcoming tremendous odds to achieve success.

Taraborrelli, J. Randy. *Cher: A Biography*. New York: St. Martin's Press, 1986. With information gleaned from interviews and magazine articles, Taraborrelli creates an entertaining and thorough account of Cher's rise to fame and the various people involved in her life.

Wickens, Barbara. "The Cher Effect." *Maclean's* 102 (March 6, 1989): 38-42. In an interview with Cher, Wickens gathers biographical information, a history of Cher's career, and a perspective of Cher's thoughts on topics ranging from acting to fame to women.

Jennifer Padgett Griffith

MARY BOYKIN CHESNUT

Born: March 31, 1823; Statesburg, South Carolina
Died: November 22, 1886; Camden, South Carolina
Area of Achievement: Literature
Contribution: In her Civil War diary and its revisions, Chesnut created—often within the contexts of women's issues—powerful literary works with enduring historical, political, and social implications.

Early Life

Born in Statesburg, South Carolina, on March 31, 1823, Mary Boykin Miller was the first child of Mary Boykin and Stephen Decatur Miller. A lawyer and former U.S. congressman, Miller was then a senator in the South Carolina legislature. His involvement in politics at many levels, especially his advocacy of states' rights, influenced his daughter Mary's political development. Since Mary's parents lived with her mother's family in the early years of their marriage, Mary was well acquainted with plantation life. When her father was elected governor of South Carolina in 1828, the family moved to Columbia. He later won a seat in the U.S. Senate in 1830, and his family returned to the Boykin plantation near Camden, South Carolina. By 1833, Mary was attending a Camden school opened by Stella Phelps, an excellent young teacher from Vermont. Claiming ill health, Mary's father resigned from the Senate in 1833 and later died in 1838. In 1835 Mary met Colonel James Chesnut, whose youngest son, James, Jr., was a senior at Princeton. That year, Mary was enrolled in Madame Talvande's French School for Young Ladies in Charleston. Mary's courses included literature, music, history, rhetoric, natural science, singing, and dancing, and she was an excellent student. Following his graduation from Princeton, James Chesnut, Jr., visited a niece at the school in the summer of 1836 and met the vivacious, thirteen-year-old Mary Miller. In spite of interference from Mary's family, James continued his interest in Mary, and on April 23, 1840, three weeks after her seventeenth birthday, Mary and James were married and went to live at Mulberry, the Chesnut plantation near Camden.

At Mulberry, Mary's lively interest in literature and the world beyond the plantation at times made her fretful. In 1848, the couple moved from Mulberry to a modest new home, named Frogvale, in Camden. James was involved in state politics, and by 1854 they moved to an elegant new home in northern Camden. This home, Kamchatka, was well suited to the entertaining that Mary enjoyed. James was elected to the U.S. Senate in 1858, and Mary cheerfully entered the Washington, D.C., social scene. James became a spokesman for states' rights, although neither James nor Mary defended slavery. With Abraham Lincoln's election to the presidency in November of 1860, civil war became a possibility. James resigned from the Senate on November 10, 1860, the first southern senator to take that step. Fearing the worst, Mary soon would begin the diary that recorded her experiences during the Civil War and established her enduring renown.

Life's Work

Although reluctant to leave Washington, D.C., Mary Boykin Chesnut supported the right of southern states to secede. In February of 1861, Mary began a diary that she was to continue until the summer of 1865. This diary records her involvement in the war, her attitudes against slavery and the limited role of women in society, her social relationships, and her continuing interest in intellectual growth as revealed through her extensive references to English, French, and American literature. No other civilian diary presents such a comprehensive insider's view of the Civil War from a southern perspective. Without the diary and its revisions, Mary Chesnut would probably have remained a mere social footnote to her husband's career. With her diary, Mary gave posterity a work of enduring literary significance, one that provides a clearer understanding of the Civil War and its appalling human consequences. At the same time, she establishes herself as a dynamic personality who did not easily abide fools.

Mary wrote her diary in many places, as she accompanied her husband from one position to another. In early 1861, she was in Montgomery, Alabama, while James attended the Confederate Provisional Congress. Next, she went to Charleston, where James was involved in negotiations over Fort Sumter. A firsthand witness to the first battle of the war, Mary viewed the shelling of the fort from a rooftop. She also heard the news of the battle of Manassas, visited the sick and wounded, and faced, for the first time, the grim reality of death for her acquaintances and compatriots. Mary fretted over the caution and indecision of some southern leaders. She particularly resented her husband's reluctance to assert his interest in diplomatic positions in London and Paris, even to the point of wishing that Jefferson Davis would post her to Paris. Back in Camden briefly, Mary was exasperated with James's apparent indifference to the battles in Virginia. She wished that she were a man so that she could take an active role in the war.

Following an illness in 1862, Mary went to Richmond, Virginia, the Confederate capital, with James, who had attained the rank of colonel and been appointed as an aide to Jefferson Davis. Mary's spirits improved as she renewed her acquaintance with Varina Davis, a friend of many years. Mary and James were to remain loyal to the Davises for life. The stress of the years in Richmond led James to arrange in 1864 for an assignment to Columbia, South Carolina, where, with the rank of brigadier general, he was put in charge of organizing reserve troops. As defeat began to seem inevitable and Sherman's troops invaded North Carolina in early 1865, Mary went as an exile to Lincolnton, North Carolina. She experienced despair and misery—news of the war was all bad. When Robert E. Lee surrendered his army at Appomattox Courthouse in April of 1865, Mary moved again to Chester, South Carolina. One of her visitors there was Varina Davis, fleeing with her four children to escape arrest.

The Chesnuts moved back to Camden without resources. Northern forces had burned one hundred bales of cotton and damaged mills and gins at Mulberry plantation. The years following the war were often financially difficult. With the death of James's father in 1866, following his mother's death two years earlier, James inherited Mulberry and Sandy Hill plantations, but the properties were heavily indebted. By

1873, however, the Chesnuts were able to build a new house named Sarsfield in Camden. There, Mary renewed her interest in her wartime diary. She attempted to write about her life and war experiences in three unpublished novels, but eventually she realized that a revised diary would best tell her story. In 1875, she worked to revise her diary, but James and another reader of the manuscript, R. M. T. Hunter, suggested that the content would be offensive to some. Plagued by poor health, Mary put the diary aside again until 1881. Her revising, which included omissions, amplifications, and stylistic improvements while retaining the form and immediacy of a diary, continued for three and a half years. During this period, Mary published "The Arrest of a Spy," an expanded piece from her diary, in the Charleston *Weekly News and Courier* series entitled "Our Women in the War." She received ten dollars for the piece, apparently her only published item during her lifetime.

Although Mary intended further revision of her diary, failing health—her own and that of her husband and her mother—intervened. During her last ten years, Mary's heart and lung ailments became more acute. In 1883, James became seriously ill. In January, 1885, James suffered a stroke and died on February 1. Five days later, Mary's mother died. These stresses added to Mary's deteriorating condition. Upon James's death, the indebted family plantations, in accordance with his father's will, were to pass to a male heir with the Chesnut name. Since Mary and James had no children, Mary was left with only Sarsfield and an income slightly exceeding one hundred dollars a year. By selling butter and eggs, she was able to earn an additional twelve dollars a month. Mary attempted another expansion of an excerpt from her diary, this time focusing on conditions in Richmond in 1864, but the piece was never published during her lifetime.

During the spring and summer of 1886, Mary was somewhat cheered by the marriage of her nephew, David Williams, to the daughter of former Governor John L. Manning, with whom Mary had flirted at the beginning of the war. Mary attended the wedding, but her heart bothered her during the festivities. A heart attack ended her life on November 22, 1886, and she was buried at Knights Hill beside her husband James.

Summary

Mary Chesnut's legacy to the world, a diary extensively revised for the public and also later published in part in the original form, went through a variety of editions beginning in 1905 (*A Diary from Dixie*) and extending into the 1980's. Early editions were faulty and incomplete, even though they were praised for their candor. What the diary reveals is the struggles and sufferings of the South as people on all levels coped with the harsh realities of war. It also reveals that Mary, the wife of a southern senator who defended states' rights, was an abolitionist who rejoiced, with her husband, at the end of slavery.

Mary made a direct connection between the structure of a slave society and the inferior political and social status of women. A married woman, she believed, was a slave, as was an unmarried woman who lived in her father's house. Her diary portrays the southern patriarchy as riddled with moral corruption, a reality plainly evident to

Mary through the example of her father-in-law's union with a slave woman. Slavery was destructive for both the enslaved and the enslaver. Mary believed that slavery intensified problems for southern women. The celebrated stereotype of southern women—their soft voices and gracious accommodation of male wishes—was evidence of their enslaved position. In Mary's view, many southern women secretly favored the abolitionist cause in reaction to the corruptions of the patriarchal system. Mary resented the North's moral posturing—the South, she believed, would soon abolish slavery without northern interference.

Her diary is also significant because it reveals Mary's solid intellectual qualities, stimulated through insatiable reading of the best works of literature and history. An Anglophile, Mary was also widely acquainted with French and American literature and philosophy. Above all, Mary Chesnut's diary reveals a witty individualist ready to advance heretical views and to laugh at the follies of society.

Bibliography
Chesnut, Mary Boykin. *A Diary from Dixie*. Edited by Isabella D. Martin and Myrta Lockett Avary. New York: D. Appleton, 1905. Prepared in haste, this book features limited selections from Chesnut's revised manuscript of the 1880's, omits content to reflect editor Martin's politically correct view of the Confederate legend, and takes liberties with the manuscript's format.

——————. *A Diary from Dixie*. Edited by Ben Ames Williams. Boston: Houghton Mifflin, 1949. This work contains more of the 1880's manuscript than the 1905 version does but it also leaves out content without acknowledgment, takes liberties with the text to improve readability, inserts the editor's own flawed beginning and concluding passages, and silently mingles a few passages from the 1860's manuscript.

——————. *Mary Chesnut's Civil War*. Edited by C. Vann Woodward. New Haven, Conn.: Yale University Press, 1981. Based on the 1880's manuscript, this book finally gives to the world all that Mary Chesnut intended for it to see. Woodward is meticulous in his editing, clearly distinguishing, for example, content from the 1860's manuscript introduced for comparison. A distinguished historian of the South, Woodward writes a thorough introduction that includes a discussion of the development of the Chesnut manuscripts, a biography of Chesnut, and an analysis of Chesnut's views. This book contains entries for all the years of the Civil War and shows that Chesnut was working from her original manuscripts, some of which apparently were lost by her first editors.

——————. *The Private Mary Chesnut: The Unpublished Civil War Diaries*. Edited by C. Vann Woodward and Elisabeth Muhlenfeld. New York: Oxford University Press, 1984. Chesnut did not intend to publish this original diary, the basis for her 1880's revision. The entries are in many respects more revealing than the revision, showing Chesnut's flirtations, her occasional disputes with and criticisms of her husband, and disharmony within the Confederacy. Since some of the original manuscripts were lost, this book has entries for only 1861 and 1865.

Muhlenfeld, Elisabeth. *Mary Boykin Chesnut: A Biography*. Baton Rouge: Louisiana State University Press, 1981. Drawing extensively on primary and secondary sources, this biography traces Chesnut's early years, her intense involvement in the Civil War as reflected in her diary, and the difficulties of her last twenty years as she experimented with novels, revised the diary, and struggled with family indebtedness and personal illness. Muhlenfeld clearly and sympathetically delineates Chesnut's historical and literary achievements.

Ray Leadbetter

JUDY CHICAGO

Born: July 20, 1939; Chicago, Illinois

Area of Achievement: Art
Contribution: A leader of the Women Artists' Movement of the 1970's, Judy Chicago has produced a body of art and writing that has been extremely influential in promoting acceptance and recognition of women artists of the past and modern times and in encouraging the development of a more expansive, inclusive view of history.

Early Life
Judith Cohen was born in Chicago in 1939 to Jewish parents who were actively involved in left-wing politics and who believed in equal rights for women. Her mother worked and her father was a union organizer. Judy began to draw by the time she was three. Her mother strongly supported her developing interest in art, and Judy took art classes at the Art Institute of Chicago beginning in 1947, continuing as a student there until she was eighteen. She often visited the galleries at the Art Institute, where she was introduced to some of the great art and artists of the past.

After Judy's father died when she was thirteen, her mother struggled to support the family and keep Judy in school. Judy's interest in art continued to grow; from 1960 to 1964, she attended the University of California at Los Angeles (UCLA) as an art major. During this period, Judy Cohen had a short marriage to Jerry Gerowitz, who was later killed in an auto accident.

While attending UCLA, Judy began to notice that females were taken less seriously than males by the predominantly male art faculty and were viewed more as potential art hobbyists than as potential professional artists. She felt pressured to prove that she could compete in the male-dominated art world of the time.

Although Judy had an interest in creating works of art that would have personal meaning and would reveal her nature as a woman, the male faculty rejected art with subject matter or content that reflected any kind of female or feminine consciousness. In an attempt to be taken seriously as an artist and to detract from her identification as a woman, she created large-scale, nonrepresentational, minimalist works of art which catered to the taste of the male-dominated art world of her time.

By 1966, Judy had staged a one-woman exhibition and her minimalist sculptures were receiving recognition in the art world. Her *Ten Part Cylinder* (1966-1967) was included in the Los Angeles County Museum of Art exhibition: "Sculpture of the Sixties" in 1967.

In 1969, Judy Gerowitz married the artist Lloyd Hamrol. By this time, she decided to make art that would affirm and express her identity as a woman, rather than mask it. That same year, she began a series called *Pasadena Lifesavers*, which consisted of hexagonal forms sprayed on acrylic sheets, meant to symbolize female emotional and sexual multiplicity.

Life's Work

Judy Gerowitz was given an important one-woman exhibition in 1970, at the California State University at Fullerton, which included her *Pasadena Lifesavers* series. It was at this time that she took the name of Judy Chicago in a symbolic act which identified her as an independent woman and revealed her growing feminist attitude. She announced her name change across the entrance wall of the gallery: "Judy Gerowitz hereby divests herself of all names imposed upon her through male social dominance and freely chooses her own name Judy Chicago."

Early in 1970, the California State University at Fresno hired Chicago to teach a female art class. This course was to become the first feminist art class in the United States. By 1970, Chicago had become painfully aware of the oppressive situation of women artists and art students and was deeply concerned about their education. Her art program included consciousness-raising and role-playing sessions that were intended to help make women artists more aware of their identities as women and of their position within the culture. She also began to research, with her students, the history of women artists in Western culture.

Chicago left Fresno in 1971 and, with the well-known Canadian-born artist and feminist, Miriam Schapiro, founded and developed the first feminist art program at the California Institute of the Arts (CalArts) in Valencia, California, (1971-1972). Out of this program, they created *Womanhouse*, the first space designed solely for the exhibition of feminist art. The *Womanhouse* building was an old house in Hollywood, California, that was renovated by the CalArts students under the direction of Chicago and Schapiro. Each room or area of the house was assigned to a different artist or group of artists, to be transformed into an environment that would reflect women's experiences, dreams and fantasies. Chicago's "Menstruation Bathroom," with its white walls, floor, toilet, and a trash can filled with used sanitary pads, was one of the first works of art to represent any aspect of this subject.

After resigning from her position at CalArts in 1973, Chicago went on to found the Los Angeles Woman's Building, which incorporated *Womanhouse* and other feminist organizations. It consisted of an exhibition space, a bookstore, and a women's art school. The Woman's Building became the leading center for feminist art, education, exhibition, and research during this period. Judy Chicago was one of the most influential leaders of what was to be called the Women Artists' Movement of the 1970's.

The first exhibition to be given at the Woman's Building was Judy Chicago's *The Great Ladies* (1972-1973), a series of abstract paintings that represented powerful queens of history, including Christina of Sweden, Marie Antoinette, Catherine the Great, and Queen Victoria. In a related series entitled *The Reincarnation Triptych* (1973), Chicago dealt with three women writers she particularly identified with: French intellectual Madame de Staël, French novelist George Sand, and British writer Virginia Woolf.

In 1973, Chicago began to write about her own experiences as a woman artist in her autobiography, *Through the Flower*. In the book, Chicago described her childhood, her education, her early art projects, and her struggles in the art world. This book was to become a major source of inspiration for women artists.

As a continuation of her efforts to discover, represent, and inform about female achievers of Western history, by 1972 Chicago had begun planning a large-scale project which would attempt to recover the identities and accomplishments of important historical women whose work had been ignored, derided, or forgotten. These plans were to result in Judy Chicago's most famous and monumental work of art: *The Dinner Party* (1973-1978).

The Dinner Party was to be the first epic feminist work of art. Thirty-nine place settings, including table runners, napkins, porcelain, silverware, goblets, and 14-inch plates were arranged on an immense, open-centered equilateral triangle table (each side measuring 46½ feet). Each plate was painted with abstract images which were to represent and symbolize an important woman of history, legend, or mythology, who was to be one of *The Dinner Party*'s thirty-nine absent guests. Needlework table runners under the plates presented the names of the guests and imagery which reflected their historical context. Sappho, Theodora, Virginia Woolf, and Georgia O'Keeffe were some of the honored guests.

The table was set on an equilateral triangular base (each side measuring forty-eight feet) which was covered with 2,300 white porcelain tiles painted with the names of 999 other women of history. Each woman identified at *The Dinner Party* was meant to suggest thousands of women whose names and accomplishments have been lost or forgotten. *The Dinner Party* was meant to be ritualistic and symbolic, with multiple social, political and religious connotations.

Judy Chicago was the originator and designer of all aspects of *The Dinner Party*, but because of the size and complexity of the project, she used hundreds of volunteers to execute it. During the creation of *The Dinner Party*, Chicago wrote a book entitled *The Dinner Party: A Symbol of Our Heritage* (1979), which documents the evolution of the project. *The Dinner Party* was first exhibited in 1979 at the San Francisco Museum of Art.

Soon after the completion of *The Dinner Party*, Chicago began another large-scale feminist work of art, *The Birth Project* (1980-1985). Again concerned with the development of female imagery, she created more than 150 designs (only half of these were completed) for fiber and textile work to be executed by some 140 needleworkers.

The images for *The Birth Project* were meant to educate about the birth process and present birth as a symbol of creation. *The Birth Project* consists of needlework panels that depict various aspects of the birth experience, including the mythic, the painful, and the celebratory. Powerful depictions of pregnancy and birth, as in "The Crowning," "Birth," and "Pregnant Amazon," were some of the first of their kind. Chicago wrote a book, *The Birth Project* (1985), which describes the creation of this project.

In a series of drawings, paintings, weavings, and bronzes, entitled *Powerplay* (completed in 1987), Chicago continued her exploration of gender issues. The images of *Powerplay* present a visual examination of the male role in society and the burden of power which has been placed upon them throughout history.

From 1985 to 1993, Chicago was at work on the research, drawing, and painting for the *Holocaust Project*. Inspired by her interest in her own Jewish heritage and her concern for those who have been oppressed, enslaved, and ignored or marginalized by history, Chicago traveled and studied extensively in preparation for her design of the project. Chicago's partner in this project was Donald Woodman, a photographer whom she married in 1986.

The *Holocaust Project* consists of a series of powerfully expressive images which combine techniques of photography and painting, as well as woven and stained glass images. In an attempt to promote a larger understanding of the Holocaust and its relation to other issues of Western history as well as its global connotations, Chicago juxtaposed depictions of the Jewish experience of the Holocaust with depictions of other experiences of victimization and persecution, such as the burning of witches during the European Inquisition and the enslavement of African Americans in the United States. The evolution of the *Holocaust Project* was described by Chicago in her book: *Holocaust Project, From Darkness into Light* (1993). The *Holocaust Project* was first exhibited at the Maurice Spertus Museum of Judaica in Chicago in 1993.

Summary

Judy Chicago's work, as a feminist artist, educator, and writer, has been extremely influential in helping women artists of the later twentieth century gain greater freedom, visibility, and awareness. In the 1970's, she was instrumental in creating a sense of identity for women artists. Chicago's art, programs, lectures, books, and exhibitions inspired many women artists to have the courage to express themselves as women.

Chicago was the first artist to teach a feminist art course in the United States. She was the founder or cofounder of many of the first organizations designed to educate and promote women artists. She was one of the first artists to recognize, study, appreciate, and adopt traditional women's art forms such as china-painting and needlework, and she created the first epic feminist work of art.

Chicago's female imagery was some of the first of its kind. It identified women's experience as a viable subject for art. She also initiated pioneering research projects on women artists of history, in an effort to find role models for twentieth century women artists.

Judy Chicago's dedication to the education of women in general and women artists in particular inspired hundreds of women, after the 1970's, to research women's history, and to continue to create female imagery and design programs and classes for the education of women artists and to create a greater awareness of women's history. *The Dinner Party* and *The Birth Project* brought women's lives, experiences, history, and imagery to the eyes of thousands of people for the first time. Through projects such as *The Dinner Party*, *The Birth Project*, and the *Holocaust Project*, Judy Chicago has been a major force in promoting the development of a larger and more inclusive view of history.

Bibliography

Chicago, Judy. *The Birth Project*. Garden City, N.Y.: Doubleday, 1985. Provides a history of the inspiration for *The Birth Project* and documents its creation through Chicago's commentary, excerpts from her journals of the period, letters and statements from others involved in the project, photographs, and color reproductions of paintings and weavings. Includes a list of sources and a "Vocabulary of Birth Project Terms."

————————. *The Dinner Party: A Symbol of Our Heritage*. Garden City, N.Y.: Anchor Press/Doubleday, 1979. An extremely thorough documentation of the planning and creation of *The Dinner Party*. Includes excerpts from Chicago's journals of the period, photographs of the work in process and color reproductions of *The Dinner Party* plates. A large section of the book presents short biographies of the thirty-nine guests and the 999 women named at *The Dinner Party*.

————————. *Holocaust Project: From Darkness into Light*. New York: Penguin Books, 1993. A beautifully written book about Chicago's developing interest in her Jewish heritage, with a history of the *Holocaust Project* from conception to completion. Includes a commentary by Chicago and excerpts from her journals of the period. Highly illustrated with Donald Woodman's photographs from travels to sites significant to a study of the Holocaust. Includes color reproductions and a bibliography.

————————. *Through The Flower: My Struggle as a Woman Artist*. Garden City, N.Y.: Doubleday, 1975. With an introduction by Anaïs Nin. This autobiography begins with Chicago's birth and childhood and chronicles her education, relationships, marriages, and art projects up to 1973. The focus of the book is on Chicago's expanding feminist consciousness. Includes 56 black-and-white photographs and reproductions of Chicago's early work, and the work of other women artists.

Lippard, Lucy. *From the Center: Feminist Essays on Women's Art*. New York: E. P. Dutton, 1976. An early, important collection of Lippard's essays on female imagery and art style, the Woman's Building in Los Angeles, and the Women Artist's Movement, as well as monographs on several individual women artists. Includes an interview with Judy Chicago. Color reproduction of "George Sand" from *The Reincarnation Triptych*.

Moore, Sylvia, ed. *Yesterday and Tomorrow: California Women Artists*. New York: Midmarch Arts Press, 1989. A collection of essays by various authors about women artists of California and feminist art issues. Chicago is discussed in several essays; her work forms the focus of the following three essays: "The Feminist Art Movement California Style, 1970-1980" by Faith Wilding, "Recalling Womanhouse" by Miriam Schapiro, and "Judy Chicago: The Dinner Party and The Birth Project" by Rita Cummings Belle.

Raven, Arlene. *Crossing Over: Feminism and Art of Social Concern*. Ann Arbor, Mich.: UMI Research Press, 1988. Half of this book documents the women's movement, with chapters on women artists of the 1970's and feminist art. Judy Chicago and her projects, such as *Womanhouse, The Dinner Party*, and *The Birth*

Project, are discussed extensively. Includes photographs of *Womanhouse*, the Woman's Building, and two reproductions of images from *The Birth Project*.

Rubinstein, Charlotte Streifer. *American Women Artists: From Early Indian Times to the Present*. Boston: G. K. Hall, 1982. This book chronicles the history of the feminist art movement and addresses the lives and work of several feminist artists, including Judy Chicago and Miriam Schapiro. An important and useful introduction to the life and work of Chicago, with an emphasis on *The Dinner Party*. Includes a bibliography.

Nannette Fabré Kelly

LYDIA MARIA CHILD

Born: February 11, 1802; Medford, Massachusetts
Died: October 20, 1880; Wayland, Massachusetts
Areas of Achievement: Social reform, literature, and women's rights
Contribution: One of the earliest American women to make her living with her pen, Lydia Maria Child wrote not only romantic fiction but also antislavery works, editorializing for fifty years both before the Civil War and after. She also wrote children's books, advice books, and histories of women and of religion.

Early Life

The youngest of six children, Lydia Maria Francis was born to David Convers Francis and Susannah Rand Francis in small-town Massachusetts. An ambitious baker, David was a well-respected citizen and the inventor of the famous "Medford Crackers." Only twelve when her mother died, Maria was reared mostly by older siblings. Her next eldest brother, Convers, fostered her love for learning and loaned her books from his library when he began his education at Harvard College. Sent to live with her married sister in frontier Norridgewock, Maine Territory, Maria continued her voracious reading while attending school there. At the age of nineteen, she began teaching in Gardiner, Maine. During this period, she encountered the writings of the eighteenth century philosopher Emanuel Swedenborg, becoming a lifelong believer in his idea of correspondences, that earthly events were emblematic of spiritual states.

Lydia Maria Francis began her literary career while teaching at the girls' school she opened in Watertown, Massachusetts, where she moved to live with her brother Convers and his wife in 1824. Her first publication was a romantic novel about Massachusetts' colonial past—a love story about a white woman and an American Indian named Hobomok. The interracial marriage theme was nearly unique for the time, a theme that she returned to later. *Hobomok: A Tale of Early Times* (1824) was a critical and financial success and persuaded the twenty-two-year-old Maria that she could write for a living. A less successful second romance, *The Rebels: Or, Boston Before the Revolution* (1825) followed. She then hit on a lucrative idea: a magazine for children, the first one ever published in the United States. In 1826, she began editing *Juvenile Miscellany*, a bimonthly magazine with stories, poems, and games. She herself wrote most of the material, and the paid subscriptions rose quickly.

In that same year, Maria was introduced to David Lee Child, a Harvard-educated, reform-minded lawyer just back from diplomatic assignment in Portugal. They were married in 1828, and Maria embarked on a lifelong attempt to keep David out of debt. He repeatedly took on charity cases or sank their small savings in questionable financial schemes. Laws protecting married women's property from seizure by their husbands' creditors were decades away, so Maria lost her own property as well as the income that she earned from writing. Small wonder, then, that she soon began assigning the copyright for her works to her father. The couple had no children. She continued to write, choosing quick income articles for magazines and advice books for women, such as *The Frugal Housewife* (1829), which eventually ran to thirty-three editions and was also popular in England and Scotland.

Life's Work

Lydia Maria Child's life was changed when she became a supporter of William Lloyd Garrison's call for the immediate abolition of slavery. Her husband helped Garrison found the New England Anti-Slavery Society. In 1833, she published the first lengthy defense of abolitionism, *An Appeal in Favor of That Class of Americans Called Africans*. It was credited with persuading orator Wendell Phillips, theologian William Ellery Channing, and politician Charles Sumner, among others. More important, it changed forever Maria's literary reputation: The sales of her earlier books fell off sharply, subscriptions to her children's magazine were canceled and the magazine failed in 1834, her Atheneum library privileges were revoked, and critics lambasted her. Abolitionism in 1833 was not popular, even in Boston, the city most sympathetic to the cause. For the rest of her life, Child labored for antislavery—organizing Women's Anti-Slavery Fairs to raise money, writing articles, editing the *National Anti-Slavery Standard*, writing letters, and attending meetings. Biographer Deborah Clifford says that Child found her true religion in the antislavery movement, "a holy cause that fulfilled her youthful dreams of romance, heroism, and faith."

In the spring of 1835, the American Anti-Slavery Society decided to send Maria and David Child to England to lecture, write, and organize. Maria's books sold better in England than in the United States, and David was an effective speaker. Friends gave them a farewell party in August, and they sold their household effects, anticipating a lengthy stay. Unfortunately, David was arrested on the dock in New York for nonpayment of debts on the day they were to sail. Ultimately the Childs did not go at all, although for eighteen months they kept rescheduling their sailing. While waiting, Maria went to Philadelphia, where she met abolitionists such as Quaker preacher Lucretia Mott and Angelina and Sarah Grimké.

In her two-volume *History of the Condition of Women* (1835), Child argued that women who go beyond private life do not necessarily develop masculine traits. She averred that woman will retain her femininity if she is free to exercise her talents. She provided evidence of the worthwhile influence of women in different cultures in history, in economics, education, and the arts, anticipating the positive "Woman as Force in History" position of twentieth century historian Mary Beard.

David did go abroad for eighteen months in October of 1836, traveling to England and the Continent in order to study sugar beet manufacture. He hoped to pioneer the cultivation and manufacture of sugar beets in New England, thus contributing to the free-produce movement and the boycott of slave-made sugar. Because the couple could barely afford one passage, Maria did not go, nor did she ever travel overseas, even though both her writings and her political ideas were widely admired by European abolitionists. She was on her own again; David, as usual, seldom wrote to her.

Maria Child attended the Women's Anti-Slavery Convention in New York in May, 1837, where she was elected a vice president, helping to draw up resolutions, including one to allow African American women membership and integrated seating in all meetings. In 1840, Maria was named to the executive committee of the American Anti-Slavery Society.

When David finally returned, Maria moved with him to Northampton, Massachusetts, where he bought land and planted sugar beets. His first sugar beet crop was a success, but his new machinery rusted on New York's docks because he could not pay for it.

In 1841, Maria was named editor of the *National Anti-Slavery Standard*, and moved alone to New York. She edited, wrote columns and articles, tried to get the publication out of debt, and struggled to avoid controversy by focusing on the paper's literary content. She resigned her editorship amidst some criticism in 1843, and was briefly succeeded as editor by her husband. Her "Letters from New York" columns for the *Boston Courier* were collected in two popular volumes. The columns discussed her ramblings in the city as well as issues such as poverty, capital punishment, women's rights, and religious toleration.

Maria preferred New York to Boston because New York was more open to varieties of people, arts, and ideas. Boston was bound by convention and an entrenched elite. In New York, she could dress as she chose, comfortably and unfashionably, and walk everywhere as she explored the city. She could be anonymous and therefore free. She often compared herself to George Sand, the unconventional French woman novelist, calling herself Sand's "twin sister." Sand wore masculine clothes in Paris to give her access to places where women were barred; Child's old clothes in New York served the same function.

When David Child gave up his failed sugar-beet venture and the farm, he declared bankruptcy, and all of their possessions were sold. Maria asked a friend to draw up the necessary papers to separate her income from her husband's, and determined to remain in New York to further her writing career. David eventually moved to Washington, D.C., to pursue a career as a journalist for the Whig Party, before returning home to Massachusetts. Disappointed by her husband's failures, she found herself exhausted in her efforts to help him, concluding that "to pump water into a sieve for fourteen years is enough to break the most energetic spirit. I must put a stop to it, or die." By 1852, however, she returned to Massachusetts, living with her husband and her ailing father in the latter's home in Wayland.

One of Child's projects in 1861 was editing and writing the introduction to *Incidents in the Life of a Slave Girl*. The book's author and narrator was Harriet Jacobs, an escaped slave who hid in a storeroom attic in Edenton, North Carolina, for seven years to escape sexual harassment by her owner. Child made clear editorial suggestions about structure, but did not rewrite the manuscript, telling Jacobs that the language was "wonderfully good." Child also helped in the book's distribution and sale, writing letters to notables such as the poet John Greenleaf Whittier. Although critics questioned its authenticity well into the twentieth century (some thought it was actually written by Child), modern critics and scholars have since verified its accuracy.

Child became embroiled in controversies surrounding the ill-fated John Brown uprising, the Fugitive Slave Act, and the Kansas referendum on slavery, writing pamphlets and articles that were widely distributed. She also wrote a three-volume history of world religions (*The Progress of Religious Ideas Through Successive Ages*, 1855), another romantic novel about racial miscegenation (*A Romance of the Republic*, 1867), and two works the proceeds of which she donated to the freedmen's movement after the Civil War.

After her husband's death in 1874, she became even more a recluse, dying of heart failure at her home in Wayland, Massachusetts, in 1880.

Summary

Lydia Maria Child's impact on the mid-nineteenth century was incalculable. Even though she did not participate in the public world except by her writing, she was one of the most influential women of her time. Her body of work—essays, pamphlets, books, letters—was enormous and encompassed many different genres, from children's stories to romantic fiction as well as sustained argument and history. In the twentieth century she is remembered more for her nonfiction, but in her own generation she was equally noted for her novels and short stories.

Ironically, her marriage to David Child may have provided her with the possibility of being both effective and prolific, able to defy conventions that restrained women of her class from working for a living. One could speculate about how much she might not have accomplished if her husband had been successful in the sugar beet business. Maria worked for the causes in which she believed to the end of her life, giving away most of the money she made. Balancing her lucrative periodical writing with her work for antislavery, Maria managed to scrape together a living, assisted by friends who often provided her with living accommodations or a new shawl.

Perhaps her greatest impact, then as now, lies in her voluminous correspondence, available to modern readers on microfilm and in print form. For it is in her letters that the energetic Maria Child appears, always working on another project, always ready with her lively wit and descriptions, perpetually optimistic about life's vicissitudes. She corresponded with everyone, never put off by class or title—from the governor of Virginia to poet-friend John Greenleaf Whittier to former slaves.

Bibliography
Child, Lydia Maria. *Lydia Maria Child: Selected Letters, 1817-1880*. Edited by Milton Meltzer and Patricia G. Holland. Amherst: University of Massachusetts Press, 1982. Autobiographical detail from one of the foremost letter writers of the nineteenth century. Helpful notes and excellent introductions to chronologically arranged sections.
Clifford, Deborah Pickman. *Crusader for Freedom: A Life of Lydia Maria Child*. Boston: Beacon Press, 1992. The first complete biography of Child, looking at all

phases of her life and giving the essential historical context for the turbulent times of the pre-Civil War struggles. Includes an excellent biography.

Crapol, Edward P. "Lydia Maria Child: Abolitionist Critic of American Foreign Policy." In *Women and American Foreign Policy: Lobbyists, Critics, and Insiders.* New York: Greenwood Press, 1987. Chronicles Child's work on foreign policy issues—the recognition of Haiti, the annexation of Texas, the attitude of England toward slavery, and other issues. Illuminates an underappreciated aspect of Child's influence.

Karcher, Carolyn L. "Patriarchal Society and Matriarchal Family in Irving's 'Rip Van Winkle' and Child's 'Hilda Silfverling.'" *Legacy* 2 (Fall, 1985): 31-44. An interesting comparison of two dystopic stories in which the protagonist sleeps for a century, awakening to a very different world. Written by one of the best contemporary critics of Child's literary work.

Osborne, William S. *Lydia Maria Child.* Boston: Twayne, 1980. An introduction to Child's life and work, this volume is a good place to begin a study of Child. It is marred, however, by its repetition of traditional assessments of her as a second-rate writer and polemicist.

Yellin, Jean Fagan. *Women and Sisters: The Antislavery Feminists in American Culture.* New Haven, Conn.: Yale University Press, 1989. A useful historical overview that includes Child in an account of the importance of women in the antislavery movement.

Margaret McFadden

SHIRLEY CHISHOLM

Born: November 30, 1924; Brooklyn, New York

Area of Achievement: Government and politics
Contribution: As the first African American woman elected to the U.S. Congress and the first to run as a candidate for the presidency, Shirley Chisholm has been an outspoken advocate for women, children, and ethnic minorities.

Early Life

Shirley Anita St. Hill was born in 1924 in the Bedford-Stuyvesant section of Brooklyn to West Indian emigrants, Charles Christopher St. Hill and Ruby Seale St. Hill. Seeking relief from the 1920 famine that besieged their Caribbean home on the island of Barbados, both parents migrated to New York City. Unable to save enough money from her work as a seamstress in the garment district or his work as an unskilled laborer in a burlap bag factory, the St. Hills sent three-year-old Shirley, along with her two younger sisters, Muriel and Odessa, back to Barbados to live on a farm with their maternal grandmother, Emmeline Seale.

The next seven years under the stern, disciplined eye of Grandma Seale, a towering woman who was more than six feet tall, shaped Shirley's compassion and concern for the well-being of others and further strengthened her understanding that commitment to one's principles, while rewarding, might be a lonely existence. The foundation of Shirley's future academic success would be based on the structured academic environment of the British-styled schools of Barbados.

The transition back into American life in 1934 at the height of the Depression was difficult for eleven-year-old Shirley. The meager resources of the St. Hill family were further divided with the arrival of baby sister Selma. The stark contrast between the warm, balmy climate of Barbados as compared to the harsh cold reality of New York winters made the adjustment even more painful.

The family moved from the predominantly Jewish neighborhood of Brownsville to the more ethnically diverse community of Bedford-Stuyvesant in Brooklyn. This half-black neighborhood would help sharpen Shirley's developing political awareness, especially as the economic conditions of the neighborhood worsened.

Shirley's fertile teenage mind was challenged by the daily lectures and discussions with her father, a largely self-educated man. Charles St. Hill, a voracious reader, daily devoured several publications. Like many working-class blacks, he was an avid follower of the charismatic Pan-Africanist leader, Marcus Garvey. Garvey's Universal Negro Improvement Association (UNIA), which promoted racial pride and encouraged self-sufficiency, was one of the most important political, cultural black movements during the early part of the twentieth century in America.

Upon returning to the New York school system, Shirley was held back in a lower grade because of her ignorance of U.S. civic history. After receiving tutoring lessons, she was promoted to her appropriate grade level and quickly surpassed the efforts of many of her classmates. Chisholm would always retain one trait from her years in the Caribbean—a slight, melodious West Indian accent. A petite young woman, Chisholm soon learned that her size tended to disguise her surprisingly forceful, straightforward manner.

Upon graduation from high school, Shirley received offers to attend college at Vassar and Oberlin. Because of her family's limited economic resources and her own desire to remain close to home, however, she accepted a scholarship to study sociology at Brooklyn College. Shirley's involvement in several campus organizations and the debating society caught the attention of one Brooklyn College professor, who encouraged her to pursue a political career. In the end, Chisholm chose to become a teacher, a more realistic career choice for African American women of her day.

In 1946, she graduated cum laude from Brooklyn College with a degree in social work. She immediately began work on a masters degree in elementary education at Columbia University's night school. During the day, she was employed at a local nursery school. At about this time, she met a recent Jamaican transplant, Conrad Chisholm, who was working as a waiter. They were married on October 8, 1950, and settled in Brooklyn. Conrad returned to school and then became an investigator for the New York City Department of Hospital Services.

For the next several years, Shirley worked for a number of schools, including Friends Day Nursery in Brownsville and the Mount Calvary Child Care Center in Harlem. From 1953 to 1959, she served as director of the Hamilton-Madison Child Care Center in Lower Manhattan. She further distinguished herself as a bilingual educator, because of her ability to communicate fluently in Spanish. Gradually, her reputation as a leading early-childhood specialist spread, resulting in increased demands for her services as a consultant to such organizations as the New York City Bureau of Child Welfare.

Life's Work

Shirley Chisholm's growing interest in the political world began in the mid-1950's when she stepped up her involvement in several organizations, including the Bedford-Stuyvesant Political League, the National Association for the Advancement of Colored People (NAACP), the Democratic Women's Workshop, and the League of Women Voters. The organization that most directly sparked Chisholm's activism was the Seventeenth Assembly District Democratic Club. She became active in the district's party politics after meeting an old college associate, Wesley Holder. Holder had carved out a reputation for getting black candidates elected while still remaining loyal to the white-dominated Democratic party agenda. Shirley's distaste for such blind allegiance to the party machine, however, soon found her at odds with Holder and on the outside of the club's inner circle. This situation rendered Chisholm politically inactive for a number of years.

She reentered politics in 1960 when she helped form the Unity Democratic Club with the express goal of destroying the grip the party held over her district. In 1964, Chisholm succeeded in winning a seat to the New York State Assembly for the

Fifty-fifth District as the first black woman from Brooklyn to serve in the state legislature. During her four years in Albany, New York, she was the only woman and one of only eight black representatives in the state assembly. As a state representative, Chisholm spearheaded the passage of a bill for unemployment insurance for domestic workers and also developed a program known as Search for Elevation, Education and Knowledge (SEEK), which was designed to increase higher educational opportunities for disadvantaged youth.

Having cut her political teeth at the state level, Chisholm went on in 1968 to beat James Farmer, former leader of the Congress of Racial Equality (CORE), who was running as a Republican candidate for the newly created Twelfth Congressional District of Brooklyn. This new congressional district included her old Bedford-Stuyvesant neighborhood, a community comprising seventy percent black and Puerto Rican residents by the late 1960's. Her victory made her the first African American woman to win a seat to the U.S. Congress.

As a champion for the underdog, Chisholm made it clear that she would always align herself with the most able candidate. So in 1969, she crossed party lines when she supported Republican candidate John Lindsay in his successful New York City mayoral bid. During her fourteen years on Capitol Hill, Chisholm served on a number of congressional committees. She was originally appointed to the Agricultural Committee, but she aggressively lobbied to be removed from this committee because it did not serve the direct interests of her urban constituents. While on the Education and Labor Committee, Chisholm worked diligently to increase the minimum wage standard and increase federal subsidies for day care centers. Her proposed bill, however, was later vetoed by President Gerald Ford. Other noteworthy legislation introduced by Chisholm called for increasing the level of federal reimbursement of state welfare programs to 70 percent and the establishment of a Department of Consumer Affairs as a cabinet-level position.

Always active in the women's movement, Chisholm was involved in the early years of the National Organization for Women (NOW). She was a founding member of the National Women's Political Caucus, was a spokeswoman for the National Abortion Rights Action League (NARAL), and served as a guiding force in the formation of the National Political Congress of Black Women (NPCBW). From 1972 to 1976, Chisholm served on the Democratic National Committee.

Convinced that the status quo power structure of American politics needed to be changed, Chisholm decided in 1972 to run for the presidency. Returning to her old campaign slogan, "Unbought and Unbossed," Chisholm waged an uphill battle against the reigning power oligarchy and many old prejudices. Despite her lack of strong financial backing, Chisholm succeeded in mounting a ground-breaking campaign, assembling a coalition of blacks, feminists, and other minority groups. Nevertheless, she failed to gain the largely symbolic yet influential support of the members of the Congressional Black Caucus. She arrived at the 1972 Democratic Convention with only 24 votes; later, she received an additional 151 votes released to her by Hubert H. Humphrey.

This particular campaign, more than any other venture, left a bitter taste in Chisholm's mouth as she came to grips with the unexpected opposition she encountered from two previously supportive sectors: women's groups and black civil rights organizations. Nevertheless, Chisholm remained convinced that her maiden journey had opened the door for future generations of women.

The year 1977 was a momentous time in Chisholm's life, highlighted by her appointment to the powerful House Rules Committee. This political success was nearly overshadowed by the dissolution of her marriage to Conrad Chisholm. After her divorce became final in 1978, she was married to Arthur Hardwick, Jr., a black businessman and an old acquaintance from her days in the New York state assembly. In 1979, Hardwick was involved in a serious car accident, sustaining injuries that necessitated a long recovery. This personal burden combined with the pressures of a changing political atmosphere in Washington, D.C., to place Chisholm at a challenging crossroad in her career. She retired from the U.S. House of Representatives in 1983. After her retirement, she essentially remained out of the political arena, limiting her involvement to endorsing and advising Jesse Jackson in his 1984 and 1988 presidential campaigns. In addition to serving as a popular speaker on the lecture circuit, Chisholm accepted an appointment as the Purington Professor at Mount Holyoke College, teaching classes in women's studies and political science from 1983 to 1987. She became a widow after Arthur Hardwick died from cancer in 1986. Although her outspoken nature created a stormy relationship between Chisholm and the Democratic Party during the 1990's, she was nominated to serve as U.S. ambassador to Jamaica by President Bill Clinton in 1993.

Summary

As an outspoken, charismatic maverick, Shirley Chisholm enjoyed a lengthy political career that witnessed many firsts. Chisholm's trailblazing journey served to inspire others to overcome seemingly insurmountable hurdles as she became the first African American woman to win a seat in the U.S. Congress and the first African American woman to mount an official campaign for the presidency of the United States.

An advocate for the rights of women, children, and racial minorities, Chisholm served as a voice for many who could not speak for themselves. Her political agenda included the introduction of legislation that improved conditions for women and their children and created employment opportunities for inner-city residents. Undaunted and confident in her ability to wage "the good fight," Chisholm continued to pursue an independent course and was proud to remain unaccountable to either a party agenda or the narrow goals of special interests. After fourteen years on Capitol Hill, Chisholm succeeded in altering and realigning portions of the Democratic Party platform to reflect her own political beliefs. Even so, she was unable to placate some interest groups and often clashed with environmentalists, whose causes often placed obstacles in the way of her efforts to secure much-needed jobs for her constituents.

Chisholm's public career served to inspire other women to pursue careers in politics, and her achievements helped shape and influence an entire generation of African American political leaders, most notably California congresswoman Maxine Waters and presidential candidate Jesse Jackson. In spite of the obstacles and petty feuds she faced throughout her political career and particularly during her unconventional run for the presidency, Shirley Chisholm could look back on nearly forty years of public service as both a legislator and an educator with great pride.

Bibliography
Brownmiller, Susan. *Shirley Chisholm: A Biography*. Garden City, N.Y.: Doubleday, 1971. A short biography for young readers covering Chisholm's life from her return to New York City up through her successful bid for a congressional seat.
Chisholm, Shirley. *The Good Fight*. New York: Harper & Row, 1973. This memoir provides Chisholm's own perspective on the prejudices and obstacles she encountered in her unsuccessful 1972 bid for the American presidency.
——————. *Unbought and Unbossed*. Boston: Houghton Mifflin, 1970. Chisholm's first autobiography profiles her early life up through her election to the U.S. House of Representatives for New York's Twelfth Congressional District in 1968.
Drotning, Philip T., and Wesley W. South. *Up from the Ghetto*. New York: Cowles, 1970. An entire chapter of this book is devoted to Chisholm's effort to succeed against all odds. Places her struggle within the context of efforts by other African Americans to carve out productive careers in the face of racial prejudice and discrimination.
Duffy, Susan, comp. *Shirley Chisholm: A Bibliography of Writings by and About Her*. Metuchen, N.J.: Scarecrow Press, 1988. A useful source for locating writings by Chisholm, this work also serves as a good starting point for surveying the variety of sources of biographical information on Chisholm.
Rennert, Richard Scott, ed. *Female Leaders*. New York: Chelsea House, 1993. A work that surveys the lives and careers of several significant African American women, this multibiography places Chisholm's achievements within the context of her era and demonstrates how her efforts inspired women who followed, including Illinois Senator Carol Moseley Braun.
Scheader, Catherine. *Shirley Chisholm: Teacher and Congresswoman*. Hillsdale, N.J.: Enslow, 1990. A well-organized biography aimed at a juvenile audience, this work provides a straightforward overview of Chisholm's career and accomplishments and includes some discussion of her activities since leaving Congress.

Donna Mungen

GREAT LIVES
FROM
HISTORY

AREAS OF ACHIEVEMENT

Margaret Sanger V-1599
Anna Howard Shaw V-1637
Elizabeth Cady Stanton V-1666
Gloria Steinem V-1677

Lucy Stone V-1687
Sojourner Truth V-1769
Sarah Weddington V-1859
Frances Willard V-1898